Towards Neuromorphic Machine Intelligence

Towards Neuromorphic Machine Intelligence

Spike-based Representation, Learning, and Applications

Hong Qu

Xiaoling Luo

Zhang Yi

Academic Press is an imprint of Elsevier
125 London Wall, London EC2Y 5AS, United Kingdom
525 B Street, Suite 1650, San Diego, CA 92101, United States
50 Hampshire Street, 5th Floor, Cambridge, MA 02139, United States

Notices

Knowledge and best practice in this field are constantly changing. As new research and experience broaden our understanding, changes in research methods, professional practices, or medical treatment may become necessary.

Practitioners and researchers must always rely on their own experience and knowledge in evaluating and using any information, methods, compounds, or experiments described herein. In using such information or methods they should be mindful of their own safety and the safety of others, including parties for whom they have a professional responsibility.

To the fullest extent of the law, neither the Publisher nor the authors, contributors, or editors, assume any liability for any injury and/or damage to persons or property as a matter of products liability, negligence or otherwise, or from any use or operation of any methods, products, instructions, or ideas contained in the material herein.

ISBN: 978-0-443-32820-6

For information on all Academic Press publications
visit our website at https://www.elsevier.com/books-and-journals

Publisher: Mara Conner
Acquisitions Editor: Chris Katsaropoulos
Editorial Project Manager: Himani Dwivedi
Production Project Manager: Anitha Sivaraj
Cover Designer: Christian Bilbow

Typeset by VTeX

Contents

Biographies of authors ix

Foreword xi

Acknowledgments xv

1. Introduction 1
   - 1.1. Computational theory of the brain 1
   - 1.2. What is neuromorphic computing 2
   - 1.3. Artificial intelligence with neuromorphic computing 2
   - References 5

2. Fundamentals of spiking neural networks 11
   - 2.1. Biological background 11
   - 2.2. Neuronal diversity and spiking neuron models 13
   - 2.3. Conclusion 17
   - References 17

3. Specialized spiking neuron model 19
   - 3.1. Resonate spiking neuron 19
   - 3.2. Rectified linear PSP-based spiking neuron 20
   - 3.3. Pyramidal structure spiking neuron 21
   - 3.4. Signed neuron with memory 22
   - 3.5. Conclusion 25
   - References 25

4. Learning algorithms for shallow spiking neural networks 27
   - 4.1. Preface 27
   - 4.2. Accuracy measure and neuron model 28
   - 4.3. First error-based supervised learning algorithm 29
   - 4.4. Recursive least squares-based learning algorithm 48

4.5. Membrane potential driven aggregate-label learning 65
4.6. Efficient threshold driven aggregate-label learning algorithm 75
4.7. Conclusions 89
References 89

5. Learning algorithms for deep spiking neural networks 95
5.1. Preface 95
5.2. Learning algorithm with neural oscillation and phase information 97
5.3. Learning algorithms with rectified linear postsynaptic potential 102
5.4. Conclusion 113
References 113

6. Neural column-inspired spiking neural networks for episodic memory 117
6.1. Preface 117
6.2. Minicolumn-based model for episodic memory 118
6.3. Columnar-structured model for temporal-sequential learning 137
6.4. Conclusion 146
References 146

7. An ANN–SNN algorithm suitable for ultra energy efficient image classification 149
7.1. Preface 149
7.2. Convert pre-trained ANNs to SNNs 149
7.3. ANN–SNN conversion with signed neuron with memory 151
7.4. Neuron-wise normalization 154
7.5. Hardware energy consumption analysis 156
7.6. Applications and results 158
7.7. Conclusions 159

References 160

8. Spiking deep belief networks for fault diagnosis 163

8.1. Preface 163

8.2. Building blocks of spiking deep belief networks 163

8.3. Event-driven spike deep belief network 167

8.4. Applications and results 171

8.5. Conclusions 186

References 186

9. Conclusions 189

9.1. Summary 189

9.2. Future outlook 191

Glossary 193

Index 197

Biographies of authors

Hong Qu

Hong Qu (Member, IEEE) received the Ph.D. degree in computer science from the University of Electronic Science and Technology of China, Chengdu, China, in 2006. From 2007 to 2008, he was a Post-Doctoral Fellow with the Advanced Robotics and Intelligent Systems Laboratory, School of Engineering, University of Guelph, Guelph, ON, Canada. From 2014 to 2015, he was a Visiting Scholar with the Potsdam Institute for Climate Impact Research, Potsdam, Germany and the Humboldt University of Berlin, Berlin, Germany. He is currently a Professor with the Computational Intelligence Laboratory, School of Computer Science and Engineering, University of Electronic Science and Technology of China. His current research interests include neural networks, machine learning, and big data.

Xiaoling Luo

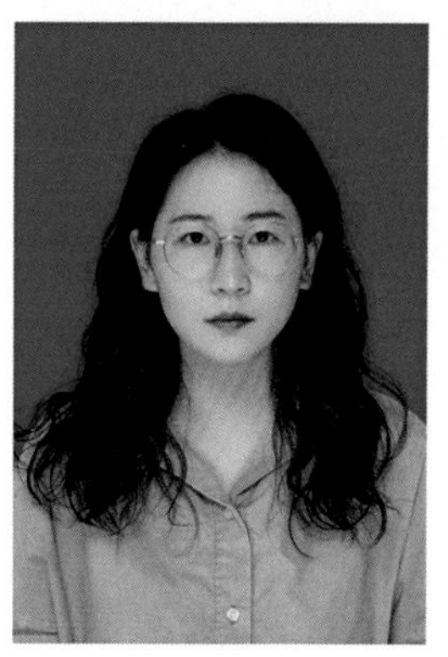

Xiaoling Luo received the Ph.D. degree in computer science from the University of Electronic Science and Technology of China, Chengdu, China, in 2023. She is currently a lecturer at the School of Computer Science and Engineering, Sichuan University of Science & Engineering. Her current research interests include machine learning and spiking neural networks.

Zhang Yi

Zhang Yi (Fellow, IEEE) received the Ph.D. degree in mathematics from the Institute of Mathematics, Chinese Academy of Science, Beijing, China, in 1994. He is currently a Professor with the Machine Intelligence Laboratory, College of Computer Science, Sichuan University, Chengdu, China. He has coauthored three books: Convergence Analysis of Recurrent Neural Networks (Kluwer Academic Publishers, 2004), Neural Networks: Computational Models and Applications (Springer, 2007), and Subspace Learning of Neural Networks (CRC Press, 2010). His current research interests include neural networks and big data. Prof. Yi was an Associate Editor of the IEEE TRANSACTIONS ON NEURAL NETWORKS AND LEARNING SYSTEMS from 2009 to 2012 and the IEEE TRANSACTIONS ON CYBERNETICS in 2014.

Foreword

Spiking neural networks (SNNs) is an emerging research field in Artificial Intelligence, which offers the potential for intelligent applications with enhanced efficiency and reduced power consumption. As the third generation of artificial neural networks (ANN), SNNs provide a more detailed simulation of neuron dynamics and information transmission in biological neural systems, bridging computer science and neuroscience. While there have been numerous notable theoretical advancements in neuron models, learning algorithms, network architectures, etc., these achievements are often scattered and lack systematic integration, posing challenges for beginners to start their studies. Therefore, this book aims to serve as a user-friendly learning tool that provides both beginners and researchers with an extensive understanding of SNNs.

The primary target audience of this book can be divided into two categories: artificial intelligence researchers who are unfamiliar with SNNs and those who possess substantial knowledge about SNNs. The former group needs to acquire fundamental knowledge about SNNs; however, the existing literature on SNNs often only briefly mentions basic concepts or lacks depth. This book addresses this issue by providing a comprehensive explanation starting from scratch. The latter group seeks to explore novel research breakthroughs in the field of SNNs; thus, this book introduces the latest findings across various aspects of SNNs while offering detailed simulation processes for readers' replication.

The structure of the book is shown below.

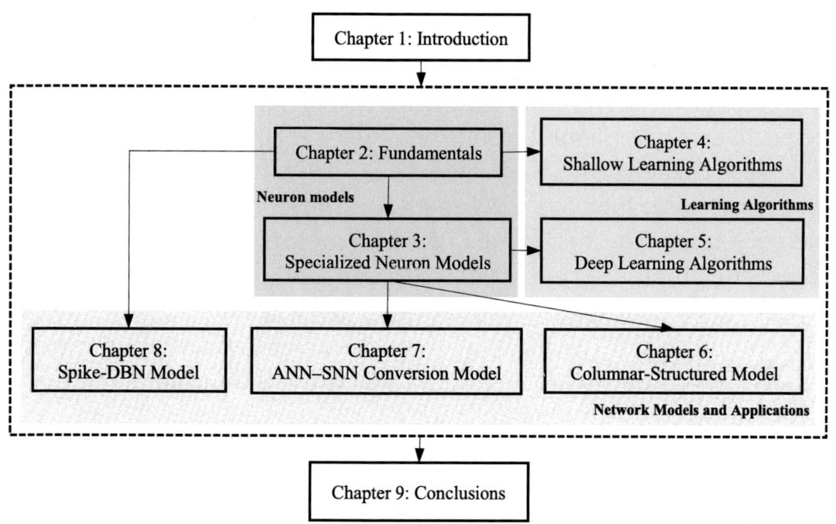

SNNs serve as the theoretical foundation for neuromorphic computing and represent a burgeoning domain within artificial intelligence. The initial chapter of this book introduces the contextual background that gave rise to SNNs, specifically focusing on the computational theory of the brain and neuromorphic computing. Subsequently, Chapter 2 delves into three primary neuron models within the realm of SNNs, while Chapter 3 introduces several novel and specialized spiking neuron models.

The models discussed in Chapter 3 aim to adapt and enhance the existing neuron models to facilitate algorithm derivation and model building. Among them, the resonate spiking neuron incorporates neural oscillation and phase-locking mechanisms into its design. Alternatively, rectified linear PostSynaptic Potential (PSP) neurons modify the PSP function to adopt a linear format, facilitating easier forward and backward propagation in deep network architectures. Drawing inspiration from the biological structure of pyramidal cells, there are also spiking neurons constructed with multiple dendrites, tailored for processing sequential information. Furthermore, signed neurons with memory are introduced for lossless conversion between ANN and SNN frameworks.

The subsequent chapter delves into the algorithms and models corresponding to these neuron models, complementing the understanding of their functionalities and applications. In Chapter 4, we introduce several learning algorithms tailored for shallow SNNs. Specifically, for sequence learning, we present the FE-Learn and RLSBLR algorithms. FE-Learn enhances efficiency by updating parameters solely at the first incorrect spike time in each iteration. Conversely, RLSBLR leverages multiple learning iterations within a single time window traversal, reducing the number of required learning rounds. For aggregate-label learning, we introduce the MPD-AL and ETDP algorithms. MPD-AL significantly reduces computational time by manually selecting the adjustment point. ETDP, meanwhile, leverages a critical threshold and demonstrates a robust capability in addressing time credit allocation challenges.

Chapter 5 introduces two learning algorithms specifically designed for deep SNNs, addressing the prevalent challenges encountered during direct training, namely, the non-differentiable spike function, gradient explosion, and dead neurons. The deep SNNs constructed with resonate neurons and rectified linear PSP neurons tackle these issues from distinct perspectives. Experimental results demonstrate the efficacy of these approaches in addressing these challenges.

In Chapter 6, we introduce two SNN models inspired by cortical neural columns for episodic memory tasks. The first model, BSTM, employs the STDP learning algorithm alongside a novel column selection method to encode input elements, and with its sequential memory algorithm, it can complete multi-sentence memory and multi-time step memory. The second model, CSTM, is tailored for sequences exhibiting variable time intervals. Remarkably, CSTM can retrieve a long sequence of thousands of elements after a single pass through the input sequence.

In Chapter 7, a nearly lossless method for converting ANNs to SNNs is introduced. This approach leverages signed spiking neurons with memory to alleviate the mismatch in information transmission between the synchronous ANN and the asynchronous SNN.

Notably, this method maintains a high degree of accuracy during the conversion process. Furthermore, a novel normalization method, known as neuron-wise normalization, is proposed, which significantly reduces the inference delay of the converted SNN.

Chapter 8 presents a fault diagnosis SNN named spike-DBN. It seamlessly integrates the event-driven approach within its framework by utilizing the Latency-Rate coding method and the reward-STDP learning rule. As a result, it adeptly captures temporal variations in multivariate time-series data, ensuring not only minimal resource consumption but also enhanced fault diagnosis capabilities.

Finally, a concise summary concludes the book in Chapter 9.

This book possesses three key features: 1) Introducing a new generation of biologically inspired artificial intelligence; 2) Keeping up with the latest research progress on SNNs; 3) Offering a comprehensive organizational structure that systematically covers essential knowledge about SNNs including neuron and network models, learning algorithms, realistic applications, etc.

We have also provided references or directly included URLs in the footnotes to make it convenient for interested readers to access the data and some of the code used in the book. Additionally, we encourage readers to attempt the experiments using programming languages such as MATLAB and Python.

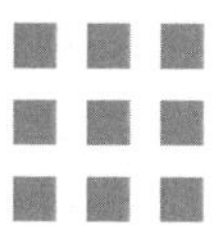

Acknowledgments

This work was supported by the National Key Research and Development Program of China under Grant Number 2018AAA0100202. We would also like to extend our sincere appreciation to our colleagues Yun Zhang, Yi Chen, Malu Zhang, Yuchen Wang, and Ying Liu for their invaluable contributions encompassing data collection, text verification, and comprehensive revision. Our heartfelt gratitude also goes to the exceptional team at Elsevier Press for their support.

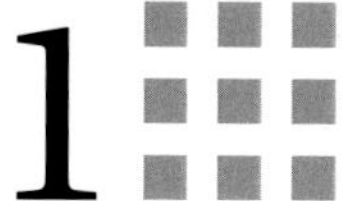

Introduction

1.1 Computational theory of the brain

Currently, the details of how the brain completes advanced functions such as perception, cognition, memory, and movement remain unknown, but it is certain that these are due to the trillions of neurons and the quadrillions of synaptic connections between neurons in the human brain. The field of artificial intelligence is committed to revealing the essence of intelligence by simulating the structure and function of the human brain and developing machines with human-like intelligence. Artificial Neural Networks (ANNs) design artificial neurons with a "weighted-sum-activation" process by highly abstracting biological neurons, and connect these neurons to construct deep networks. Through repeated training on a large number of manually labeled data, ANNs have achieved great success in applications such as image recognition [HZRS16], object detection [CFFV16,ZZXW19], and speech recognition [LXH$^+$19], sparking a boom in artificial intelligence. However, the development of ANNs is also hindered by multiple obstacles. On the one hand, the training of ANNs requires a large amount of manually labeled data, which has a high cost; on the other hand, ANNs also have a high demand for computational resources (such as GPUs and computing clusters), which limits their application in power-constrained platforms (such as edge computing); in addition, the current von Neumann architecture used by computers has separate storage and computation, which exacerbates computational consumption. With the gradual failure of Moore's Law, issues such as heat dissipation, leakage, and power consumption have also become important factors restricting the development of ANNs.

In order to achieve truly human-level and low-power artificial intelligence, countries around the world have focused on brain-inspired computing based on brain research. In 2013, the EU proposed a ten-year "Human Brain Project" aimed at studying the brain and brain diseases using advanced technologies in neuroscience and artificial intelligence, and promoting the innovation of brain-inspired computing and intelligent robotics related technologies. In the same year, the United States also launched the "BRAIN" project to carry out work on characterizing and mapping nerve and non-nerve cells of the human brain, and support the development and application of innovative technologies to gain a deeper understanding of the functioning of the brain. In 2014, Japan also launched its own Brain/MINDS project, which focuses on studying the brains of marmosets, developing brain mapping technology, and creating human brain atlases. Subsequently, South Korea, Canada, Australia, and China have also launched their own brain projects. As an important research content of brain projects, brain-inspired computing constructs computational theories by borrowing information processing methods from the brain's nervous system, creating brain-inspired intelligent models and algorithms, and building neuromorphic

Towards Neuromorphic Machine Intelligence. https://doi.org/10.1016/B978-0-44-332820-6.00008-2

chip systems. This is expected to bridge the gap between neuroscience and artificial intelligence and become a breakthrough in the future development of artificial intelligence.

1.2 What is neuromorphic computing

Neuromorphic computing began in the 1980s. Carver Mead, a professor of American scientists, engineers, and microprocessor pioneers, proposed the concept of neuromorphic engineering. Neuromorphic systems attempt to mimic the operation of the human nervous system. Neuromorphic computing implements various aspects of biological neural networks as electronic analog circuits, creating energy-saving hardware for information processing that enables it to perform highly complex tasks.

Neuromorphic computing encompasses the generation and utilization of neural networks. In the human brain, neural synapses provide the ability for neurons to directly access memory for processing information. This is how the brain achieves impressive computational power and speed with minimal power consumption. By mimicking this architecture, neuromorphic computing offers a path to building intelligent neuromorphic chips that consume little energy and have high computational speeds.

A typical example of neuromorphic chips is Intel's Loihi chips [DSL+18,IC20]. Loihi is a neuromorphic multi-core processor with on-chip learning capabilities, and this 14-nm chip contains over 2 billion transistors, 130 000 artificial neurons, and 130 million synapses. It incorporates various novel features in the field of spiking neural networks, such as hierarchical connectivity, dendritic compartments, synaptic delays, and most importantly, programmable synaptic learning rules. By running a spiking convolutional form of the local competition algorithm, Loihi can solve LASSO optimization problems with an energy-delay product that is three orders of magnitude higher compared to conventional solvers running on processors such as CPUs.

Although neuromorphic technology is still in its infancy, the field is rapidly developing. In the near future, neuromorphic chips on the market are likely to have an impact on edge devices, robots, and Internet of Things (IoT) systems. Neuromorphic computing is moving towards low-power, miniaturized chips that can infer and learn in real time.

1.3 Artificial intelligence with neuromorphic computing

Whereas traditional computer chips provide powerful computing capabilities for traditional artificial intelligence methods, such as ANNs, neuromorphic chips are specifically designed to provide hardware support for the new artificial intelligence computing paradigm of Spiking Neural Networks (SNNs). SNNs can only achieve their brain-like, low-power information processing advantages when running on neuromorphic chips.

SNNs have different component units, input and output forms, and operation modes from traditional ANNs. Many spiking neural models were proposed in the last century to more biologically abstract and simulate the structure and function of biological neurons, and many of these models are widely used in current SNNs. In addition, the need for new intelligent applications such as pattern recognition and directional localization has led to the emergence of new encoding strategies for input information such as images, sounds, and texts, which has suggested new requirements for spiking network models and learning algorithms. How to build appropriate network models and learning algorithms to fully utilize the temporal processing capabilities of SNNs is a long-term research goal of SNNs. In the past few decades, many excellent results have emerged. Among them, the research on shallow and deep feedforward networks has the most abundant results, and also includes some special network structures.

The structures of shallow SNNs are simple, typically containing only one decision layer fully connected with the input layer. Some models also add a group of inhibitory neurons connected to the decision layer. The representative of unsupervised learning algorithms for shallow neural network models is the Spike-Timing Dependent Plasticity (STDP) rule [BP98,MGT09]. The idea is that if the presynaptic neuron fires a spike before the postsynaptic neuron, the synaptic strength between them is enhanced, and vice versa. In addition to the classic STDP rule, there are also exponential weight-dependent STDP [BMLW13,QBDG13], power-law weight-dependent STDP [BMLW13,QBDG13], pre- and post-STDP [DM15], and three-factor STDP [PG06]. Although these unsupervised learning algorithms train shallow networks with only one (or two) layers of neurons and without additional guidance signals, they still achieve good results in pattern recognition tasks [DM15]. On the other hand, there are also many supervised learning algorithms based on STDP rules [TRT08,MGT09,PK10,ASSN12,SF13,YTTL13]. The typical algorithm is the Remote Supervised Method (ReSuMe) [PK10]. ReSuMe applies STDP to increase synaptic weights at desired output spike times and anti-STDP to decrease weights at non-desired output spike times, prompting neurons to fire spikes at specified times. Following the idea of ReSuMe, the Spike Pattern Association Neuron (SPAN) [ASSN12] and Precision Spike Driven (PSD) [YTTL13] methods convert discrete spike sequences into continuous signals to guide synaptic weight adjustments. In addition, combining ReSuMe with particle swarm optimization and delay learning has also further improved ReSuMe's learning performance [XHLL14,TBLM15a,TBLM15b,TBLM18]. Compared to these algorithms, the Perceptron-Based Spiking Neuron Learning Rule (PBSNLR) [XZZ13,QXL$^+$15] and the Normalized Perceptron-Based Learning Rule (NPBLR) [XQLZ17] only adjust weights based on synaptic input contributions, making them easier to compute. Overall, shallow SNNs learning algorithms have low computational complexity and are biologically reasonable, but they are not very efficient in learning spatial and temporal spike patterns because of the limited nonlinear expression capabilities of shallow networks.

Most practical applications rely on deep networks, so it is necessary to build deep SNNs. However, due to the non-differentiability of the spike activation function, deep-structured SNNs (multi-layer fully connected structures, convolutional structures, etc.) are difficult to train using the Error Backpropagation (BP) algorithm [RHW86] like ANNs. The temporal dynamic nature of spiking neurons makes the spike activation uncertain in time, and the error needs to be backpropagated not only in the spatial scale but also in the temporal scale, which brings difficulties to the learning of deep SNNs. The SpikeProp algorithm [BKLP02] assumes that each neuron can only be excited once, and the membrane voltage is assumed to increase linearly in a small neighborhood around the spike excitation time to deal with the non-differentiability of spikes. Therefore the weight update rule is derived based on the BP algorithm. However, this single-spike assumption greatly limits the application capabilities of the network. Therefore subsequent work has proposed improved multi-spike versions [GDA09,XZHY13]. The authors of [HS18] proposed an augmented LIF model that replaces the spike activation function with a continuous gate function to avoid the issue of non-differentiability. However, the most popular approach to this problem so far has been to use surrogate gradients, which approximate the derivative of spike time with respect to membrane voltage as a function related to threshold and membrane voltage. These algorithms are also called surrogate gradient algorithms, such as SLAYER [SO18], STBP (Spatio-Temporal Backpropagation) [WDL+18,WDL+19], SuperSpike [ZG18], TSSL-BP [ZL20], BackEISNN [ZZL22] and others [ZWW+22]. Like some algorithms using recurrent network structures [ZL19,BSS+18,YCB21], these algorithms update synaptic weights using the idea of Backpropagation Through Time (BPTT) [Wer90], which can directly train SNNs. However, these algorithms require storing a large number of intermediate variables for reverse gradient calculation, which places considerable demands on computation and storage. Therefore algorithms inspired by dynamic systems have been proposed [CRBD18,BKK19,DDT19,XMZ+21]. These algorithms treat the entire network as a dynamic system represented by ordinary differential equations. Therefore both the feedforward and feedback processes of the network can be viewed as numerical solution processes of differential equations, which can save a lot of storage consumption. In contrast to these directly trained algorithms, there are indirect training algorithms based on transformation, namely ANN2SNN methods [RLH+17,SYW+19,DWH+20,DG21,WZCQ22]. By treating the continuous output values of ANNs as the firing rates of spike neurons in SNNs, ANN2SNN methods transplant the trained weights of ANNs to SNNs with the same structure, aiming to make SNNs achieve inference results similar to those of ANNs. However, the transformation process usually comes with a loss of accuracy. To reduce the transformation loss, the simulation time length needs to be increased, which in turn leads to more inference latency in SNNs and reduces the real-time processing capabilities of the model. Additionally, input needs to be encoded using frequency encoding, which makes ANN2SNN methods perform well on static data tasks but lack processing capabilities for sequential tasks [FYC+21].

In addition to the above common structures of SNNs, there are also some special network models, such as reservoir structures and columnar structures. In the reservoir structure networks, there are a large number of recurrent connections, which are usually randomly generated and generally not adjusted. Most of the learning of the network relies on the connection between the reservoir and a (or a group of) readout unit(s). This network's learning algorithm is represented by the First-Order Reduced and Controlled Error (FORCE) algorithm [SA09,NC17], using recursive least squares to derive the weight update strategy. This model can simulate neural circuits in the brain and reproduce neural activity in the motor cortex. Columnar structure models simulate neural columns in the brain cortex, proposing that multiple identical neurons are stacked into columns to represent the same object, often used to simulate sequential memory [HAD+11,CAH17,LZX20,HSG17,SMH20,BSH19]. The Hierarchical Temporal Memory (HTM) model [HAD+11] is representative of this kind of network. The learning in this network is often one-time, occurring at the same time as input reception, with connections in the network constantly being generated or eliminated. These special structure network models usually have their specific application scenarios. Starting from these models, exploring models and algorithms suitable for more applications is one of the research directions of SNNs.

It is worth noting that in addition to the above synaptic weight plasticity-based methods for SNNs learning, there are many algorithms that also consider other parameters adjustments, such as synaptic delay, membrane time constant, threshold, etc. Neuroscience research shows that synaptic delay can be modulated and plays an important role in the learning process [KM65,LF02]. However, there are many different ways to incorporate synaptic delay into network training. For example, multiple sub-connections with different delays can be established between every pre- and postsynaptic neuron pair. These delays are fixed and not adjustable. During learning, the connection strength of synapses with appropriate delay sizes is enhanced, while the connection strengths of synapses with inappropriate delay sizes are reduced [BKLP02,GDA09,GDA07,XZHY13]. Conversely, it is also possible to consider only the plasticity of synaptic delays while keeping synaptic weights constant [AMS05,PPC08]. In addition, there are also methods that simultaneously adjust both synaptic delays and synaptic weights. DL-ReSuMe [TBLM15a] and its variants [TBLM15b,ZWB+20] introduce delay learning into ReSuMe, but limit each delay to only being adjustable once during learning. This method was later improved to allow multiple adjustments [TBLM18,Mat16,SS16,WLD19], and adaptation to multi-layer network structures [TBLM18]. In addition, there are also algorithms that turn fixed membrane time constants into adjustable parameters [FYC+21] to increase neural diversity and expression ability of the network, or modify weights with threshold adjustment as the goal to enable temporal credit assignment capability [Güt16] in the model.

SNNs have high biological plausibility, and when deployed on neuromorphic hardware, they have advantages such as low power consumption and high response speed. However, so far, SNNs models and algorithms can only be used to achieve pattern recognition tasks on partial static or neuromorphic data. How to effectively utilize the inherent time-series processing capability of SNNs and develop new SNNs models and learning algorithms suitable for various application scenarios still needs to be studied.

References

[AMS05] Peyman Adibi, Mohammad Reza Meybodi, Reza Safabakhsh, Unsupervised learning of synaptic delays based on learning automata in an rbf-like network of spiking neurons for data clustering, Neurocomputing 64 (2005) 335–357.

[ASSN12] A. Mohemmed, S. Schliebs, S. Matsuda, N. Kasabov, Span: spike pattern association neuron for learning spatio-temporal spike patterns, International Journal of Neural Systems 22 (04) (2012) 1659–1685.

[BKK19] Shaojie Bai, J. Zico Kolter, Vladlen Koltun, Deep equilibrium models, in: Advances in Neural Information Processing Systems, vol. 63, 2019, pp. 690–701, Vancouver, Canada.

[BKLP02] Sander M. Bohte, Joost N. Kok, Han La Poutre, Error-backpropagation in temporally encoded networks of spiking neurons, Neurocomputing 48 (1–4) (2002) 17–37.

[BMLW13] B. Nessler, M. Pfeiffer, L. Buesing, W. Maass, Bayesian computation emerges in generic cortical microcircuits through spike-timing-dependent plasticity, PLoS Computational Biology 9 (4) (2013).

[BP98] Guo-qiang Bi, Mu-ming Poo, Synaptic modifications in cultured hippocampal neurons: dependence on spike timing, synaptic strength, and postsynaptic cell type, Journal of Neuroscience 18 (24) (1998) 10464–10472.

[BSH19] Basawaraj, Janusz A. Starzyk, Adrian Horzyk, Episodic memory in minicolumn associative knowledge graphs, IEEE Transactions on Neural Networks and Learning Systems 30 (11) (2019) 3505–3516.

[BSS+18] Guillaume Bellec, Darjan Salaj, Anand Subramoney, Robert Legenstein, Wolfgang Maass, Long short-term memory and learning-to-learn in networks of spiking neurons, Advances in Neural Information Processing Systems 31 (2018).

[CAH17] Yuwei Cui, Subutai Ahmad, Jeff Hawkins, The HTM spatial pooler—a neocortical algorithm for online sparse distributed coding, Frontiers in Computational Neuroscience 11 (2017).

[CFFV16] Zhaowei Cai, Quanfu Fan, Rogerio S. Feris, Nuno Vasconcelos, A unified multi-scale deep convolutional neural network for fast object detection, in: European Conference on Computer Vision, Amsterdam, Netherlands, 2016, pp. 354–370.

[CRBD18] Ricky T.Q. Chen, Yulia Rubanova, Jesse Bettencourt, David Duvenaud, Neural ordinary differential equations, in: Advances in Neural Information Processing Systems, vol. 31, 2018, pp. 6572–6583, Montréal, Canada.

[DDT19] Emilien Dupont, Arnaud Doucet, Yee Whye Teh, Augmented neural odes, in: Advances in Neural Information Processing Systems, vol. 32, 2019, pp. 3140–3150, Vancouver, Canada.

[DG21] Shikuang Deng, Shi Gu, Optimal conversion of conventional artificial neural networks to spiking neural networks, arXiv preprint, arXiv:2103.00476, 2021.

[DM15] Peter U. Diehl, Cook Matthew, Unsupervised learning of digit recognition using spike-timing-dependent plasticity, Frontiers in Computational Neuroscience 9 (429) (2015) 99.

[DSL+18] Mike Davies, Narayan Srinivasa, Tsung-Han Lin, Gautham Chinya, Yongqiang Cao, Sri Harsha Choday, Georgios Dimou, Prasad Joshi, Nabil Imam, Shweta Jain, Yuyun Liao, Chit-Kwan Lin, Andrew Lines, Ruokun Liu, Deepak Mathaikutty, Steven McCoy, Arnab Paul, Jonathan Tse, Guruguhanathan Venkataramanan, Yi-Hsin Weng, Andreas Wild, Yoonseok Yang, Hong Wang, Loihi: a neuromorphic manycore processor with on-chip learning, IEEE Micro 38 (1) (2018) 82–99.

[DWH+20] Lei Deng, Yujie Wu, Xing Hu, Ling Liang, Yufei Ding, Guoqi Li, Guangshe Zhao, Peng Li, Yuan Xie, Rethinking the performance comparison between snns and anns, Neural Networks 121 (2020) 294–307.

[FYC+21] Wei Fang, Zhaofei Yu, Yanqing Chen, Timothée Masquelier, Tiejun Huang, Yonghong Tian, Incorporating learnable membrane time constant to enhance learning of spiking neural networks, in: IEEE/CVF International Conference on Computer Vision, Montreal, Canada, October 2021, pp. 2641–2651.

[GDA07] S. Ghosh-Dastidar, H. Adeli, Improved spiking neural networks for eeg classification and epilepsy and seizure detection, Integrated Computer-Aided Engineering 14 (3) (2007) 187–212.

[GDA09] Samanwoy Ghosh-Dastidar, Hojjat Adeli, A new supervised learning algorithm for multiple spiking neural networks with application in epilepsy and seizure detection, Neural Networks the Official Journal of the International Neural Network Society 22 (10) (2009) 1419–1431.

[Güt16] Robert Gütig, Spiking neurons can discover predictive features by aggregate-label learning, Science 351 (6277) (2016) aab4113.

[HAD+11] Jeff Hawkins, Subutai Ahmad, Donna Dubinsky, et al., Cortical learning algorithm and hierarchical temporal memory, Numenta Whitepaper 1 (2011) 68.

[HS18] Dongsung Huh, Terrence J. Sejnowski, Gradient descent for spiking neural networks, in: Advances in Neural Information Processing Systems, vol. 31, 2018, pp. 1433–1443, Montréal, Canada.

[HSG17] Adrian Horzyk, Janusz A. Starzyk, James Graham, Integration of semantic and episodic memories, IEEE Transactions on Neural Networks and Learning Systems 28 (12) (2017) 3084–3095.

[HZRS16] Kaiming He, Xiangyu Zhang, Shaoqing Ren, Jian Sun, Deep residual learning for image recognition, in: The IEEE Conference on Computer Vision and Pattern Recognition, Las Vegas, USA, June 2016, pp. 770–778.

[IC20] Nabil Imam, Thomas A. Cleland, Rapid online learning and robust recall in a neuromorphic olfactory circuit, Nature Machine Intelligence 2 (3) (2020) 181–191.

[KM65] Bernard Katz, Ricardo Miledi, The measurement of synaptic delay, and the time course of acetylcholine release at the neuromuscular junction, Proceedings of the Royal Society of London. Series B, Biological Sciences 161 (985) (1965) 483–495.

[LF02] Jen-Wei Lin, Donald S. Faber, Modulation of synaptic delay during synaptic plasticity, Trends in Neurosciences 25 (9) (2002) 449–455.

[LXH+19] Max W.Y. Lam, Chen Xie, Shoukang Hu, Jianwei Yu, Helen M. Meng, Gaussian process lstm recurrent neural network language models for speech recognition, in: IEEE International Conference on Acoustics, Speech and Signal Processing, Brighton, United Kingdom, 2019, pp. 7235–7239.

[LZX20] Q. Liang, Y. Zeng, B. Xu, Temporal-sequential learning with a brain-inspired spiking neural network and its application to musical memory, Frontiers in Computational Neuroscience 14 (2020).

[Mat16] S. Matsuda, Bpspike: a backpropagation learning for all parameters in spiking neural networks with multiple layers and multiple spikes, in: International Joint Conference on Neural Networks, 2016, pp. 293–298.

[MGT09] T. Masquelier, R. Guyonneau, S.J. Thorpe, Competitive STDP-based spike pattern learning, Neural Computation 21 (5) (2009) 1259.

[NC17] Wilten Nicola, Claudia Clopath, Supervised learning in spiking neural networks with force training, Nature Communications 8 (2017) 2208.

[PG06] Jean-Pascal Pfister, Wulfram Gerstner, Triplets of spikes in a model of spike timing-dependent plasticity, The Journal of Neuroscience 26 (38) (2006) 9673–9682.

[PK10] Filip Ponulak, Andrzej Kasiński, Supervised learning in spiking neural networks with resume: sequence learning, classification, and spike shifting, Neural Computation 22 (22) (2010) 467–510.

[PPC08] D.T. Pham, M.S. Packianather, E.Y.A. Charles, Control chart pattern clustering using a new self-organizing spiking neural network, Proceedings of the Institution of Mechanical Engineers. Part B, Journal of Engineering Manufacture 222 (B10) (2008) 1201–1211.

[QBDG13] Damien Querlioz, Olivier Bichler, Philippe Dollfus, Christian Gamrat, Immunity to device variations in a spiking neural network with memristive nanodevices, IEEE Transactions on Nanotechnology 12 (3) (2013) 288–295.

[QXL+15] Hong Qu, Xiurui Xie, Yongshuai Liu, Malu Zhang, Lu Li, Improved perception-based spiking neuron learning rule for real-time user authentication, Neurocomputing 151 (2015) 310–318.

[RHW86] David E. Rumelhart, Geoffrey E. Hinton, Ronald J. Williams, Learning representations by back-propagating errors, Nature 323 (6088) (1986) 399–421.

[RLH+17] Bodo Rueckauer, Iulia-Alexandra Lungu, Yuhuang Hu, Michael Pfeiffer, Shih-Chii Liu, Conversion of continuous-valued deep networks to efficient event-driven networks for image classification, Frontiers in Neuroscience 11 (2017) 682.

[SA09] David Sussillon, L.F. Abbott, Generating coherent patterns of activity from chaotic neural networks, Neuron 63 (4) (2009) 544–557.

[SF13] Scarpetta Silvia, Giacco Ferdinando, Associative memory of phase-coded spatiotemporal patterns in leaky integrate and fire networks, The Journal of Neuroscience 34 (2) (2013) 319–336.

[SMH20] Janusz A. Starzyk, Lukasz Maciura, Adrian Horzyk, Associative memories with synaptic delays, IEEE Transactions on Neural Networks and Learning Systems 31 (1) (2020) 331–344.

[SO18] Sumit Bam Shrestha, Garrick Orchard, SLAYER: spike layer error reassignment in time, in: Advances in Neural Information Processing Systems, vol. 31, 2018, pp. 1412–1421, Montréal, Canada.

[SS16] S.B. Shrestha, Q. Song, Adaptive delay learning in spikeprop based on delay convergence analysis, in: International Joint Conference on Neural Networks, 2016, pp. 277–284.

[SYW+19] Abhronil Sengupta, Yuting Ye, Robert Wang, Chiao Liu, Kaushik Roy, Going deeper in spiking neural networks: Vgg and residual architectures, Frontiers in Neuroscience 13 (2019) 95.

[TBLM15a] Aboozar Taherkhani, Ammar Belatreche, Yuhua Li, Liam P. Maguire, Dl-resume: a delay learning-based remote supervised method for spiking neurons, IEEE Transactions on Neural Networks and Learning Systems 26 (12) (2015) 3137–3149.

[TBLM15b] Aboozar Taherkhani, Ammar Belatreche, Yuhua Li, Liam P. Maguire, Multi-dl-resume: multiple neurons delay learning remote supervised method, in: 2015 International Joint Conference on Neural Networks (IJCNN), IEEE, 2015, pp. 1–7.

[TBLM18] Aboozar Taherkhani, Ammar Belatreche, Yuhua Li, Liam P. Maguire, A supervised learning algorithm for learning precise timing of multiple spikes in multilayer spiking neural networks, IEEE Transactions on Neural Networks and Learning Systems 29 (11) (2018) 5394–5407.

[TRT08] Masquelier Timothée, Guyonneau Rudy, Simon J. Thorpe, Spike timing dependent plasticity finds the start of repeating patterns in continuous spike trains, PLoS ONE 3 (1) (2008) e1377.

[WDL+18] Yu Jie Wu, Lei Deng, Guo Li Qi, Jun Zhu, Lu Ping Shi, Spatio-temporal backpropagation for training high-performance spiking neural networks, Frontiers in Neuroscience 12 (331) (2018) 1–12.

[WDL+19] Yujie Wu, Lei Deng, Guoqi Li, Jun Zhu, Yuan Xie, L.P. Shi, Direct training for spiking neural networks: faster, larger, better, in: Proceedings of the AAAI Conference on Artificial Intelligence, 2019, pp. 33:1311–1318, 07.

[Wer90] P.J. Werbos, Backpropagation through time: what it does and how to do it, Proceedings of the IEEE 78 (10) (1990) 1550–1560.

[WLD19] Xiangwen Wang, Xianghong Lin, Xiaochao Dang, A delay learning algorithm based on spike train kernels for spiking neurons, Frontiers in Neuroscience 13 (2019).

[WZCQ22] Yuchen Wang, Malu Zhang, Yi Chen, Hong Qu, Signed neuron with memory: towards simple, accurate and high-efficient ann-snn conversion, in: Proceedings of the Thirty-First International Joint Conference on Artificial Intelligence, 2022, pp. 2501–2508.

[XHLL14] Xiurui Xie, Qu Hong, Guisong Liu, Lingshuang Liu, Recognizing human actions by using the evolving remote supervised method of spiking neural networks, in: International Conference on Neural Information Processing, Kuching, Malaysia, vol. 8834, 2014, pp. 366–373.

[XMZ+21] Mingqing Xiao, Qingyan Meng, Zongpeng Zhang, Yisen Wang, Zhouchen Lin, Training feedback spiking neural networks by implicit differentiation on the equilibrium state, in: Advances in Neural Information Processing Systems, vol. 34, 2021, pp. 14516–14528, virtual-only.

[XQLZ17] Xiurui Xie, Hong Qu, Guisong Liu, Malu Zhang, Efficient training of supervised spiking neural networks via the normalized perceptron based learning rule, Neurocomputing 241 (2017) 152–163.

[XZHY13] Yan Xu, Xiaoqin Zeng, Lixin Han, Jing Yang, A supervised multi-spike learning algorithm based on gradient descent for spiking neural networks, Neural Networks 43 (2013) 99–113.

[XZZ13] Yan Xu, Xiaoqin Zeng, Shuiming Zhong, A new supervised learning algorithm for spiking neurons, Neural Computation 25 (6) (2013) 1472–1511.

[YCB21] Bojian Yin, Federico Corradi, Sander M. Bohté, Accurate and efficient time-domain classification with adaptive spiking recurrent neural networks, Nature Machine Intelligence 3 (10) (2021) 905–913.

[YTTL13] Qiang Yu, Hua Jin Tang, Kay Chen Tan, Hai Li Zhou, Precise-spike-driven synaptic plasticity: learning hetero-association of spatiotemporal spike patterns, PLoS ONE 8 (11) (2013) 65–87.

[ZG18] Friedemann Zenke, Surya Ganguli, Superspike: supervised learning in multilayer spiking neural networks, Neural Computation 30 (6) (2018) 1514–1541.

[ZL19] Wenrui Zhang, Peng Li, Spike-train level backpropagation for training deep recurrent spiking neural networks, in: Advances in Neural Information Processing Systems, vol. 32, 2019, pp. 7800–7811, Vancouver, Canada.

[ZL20] Wenrui Zhang, Peng Li, Temporal spike sequence learning via backpropagation for deep spiking neural networks, arXiv preprint, arXiv:2002.10085, 2020.

[ZWB+20] Malu Zhang, Jibin Wu, Ammar Belatreche, Zihan Pan, Xiurui Xie, Yansong Chua, Guoqi Li, Hong Qu, Haizhou Li, Supervised learning in spiking neural networks with synaptic delay-weight plasticity, Neurocomputing (2020) 103–118.

[ZWW+22] Malu Zhang, Jiadong Wang, Jibin Wu, Ammar Belatreche, Burin Amornpaisannon, Zhixuan Zhang, Venkata Pavan Kumar Miriyala, Hong Qu, Yansong Chua, Trevor E. Carlson, Haizhou Li, Rectified linear postsynaptic potential function for backpropagation in deep spiking neural networks, IEEE Transactions on Neural Networks and Learning Systems 33 (5) (2022) 1947–1958.

[ZZL22] Dongcheng Zhao, Yi Zeng, Yang Li, Backeisnn: a deep spiking neural network with adaptive self-feedback and balanced excitatory–inhibitory neurons, Neural Networks 154 (2022) 68–77.

[ZZXW19] Z. Zhao, P. Zheng, S. Xu, X. Wu, Object detection with deep learning: a review, IEEE Transactions on Neural Networks and Learning Systems 30 (11) (2019) 3212–3232.

2 Fundamentals of spiking neural networks

2.1 Biological background

As a prelude to discussing spiking neuron models, we first introduce their biological basis, that is, the basic structure of biological neurons, the information transmission mechanism, and spike generation process.

2.1.1 Basic structure and information transmission mechanism of biological neurons

Neurons (nerve cells) are the basic structure and functional unit of the brain's nervous system, which mainly includes soma (cell body), dendrites, and axons, as shown in Fig. 2.1.

The soma is the roughly spherical central part of a neuron, containing important organelles such as the nucleus and mitochondria, and is considered to be the information processing center of the neuron. The axon is a structure that only exists in neurons, is highly specialized for transmitting information over long distances, and is considered to be the output device of the neuron. The ends of the axons have many short branches, which contact and transmit information to other neurons' dendrites or cell bodies at points called synapses. The dendrite is expanded and protrudes from the cell body, forming a dendritic shape, which is the antenna of the neuron. It contacts with the axon terminals of other neurons to form thousands of synapses, receiving information transmitted by other neurons. It is considered to be the input device of the neuron. The synapse is the key to the infor-

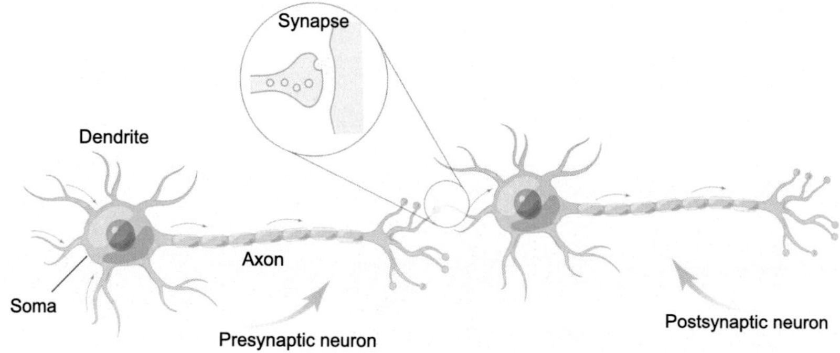

FIGURE 2.1 Biological neuron structure and information transmission. The presynaptic neuron transmits electrical signals to the postsynaptic neuron through the synaptic structure. This figure is drawn by Figdraw (https://www.figdraw.com/static/index.html).

Towards Neuromorphic Machine Intelligence. https://doi.org/10.1016/B978-0-44-332820-6.00009-4

mation transmission of neurons. The presynaptic side is usually composed of the axon terminals, while the postsynaptic side is the dendrite or cell body of another neuron. The neuron that transmits information is called the presynaptic neuron, and the neuron that receives information is called the postsynaptic neuron.

2.1.2 The generation of action potentials: spikes

When a postsynaptic neuron does not receive any signals from its presynaptic neurons, the potential difference between the inner and outer membranes of the neuron, i.e., the membrane voltage, is at the resting state.

The electrical signals transmitted by the presynaptic neuron along the axon are converted to chemical signals (i.e., neurotransmitters) at the terminals. The neurotransmitters cross the synaptic cleft and bind to proteins on the postsynaptic membrane, causing the ion channels on the postsynaptic membrane to open or close, thereby causing changes in the membrane voltage of the postsynaptic neuron.

The changes in the membrane voltage of postsynaptic neurons caused by a single electrical impulse are called postsynaptic potentials (PSPs), and their amplitude is determined by the strength of the synaptic connection. PSPs are divided into excitatory PSPs and inhibitory PSPs, which enhance and weaken the membrane voltage, respectively, as shown in Fig. 2.2. When the membrane voltage accumulates to exceed a threshold, the neuron produces an action potential, also called a spike, and transmits the spike to its postsynaptic neurons along its axon.

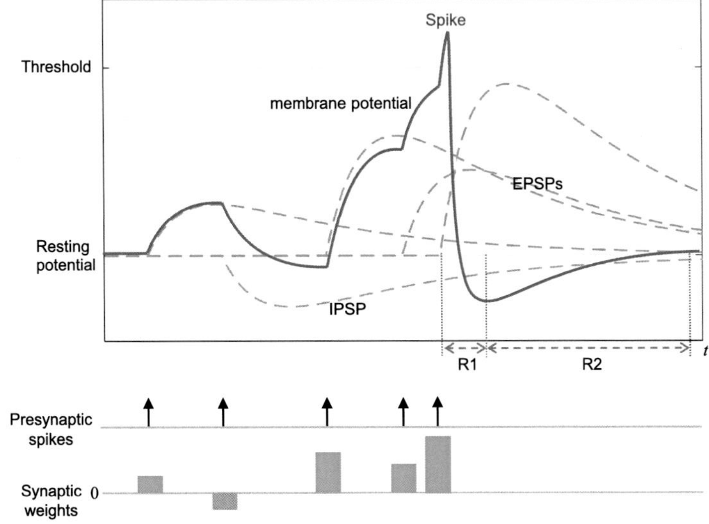

FIGURE 2.2 Variation of neuronal membrane voltage and the process of generating spike. IPSP reduces the membrane voltage, while EPSP increases the membrane voltage. R1: absolute refractory period, R2: relative refractory period.

The action that produces the spike is also called firing. After firing the spike, the neuron enters an absolute refractory period, during which the neuron cannot fire again. Then, the membrane voltage slowly returns to the resting state, a period called the relative refractory period, during which firing is difficult unless strongly stimulated.

2.2 Neuronal diversity and spiking neuron models

To simulate the above properties of biological neurons, many spiking neuron models have been proposed, which have different levels of detailed characterization and therefore different levels of complexity, or computational efficiency. In general, the higher the simulation detail, the lower the computational efficiency. For example, the Leaky Integrate-and-Fire (LIF) [MB99,GK02] model, which describes the membrane dynamics using first-order ordinary differential equations, balances simulation detail and computational efficiency, and thus has become the most widely used spiking neuron in the field of SNNs. The Hodgkin and Huxley (HH) [HH52,MB99,GK02] model, which simulates the details of three ion channels on the membrane, has a high degree of biological rationality, but is more complex in calculation, and is more commonly used among biophysiological researchers than in the artificial intelligence community.

2.2.1 Hodgkin and Huxley model

The HH model is one of the most biologically plausible spiking neuron models. In experiments on the giant axons of squid, the researchers found that there are three types of ion currents inside and outside the cell membrane: sodium (Na) ion currents, potassium (K) ion currents, and other currents (hereafter called leakage currents), mainly chloride ions. By analyzing the three types of current, the differential equation model of membrane voltage u is given as Eq. (2.1):

$$C\frac{\mathrm{d}u}{\mathrm{d}t} = I(t) - g_{Na}m^3h\left(u - E_{Na}\right) - g_K n^4\left(u - E_K\right) - g_L\left(u - E_L\right), \tag{2.1}$$

where C is capacitance, $I(t)$ represents the total input current. The last three items on the right of the equation represent the currents of each of the three ion channels. g_{Na}, g_K, and g_L represent the conductivity of sodium ion, potassium ion, and leakage channel, respectively. E_{Na}, E_K, and E_L, respectively, represent their corresponding equilibrium potentials, all of which are constants. The circuit diagram corresponding to this formula is shown in Fig. 2.3(a). The parameters m, h, n are used to control the opening and closing of each ion channel, which is affected by the membrane voltage u and expressed by Eq. (2.2):

$$\frac{\mathrm{d}x}{\mathrm{d}t} = \alpha_x(u)(1 - x) - \beta_x(u)x, \quad x \in \{m, h, n\}. \tag{2.2}$$

The settings of α and β as well as g and E are shown in Table 2.1, obtained from the experimental data from the squid axon.

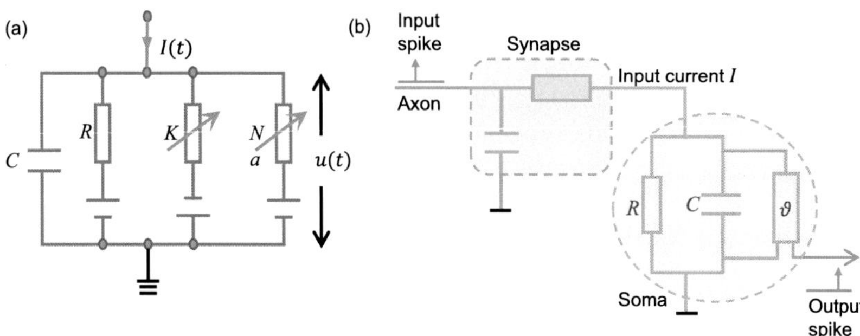

FIGURE 2.3 Circuit diagram of HH model and LIF neuron model [MB99,GK02]. (a) HH model. (b) LIF model.

Table 2.1 The setting of parameters α and β in the HH model [GK02].

x	α_x **(u/mV)**	β_x **(u/mV)**
m	$(2.5-0.1u)/[\exp(2.5-0.1u)-1]$	$4\exp(-u/18)$
h	$0.07\exp(-u/20)$	$1/[\exp(3-0.1u)+1]$
n	$(0.1-0.01u)/[\exp(1-0.1u)-1]$	$0.125\exp(-u/80)$
x	E_x **(mV)**	g_x **(mS/cm^2)**
Na	50	120
K	−77	36
L	−54.4	0.3

HH model's simulation of ion channels accurately reflects the activity of biological neurons, and models with varying levels of detail can be obtained by adding, deleting, or modifying the types of ion currents in the HH model. However, the model contains many differential equations, which is difficult to calculate in practice.

2.2.2 Leaky integrate-and-fire model

As mentioned earlier, the electrical signal transmitted by the presynaptic neuron will generate a PSP on the postsynaptic neuron and accumulate to the membrane voltage, which will ignite the neuron when the membrane voltage exceeds the threshold. The "integrate" in the LIF refers to the accumulation of PSPs, while the "leakage" refers to the action of the membrane voltage gradually attenuating to the resting potential without receiving a new PSP. If there is no membrane voltage leakage, it is called the Integrate-and-Fire (IF) model.

The LIF model can be represented by a classical RC circuit, as shown in Fig. 2.3(b), in which the spike transmitted by the presynaptic neuron through the axon is low-pass filtered into an input current I, which charges the circuit on the right. Consider the capacitor as the cell membrane, and the voltage on it is the neuron membrane voltage u. Let $\tau_m = RC$, and according to the circuit diagram on the right of Fig. 2.3(b), Eq. (2.3) can be obtained:

$$\tau_m \frac{\mathrm{d}u}{\mathrm{d}t} = -u(t) + RI(t), \tag{2.3}$$

where τ_m is the membrane time constant. When the voltage through the capacitor exceeds the threshold value ϑ at a certain time t^f, the circuit will shunt, and a spike will be generated and sent to other neurons. Eq. (2.4) characterizes the firing of spikes:

$$s(t) = H(u(t) - \vartheta), \tag{2.4}$$

where $H(x)$ is the Heaviside function, which is equal to 1 when $x < 0$ and 0 when $x > 0$. The value of $s(t^f) = 1$ indicates that the spike is generated at time t^f. After the spike is excited, the membrane voltage is reset to the resting potential u_{rest} and the accumulation process starts again. The forced resetting of the membrane voltage to the resting potential is called a "hard reset", and the corresponding "soft reset" will be introduced in the next section. For the charging current I, it is usually expressed as the weighted sum of the PSPs triggered by spikes transmitted by multiple synapses, as shown in Eq. (2.5):

$$I(t) = \sum_i w_i \sum_f \varepsilon\left(t - t_i^f\right), \quad s(t_i^f) = 1, \tag{2.5}$$

where w_i represents the weight of the ith synapse, t_i^f is the fth impulse excitation time of the ith presynaptic neuron, $\varepsilon(\cdot)$ represents the low-pass filtering of the input spikes, which can be taken in a variety of different forms of functions. Several commonly used functions will be given in the next section.

The LIF model has become one of the most widely used spiking neuron models due to its simple calculation and a certain degree of bionics.

2.2.3 Spike response model

The Spike Response Model (SRM) model uses two spike response kernels to characterize the temporal-dependent membrane dynamics of neurons. One kernel characterizes the response to the input spikes transmitted by the presynaptic neurons, expressed as $\varepsilon(\cdot)$, and the other characterizes the response to the postsynaptic neuron's own firing spikes, expressed as $\eta(\cdot)$.

Assuming that the set of postsynaptic neuron i is Γ_i, and I^{ext} is the external excitation current, then the total postsynaptic potential of i is expressed as Eq. (2.6):

$$h_i(t) = \sum_{j \in \Gamma_i} w_{ij} \sum_f \varepsilon(t - \hat{t}_i, t - t_j^f) + \int_0^{\infty} \kappa\left(t - \hat{t}_i, s\right) I^{ext}(t - s)\, ds, \tag{2.6}$$

where w_{ij} represents the synaptic connection weight between the jth presynaptic neuron and neuron i. $\hat{t}_i$ is the time of the most recent spike of neuron i. The first term on the right side of the equation represents the PSP generated by all presynaptic spikes, and the second term represents the linear response of the membrane voltage to the external excitation current. When the effect of $\hat{t}_i$ on PSP is not considered, and the external excitation is not considered, Eq. (2.6) and Eq. (2.5) are the same.

Another important part of the SRM model is the response to the spike generated by the neuron itself, which controls the membrane voltage reset after the neuron fires, and is also a description of the refractory period, expressed as $\sum_k \eta\left(t - t_i^k\right)$. It is possible to consider only the most recently generated spike, i.e., $\eta\left(t - \hat{t}_i\right)$. Thus the membrane voltage of the neuron is the sum of the two parts, as shown in Eq. (2.7):

$$u_i(t) = h_i(t) + \sum_k \eta\left(t - t_i^k\right). \tag{2.7}$$

The kernel $\eta(\cdot)$ is often set to an exponential decay function such as $H(\cdot)$:

$$\eta(x) = -\vartheta e^{(-x/\tau_s)} H(x), \tag{2.8}$$

where τ_s is the decay constant and $H(\cdot)$ is the Heaviside function. Such a kernel will cause the membrane voltage to be reduced by ϑ immediately after firing, and then this "reduction" will gradually weaken, allowing the membrane voltage to gradually recover. Unlike the hard reset in the previous section, this method will preserve the membrane voltage above the threshold during the reset, which is called a "soft reset".

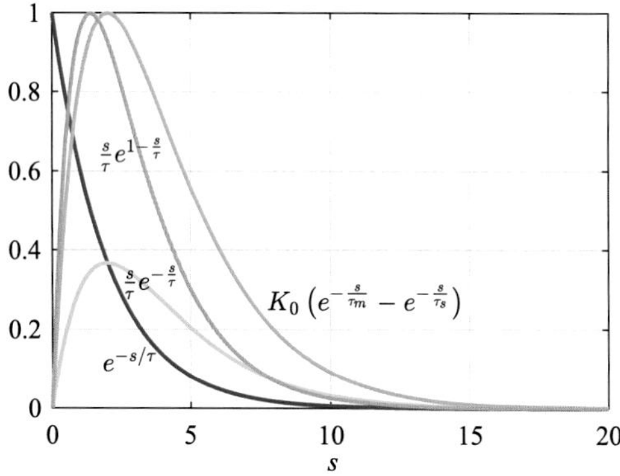

FIGURE 2.4 Common PSP function. $\tau = 2,\ \tau_m = 2,\ \tau_s = 1,\ K_0 = 4,\ H(s) = 1.$

The kernel $\varepsilon(\cdot)$ that performs filtering operations on the input spikes is commonly represented by several functions, as shown in Eq. (2.9):

$$\varepsilon(s) = \begin{cases} e^{-s/\tau} H(s), \\ \frac{s}{\tau} e^{-\frac{s}{\tau}} H(s), \\ \frac{s}{\tau} e^{1-\frac{s}{\tau}} H(s), \\ K_0\left(e^{-\frac{s}{\tau_m}} - e^{-\frac{s}{\tau_s}}\right) H(s), \end{cases} \tag{2.9}$$

where τ, τ_m, τ_s are the corresponding time constants. The shapes of these functions are shown in Fig. 2.4. It can be shown that the SRM model is equivalent to the LIF model when the appropriate kernel function is selected [GK02].

2.3 Conclusion

This chapter briefly introduced the structure of biological neurons and the process of spike reception, processing, generation, and transmission. Then, we introduced several classical spiking neuron models, including the HH model, the LIF model, and the SRM model. Various spiking neural network algorithms based on the latter two models will be discussed in subsequent chapters of this book.

References

[GK02] Wulfram Gerstner, Werner M. Kistler, Spiking Neuron Models: Single Neurons, Populations, Plasticity, Cambridge University Press, Cambridge, 2002.

[HH52] A.L. Hodgkin, A.F. Huxley, A quantitative description of membrane current and its application to conduction and excitation in nerve, Journal of Physiology 117 (4) (1952) 500–544.

[MB99] W. Maass, C.M. Bishop, Pulsed Neural Networks, The MIT Press, 1999.

3 Specialized spiking neuron model

3.1 Resonate spiking neuron

Inspired by the findings that neural oscillation and phase information play a critical role in information processing in the brain, a Resonate Spiking Neuron (RSN) with Oscillation Postsynaptic Potential (Os-PSP) and phase-locking active function was proposed [CQZW21]. Instead of the binary spike representation, the number of ions a_i^{l-1} released by spiking neuron i in one spike is used to increase the encoding capacity of spike trains. The oscillation membrane potential $V_j^l(t)$ of RSN j in layer l at time t can be written as:

$$V_j^l(t) = \sum_i w_{ij}^l a_i^{l-1} K\left(t - \left(t_i^{l-1} + d_{ij}^l\right)\right), \tag{3.1}$$

$$K(s) = a_i^{l-1} \cos(s), \quad t_i^{l-1} + d_{ij}^l \le t, \tag{3.2}$$

where w_{ij}^l is the synaptic weight from presynaptic neuron i in layer $l-1$ to postsynaptic neuron j in layer l, and d_{ij}^l is the spike transmission delay on this synapse. t_i^{l-1} is the time that the neuron i in layer $l-1$ fires the spike.

As shown in Fig. 3.1, an RSN contains two phases: the collecting phase and the resonating phase. During the collecting phase, the RSN will receive all the ions from presynaptic neurons and its membrane potential starts oscillating. In the resonating phase, the membrane potential of the neuron will gradually stabilize and show periodicity. The neuron will spike when the membrane potential reaches its maximum V_{max}^j in one cycle, the magnitude of the spike $a(t)$ is related to V_{max}^j at the moment of firing, and then enters a resting state. In Fig. 3.1 upper, the amplitude of neural oscillation is reduced when the 3rd and 4th spikes occur because the time of the last two spikes is about half a period T different from the time of the first two spikes. On the contrary, in Fig. 3.1 lower, with proper delays, all presynaptic potentials are resonated and generate a much larger membrane potential oscillation.

The information accuracy that a standard binary spike train can encode is limited by its breadth (number of neurons, e.g., population coding) and length (time step, e.g., temporal-based coding or rate-based coding). Inspired by the phase-lock mechanism found in the auditory system, a phase-locking active function was proposed. The relation between ion amount $a_j(t)$ of the RSN j and firing time t can be defined by:

$$a_j(t) = \begin{cases} F(V_j(t)), & V_j(t) = V_j^{max}, \\ 0, & \text{others}, \end{cases} \tag{3.3}$$

Towards Neuromorphic Machine Intelligence. https://doi.org/10.1016/B978-0-44-332820-6.00010-0

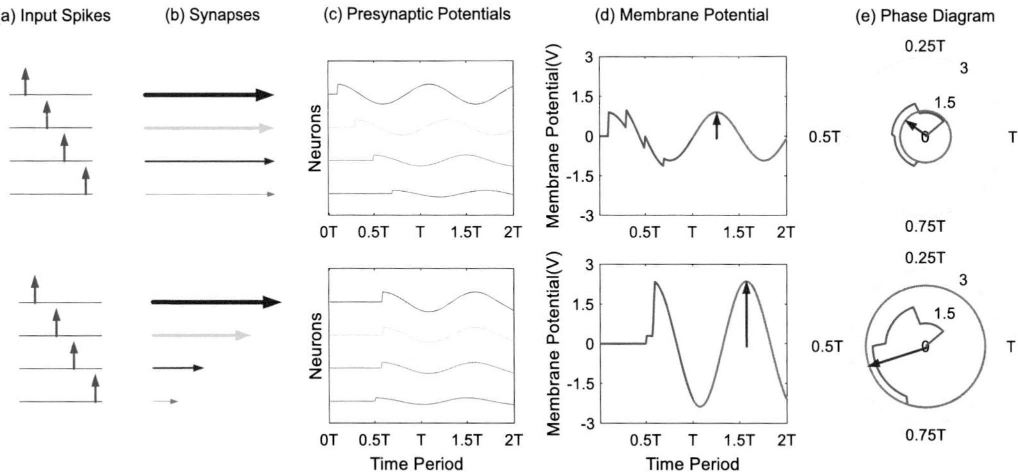

FIGURE 3.1 Resonate Spiking Neuron. (a) Input spike train generated by four input neurons. (b) Synaptic weights and delays are represented by the thickness and length of the arrows, respectively. (c) The presynaptic potential is not only related to the number of ions in the spike but also to the spike time and synaptic delay. (d) The resonate spiking neuron accumulates membrane potential in the first cycle T and then releases a pulse at the crest of the next cycle. (e) The phase diagram corresponds to (d). The amplitude of neural oscillation is represented by the radius in the figure. The length and radius of the red arrows indicate the spike size and time, respectively.

where V_j^{max} is the maximum membrane potential in one cycle. The function F is defined to represent the relation between ion amount $a_j(t)$ and $V_j(t)$. The specific formula for the function F can be set as needed. In this chapter, the function F is defined as $F(V) = V$.

According to Eq. (3.1), the RSN membrane potential is not only related to the number of ions in spikes but also to the time between spikes. When all input neurons fire spikes simultaneously, the resonance scale of the neuron is the largest, then the RSN will be completely equivalent to ANN. In contrast, when the time difference between the two input spikes is precisely half a cycle, the membrane potential oscillations generated by them will inhibit each other, resulting in the decreased amplitude of the membrane potential oscillations of the neurons.

Through the above mechanism, spike trains between RSN neurons convey two kinds of information: one is the size of the spike, which represents the activity level of neurons; the other is the relative time of the spike, which represents the degree of association between different neurons. By adjusting the relative delay between neurons, a single neuron can show both excitation and inhibition.

3.2 Rectified linear PSP-based spiking neuron

Error backpropagation, specifically stochastic gradient descent, is the workhorse of learning in DNNs. However, the dynamics of a typical artificial neuron used in Deep Neural

Networks (DNNs) differ significantly from their spiking neuron counterparts, therefore the well-known BP algorithm cannot be directly applied to deep SNNs.

To overcome this problem, a simple yet efficient Rectified Linear Postsynaptic Potential (ReL-PSP)-based spiking neuron model is proposed [ZWW+22], whose dynamics is defined as follows:

$$V_j^l(t) = \sum_i w_{ij}^l K\left(t - t_i^{l-1}\right), \tag{3.4}$$

where $V_j^l(t)$ is the membrane voltage of the neuron j in the layer l at time t, and w_{ij}^l is the synaptic weight between the neuron j and its ith presynaptic neuron in the layer $l-1$. $K(t - t_i^{l-1})$ is the kernel of the PSP function, which is defined as

$$K(t - t_i^{l-1}) = \begin{cases} t - t_i^{l-1}, & \text{if } t > t_i^{l-1}, \\ 0, & \text{otherwise}, \end{cases} \tag{3.5}$$

where t_i^{l-1} is the spike time of neuron i.

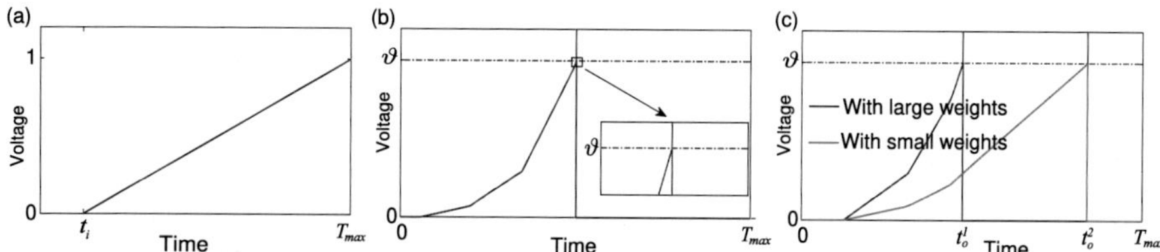

FIGURE 3.2 Membrane voltage of ReL-PSP neuron. There are three input spikes denoted as t_1, t_2, t_3. (a) ReL-PSP function. (b) Trace of the neuron membrane voltage during threshold crossing. (c) Trace of the ReL-PSP neuron membrane voltages with large and small synaptic weights, and the neuron generates spikes at t_o^1 and t_o^2, respectively ($t_o^1 < t_o^2$).

As shown in Fig. 3.2, given an input spike at t_i^{l-1}, the membrane potential after t_i^{l-1} is a linear function of time t. Since the shape of the proposed PSP function resembles that of a rectified linear function, it is called a ReL-PSP function.

3.3 Pyramidal structure spiking neuron

Referring to the biological structure of pyramidal neurons, a Bionic Spiking Temporal Memory (BSTM) neuron model was proposed [ZCZ+22]. There are a large number of pyramidal neurons in both CA3 and CA1 regions of the hippocampus [MHCJ98,SSC+17, MEFG01], and the biological structure of a pyramidal neuron is shown in Fig. 3.3(a). The pyramidal neuron receives the feedforward inputs from the lower layer by the proximal dendrite (red rectangle), lateral inputs from the same layer by the distal dendrite, and the feedback inputs from the higher layer by the apical dendrite. When the neuron receives enough inputs, it generates a spike that transmits to neurons through the axon.

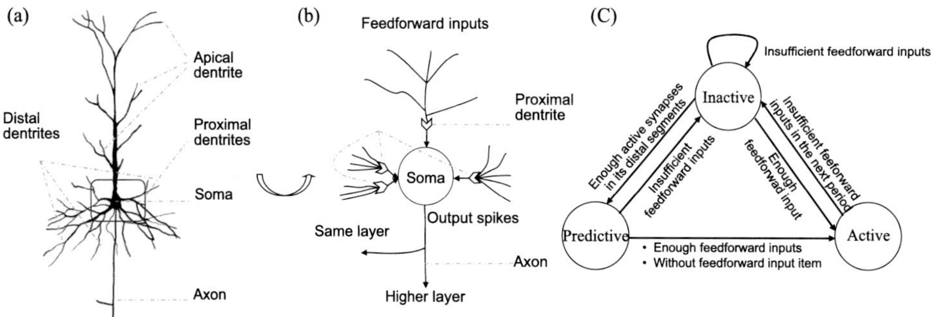

FIGURE 3.3 (a) The structure of a biological pyramidal neuron. (b) The structure of a BSTM neuron. (c) The state transition between the BSTM neurons.

Inspired by the pyramidal neuron, the BSTM neuron model has one proximal dendrite and multiple (sometimes zero) distal dendrites, as shown in Fig. 3.3(b). Similarly, it receives feedforward input spikes by the proximal dendrite and receives lateral inputs by distal dendrites. When enough feedforward input spikes are received, it generates an output spike that is transmitted from the axon to the neurons of higher layers and the same layer.

The pyramidal structure neurons are in three states: active, predictive, and inactive, and these states can be dynamically switched, as shown in Fig. 3.3(c). The default state of neurons for each period is inactive. The neuron becomes active after receiving enough feedforward inputs. While enough active synapses on its distal dendrite from other active neurons will depolarize it into a predictive state. The predictive neurons become active (inactive) in the next period with enough (insufficient) feedforward inputs. However, if there are no feedforward inputs in the next period, the predictive neurons will become active to make further predictions.

The computation of this kind of neuron with dendritic structure is complex, and its computation also varies for different tasks. The specific implementation details will be introduced in Chapter 6.

3.4 Signed neuron with memory

Thalamocortical neurons are a type of neuron that connect the thalamus to the cerebral cortex, located between the thalamus and cortex. They play a crucial role in sensory processing and perception by transmitting information from the cortex to the thalamus, thereby facilitating functions such as cognition and motor control. There are several types of thalamocortical neurons, including projection neurons, which transmit information from the cortex to the thalamus. These neurons usually send out fibers that go to the hypothalamus, specifically the amygdala and hippocampus. Another type is afferent neurons, which carry information from the hypothalamus to the cortex. These neurons usually send fibers toward the surface of the cortex, especially the motor area.

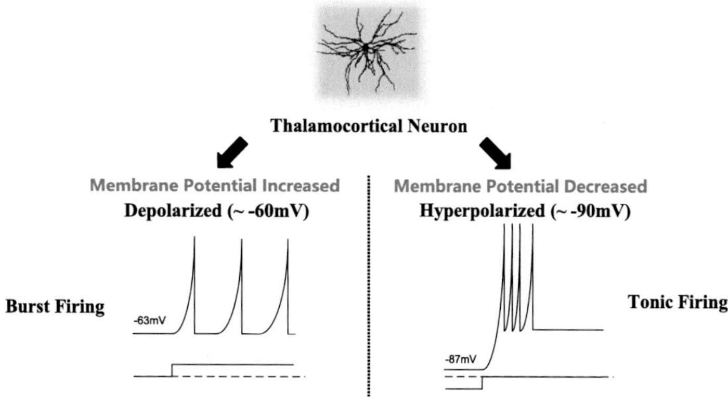

FIGURE 3.4 Explanation of two firing patterns of a thalamocortical neuron.

Thalamocortical neurons are also involved in higher cognitive functions such as emotion and learning. For example, they may play a role in recognizing and understanding emotional signals and in modulating cortical activity during learning and memory. Due to their central role in the brain, thalamocortical neurons have been the focus of research in many neuroscience and psychiatric disorders, such as anxiety, depression, cognitive impairment, and epilepsy.

Thalamocortical neurons have more than one firing threshold [Izh03], the higher threshold is around the resting potential, about -60 mV, and the lower threshold is about -90 mV, as shown in Fig. 3.4. When a thalamocortical neuron receives a positive current and reaches the higher threshold it will exhibit tonic firing, while when it receives a negative current and reaches the lower threshold it will fire different pattern spikes.

Inspired by the thalamocortical neuron with multiple firing patterns, the signed neuron with memory (SNM) neuron was proposed [WZCQ22]. The neuron has two firing thresholds, a higher threshold θ^+ that is greater than 0 and a lower threshold θ^- that is smaller than 0. In addition, to regulate the release of spikes, a memory mechanism is further added into neurons. As shown in Fig. 3.5, when the membrane potential of the SNM exceeds the positive threshold θ^+, a positive spike is fired regardless of the memory value. When the

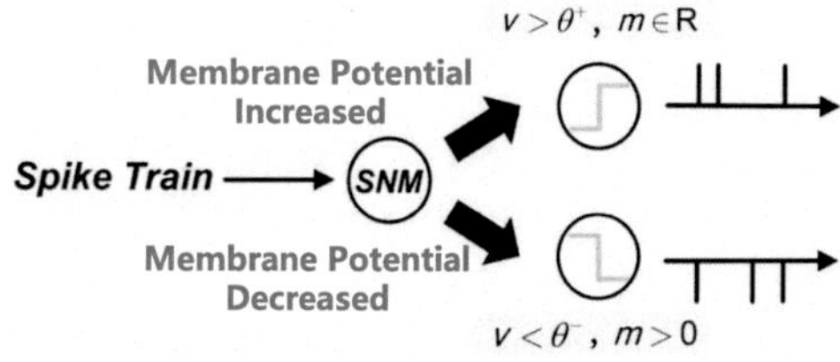

FIGURE 3.5 A description of the conditions of SNM under which different spikes are fired.

SNM membrane potential is lower than the negative threshold θ^-, only if the memory value is greater than zero will the negative spike be emitted. Other basic characteristics of this neuron are consistent with Integrate-Fire (IF) neurons. By this means, the dynamic of the SNM neuron is described by:

$$\tilde{v}_j^l(t) = v_j^l(t-1) + \sum_i w_{ij}^l s_i^{l-1}(t) + b_j, \tag{3.6}$$

where s_i^{l-1} is the spike from presynaptic neuron i, w_{ij}^l is the synaptic weight from presynaptic neuron i in layer $l-1$ to postsynaptic neuron j in layer l. Similar to ordinary neural networks, neurons have learnable bias, denoted as b_j. A temporary memory $\tilde{m}_j^l(t)$ at time t is defined as:

$$\tilde{m}_j^l(t) = m_j^l(t-1), \tag{3.7}$$

where $m_j^l(t-1)$ is the memory value of neuron j in layer l at time $t-1$. $\tilde{m}_j^l(t)$ is used to control whether the negative spike is fired:

$$s_j^l(t) = \begin{cases} \theta_j^l, & \tilde{v}_j^l(t) \geq \theta_j^l, \\ -\theta_j^l, & \tilde{v}_j^l(t) \leq -\theta_j^l \quad \text{and} \quad \tilde{m}_j^l(t) > 0, \\ 0, & \text{otherwise}. \end{cases} \tag{3.8}$$

When $\tilde{v}_j^l(t)$ exceeds the higher firing threshold θ_j^l, neuron j will send a spike $s_j^l(t)$ to its postsynaptic neuron. Unlike traditional IF and LIF neurons, SNM neurons use the soft-reset mechanism:

$$v_j^l(t) = \tilde{v}_j^l(t) - s_j^l(t). \tag{3.9}$$

In terms of the hard-reset neuron, the membrane potential will immediately return to the resting potential after firing a spike. Therefore hard-reset neurons ignore residual potential at firing instants, resulting in an accuracy drop for the converted SNN. Soft-reset neurons avoid the above problem and are widely used in various models. The memory value at the current moment t will be updated according to the release of the spike, which is described in the following equation:

$$m_j^l(t) = \tilde{m}_j^l(t) + s_j^l(t). \tag{3.10}$$

The negative spike of SNM can enable SNN to maintain both asynchronous transmission and synchronous transmission capabilities while effectively solving the problem of excessively high output rate. Usage of the memory mechanism allows SNM to remember the sum of its transmitted spikes (positive and negative spikes can be offset). Only when the memory value is greater than zero can the negative spikes be transmitted to the next layer.

3.5 Conclusion

This chapter introduced specialized spiking neuron models. The resonate spiking neuron is proposed by borrowing the neural oscillation and phase-locking phenomenon in biological neurons. This neuron can transmit spikes with different sizes. The rectified linear PSP neuron does not use the common nonlinear PSP, but uses the linear growth PSP, which makes the backpropagation calculation of gradients in deep SNNs simpler. How to build a network with these two types of neurons for real-world applications is described in Chapter 5. Neurons with dendritic structures have a rather complex structure and can be used to implement sequential memory, which will be explained in Chapter 6. The signed neurons with memory are designed for the ANN-SNN algorithm, which can realize almost lossless conversion from ANNs to SNNs, which will be introduced in Chapter 7.

References

[CQZW21] Yi Chen, Hong Qu, Malu Zhang, Yuchen Wang, Deep spiking neural network with neural oscillation and spike-phase information, in: Proceedings of the AAAI Conference on Artificial Intelligence, vol. 35, 2021, pp. 7073–7080.

[Izh03] E.M. Izhikevich, Simple model of spiking neurons, IEEE Transactions on Neural Networks 14 (6) (2003) 1569–1572.

[MEFG01] M. Megıas, Z.S. Emri, T.F. Freund, A.I. Gulyas, Total number and distribution of inhibitory and excitatory synapses on hippocampal ca1 pyramidal cells, Neuroscience 102 (3) (2001) 527–540.

[MHCJ98] Jeffrey Magee, Dax Hoffman, Costa Colbert, Daniel Johnston, Electrical and calcium signaling in dendrites of hippocampal pyramidal neurons, Annual Review of Physiology 60 (1) (1998) 327–346.

[SSC+17] Qian Sun, Alaba Sotayo, Alejandro S. Cazzulino, Anna M. Snyder, Christine A. Denny, Steven A. Siegelbaum, Proximodistal heterogeneity of hippocampal ca3 pyramidal neuron intrinsic properties, connectivity, and reactivation during memory recall, Neuron 95 (3) (2017) 656–672.

[WZCQ22] Yuchen Wang, Malu Zhang, Yi Chen, Hong Qu, Signed neuron with memory: towards simple, accurate and high-efficient ann-snn conversion, in: Proceedings of the Thirty-First International Joint Conference on Artificial Intelligence, 2022, pp. 2501–2508.

[ZCZ+22] Yun Zhang, Yi Chen, Jilun Zhang, Xiaoling Luo, Malu Zhang, Hong Qu, Zhang Yi, Minicolumn-based episodic memory model with spiking neurons, dendrites and delays, IEEE Transactions on Neural Networks and Learning Systems (2022) 1–15.

[ZWW+22] Malu Zhang, Jiadong Wang, Jibin Wu, Ammar Belatreche, Burin Amornpaisannon, Zhixuan Zhang, Venkata Pavan Kumar Miriyala, Hong Qu, Yansong Chua, Trevor E. Carlson, Haizhou Li, Rectified linear postsynaptic potential function for backpropagation in deep spiking neural networks, IEEE Transactions on Neural Networks and Learning Systems 33 (5) (2022) 1947–1958.

4

Learning algorithms for shallow spiking neural networks

4.1 Preface

The research of SNNs has gained extensive attention in recent years [WCZ$^+$18,ZWW$^+$21]. Although their development is not as mature as that of ANN on many standard benchmarks, there are many promising results, especially in terms of their learning algorithm.

A considerable part of SNN learning algorithms is inspired by biological mechanisms, and the Spike-Timing Dependent Plasticity (STDP) rule [BP98] is the most notable. Many learning algorithms based on STDP were proposed successively [TRT08,MGT09, PK10,ASSN12,SF13,YTTL13]. However, the learning performance of STDP based algorithms is relatively poor because they rely on the local neuronal activities rather than the global monitoring signal [WDL$^+$18]. In contrast, there are a large number of gradient-based global learning algorithms [BKLP02,GDA09,XZHY13,SO18,ZG18,WDL$^+$18,BSS$^+$18, WDL$^+$19] that were transplanted from ANNs, which are based on the idea of Backpropagation Through Time (BPTT) [Wer90]. However, this makes them often have a considerable requirement for calculation and storage because the entire sequence needs to be stored to facilitate calculation.

The above-mentioned learning methods are all based on synaptic weight plasticity. While the learning of delay [BKLP02,GDA09,GDA07,XZHY13] parameters can bring new possibilities for SNN algorithms, and more efficient delay learning algorithms remains to be explored. In some methods [BKLP02,GDA09,GDA07,XZHY13], the synaptic delays are regarded as constants and only the synaptic weights can be adjusted. Some other methods [AMS05,PPC08] only consider the plasticity of synaptic delays and keep the synaptic weights unchanged. The remaining methods [TBLM18,Mat16,SS16,WLD19], such as DL-ReSuMe [TBLM15b] and its variations [TBLM15c,ZWB$^+$20], integrate delay learning to existing algorithms to perform the plasticity of both synaptic delays and weights. However, these algorithms are usually more computationally expensive and therefore less efficient.

Moreover, the algorithms with ambiguous guidance signals are also worth exploring. Aggregate-label learning algorithms, such as Multi-Spike Tempotron (MST) [Güt16] and Threshold-Driven Plasticity (TDP) [YLT18], train the neuron to produce the desired number of spikes proportional to the number of available clues, regardless of the precise timing of spikes. They first transform the difference between the actual and desired number of spikes to the distance between the fixed biological firing threshold ϑ and the closest hypothetical threshold ϑ^*, and then update the synaptic weights by gradient descent strategy. This substitute makes learning more efficient, but the learning process becomes less straightforward and greatly increases computational complexity.

Towards Neuromorphic Machine Intelligence. https://doi.org/10.1016/B978-0-44-332820-6.00011-2

On the whole, the research of efficient learning algorithms for SNNs is still a nontrivial problem. In this chapter, we first introduce a joint weight-delay learning algorithm—First Error Learning (FE-Learn) [LQZC19], which is inspired by the finite precision learning [MROS14]. Then, a Recursive Least Squares-Based Learning Rule (RLSBLR) [ZQL+21] is described, where the weight modification depends on the influence of the current error function and the historical error function. In the following two sections, we introduce a Membrane-Potential Driven Aggregate-Label learning algorithm (MPD-AL) [ZWC+19] and an Efficient Threshold-Driven Plasticity rule (ETDP) [ZLC+20]. The MPD-AL algorithm constructs an error function based on the membrane potential trace and the fixed firing threshold ϑ of the neuron, and its learning speed is faster than the TDP and the MST algorithms. ETDP enables spiking neurons to generate the desired number of spikes that match the magnitude of delayed feedback signals and to learn useful multimodal sensory clues embedded within spontaneous spiking activities.

4.2 Accuracy measure and neuron model

Before starting the topic, we first introduce an evaluation metric commonly used in sequence learning, which is used in experiments with FE-Learn and RLSBLR algorithms. Then, the neuron model used in all four algorithms is introduced, which is essentially an example of the SRM model.

4.2.1 Spike metric

For sequential learning tasks, the learning accuracy can be measured by the spike metric C $(0 < C < 1)$ [SFW+03], which measures the similarity between the actual and desired output spike train. This metric is efficient and faithful in characterizing spike time reliability and is a common evaluation criterion. It has been employed by many algorithms [ZQB+18,LQZC19,PK10,TBLM15a,XLC+18,ZQX18,XZZ13,ZGZ+18,AR15].

The closer the actual output spike train is to the expected spike train, the closer the metric C approaches 1. The metric is defined as:

$$C = \frac{\vec{v}_d \cdot \vec{v}_a}{|\vec{v}_d|\,|\vec{v}_a|}, \tag{4.1}$$

where $\vec{v}_a$ and $\vec{v}_d$ are vectors that are the convolution (in discrete time) of actual and desired output spike trains by a symmetric Gaussian filter given as $f(t,\sigma) = \exp\left(-t^2/2\sigma^2\right)$, respectively. The parameter σ, determining the width of the filter, is usually set to 2. $\vec{v}_d \cdot \vec{v}_a$ is the inner product of these two vectors, while $|\vec{v}_d|$ and $|\vec{v}_a|$ are their L_2-norms.

4.2.2 Neuron model

Many spiking neuron models have been proposed over the years, among which conductance-based models can simulate biological neurons' dynamics accurately to a large extent, but require considerable computational cost because of the inherent complexity of their expressions. By contrast, the current-based leaky integrate-and-fire (LIF) [GK02] model can well simulate the dynamics of biological neurons with lower computation cost, which makes it a widely used model in many papers.

In the LIF model, learning neuron accumulates its membrane voltage $V(t)$ by integrating synaptic currents from N upstream neurons, yielding

$$V(t) = V_{rest} + \sum_{i=1}^{N} w_i \sum_{t_i^j < t} K\left(t - t_i^j\right) - \vartheta \sum_{t_s^j < t} \exp\left(-\frac{t - t_s^j}{\tau_m}\right), \quad x > 0, \tag{4.2}$$

where V_{rest} is the resting potential, which is usually set to 0. t_i^j is the firing time of the jth spike from the ith synapse, t_s^j is the firing time of the jth spike generated by the learning neuron. ϑ is the firing threshold. w_i represents the synaptic strength of the ith synapse, and it controls the amplitude of the postsynaptic potential induced by its spike, while the kernel $K(\cdot)$ controls the shape, and it is defined as

$$K(x) = V_{norm}\left[\exp\left(-\frac{x}{\tau_m}\right) - \exp\left(-\frac{x}{\tau_s}\right)\right], \tag{4.3}$$

where τ_m and τ_s are the time constants of the membrane potential and the synaptic current, respectively. V_{norm} is the normalization constant that stretches the peak value of $K(\cdot)$ to unity, and it is calculated by

$$V_{norm} = \frac{\beta^{\beta/(\beta-1)}}{\beta - 1}, \tag{4.4}$$

with $\beta = \tau_m/\tau_s$. If the voltage $V(t)$ reaches the firing threshold, it triggers a spike immediately, then this new spike causes the membrane voltage of the neuron to encounter a reset operation, which is expressed by the second term in Eq. (4.2).

4.3 First error-based supervised learning algorithm

Neural circuits respond to multiple sensory stimuli by firing precisely timed spikes. Inspired by this phenomenon, the spike timing based SNNs are proposed to process and memorize the spatiotemporal spike patterns. However, the response speed and accuracy of the existing learning algorithms of SNNs are still lacking compared to the human brain. To further improve the performance of learning precisely timed spikes, the learning algorithm First Error Learning (FE-Learn) that always adjusts the synaptic parameters at the first wrong output spike time is proposed [LQZC19]. It can accurately adjust the synaptic weights and delays that contribute to the membrane potential of desired and non-desired firing time.

4.3.1 First error learning rule

The aim of the vanilla FE-Learn algorithm is to modify the neuron's synaptic weights so that it can generate the target spike sequence corresponding to the given input spike pattern. Most existing algorithms train the neuron to fire spikes directly towards the desired times, but FE-Learn sets a tolerance window with a small width ε (less than the distance between any two desired spike times) at each desired time, and by training the neuron to emit a spike within the corresponding tolerance window in chronological order, the requirement of firing the target spike sequence is finally achieved. Accordingly, the learning method takes advantage of the idea that running synaptic modification rules only at the first wrong spike time in each trial in [MROS14].

There are different types of wrong spike times, but in general, they all fall into one of three categories and are shown in Fig. 4.1:

- If there is a spike fired outside all tolerance windows, this spike time is a wrong spike time of type a.
- If more than one spike is generated in the same window, then each spike except the first one in the window is a wrong spike time of type b.
- If there is no spike within the desired tolerance window, the desired spike time is a wrong spike time of type c.

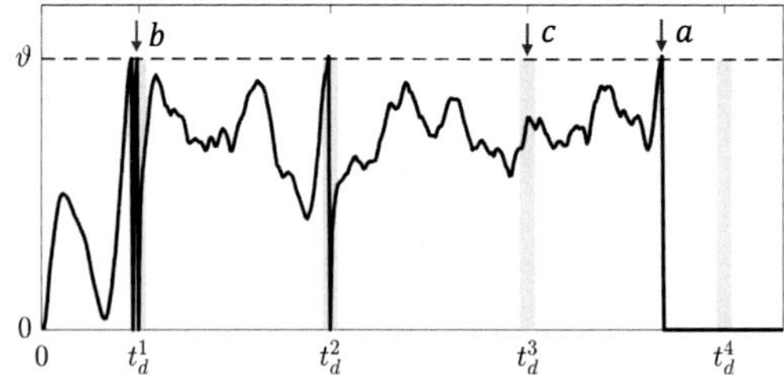

FIGURE 4.1 Three error types: undesired spike outside the tolerance window (a), undesired spike inside the tolerance window (b), and missed spike within the tolerance window (c). The gray vertical bars near the desired spike times t_d^j are the respective tolerance windows.

Following the idea that running synaptic modification rules only at the first wrong spike time in each trial, FE-Learn calculates weight adjustment in a new way that utilizes more temporal information between the input and output spike trains. Based on the different error types, it employs two weight updating processes. The cost function is defined as

$$E = \pm \left(\vartheta - V\left(t_e\right)\right), \tag{4.5}$$

where t_e is the first wrong spike time, and the $\pm$ sign corresponds to weight increment and decrement, respectively. In terms of error type c, a spike is supposed to be emitted within the tolerance window of a desired output spike time t_d^j, but if it is not, t_e is equal to t_d^j. Then, the contributory synaptic weights should be strengthened to stretch the membrane potential at time t_e to the threshold ϑ, so the error type c corresponds to the "+" case in

Eq. (4.5). When there is a spike fired outside the tolerance window (error type a) or there are more than one spike fired inside the same tolerance window (error type b), the contributory synaptic weights should be weakened to prevent the extra spike. Hence, the error types a and b correspond to the "–" case in Eq. (4.5).

According to the definition of the cost function, the membrane voltage at t_e dominates the parameter adjustment. In gradient-based learning, the weight modification Δw_i is proportional to the negative of the derivative of the cost function with respect to w_i:

$$\Delta w_i = -\lambda \frac{\mathrm{d}E}{\mathrm{d}w_i} = \pm\lambda \frac{\mathrm{d}V\,(t_e)}{\mathrm{d}w_i}, \tag{4.6}$$

where $\lambda > 0$ is the learning rate that defines the size of the weight adjustment. From Eq. (4.2), the membrane potential $V\,(t_e)$ not only receives the direct influence of the synaptic weights, but also the indirect influence of them, which is transmitted by the previous output spike times $t_o^j < t_e$, $j = 1, 2, \cdots, m$. The derivative term in Eq. (4.6) is hence given by

$$\frac{\mathrm{d}V\,(t_e)}{\mathrm{d}w_i} = \frac{\partial V\,(t_e)}{\partial w_i} + \sum_{j=1}^{m} \frac{\partial V\,(t_e)}{\partial t_o^j} \frac{\mathrm{d}t_o^j}{\mathrm{d}w_i}. \tag{4.7}$$

From Eq. (4.2), the first term of Eq. (4.7) can be expressed as

$$\frac{\partial V\,(t_e)}{\partial w_i} = \sum_{t_i^j < t_e} K\left(t_e - t_i^j\right), \tag{4.8}$$

and the partial derivative in the second term is

$$\frac{\partial V\,(t_e)}{\partial t_o^j} = -\frac{\vartheta}{\tau_m} \exp\left(-\frac{t_e - t_o^j}{\tau_m}\right), \tag{4.9}$$

while for the derivative $\mathrm{d}t_o^j/\mathrm{d}w_i$, applying the chain rule,

$$\frac{\mathrm{d}t_o^j}{\mathrm{d}w_i} = \frac{\partial t_o^j}{\partial V(t_o^j)} \frac{\mathrm{d}V(t_o^j)}{\mathrm{d}w_i} = \frac{\partial t_o^j}{\partial V(t_o^j)} \left(\frac{\partial V(t_o^j)}{\partial w_i} + \sum_{k=1}^{j-1} \frac{\partial V(t_o^j)}{\partial t_o^k} \frac{\mathrm{d}t_o^k}{\mathrm{d}w_i} \right) \approx \frac{\partial t_o^j}{\partial V(t_o^j)} \frac{\partial V(t_o^j)}{\partial w_i}, \tag{4.10}$$

in order to save the computation cost, the iterative computation term in Eq. (4.10) is eliminated. $\partial V(t_o^j)/\partial w_i$ can be solved by Eq. (4.8). Then, following the linear assumption of threshold crossing [BKLP02], the neuron's membrane potential is thought to increase linearly in the infinitesimal time step before the firing time. Hence, there is

$$\frac{\partial t_o^j}{\partial V(t_o^j)} = -\left[\left.\frac{\partial V(t)}{\partial t}\right|_{t=t_o^{j-}} \right]^{-1}, \tag{4.11}$$

where

$$\frac{\partial V(t)}{\partial t} = \sum_{i=1}^{N} w_i \sum_{t_i^j < t} \kappa(t - t_i^j) + \frac{\vartheta}{\tau_m} \sum_{t_o^k < t} \exp\left(-\frac{t - t_o^k}{\tau_m}\right), \tag{4.12}$$

with

$$\kappa(x) = \frac{\partial K(x)}{\partial x} = V_{norm}\left[\frac{1}{\tau_s}\exp\left(-\frac{x}{\tau_s}\right) - \frac{1}{\tau_m}\exp\left(-\frac{x}{\tau_m}\right)\right], \quad x > 0. \tag{4.13}$$

In the FE-Learn algorithm, as long as the spike is fired within the tolerance window of the desired time, it is considered to be correct.

4.3.2 Extended first error learning rule

As can be seen from the previous section, in each round of learning, the FE-Learn algorithm needs to find the first mismatch time point between the actual output spike train and the desired output spike train, and modify the weight according to its error type to enhance or weaken the membrane voltage at that moment, so as to correct the misfired spike. Under this premise, the FE-Learn algorithm is extended.

4.3.2.1 Synaptic delay learning

Neuroscience research shows that synaptic delay also has plasticity, so synaptic delay learning is added to FE-Learn to obtain the synapse weight-delay joint learning rules.

Similar to synaptic weight learning, the adjustment of synaptic delay d_i between a postsynaptic neuron and its ith presynaptic neuron is calculated as

$$\Delta d_i = -\eta \frac{\mathrm{d}E}{\mathrm{d}d_i} = \pm\eta \frac{\mathrm{d}V(t_e)}{\mathrm{d}d_i}, \tag{4.14}$$

where $\eta > 0$ is the learning rate of delay updating. The derivative of the membrane voltage at the first wrong time with respect to the delay is

$$\frac{\mathrm{d}V(t_e)}{\mathrm{d}d_i} = \frac{\partial V(t_e)}{\partial d_i} + \sum_{j=1}^{m} \frac{\partial V(t_e)}{\partial t_o^j} \frac{\mathrm{d}t_o^j}{\mathrm{d}d_i}. \tag{4.15}$$

It is easy to see that the derivation of this equation is the same as that for Eq. (4.7). $\partial V(t_e)/\partial t_o^j$ in the second term on the right side of the equation can be obtained by Eq. (4.9). $\mathrm{d}t_o^j/\mathrm{d}d_i$ can be solved by referring to Eqs. (4.10)–(4.13), the only difference lies in the first term on the right side of the equation, that is, the partial derivative of the membrane voltage of the postsynaptic neuron with respect to the synaptic delay directly connected with it (corresponding to Eq. (4.8)) is

$$\frac{\partial V(t_x)}{\partial d_i} = -w_i \sum_{t_i^j} \kappa(t_x - t_i^j - d_i), \tag{4.16}$$

where $t_x = t_o^1,\ t_o^2,\ \cdots,\ t_o^m,\ t_e$.

4.3.2.2 Multi-layer network learning

In view of the limitations of shallow networks, the algorithm is further extended to multi-layer SNNs. Assume that the network has L layers and is fully connected. The following derivation is based on a single neuron in the output layer. Let $V(t_e)$ be the membrane voltage of the first error spike time of this neuron. The parameters of the output layer are adjusted in exactly the same way as those of the single-layer network. Therefore only the parameter update formulas for the hidden layer are derived later (i.e., $1 \leq l \leq L-1$).

Assuming that w_{ih}^{l}, d_{ih}^{l} are the connection weight and delay between the neuron i in the $(l-1)$th layer and the neuron h in the lth layer, they will affect the output spike time $t_h^{m,l}$ of the neuron h, then $t_h^{m,l}$ will affect the output spike times of all subsequent layers. Therefore the derivative of the membrane voltage at the wrong time with respect to the parameter of the lth layer is

$$\frac{\mathrm{d}V(t_e)}{\mathrm{d}w_{ih}^{l}(d_{ih}^{l})} = \sum_{t_h^{m,l}<t_e} \frac{\mathrm{d}V(t_e)}{\mathrm{d}t_h^{m,l}} \frac{\mathrm{d}t_h^{m,l}}{\mathrm{d}w_{ih}^{l}(d_{ih}^{l})}, \tag{4.17}$$

where $t_h^{m,l}$ is the mth spike time of neuron h in the lth layer. $\mathrm{d}t_h^{m,l}/\mathrm{d}w_{ih}^{l}(d_{ih}^{l})$ can be solved by Eq. (4.10), so the only term that needs to be solved in Eq. (4.17) is $\mathrm{d}V(t_e)/\mathrm{d}t_h^{m,l}$, which is the key term for error transfer between layers.

Since the gradient derivation process of synaptic delay and synaptic weight is exactly the same, this section only takes synaptic weight as an example to deduce its updating process. For writing purposes, all delays are assumed to be 0 in the following equations. Now, define the error transitive term to be $\delta_h^{m,l}$. As for $1 \leq l < L-1$,

$$\delta_h^{m,l} \triangleq \frac{\mathrm{d}V(t_e)}{\mathrm{d}t_h^{m,l}} = \sum_{j=1}^{n^{l+1}} \sum_{t_h^{m,l}<t_j^{k,l+1}<t_e} \frac{\mathrm{d}V(t_e)}{\mathrm{d}t_j^{k(l+1)}} \frac{\mathrm{d}t_j^{k,l+1}}{\mathrm{d}t_h^{m,l}} = \sum_{j=1}^{n^{l+1}} \sum_{t_h^{m,l}<t_j^{k,l+1}<t_e} \delta_j^{k,l+1} \cdot \frac{\mathrm{d}t_j^{k,l+1}}{\mathrm{d}t_h^{m,l}}, \tag{4.18}$$

where n^l represents the number of neurons in the lth layer. As for $l = L-1$, only a single neuron j in the output layer is discussed (as mentioned above):

$$\delta_h^{m,L-1} = \frac{\partial V(t_e)}{\partial t_h^{m,L-1}} + \sum_{t_h^{m,L-1}<t_j^{k,L}<t_e} \frac{\mathrm{d}V(t_e)}{\mathrm{d}t_j^{k,L}} \frac{\mathrm{d}t_j^{k,L}}{\mathrm{d}t_h^{m,L-1}}. \tag{4.19}$$

For the first term on the right of the equation, according to the formula (4.2), the partial derivative of the membrane voltage of a postsynaptic neuron with respect to its input spike time is expressed as

$$\frac{\partial V(t_e)}{\partial t_h^{m,L-1}} = -w_{hj}^{L} \cdot \kappa\left(t_e - t_h^{m,L-1}\right), \tag{4.20}$$

while $\mathrm{d}V(t_e)/\mathrm{d}t_j^{k,L}$ in the second term can be solved by Eq. (4.9).

As the calculation of $\delta_h^{m,l}$ actually includes the transmission on the spatial scale (transmission between layers) and the time scale (transmission between multiple spikes of the same neuron), the cycle term of spike time is omitted in the solving process, similar to the formula (4.10). Hence, for $1 \leq l \leq L-1$:

$$\begin{aligned}\frac{\mathrm{d}t_j^{k,l+1}}{\mathrm{d}t_h^{m,l}} &= \frac{\partial t_j^{k,l+1}}{\partial V\left(t_j^{k,l+1}\right)} \frac{\mathrm{d}V(t_j^{k,l+1})}{\mathrm{d}t_h^{m,l}} \approx \frac{\partial t_j^{k,l+1}}{\partial V\left(t_j^{k,l+1}\right)} \frac{\partial V\left(t_j^{k,l+1}\right)}{\partial t_h^{m,l}} \\ &= \left(\frac{\partial V\left(t_j^{k,l+1}\right)}{\partial t_j^{k,l+1}}\right)^{-1} w_{hj}^{l+1} \cdot \kappa\left(t_j^{k,l+1} - t_h^{m,l}\right),\end{aligned} \tag{4.21}$$

where $\partial V\left(t_j^{k,l+1}\right)/\partial t_j^{k,l+1}$ can be solved by Eq. (4.12).

4.3.3 Algorithm analysis

Assuming t_o^k $(k = 1,\ 2,\ \cdots, M)$ is the kth actual output spike time of the output layer neuron o, t_d^k $(k = 1,\ 2,\ \cdots,\ N)$ is its kth desired output spike time. This section puts forward some key points in the experimental process from the theoretical point of view, and analyzes their causes and solutions.

4.3.3.1 Replace t_o^k with t_d^k when calculating the gradient

Note that each actual output spike time t_o^k before the t_e is within the tolerance window of the corresponding desired spike time t_d^k, and there is usually a slight deviation between t_o^k and t_d^k. Hence, the weight modification strategy based on Eq. (4.7) may exacerbate this deviation after multiple updates, resulting in more unnecessary adjustments. In order to address this, in the actual weight adjustment, t_o^j is replaced with t_d^j in Eqs. (4.7)–(4.11).

4.3.3.2 Control the influence of spike before t_e on weight update

In order to flexibly control the influence of output spike triggered before t_e on parameter adjustment, a scaling factor S_r (> 0) is given to the second term of Eq. (4.7), which is proven to be meaningful and vital by experiments. For the case where the membrane voltage needs to be reduced, S_r is set to 0 to avoid interfering with the output spike correctly fired before t_e. That is, the synaptic adjustment at the undesired time only depends on the error spike time t_e, and the influence of the past output spikes is discarded.

4.3.3.3 Initialize parameters appropriately

It can be seen from the above derivation that all parameter updates are carried out based on spikes. If a hidden layer neuron does not emit spikes initially, the synapses that come out of the neuron cannot be adjusted. In the synthetic data experiment of spike sequence learning, there is only one input pattern for a trial, which means that the hidden neurons that are not fired initially will not be adjusted and will remain silent all the time, unless there is an additional forced adjustment strategy. Although this is less likely in real-world data experiments (because hidden neurons that do not fire for one input sample may fire when stimulated by other samples), an appropriate initialization that enables most hidden neurons to fire is still helpful.

4.3.3.4 Avoid gradient explosion

Take weight adjustment as an example, and the delays are all fixed at 0. The value of Eq. (4.12) denotes the slope of the membrane potential around a spike time. When the membrane potential slowly and barely reaches the firing threshold, the value of Eq. (4.12) is very small, i.e., $\partial V(t_x)/\partial t_x \approx 0$. This causes a gradient explosion, since Eq. (4.12) is the denominator of Eq. (4.11). In the following, the circumstances that may cause the value of Eq. (4.12) to be abnormal will be discussed. Here, the first term is simply written as $\sum_i w_i \kappa_i$, where $\kappa_i(t) = \sum_j \kappa\left(t - t_i^j\right)$.

- $\sum_i w_i \kappa_i \geq 0, 0 < \partial V(t_x)/\partial t_x < \vartheta_P$: A single-layer network consisting of a learning neuron with two input synapses is shown in Fig. 4.2. The blue and purple dashed lines in Fig. 4.2 are the κ_i $(i = 1, 2)$ curves of the two inputs. The blue and purple arrows at the bottom represent input spikes of the two neurons. As shown in the figure, the κ_1 curve (blue) decays from the time of its input spike, and after time $a = \frac{\tau_m \tau_s ln(\tau_m/\tau_s)}{\tau_m - \tau_s}$, it decays to 0. After that, its value is always less than 0, but it decreases first, then rises, and finally approaches 0. The κ_2 curve (purple) also shows the same trend. According to Eq. (4.12), the curve of the partial derivative term $\partial V(t)/\partial t$ (red solid line) equals the weighted sum of the two κ curves, and its value at the output spike time, i.e., $\partial V(t_x)/\partial t_x$ (red solid point) is a crucial intermediate variable of gradient calculation. When this value is very small, the reciprocal will be very large, then it will lead to the gradient explosion and disrupt the weight adjustment. Hence, its value must be limited: when the value is less than a threshold ϑ_P ($\vartheta_P > 0$, usually set to 0.05), make it equal to ϑ_P.

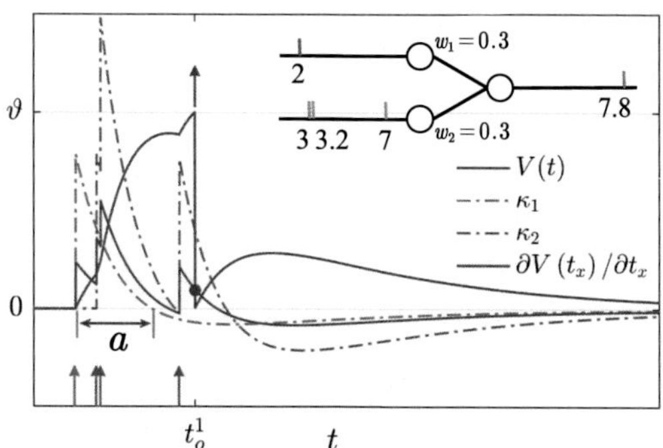

FIGURE 4.2 Schematic of the partial derivatives $\partial V(t_x)/\partial t_x$ that may result in a gradient explosion. The arrows represent input and output spikes, and their colors correspond to the network in the upper-right corner. $\kappa_i(t) = \sum_j \kappa\left(t - t_i^j\right)$. The value of the red point is $\partial V\left(t_o^1\right)/\partial t_o^1$, with $t_o^1 = 7.8$.

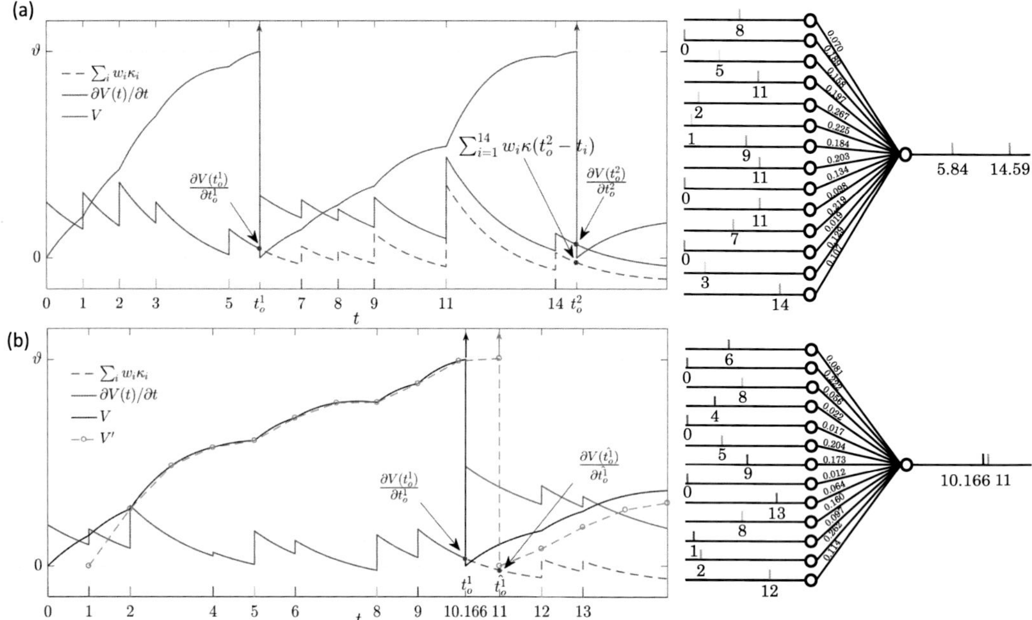

FIGURE 4.3 The effect of the output spike and the resolution of time step on the partial derivatives $\partial V(t_x)/\partial t_x$. (a) Due to the influence of the first output spike t_o^1, the partial derivative curve value at the second output spike time t_o^2 is larger than 0. (b) The black and gray curves represent the voltage curves when the time step is 0.001 and 1, respectively. When the time step is 1, the neuron fires at $\hat{t}_o^1 = 11$, and the sign of the corresponding partial derivative value is opposite to that of the true output spike time $t_o^1 = 10.166$, resulting in abnormal parameter adjustment. The symbol representation is the same as in Fig. 4.2.

- $\sum_i w_i\kappa_i < 0, 0 < \partial V(t_x)/\partial t_x < \vartheta_P$: The red solid line in Fig. 4.3(a) is the partial derivative curve of $\partial V(t)/\partial t$, the red dashed line is the weighted sum of the κ curves of the input neurons. Before the first output spike time t_o^1, they overlap. Then, because of the influence of the previous output spike (the second term of Eq. (4.12)), the partial derivative curve is higher than the weighted κ curve after t_o^1, and the partial derivative value at the second output spike time t_o^2 is avoid to be less than 0. However, the positive and negative terms cancel out, causing the value of Eq. (4.12) to be very close to 0. This case is treated in the same way as the first one.
- $\partial V(t_x)/\partial t_x > 0$, $\partial V(\hat{t_x})/\partial \hat{t_x} \leq 0$: As shown in Fig. 4.3(b), the time resolution will affect the sign of the partial derivative $\partial V(t_x)/\partial t_x$. When the time step is 0.001, the neuron fires at $t_o^1 = 10.166$ (the solid black line), and the partial derivative term $\partial V(t_o^1)/\partial t_o^1$ is positive. However, when the time resolution is 1, the membrane voltage of the neuron at $t = 10$ is below the threshold, then we can only detect that the membrane voltage at $\hat{t}_o^1 = 11$ is higher than the threshold. Hence, $\hat{t}_o^1$ is a pseudo-firing time. Although the difference between it and the real firing time t_o^1 is less than the time resolution, the sign

of $\partial V(\hat{t_o^1})/\partial \hat{t_o^1}$ is opposite to the real one, resulting in an abnormal weight adjustment. For this case where the partial derivative is negative, we set its reciprocal equal to zero.

To sum up, in order to avoid gradient explosion, the following strategy is applied:

$$\frac{\partial t_x}{\partial V(t_x)} = \begin{cases} -\frac{1}{\vartheta_P}, & 0 < \frac{\partial V(t_x)}{\partial t_x} \leq \vartheta_P, \\ 0, & \frac{\partial V(t_x)}{\partial t_x} \leq 0, \\ -\left(\frac{\partial V(t_x)}{\partial t_x}\right)^{-1}, & \text{otherwise.} \end{cases} \tag{4.22}$$

4.3.4 Applications and results

This section first explores the learning effect of the FE-Learn algorithm and other single-layer sequence learning algorithms. Then, experiments are conducted to further explore the improvement of the extended FE-Learn compared with the original FE-Learn.

4.3.4.1 Performance evaluation of FE-learn

The effects of several important parameters on the learning performance are investigated, including the time duration of spike trains, the number of synaptic inputs, and the firing rates of input and output spike trains. In these simulations, the time constant of the membrane potential and the synaptic currents, τ_m and τ_s, are set to 10 ms and 2.5 ms, respectively. The firing threshold and the time step are set to 1 mV and 1 ms, respectively. The synaptic weights are randomly initialized by the Gaussian distribution $N(0.01, 0.01)$. 20 trials with different input and desired output pairs are conducted for each experiment.

A. Effect of the time duration: In this section, the learning neuron has 400 synaptic afferents. The aim is to train the neuron to reproduce a desired spike train with a time duration of 200–3000 ms and the length of the interval is 200 ms. When the time duration of spike trains is in the ranges [200, 1000], [1200, 2000], [2200, 3000] ms, the corresponding width of the tolerance window is 1, 3, and 5 ms, respectively. Before each training trial, the desired output spike train with a firing rate of 100 Hz, and input spike train with a firing rate of 10 Hz are generated according to the homogeneous Poisson processes. During each training, the maximum value of C and the running time required to reach it are recorded. After 20 training trials, the average values of all maximum C and corresponding running times are reported.

Fig. 4.4(a) shows the variation trend in learning accuracies of FE-Learn, SPAN, and ReSuMe. The learning accuracies of the three algorithms can reach one when the time duration of spike trains varies from 200 to 600 ms, but when the time duration exceeds 800 ms, the learning accuracies of SPAN and ReSuMe start to decline, and the learning times increase gradually. While the learning accuracy of FE-Learn is limited by the width of the tolerance window ε, it can remain constant at 1 when $\varepsilon = 1$, $C \approx 0.96$ when $\varepsilon = 3$, and $C \approx 0.89$ when $\varepsilon = 5$, and the learning accuracy drops significantly when the width of the tolerance window changes. Under the same width of the tolerance window, the learning time increases with the increase of spike train length. The general trend is that FE-Learn can obtain higher learning accuracy than SPAN and ReSuMe with less time.

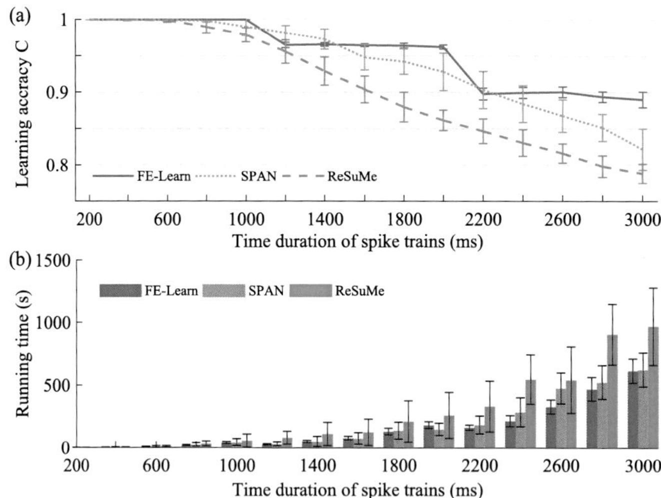

FIGURE 4.4 Effect of the time duration of spike trains on learning performance.

B. Effect of the number of the synaptic inputs: The effect of the number of the synaptic inputs is investigated in this section, and it varies from 100 to 500 in intervals of 50. When the synaptic input is in 100, [150, 250], [300, 500], the corresponding width of the tolerance window is 5, 3, and 1, respectively. The time duration of the spike trains is set to 800 ms. The desired output spike train with a firing rate of 100 Hz and input spike train with a firing rate of 10 Hz are generated according to the homogeneous Poisson processes at the beginning of each training trial.

Fig. 4.5 shows the experimental results. As shown in Fig. 4.5(a), a small number of synaptic inputs lead to a low learning accuracy for both SPAN and ReSuMe, for instance, the learning accuracy of SPAN is only 0.81 and for ReSuMe is 0.79 when the neuron is trained with only 100 synaptic inputs, but SPAN takes a very short time, and although FE-Learn with $\varepsilon = 5$ takes longer time, it can achieve higher accuracy. When the number of synaptic inputs is greater than or equal to 300, the width of the tolerance window of FE-Learn is set to 1 ms, then the learning accuracy of it can reach 1, while the learning accuracies of SPAN and ReSuMe slowly increase to 1 with the increase of the number of synaptic inputs. Additionally, under the same width of the tolerance window, the learning time of FE-Learn can decrease with the increase of the number of the synaptic inputs. In short, FE-Learn performs better than ReSuMe both in terms of accuracy and running time, and obtains higher accuracy than SPAN in a comparable time.

C. Effect of the firing rate: The effect of the firing rate of the spike trains is evaluated in the following experiments. For the input spike trains, the firing rates (r_{in}) are varied from 6 to 18 Hz in intervals of 4 Hz, while for the desired output spike trains, the firing rates (r_{out}) are varied from 20 to 160 Hz in intervals of 20 Hz. The time duration of the spike trains is 800 ms and the number of synaptic inputs is set to 400. In each trial, the learning continues

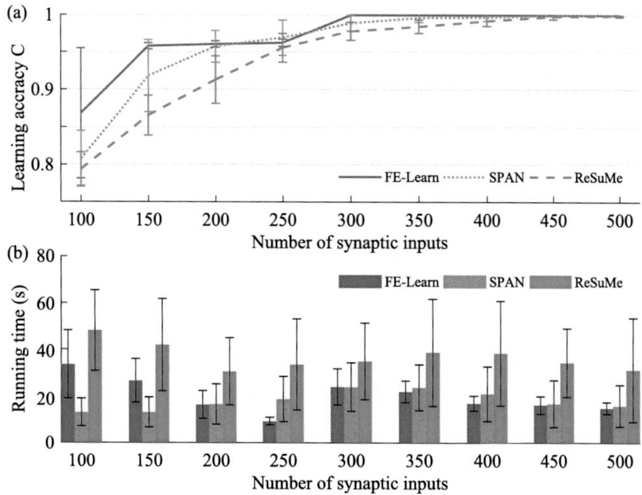

FIGURE 4.5 Effect of the number of the synaptic inputs on learning performance.

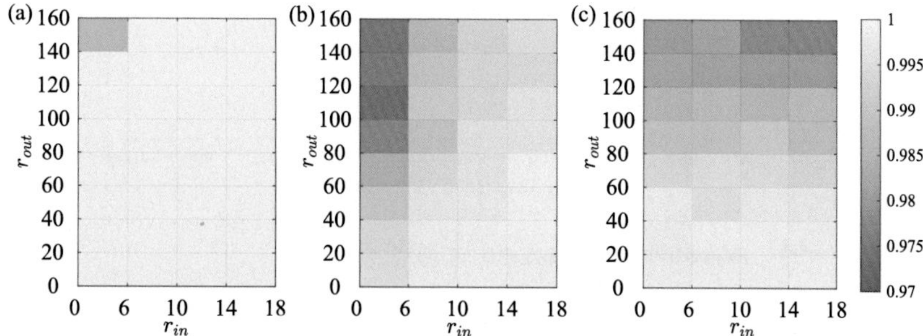

FIGURE 4.6 Effect of the firing rate of the spike trains on learning performance of FE-Learn (a), SPAN (b), and ReSuMe (c). All parameters except the firing rates of input spike trains r_{in} and the desired output spike trains r_{out} are fixed. The width of the tolerance window ε is set to 1.

until the algorithm converges and the averages of the maximum obtained C from 20 trials are reported in Fig. 4.6.

From Fig. 4.6(a), the learning accuracy of FE-Learn can achieve 1 except when the firing rates of the input spike train and the desired output spike trains are 6 Hz and 160 Hz, respectively, but even in this worst case, the accuracy still reaches 0.986. However, the performances of SPAN and ReSuMe become worse with the decrease of r_{in} and the increase of r_{out}, and their lowest accuracy are about 0.97, as shown in Fig. 4.6(b).

4.3.4.2 Performance evaluation of extended FE-learn

First, whether the proposed FE-Learn with joint synaptic weight-delay plasticity algorithm can improve the sequence learning ability of a single neuron is discussed. Then, several practical datasets are used to further verify the effectiveness of the proposed algorithm.

Finally, a multimodal pattern recognition experiment based on visual and auditory dual-channel information fusion is conducted.

In sequential learning tasks on synthetic data, unless otherwise stated, the parameters are set as follows: the time constants of the membrane (τ_m) and synapse current (τ_s) are 5 ms and 1.25 ms, respectively. The time step and tolerance window of delay FE-Learn are 1 ms. The learning neuron receives input spikes from 400 presynaptic neurons, and the time duration is 400 ms. The input spike patterns and desired output spike patterns are generated by a 2 Hz and 50 Hz Poisson process, respectively. For each set of experimental conditions, the mean and standard deviation of highest learning accuracy C for 20 trials (with an upper limit of 12 000 rounds per trial) are reported.

A. Effect of the time duration: The influence of the time duration on the sequence learning performance is investigated in this experiment, so the time duration of the spike trains varies from 100 ms to 1000 ms in intervals of 100 ms. For different time lengths, the tolerance window width of FE-Learn is [1, 1, 3, 3, 3, 5, 5, 5, 5] ms.

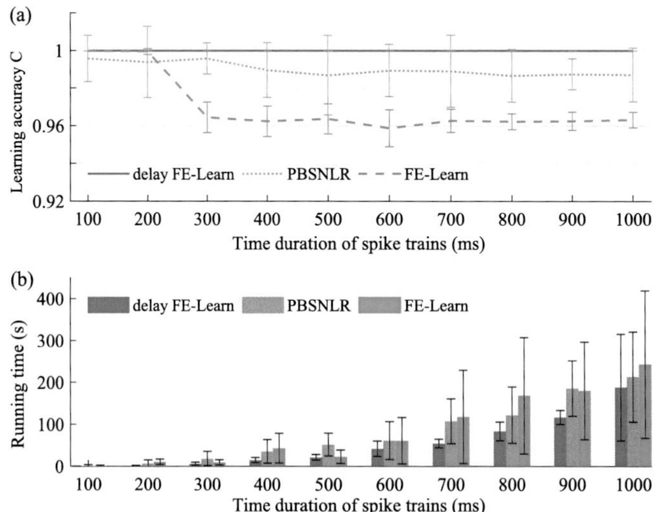

FIGURE 4.7 The effect of the length of the time duration on learning performance. (a) The highest learning accuracy under different lengths of time duration. (b) The running time required to achieve the highest accuracy.

From Fig. 4.7, as the length of the time duration increases, the time required by all three algorithms to achieve the highest accuracy will increase. According to the preliminary experiment, when the input is sparse and the length exceeds 200, FE-Learn cannot converge to 1, so the width of its tolerance window is widened to ensure its convergence. The wider the tolerance window, the looser the convergence condition. When the time step is 1 ms, a width of 1 ms means that the actual output spike train is required to be strictly equivalent to the expected output spike train, while a width of 3 ms means that if all the output spike times are located in the open intervals $(t_d^k - 3/2, t_d^k + 3/2)$ of the corresponding desired spike times, the output is correct (convergent), but according to (4.2.1), the accuracy metric C cannot reach 1. This is why the accuracy of FE-Learn remains at around 0.962 when the time length is greater than 200 ms. On the other hand, the accuracy of PBSNLR [XZZ13] decreases with the increase of duration time, while the delay FE-Learn can maintain convergence even when the tolerance window width is 1 ms. Although it has adjustments for synaptic delays that the other two algorithms do not have, it takes less time due to fewer training rounds required for convergence. This shows the superiority of the algorithm.

B. Effect of the synaptic input quantities: In this experiment, the number of input neurons varies from 100 to 400 in intervals of 50. The smaller the number of synaptic inputs, the more difficult the sequence learning. Therefore corresponding to the different number of synaptic inputs, the tolerance window width of the FE-Learn is set to [5, 5, 5, 3, 3, 3, 1, 1] ms to ensure its convergence.

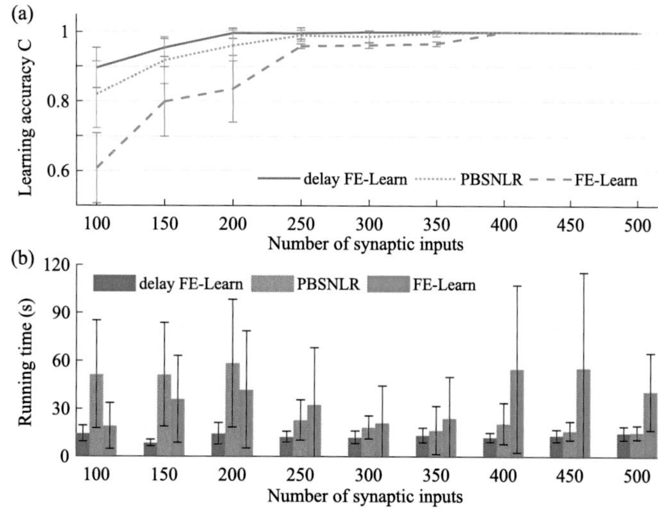

FIGURE 4.8 The effect of the number of synaptic inputs on learning performance. (a) The learning accuracy of delay FE-Learn, PBSNLR, and FE-Learn with different numbers of synaptic inputs. (b) The running time required to achieve the highest accuracy.

As shown in Fig. 4.8, when the number of input neurons is less than 200, FE-Learn is difficult to converge and the learning accuracy is low. PBSNLR is relatively good, but it needs more learning time. However, even when the number of input neurons is only 100, the average accuracy of delay FE-Learn is still about 0.9, and its running time is less than PBSNLR. With the increase of the number of synaptic inputs, the learning accuracy of the three algorithms gradually increases. When the number of synaptic inputs is greater than or equal to 250, the learning accuracy of delay FE-Learn can converge to 1, while PBSNLR can ensure complete convergence to 1 only when the number of input synapses exceeds 400. The accuracy and running time of FE-Learn are related to the width of its tolerance window. When the window width changes, there will be a sudden increase in the accuracy and the corresponding running time, for example when the number of synaptic input is

250 and 400. Obviously, delay FE-Learn has more stable and excellent performance under different synaptic input numbers.

C. Effect of the firing rate: The input spike frequency varies from 1 Hz to 5 Hz in intervals of 1 Hz, while the desired output spike frequency varies from 20 Hz to 160 Hz in intervals of 20 Hz. For FE-Learn and delay FE-Learn, the widths of the tolerance window are set to 1 ms.

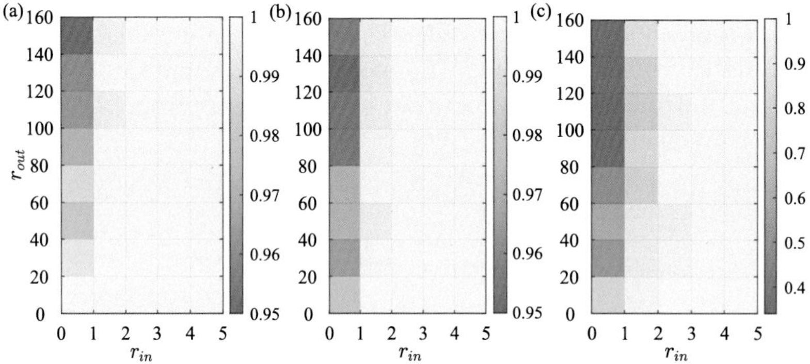

FIGURE 4.9 The average learning accuracy of delay FE-Learn (a), PBSNLR (b), and FE-Learn (c) in 20 experiments. r_{in} denotes the input spike frequency and r_{out} denotes the desired output spike frequency.

The lower the input spike frequency and the higher the output spike frequency, the more difficult it is to learn. Therefore the top-left corner of the result graph has the deepest color, representing the lowest learning accuracy. From the color blocks of Fig. 4.9, the performance of delay FE-Learn is better than PBSNLR and FE-Learn. When the input spike frequency is less than or equal to 2 Hz, the accuracy of delay FE-Learn and PBSNLR can reach 0.95. However, when the input spike frequency is extremely low and the output spike frequency is extremely high, FE-Learn faces collapse, with the lowest accuracy about 0.4.

4.3.4.3 Classification of UCI datasets

The UCI machine learning repository [DG17] is often used to train machine learning models, and has also been widely used to test the SNN models. This repository consists of 488 data sets, of which five common ones are selected for our experiments. To evaluate the effectiveness of the proposed delay learning algorithm and the multi-layer learning algorithm, we compare them with FE-Learn and other competitive methods.

A. Data encoding and output decoding: Before feeding the data into the SNN for classification, the real value of the data should be encoded into the spike that SNNs can process. The Gaussian Receptive Field Population Coding method [BKLP02] is adopted here. Assuming that each attribute is encoded by N_E neurons, a data sample with N_A attributes will be encoded into an input spike pattern by $N_E N_A$ coding neurons (each coding neuron encodes a spike time). For an attribute, each of its N_E coding neurons corresponds to a Gaussian Receptive Field, which overlap with each other and act together to cover the whole coding time interval T. These fields are of the same width, $\frac{1}{\gamma}\frac{I_{max}-I_{min}}{N_A-2}$ ($\gamma = 1.5$ as in most literature), and the center of the ith coding neuron is $I_{min} + \frac{2i-3}{2}\frac{I_{max}-I_{min}}{N_A-2}$, where I_{max} and I_{min} are the maximum and minimum values of the attribute in all samples, respectively. Attribute values are input into these Gaussian functions, and the resulting output values will be inversely mapped to the time interval T, that is, the larger the output value, the earlier the firing time. Neurons whose spike times are later than $0.9T$ are considered to be silent.

Moreover, we also need to decode the network output, i.e., define the corresponding relationship between the output spike train of the output layer and the category of the input sample. In this work, the number of neurons in the output layer is equal to the number of data categories, and each output neuron corresponds to a category. It is generally necessary to define a specific desired output spike train $\boldsymbol{t_d}$ for each class in advance, then the class of the sample is considered to be the class of the output neurons whose output most closely resembles $\boldsymbol{t_d}$ (similarity is measured by metric C). However, in practical applications, since samples from the same category differ from one another, defining an identical and fixed desired output spike train for them is not ideal. In our experiments, we adopt the dynamic decoding method [LQZC19] to set the desired spike trains. The details of the decoding strategy are shown as follows.

During training, for an input sample, the maximum subthreshold membrane voltage V_{max} and its corresponding time t_{max}, and the actual output spike train $\boldsymbol{t_o}$ of each output neuron are recorded. The desired output spike train $\boldsymbol{t_d}$ and the first error spike time t_e of an output neuron are defined as follows:

- For the non-target neuron, it should be silent, i.e., $\boldsymbol{t_d}$ does not exist, then
  a. If no spike is generated, no learning is required.
  b. If the neuron fires, then obviously t_e is the first firing time.
- For the target neuron, $\boldsymbol{t_d}$ is dynamically determined. ϑ_e $(< \vartheta)$ is a pre-defined decoding threshold:
  a. If no spike is generated, $\boldsymbol{t_d} = \{t_{max}\}$, then obviously, $t_e = t_{max}$.
  b. If the neuron fires and $V_{max} \geq \vartheta_e$, then $\boldsymbol{t_d} = \boldsymbol{t_o} \cup \{t_{max}\}$, $t_e = t_{max}$.
  c. If the neuron fires and $V_{max} < \vartheta_e$, then $\boldsymbol{t_d} = \boldsymbol{t_o}$ and no learning is required.

After full training, the non-target neuron tends to be silent. Then, the input sample is considered to belong to the class corresponding to the output neuron with the largest number of firings. If all the output neurons are silent, it belongs to the class corresponding to the neuron with the highest membrane voltage.

B. Comparison of classification performance on UCI datasets: The details of five UCI datasets (the Iris dataset, the Wisconsin Breast Cancer diagnostic dataset, BUPA Liver Disorders dataset, Pima Diabetes dataset, and Ionosphere datasets) are listed in Table 4.1. Considering the different partition ratio of training set and test set in different literatures, we choose the most commonly used ratio of 1:1 (the same as SpikeProp [SS15], SWAT [WMSS10], and SRESN [DSSS16]). The network structures and the number of training epochs of different methods are summarized in the upper part of Table 4.2, the accuracy

Table 4.1 Parameters of several UCI datasets.

Dataset	Iris	Breast cancer	Liver disorders	Pima diabetes	Ionosphere
#Instances	150	683	345	768	351
#Training	75	341	172	384	175
#Test	75	342	173	384	176
#Categories	3	2	2	2	2
#Attributes	4	9	6	8	33
#Encoders	40	15	25	10	7

(with standard deviation) is given in the lower part of Table 4.2, where the accuracy of our algorithms is the average result of 20 independent trials.

As shown in Table 4.2, the performance of our algorithms clearly outperforms others as it achieved the best accuracy in the Iris and Ionosphere datasets, and the sub-optimal performance in the remaining three datasets. Specifically, the proposed algorithms always outperform the SWAT, SRESN, and Multi-layer DL-ReSuMe [TBLM18] (abbreviated as MDL in Table 4.2) in terms of accuracy and efficiency. SpikeProp achieves the best accuracy in the BUPA Liver Disorders dataset and the Pima Diabetes dataset, but it requires 15 times as many training epochs as our methods and its performance in the other three datasets is mediocre. As for SpikeTemp [WBMM17], it can only achieve the optimal result in the Breast Cancer dataset, and the performance in the other four datasets is inferior to our methods. On the whole, there is no method that can achieve the best accuracy in all five datasets, but the overall performance of our algorithms is better than other algorithms.

4.3.4.4 Classification of multimodal data

In order to further verify the capability of the proposed methods in practical applications, experiments on larger real datasets are required. On the other hand, many neurophysiological studies have suggested that different areas of the mammalian brain can work together to better perform cognitive tasks [CCB00,CT04,BNN21]. For example, a person in a conversation can obtain information about the other person's mood and the implications of his/her words from their facial expressions, language, and even gestures. Inspired by this, an audio-visual bimodal spiking neural network structure driven by the proposed learning algorithm is applied here to perform an audio-visual bimodal recognition task.

A. Audio and visual datasets: Here, the bimodal architecture is expected to process two forms of input, i.e., images from MNIST [LBBH98] and sounds from TIDIGITS [LD93] separately, then the two high-level presentations are combined for the final decision.

MNIST is a handwritten digital dataset containing 10 numbers from 0 to 9. In the dataset, 60 000 images are used as the training set and 10 000 images are used as the test set. Each image is a gray image of 28×28. The gray values are encoded into spikes and fed into the visual pathway of the framework, as shown in Fig. 4.10. Latency coding [Hop95] is used to convert the image information into spike patterns. Specifically, each pixel is encoded to a spike by $t_i = \alpha(-p_i + 255)/255$, where p_i is the value of the ith pixel, t_i is the encoded spike time and α is a scaling factor. In our experiments, $\alpha = 30$ ms.

Table 4.2 Comparison of classification results for UCI datasets.

Dataset	Iris		Breast cancer		Liver disorders		Pima diabetes		Ionosphere	
	Architecture	Epochs	Architecture	Epochs	Architecture	Epochs	Architecture	Epochs	Architecture	Epochs
SpikeProp	25-10-3	1000	55-15-2	1000	37-15-2	3000	55-20-2	3000	205-25-2	3000
SWAT	24-312-3	500	54-702-2	500	36-468-2	500	54-702-2	500	204-2652-2	500
SRESN	24-(6-10)	102	54-(8-12)	306	36-(6-9)	715	54-(9-14)	254	204-(16-23)	1018
SpikeTemp	120-87	/	135-306	/	150-226	/	80-431	/	231-223	/
MDL	169-360-3	100	/	100	246-360-2	100	/	100	/	100
FE-Learn	160-3	200	135-2	200	150-2	200	80-2	200	231-2	200
Delay FE	160-3	200	135-2	200	150-2	200	80-2	200	231-2	200
Two-layer FE	160-360-3	200	135-360-2	200	150-360-2	200	80-360-2	200	231-360-2	200
	Train (%)	Test (%)	Train (%)	Test (%)	Train (%)	Test (%)	Train (%)	Test (%)	Train (%)	Test (%)
SpikeProp	97.2(1.9)	96.7(1.6)	97.3(0.6)	97.2(0.6)	71.5(5.2)	65.1(4.7)	78.6(2.5)	76.2(1.8)	89.0(7.9)	86.5(7.2)
SWAT	96.7(1.4)	92.4(1.7)	96.5(0.5)	95.8(1.0)	74.8(2.1)	60.9(3.2)	77.0(2.1)	72.1(1.8)	86.5(6.7)	90.0(2.3)
SRESN	96.9(1.0)	97.3(1.3)	97.7(0.6)	97.2(0.7)	60.4(1.7)	59.7(1.7)	70.5(2.4)	69.9(2.1)	91.9(1.8)	88.6(1.6)
SpikeTemp	100.0(/)	96.7(/)	99.1(/)	98.3(/)	93.0(/)	58.3(/)	77.5(/)	67.6(/)	86.8(/)	91.5(/)
MDL	99.8(/)	95.7(/)	98.2(/)	96.4(/)	69.9(/)	61.8(/)	72.1(/)	70.6(/)	96.0(/)	90.5(/)
FE-Learn	96.4(1.6)	95.1(2.5)	94.8(0.9)	94.3(1.7)	72.2(5.0)	61.2(3.6)	79.3(1.2)	71.2(2.0)	99.6(0.3)	92.1(2.0)
Delay FE	98.2(1.2)	97.3(1.2)	97.6(0.6)	97.4(0.5)	71.6(2.3)	62.0(3.7)	77.4(1.3)	72.2(1.4)	98.0(1.8)	92.5(1.2)
Two-layer FE	99.4(0.9)	98.0(1.3)	100.0(0.0)	97.5(0.5)	96.6(0.7)	64.8(2.3)	90.6(1.4)	72.5(1.5)	96.3(1.5)	92.7(1.6)

TIDIGITS is a widely used speech recognition dataset that contains the utterances of 11 words from the digits "zero" to "nine" and "oh". It contains a training set of 2464 samples and a test set of 2486 samples. The threshold encoding mechanism [GS09] is used to encode the audio information into a spike pattern. First, the original sound wave is filtered by a Constant-Q Transform (CQT) cochlear filter bank (20 cochlear filters ranging from 200 Hz to 8 kHz) to obtain a spectrogram. Next, for each spectrogram bin corresponding to a cochlear nucleus, 31 neurons are used to encode its energy changes as spikes. Hence, a total of 620 neurons are used to encode an audio sample (for more details, see [GS09,ZWC+19]). It is worth mentioning that in order to match the MNIST image dataset, we excluded the extra category of "oh" in the TIDIGITS speech dataset in the hybrid testing process, and the size of this dataset is expanded to the same size as MNIST by random sampling.

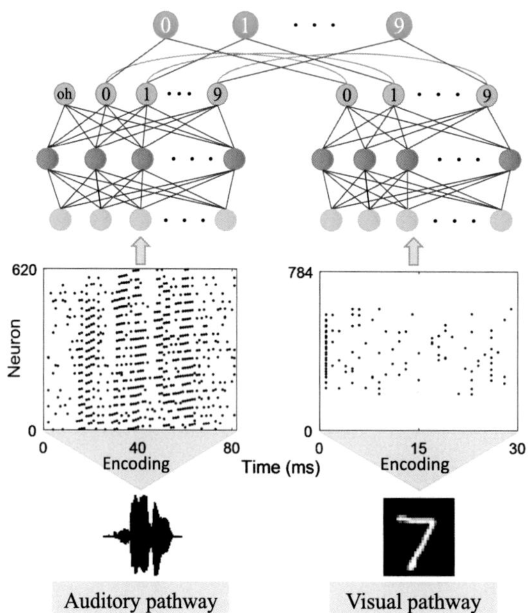

FIGURE 4.10 Audio-visual bimodal network architecture.

B. Audio-visual bimodal architecture and learning:

The entire processing architecture is built by SRM neurons as described in subsection 4.2.2. Before the fusion of the different modals, the encoded speech and image data are fed into the corresponding audio and visual path for separate, non-interference processing. As shown in Fig. 4.10, the unimodal ensemble topology of the image is the same as that of the speech, they are both fully connected networks, and the network structures are 784-800-10, 620-800-10, respectively. The established unimodal ensembles are trained with the proposed multi-layer learning algorithm, and the desired output spike train during training is decided in the same way as in subsubsection 4.3.4.3.

Table 4.3 Comparison of the proposed learning algorithms with other unimodal approaches.

Data	Model	Layers	Accuracy (%)
MNIST	Zhang et al. [ZLG+21]	1	75.0
	Pierre et al. [FTB+18]	1	88.2
	Hussain et al. † [HLB14]	1	90.26
	ROL † [LMMC18]	1	90.34
	Diehl et al. [DM15] *	2	95.0
	Mostafa [Mos17]	2	97.2
	S4NN [KM20]	2	97.4
	BP-STDP [TM18]	2	97.2
	Hong et al. [HWW+20]	2	97.4
	FE-Learn	1	91.9
	Delay FE-Learn	1	94.3
	Multi-layer FE-Learn	2	98.2
TIDIGITS	Neil et al. [NL16]	3	96.1
	Tavanaei et al. [TM17a]	3	96.0
	PBSNLR-DW [ZWB+20]	1	96.5
	MPD-AL [ZWC+19]	1	97.5
	FE-Learn	1	96.4
	Delay FE-Learn	1	96.8
	Multi-layer FE-Learn	2	98.1
Bimodal	Rathi et al. [RR18]*	2	98.0
	Zhang et al. [ZLC+20]	2	98.9
	This work	2	99.6(0.24)

* The model is unsupervised, otherwise it is supervised.

† The model only uses 10 000 samples for training and in [HLB14], only 5000 samples were tested.

Then, we implement mutual assistance by establishing cross-modal connections on the output neurons of the two unimodal networks. It is intuitive that two neurons belonging to different modals but corresponding to the same class will excite each other, two neurons belonging to different modals and corresponding to a different class will inhibit each other. However, only the former kind of cross-modal connections, that is, excitatory connections between pairs of neurons corresponding to the same category, are established. The exclusion of later inhibitory connections is due to the fear of damaging what has been learned. The excitatory cross-modal connection is bidirectional and, once determined, fixed. The connected pair of neurons renew at the same time. In addition, a supramodal layer is needed to integrate the output of 10 decision neurons of two modals, and it acts as an AND gate, i.e., each neuron of the supramodal layer corresponds to two neurons, which come from different modals but correspond to the same category. Hence, there are also 10 neurons in this layer, corresponding to 10 categories. When an input sample is fed into the network, the category of the neuron that emits most spikes is the result of the recognition.

Since the TIDIGITS dataset is expanded to the same size as the MNIST dataset by random sampling, we report the average classification accuracy for the bimodal network after 10 random extensions.

As shown in Table 4.3, the proposed delay learning algorithm significantly improves the performance of FE-Learn. For example, delay FE-Learn achieves an accuracy of 94.3% in the MNIST dataset, which is much higher than the 91.9% of FE-Learn, thus verifying the effectiveness of the proposed delay learning method. On the other hand, the multi-layer FE-Learn achieves an accuracy of 98.2% and 98.1% on MNIST and TIDIGITS, respectively. These results are better than other spike temporal-based learning algorithms [Mos17,KM20,TM18,HWW+20]. The lower part of Table 4.3 shows the results of the recent SNN-based multimodal computational models. We can see that the multimodal models achieve superior accuracy to other unimodal frameworks. In addition, the multimodal framework equipped with our learning algorithm also achieves the best accuracy (99.6%) among the existing multimodal frameworks.

4.4 Recursive least squares-based learning algorithm

In this section, a Recursive Least Squares-Based Learning Rule (RLSBLR) for SNNs is shown to generate the desired spatiotemporal spike train [ZQL+21]. During the learning process, the weight update is driven by the cost function defined by the difference between the membrane potential and the firing threshold. The amount of weight modification depends not only on the impact of the current error function, but also on the previous error functions that are evaluated by current weights. In order to improve the learning performance, a modified synaptic delay learning is integrated to the proposed RLSBLR.

4.4.1 RLSBLR learning rule

The RLSBLR learning rule also uses the neuron model described in subsection 4.2.2. For convenience of description, Eq. (4.2) is rewritten as follows:

$$V(t) = V_{rest} + \mathbf{W}^{\mathsf{T}}(t)\,\mathbf{PSP}(t) + \eta(t), \tag{4.23}$$

where $\mathbf{W} = [w_1, \ \cdots, \ w_n]^{\mathsf{T}}$ is the synaptic weight vector of the neuron and its n presynaptic neuron. $\mathbf{PSP}(t) = [PSP_1(t), \cdots, PSP_i(t), \cdots, PSP_n(t)]^{\mathsf{T}}$ is the PSPs of presynaptic neurons. $PSP_i(t) = \sum_j K\left(t - t_i^j - d_i\right)$ (from the definition of K in Eq. (4.3), $t_i^j + d_i < t$) is induced by the spike train $\mathbf{T}_{in}^i = \{t_i^1, \ t_i^2, \ \cdots, \ t_i^m\}$ of input neuron i, where t_i^j is the jth spike time in $\mathbf{T}_{in}^i$. d_i is the synaptic delay time of neuron i, which causes the input spike t_i^j $(j = 1, \ 2, \ \cdots, \ m)$ to induce PSP on the output neuron after d_i time. $\eta(t) = -\vartheta \sum_{t_a^f < t} \exp\left(-\frac{t - t_a^f}{\tau}\right)$ characterizes the refractory period of the output neuron, where t_a^f is the spike in the actual output spike train $\mathbf{T_a} = \{t_a^1, \ t_a^2, \ \cdots, \ t_a^l\}$, and τ is a time decay constant. The description of the remaining symbols is the same as in subsection 4.2.2.

The RLSBLR supervised learning rule trains the output neuron to emit spikes at the desired times by its input spike trains. Similarly, the desired spike train is represented as $\mathbf{T}_d = \{t_d^1, t_d^2, \cdots, t_d^p\}$. $\mathbf{T}_s = \mathbf{T}_a \cup \mathbf{T}_d - \mathbf{T}_a \cap \mathbf{T}_d = \{t_s^1, t_s^2, \cdots, t_s^q\}$ is an incorrect output spike set. To emit spikes at the desired times, RLSBLR learns from two aspects: the weight learning and the delay learning.

4.4.1.1 The weight learning rule

Instead of updating the weights $\mathbf{W}$ after all the input spikes have been transmitted, $\mathbf{W}$ changes at each incorrect spike time t_s^f. Suppose t^* ($t^* \in \mathbf{T}_s$) is the current weight updating time, then it falls into one of the following two categories: t^* belongs to an undesired spike time ($t^* \in \mathbf{T}_s^a = \mathbf{T}_a - \mathbf{T}_d$), which means that the output neuron generates a spike at the wrong time, or t^* belongs to the desired spike time ($t^* \in \mathbf{T}_s^d = \mathbf{T}_d - \mathbf{T}_a$), which means that the output neuron does not generate a spike at the desired spike time.

The previous weight updating time before t^* is defined as t_s^k ($k = 1, 2, \cdots, last$) and $t^* = t_s^{last+1}$, and the membrane potential is recalculated at these moments with the current weights $\mathbf{W}(t^*)$:

$$V_e(t_s^k) = V_{rest} + \mathbf{W}(t^*)^{\mathsf{T}}\mathbf{PSP}(t_s^k) + \eta(t_s^k), \qquad k = 1, 2, \cdots, last + 1. \tag{4.24}$$

Then, what needs to be done is to make $V_e(t_s^k)$ equal to ϑ at $t_s^k \in \mathbf{T}_s^d$ and $V_e(t_s^k)$ below ϑ at $t_s^k \in \mathbf{T}_s^a$. Hence, the error signal at t_s^k, $k = 1, 2, \cdots, last + 1$ (Fig. 4.11(a)) is defined as:

$$e(t_s^k) = \begin{cases} V_e(t_s^k) - \vartheta, & \text{if } t_s^k \in \mathbf{T}_s^d, \\ V_e(t_s^k) - \rho\vartheta, & \text{if } t_s^k \in \mathbf{T}_s^a, \end{cases} \tag{4.25}$$

where ρ ($0 < \rho < 1$) is used to control the distance of the membrane voltage relative to ϑ at $t_s^k \in \mathbf{T}_s^a$. The reason why the parameter ρ is given is that, obviously, the membrane potential at time $t_s^k \in \mathbf{T}_s^a$ is greater than or equal to ϑ, while the expectation is to make it lower than ϑ, and the farther the moment is from the desired firing time, the lower its membrane potential should be. To achieve this, ρ is set as a variable related to the distance to the nearest desired firing time, as defined below:

$$\rho = \begin{cases} \exp\left(-\frac{|t^* - t_{nrst}|}{\tau_n}\right), & \text{if } 0 < |t^* - t_{nrst}| < t_{len}, \\ \exp\left(-\frac{t_{len}}{\tau_n}\right), & \text{if } |t^* - t_{nrst}| \geq t_{len}, \end{cases} \tag{4.26}$$

where τ_n is a time constant to adjust the declining speed of ρ, t_{nrst} is the nearest desired spike time to t^*, t_{len} is a constant that is used to control the longest distance between t^* and t_{nrst}. The change in ρ is shown in Fig. 4.11(b).

The cost function is the accumulation of all the previous error signals:

$$J(t^*) = \sum_{k=1}^{last+1} e^2(t_s^k) + \lambda \|\mathbf{W}(t^*)\|^2, \tag{4.27}$$

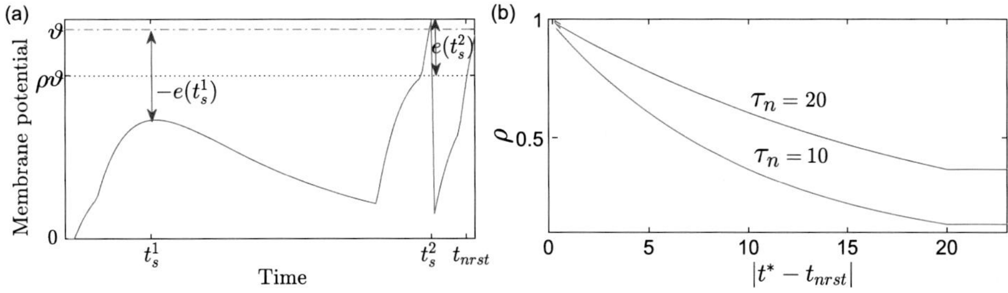

FIGURE 4.11 (a) The membrane potential of the output neuron. The error signal is $e(t_s^1)$ at the desired time $t_s^1 \in \mathbf{T}_s^d$ and is $e(t_s^2)$ at an undesired time $t_s^2 \in \mathbf{T}_s^a$. (b) The change in parameter ρ. The declining speed of ρ is related to τ_n, and t_{len} limits the decay lower bound of ρ so that it does not keep decaying, which avoids the over-adjustment of $\mathbf{W}$.

where $\|\mathbf{W}(t^*)\|$ is the L_2 norm of weights vector $\mathbf{W}(t^*)$, and λ is the regularization parameter. It is easy to understand that the regularization term is added to prevent over-fitting and enhance the generalization ability of the method. Current learning should not destroy previously learned information, the errors at previous incorrect times $(e(t_s^k), k = 1, 2, \cdots, last)$ are calculated by the current weights $\mathbf{W}(t^*)$ to ensure the correctness of the current learned information as far as possible, as shown in Fig. 4.12(a).

The recursive least-squares (RLS) [Hay95] method is used to minimize the cost function, by differentiating $J(t^*)$ of Eq. (4.27), the weight updating formula can be obtained as:

$$\mathbf{W}(t^*) = \mathbf{W}(t_s^{last}) - e(t^*)\mathbf{P}(t^*)\mathbf{PSP}(t^*), \tag{4.28}$$

$$\begin{aligned}\mathbf{P}(t^*) &= \left[\lambda\mathbf{E} + \sum_{k=1}^{last+1} \mathbf{PSP}\left(t_s^k\right)\mathbf{PSP}^{\mathsf{T}}\left(t_s^k\right)\right]^{-1} \\ &= \mathbf{P}(t_s^{last}) - \frac{\mathbf{P}(t_s^{last})\mathbf{PSP}(t^*)\mathbf{PSP}(t^*)^{\mathsf{T}}\mathbf{P}(t_s^{last})}{1 + \mathbf{PSP}(t^*)^{\mathsf{T}}\mathbf{P}(t_s^{last})\mathbf{PSP}(t^*)},\end{aligned} \tag{4.29}$$

where $\mathbf{P}(t^*)$ contains previously learned information, and it is initialized as $\mathbf{P}(0) = \frac{1}{\lambda}\mathbf{E}$ at the beginning of each epoch since no error occurs when $k = 0$ and $[\lambda\mathbf{E}]^{-1} = \frac{1}{\lambda}\mathbf{E}$, $\mathbf{E}$ is the unit matrix. Note that the parameter λ is used to initialize $\mathbf{P}$ as $\mathbf{P}(0)$, and different initialization values can cause different learning speeds, so $\frac{1}{\lambda}$ functions as the learning rate: the smaller the value $\frac{1}{\lambda}$ is, the slower the learning is, and vice versa. However, $\frac{1}{\lambda}$ is only used once at the period of initialization rather than every weight update, which differs from the usual learning rate.

The updating process of a synaptic weight w_i is shown schematically in Fig. 4.12(a). To simplify the representation, the delay d_i is 0 and assume that each element of $\mathbf{P}(t)$ is always greater than or equal to 0 from $t = 0$ to $t = t_s^3$. When $t^* \in \mathbf{T}_s^d$, $V(t^*)$ is below ϑ, hence, $-e(t^*) > 0$, and $PSP_i(t^*) > 0$ since there are input spikes before t^*, according to Eq. (4.28),

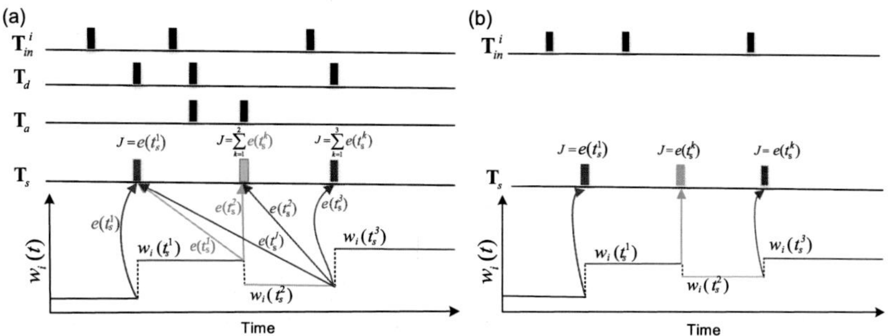

FIGURE 4.12 Comparison of weight updating processes. (a) Weight updating process of a neuron i in RLSBLR. $\{t_s^1, t_s^3\} \in \mathbf{T}_s^d$, $t_s^2 \in \mathbf{T}_s^a$, the different colored arrows represent different error $e(t_s^k)$ calculated with the unchanged current weight $w_i(t^*) = w(t_s^{last})$, and the cost function J is the sum of the errors (same colors). The weight $w_i(t)$ changes only at incorrect times t_s^k, which is calculated by Eq. (4.28), and it remains the same until next incorrect spike time. (b) Weight updating processes of ReSuMe and PBSNLR. Their cost functions J are only based on the current incorrect time, i.e., $t^* = t_s^1 / t_s^2 / t_s^3$.

the weight $w_i(t)$ at the desired time is increased to bring the $V(t^*)$ close to ϑ. When $t^* \in \mathbf{T}_s^a$, since $V(t^*)$ is higher than ϑ, $-e(t^*) < 0$, $PSP_i(t^*) > 0$, so as to decrease the weight $w_i(t)$ at an undesired time to achieve the purpose of reducing $V(t^*)$ below ϑ. The weights remain unchanged until the next incorrect spike time.

4.4.1.2 The delay learning rule

Inspired by DL-ReSuMe [TBLM15a], its delay learning method is modified and integrated with the RLSBLR. During the learning process, the modified delay learning rule helps the neuron to generate spikes at the desired time and remain silent at other time. Specifically, the modified delay learning consists of two learning processes.

On the one hand, if the current time is a desired spike time ($t^* \in \mathbf{T}_s^d$) and the membrane potential is below the firing threshold:

(1) Finding all positive synapses i ($w_i > 0$).

(2) Calculating the time $t_i^f + t_{max}$ of every positive synapse, where $t_{max} = \frac{\tau_m \tau_s[\ln(\tau_m) - \ln(\tau_s)]}{\tau_m - \tau_s}$ is the time required for the PSP function to reach the maximum value, shown in Fig. 4.13(a).

(3) Finding the synapse j with the minimum positive distance between $t_j^f + t_{max}$ and t^*: $j = \arg\min_i \{t^* - (t_i^f + t_{max})\}, t^* > t_i^f + t_{max}$.

(4) Checking whether the delay d_j of this synapse has been updated. If not, update it: $d_j \leftarrow t^* - t_j^f - t_{\max}$. If the delay of this synapse has been updated, no delay adjustment is made for this round. Note that each synapse's delay can only be adjusted once at most during the entire learning process.

On the other hand, if the membrane potential reaches the firing threshold at a wrong spike time ($t^* \in \mathbf{T}_s^a$), find all the negative synapses i ($w_i < 0$), and then repeat the above steps (2)–(4).

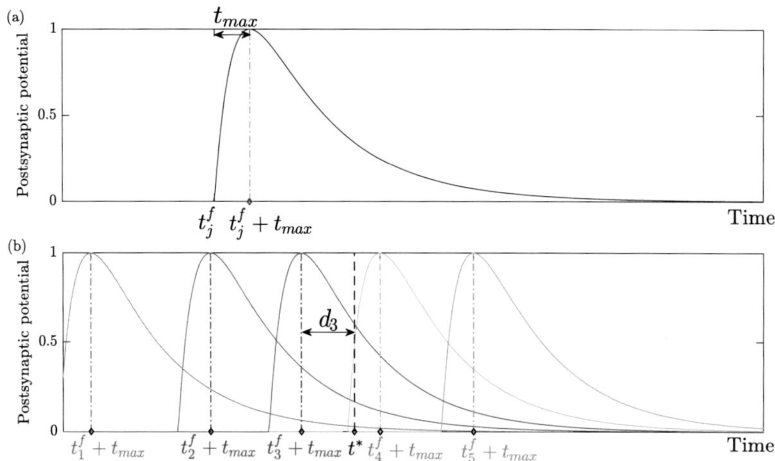

FIGURE 4.13 The delay adjustment of the modified delay learning. (a) Postsynaptic potential induced by an input spike t_j^f (the fth spike of input neuron j). t_{max} is the time interval from t_j^f to the time of its maximum postsynaptic potential. (b) Postsynaptic potentials of 5 input neurons with positive synapses. t^* is the current time. The neuron j with maximum time $t_j^f + t_{max}$ before t^* is chosen (here $j = 3$), then its delay d_j is adjusted as $t^* - t_j^f - t_{\max}$ if it has not been updated before.

Fig. 4.13(b) shows the delay adjustment of the modified delay learning. With the help of the delay learning, the maximum PSP of the chosen neuron j is transferred from $t_j^f + t_{max}$ to t^*. When $t^* \in \mathbf{T}_s^d$, the chosen synapse has a positive weight, increasing its PSP is equivalent to increasing the membrane potential at the desired time. While if the synapse j is selected from the negative synaptic weight, the weighted PSP will reduce the membrane potential at an undesired spike time, and eventually remove the undesired spike.

4.4.2 Comparison with the existing learning methods

ReSuMe, PBSNLR, and RLSBLR are single-layer spiking learning algorithms used to train the output neuron to generate the desired spike train, which is a fundamental computation task in many SNN-based neural systems. The weight updates of ReSuMe and PBSNLR are shown in Fig. 4.12(b). However, they are implemented differently for generating desired spikes, and the differences among them are shown as follows.

First, their cost function is different. ReSuMe and PBSNLR are based on the error at the current time (Fig. 4.12(b)), the weight adjustment may destroy the features learned in the previous spike times. However, the RLSBLR method calculates the total errors (Fig. 4.12(a)). In other words, the total errors not only calculate the error at the current time t^*, but also the previous errors at $t_s^1, t_s^2, \cdots, t_s^{last}$. The cost function of this method includes more information, so it converges faster. In addition, the cost function of this method includes the regularization item $\lambda\|\mathbf{W}(t^*)\|^2$ that is a technique to improve the generalization ability of the learning algorithm and prevent over-fitting [BVDG11].

Secondly, a modified delay learning is integrated in the RLSBLR method. Biological researches have shown that delays exist in neural networks [KM65,MKS12,PP10]. There is evidence to support the view that the delays can be adjusted rather than fixed [LF02,BFMD11]. Delay learning has a good performance even if the desired spike time is in a silent window [ZWB+20]. For example, t_d^3 is in the silent window (Fig. 4.14(a)), the output neuron is difficult to fire at this time since the input spikes are well before this time and the PSPs are almost zero. However, the input spikes are shifted near the desired spike time by learned delays. Therefore t_d^3 is able to be learned by updating synaptic weights, and the delay learning improves the learning accuracy. In addition, experimental results [TBLM15a,TBLM15c,TBLM18,TBLM15b] show that the delay adjustment can improve the learning accuracy and the efficiency of learning algorithms.

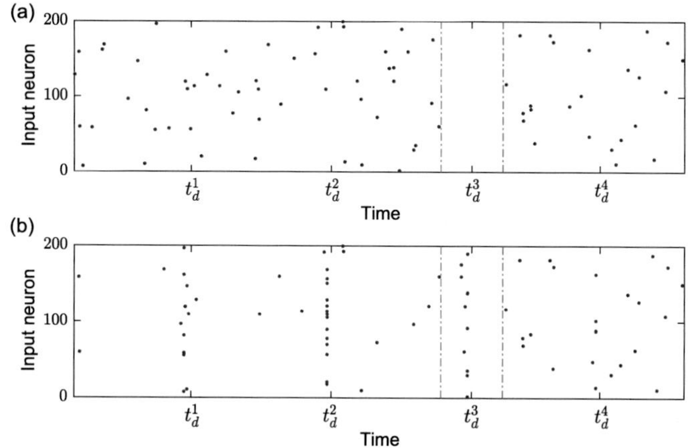

FIGURE 4.14 (a) The input spike trains of 200 input neurons and the desired spike train of the output neuron containing 4 spikes. The silent window is the time interval between two green lines, where no input spike is within this window. t_d^3 is in the silent window, and the learning is very difficult if only the weights are adjusted. (b) The delay learning changes the distribution of input spikes since many input spikes are shifted to their adjacent desired spikes.

Thirdly, compared with spike-driven methods, such as ReSuMe, the RLSBLR is a membrane-potential method. Since the cost function of a spike-driven method is based on spike time, it takes spike time to differentiate the membrane potential first, and then takes the membrane potential to differentiate weights. The weight adjustment in the method is more direct, which reduces the learning difficulty and complexity. In addition, the weight adjustment of this method follows the BPBA principle [XZHY13] (the Bigger PSP is, the Bigger is the Adjustment): the spikes introduce bigger PSP, the weight adjustment of the corresponding input neurons needs to be bigger. It is confirmed that this principle is able to effectively decrease the interference among multiple spikes during learning.

Fourthly, compared with existing membrane potential-driven learning algorithms, such as PBSNLR, this method follows the natural spiking dynamics of the neuron. PBSNLR relies on forcing the reset times to the desired output spike times, transforming the problem to that of fulfilling linear constraints imposed on the synaptic weights. However, incorporating such forced resets in a plausible synaptic learning rule is problematic, since it requires a mechanism that overrules the natural spiking dynamics of the neuron during learning.

As mentioned, there are mainly four differences between the RLSBLR method and the other two learning algorithms, which contribute to the better performance of the RLSBLR method. Fig. 4.15 and Fig. 4.16 show the learning curves among RLSBLR, PBSNLR, and ReSuMe, recording the weight change of each input neuron at the current time. Every input neuron has only one input spike, and input neurons are rearranged in ascending order of spiking time. Fig. 4.15(a) and Fig. 4.16(a) show the learning curves at a desired time $t^* \in \mathbf{T}_s^d$ and an undesired spiking time $t^* \in \mathbf{T}_s^a$, respectively. Fig. 4.15 (b) and Fig. 4.16 (b) show the PSPs for input neurons with delays or not at the current time t^*. The hollow circles and black dots with the same abscissa values represent the same input neurons with delay or not, respectively, whose x-coordinate is the spike time and the y-coordinate is the PSP at t^*. The two ends of the dotted red line are the incorrect time t_s^k and the PSP of the chosen input neuron that has updated delay at t_s^k. The PSP of the chosen neuron without delay is shown as a pink '◊', and that with the delay is expressed as red '*' (e.g., neurons 66 and 87).

Next, the learning curves will be carefully analyzed to determine the differences among RLSBLR, ReSuMe, and PBSNLR, whether these differences improve the performance of the RLSBLR algorithm and which aspect of the performance they improve.

1) The shape of the learning curve (Fig. 4.15(a) and Fig. 4.16(a)) is related to the cost function (first difference), which is based on total errors, thus it can improve the learning efficiency and robustness.

- For learning efficiency: As can be seen from Fig. 4.15(a) and Fig. 4.16(a), the weight change of ReSuMe and PBSNLR monotonically increases (decreases) before reaching the maximum (minimum) value, while for the RLSBLR algorithm, its cost function is global based and contains all errors, which are calculated repeatedly to re-correct the previously learned information as much as possible. Therefore the combinations of all the previous errors determine how much a neuron's weight changes, rendering the weight adjustments to be positive or negative, so that some bumps (concave or convex shape) are shown in the learning curve. For example, in Fig. 4.15, t^* belongs to the desired time, and the weights need to be increased to make the output neuron fire at t^*, so that most of the changed weights are positive. By integrating all the previous errors, some neurons' weight changes and becomes negative to maintain the output neuron silent at any undesired time. Therefore it can be concluded that this method carries more learning information in every weight update, and can obtain higher learning efficiency with fewer training epochs.
- For learning robustness: Due to the definition of the cost function, the errors are calculated multiple times, so the weights of some neurons with spike time around $\mathbf{T}_s^a$ and $\mathbf{T}_s^d$ are decreased or increased repeatedly. Accordingly, the membrane potential is adjusted to be much lower than the threshold at each undesired time and much higher than the threshold at any desired time. Hence, it is difficult to trigger an incorrect spike

at the undesired time. Meanwhile, as the membrane potential is strong enough around the desired spike time, the neuron will still correctly fire a desired spike even when the noise is added. Therefore the noise has less influence on the firing of the neuron, causing better robustness for this algorithm.

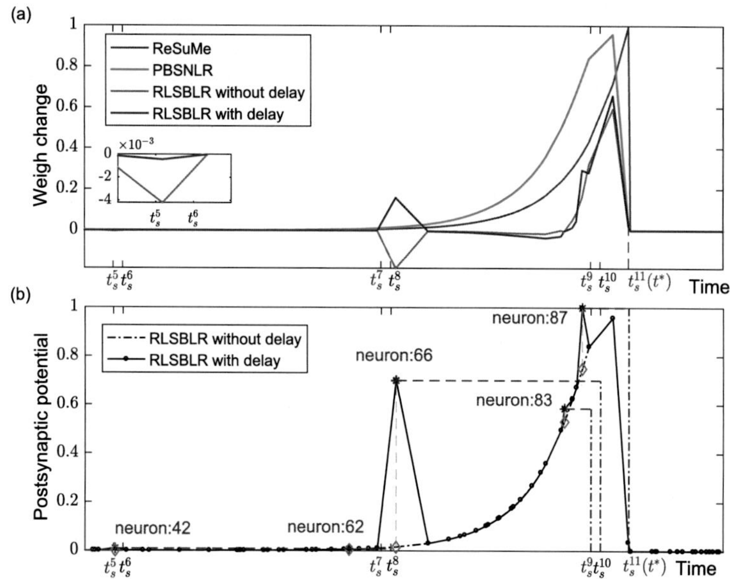

FIGURE 4.15 The learning curves of three methods (a) and the PSPs of RLSBLR's input neurons (b) at a desired spike time $t^* \in \mathbf{T}_s^d$. $\{t_s^5, t_s^7, t_s^9, t_s^{11}\} \in \mathbf{T}_s^d$, which are shown in red, and $\{t_s^6, t_s^8, t_s^{10}, t_s^{11}\} \in \mathbf{T}_s^a$, which are shown in black. For the sake of illustration, the learning curve and the PSP near t^* are drawn. In (a), the previous errors of the RLSBLR method cause some bumps on the learning curve, and the delay learning will change these bumps by affecting the PSPs of the corresponding neurons. The learning curve from t_s^5 to t_s^6 is not obvious from the figure, so this time area (zoom in) is enlarged. In (b), the solid line and dotted line are the PSPs form input neurons with and without delay, respectively. The added-delay neurons are shown in colored symbols, where the red '*' is the PSP of a neuron with a delay while the pink '◇' that are connected to it by the gray line is the PSP of the same neuron without delay, and the number is its index. The input neuron connected with incorrect time t_s^k by the red dashed line means this neuron learns delay at that time.

2) The delay learning (second difference) helps improve learning accuracy and convergence speed. In Fig. 4.15(b) and Fig. 4.16(b), the input neurons with delay make the PSPs produce some new bumps by shifting their input spikes towards t_s^k. Combining all the errors, the direction and magnitude of these bumps in the RLSBLR learning curve with delay change, which makes the curve different from that of RLSBLR without delay. For example, the delays change the direction of the bump of neuron 66 in Fig. 4.15(a) (neuron 75 in Fig. 4.16(a)), and change the magnitude of the bump of neuron 42 in Fig. 4.15(a) (neuron 91 in Fig. 4.16(a)). The shift of these input spikes caused by their delays makes the credit assignment of weights more reasonable, and also solves the silent window problem, thus improving the accuracy of the delay learning rule. Furthermore, both the weight update and the delay update can help the membrane potential increase at $\mathbf{T}_s^d$ and decrease at $\mathbf{T}_s^a$,

which means the delay learning is able to help the output neuron fire faster at the desired time.

3) Compared with ReSuMe, the RLSBLR method follows the BPBA principle, which improves the learning accuracy and efficiency. The learning curve of ReSuMe in Fig. 4.15(a) (Fig. 4.16(a)) is monotonically increasing (decreasing) with an exponential shape. However, the contribution of an input spike to the membrane potential of SRM neuron first increases and then decreases. Therefore the weight update of ReSuMe is unmatched with the membrane potential contribution of input neurons, which is not conducive to its learning efficiency and accuracy. However, the learning curve of RLSBLR is basically anastomotic with the input contribution, that is, RLSBLR follows the BPBA principle. Thereupon, the learning accuracy and efficiency of the RLSBLR algorithm are better than ReSuMe.

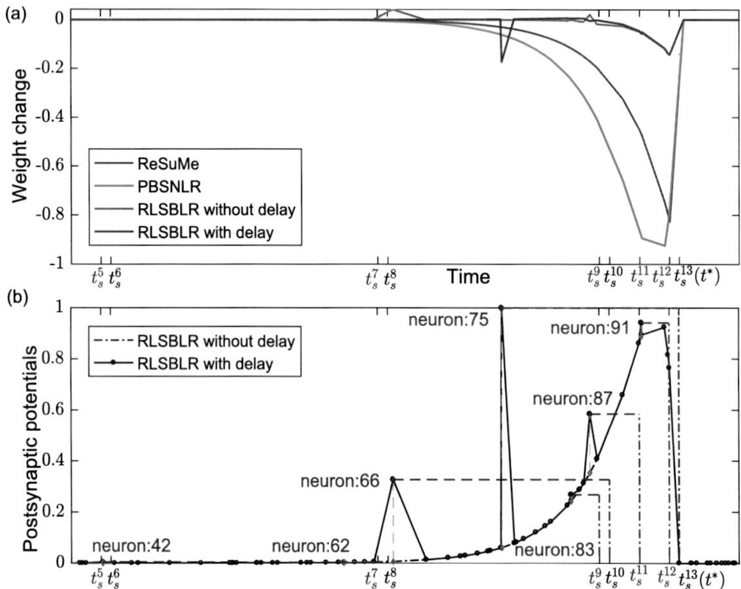

FIGURE 4.16 The learning curves of three methods at an actual output spike time $t^* \in \mathbf{T}_s^a$ in (a) and the PSPs of input neurons at t^* (b). The symbolic representation in this figure is the same as Fig. 4.15. $\{t_s^5, t_s^7, t_s^9, t_s^{11}, t_s^{12}\} \in \mathbf{T}_s^d$, and $\{t_s^6, t_s^8, t_s^{10}, t_s^{11}, t_s^{13}\} \in \mathbf{T}_s^a$. Most of the changed weights are negative to make the output neuron silent at $t^* \in \mathbf{T}_s^a$, and the positive weight changes make the output neuron fire at $\mathbf{T}_s^d$.

4.4.3 Applications and results

A number of simulations are conducted to demonstrate the characteristics of the RLSBLR learning rule in this section. Its performance compared with PBSNLR and ReSuMe methods is evaluated by exploring the parameters (such as the length of spike trains, the number of inputs, the firing rates, and the noise strength) on synthetic data. Furthermore, the algorithm is applied to a real-world classification task.

4.4.3.1 Performance evaluation of RLSBLR

The default parameters for all algorithms are shown in Table 4.4 (any parameter that differs from the default one would be declared otherwise). For the synthetic data tasks, there are 400 input neurons to make an output neuron produce a desired spike train ($\mathbf{T}_d$), and the firing rates of the Poisson distributed input spike trains $\mathbf{T}_{in}$ and $\mathbf{T}_d$ are $r_i = 4$ Hz and $r_d = 40$ Hz, respectively. The length of spike trains is 400 ms (t_{length}) and the time step is 1 ms. Empirically, the default parameters of the neuron model are: $\tau_m = 5$, $\tau_s = 1.25$, $\tau = 7$, $\vartheta = 1$. 20 trials are generated to train the networks for 1000 epochs to learn $\mathbf{T}_d$ and the initial weights $\mathbf{W}(0) = \mathbf{0}$. The delay $\mathbf{d} = [d_1, d_2, \cdots, d_n]$ of synapses is initialized to $\mathbf{0}$. The parameters in each learning rule are also shown in Table 4.4, and the learning rates in comparison experiments are shown in Table 4.5.

The input $\mathbf{T}_{in}$ and desired $\mathbf{T}_d$ spike trains are generated by Poisson distributions in synthetic data tasks. An experiment is trained with the specified trials with different input spike trains and desired output spike trains. For each trial, $\mathbf{P}$ and $\mathbf{T}_a$ are reset at the beginning of each epoch. The membrane potential $V(t)$ is calculated from time 0 to t_{length} with time step t_{step}, the actual output spike time is added to $\mathbf{T_a}$ when $V(t) \geq \vartheta$. At each time t, we judge whether t belongs to $\mathbf{T}_s$. If so, the weight rule and the delay rules are learned. At the end of each epoch, the accuracy C is measured, and the learning of this trial stops when the C is 1 or when the specified epoch $maxEpoch$ is reached.

Table 4.4 Parameters for the algorithms.

Parameter description	Symbol	Value
Number of inputs	n	400
Time step	t_{step}	1 ms
Threshold	ϑ	1
Firing rate of the input spike trains	r_i	4 Hz
Firing rate of the desired output spike train	r_d	40 Hz
Maximum trained epochs	$maxEpoch$	1000
Length of spike trains	t_{length}	400 ms
Number of trials	$trialsNum$	20
Initial weights	$\mathbf{W}(0)$	**0**
Delay of inputs	$\mathbf{d}$	**0**
	τ_m	5 ms
Time constants of neuron model	τ_s	1.25 ms
	τ	7 ms
	a	0.00001
Parameters of ReSuMe	A	1
	τ_+	5 ms
	τ_p	7 ms
Parameters of PBSNLR	τ_R	5 ms
	η_0	2

Table 4.5 The learning rates of the experiments.

	ReSuMe	PBSNLR(β)	RLSBLR($\frac{1}{\lambda}$)
Fig. 4.17	0.005(200)–0.0005(2000)	0.4(200)–0.02(2000)	0.4(200–2000)
Fig. 4.18	0.0005(50)–0.005(500)	0.005(50)–0.2(500)	0.6(50)–0.3(500)
Fig. 4.19	0.005	0.1	0.2
Table 4.6 & Fig. 4.21	0.005	0.01	0.075
Table 4.7	0.005	0.005	0.075

A. Effect of the time duration: The length of spike trains (t_{length}) is the varied parameter in this experiment, which varies from short to long and makes the output neuron more difficult to learn the desired spike train. t_{length} ranges from 200 ms to 2000 ms with the interval of 200 ms. The learning rates of all three methods are shown in Table 4.5, and $\tau_n =$ 10 ms, $t_{len} = 50$ ms. The maximum learning accuracy and the corresponding epoch and time are reported in Fig. 4.17.

As shown in Fig. 4.17(a), the learning accuracy of PBSNLR and ReSuMe decreases with increasing length of desired spike train. Since the RLSBLR method and PBSNLR are both potential-driven methods, the learning accuracy curves of these two methods are higher than ReSuMe. With the same firing rate, a longer spike train contains more desired spikes to learn, which is obviously more difficult. For example, when the output firing rate r_d is 40 Hz, the output neuron is trained to averagely generate 16 spikes with 400 ms and 80 spikes with 2000 ms. However, the accuracy of the RLSBLR algorithm is better than PBSNLR and ReSuMe with the increasing length of spikes.

Learning efficiency is investigated in Fig. 4.17(b) and (c). The needed learning epochs increase with longer multi-spike trains. The number of learning epochs of RLSBLR is smaller than PBSNLR and ReSuMe in all experimental lengths, which means RLSBLR converges faster than the other two methods. Meanwhile, the total actual computation time of the RLSBLR method is the shortest among all the three methods, and the total time of RLSBLR with delay is less than that without delay. In fact, the RLSBLR needs more computation than PBSNLR per epoch since the weight updating of $\mathbf{P}$ required additional computation. However, since the RLSBLR algorithm converges much faster, it required many fewer epochs and less total training time.

B. Effect of the number of the synaptic inputs: In this experiment, the influence of the number of inputs (n) on learning performance is tested, and in ranges from 50 to 500. The learning rates of all three methods are shown in Table 4.5, and $\tau_n = 5$ ms, $t_{len} = 4$ ms. Fig. 4.18 shows the average maximum learning accuracy C, the corresponding minimum epoch and training time required for the maximum C.

The learning accuracy of RLSBLR, together with that of PBSNLR and ReSuMe, grows with the number of inputs, as shown in Fig. 4.18(a). The learning accuracy curve of RLSBLR with delay is significantly higher than the other two algorithms when the number of inputs is small, which depicts that the RLSBLR algorithm can still learn features with relatively less input information. In addition, the RLSBLR could attain a very high learning accuracy (close to 1) quickly with only 150 input neurons, while the neuron numbers

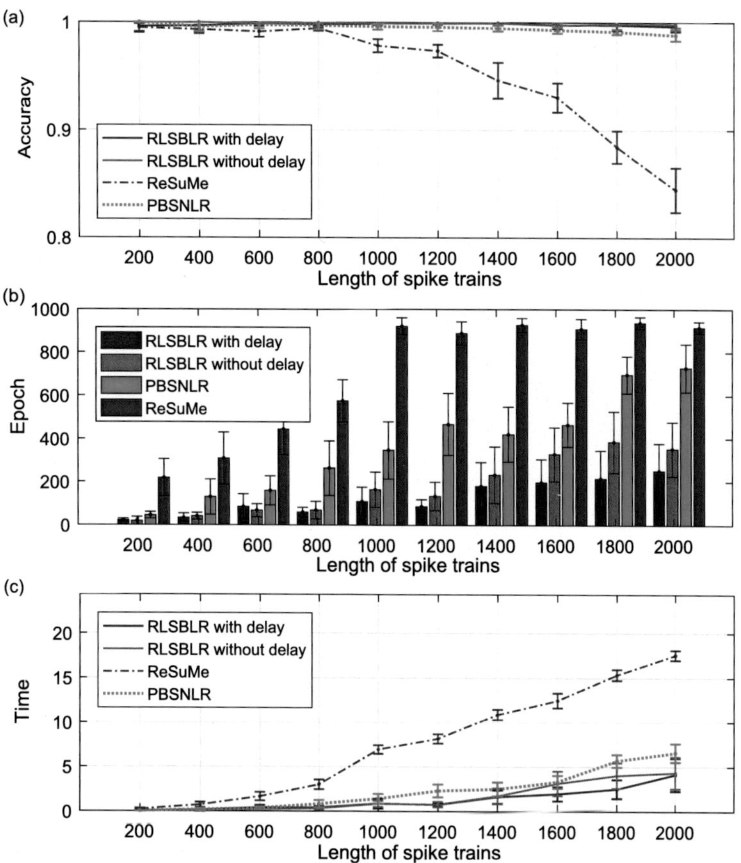

FIGURE 4.17 Effect of the length of spike trains on learning performance in RLSBLR, PBSNLR, and ReSuMe. (a) The average maximum learning accuracy. (b) The average epoch required for the maximum learning accuracy. (c) The average run time required for the maximum learning accuracy.

for PBSNLR and ReSuMe are 350 and 400, respectively. The learning effect of the RLSBLR method is more stable than ReSuMe and PBSNLR with a smaller standard deviation. In a word, RLSBLR outperforms ReSuMe and PBSNLR in the learning accuracy.

As shown in Fig. 4.18(b) and (c), learning with a small number of inputs is difficult and requires many more epochs and time. Therefore the learning epochs and time required for all the three methods slowly grow and quickly fall with the number of inputs increasing. However, overall, the learning epochs for RLSBLR with delay are less than the other two algorithms and its descending tendency of learning epochs is more significant than them, and the training time is the shortest. Since the computing time of the RLSBLR method is slightly higher than PBSNLR in every epoch, the training time of RLSBLR without delay is more than PSSNLR when their required epochs are about the same. From Fig. 4.18, it can be seen that the RLSBLR can achieve the maximum accuracy with fewer input neurons,

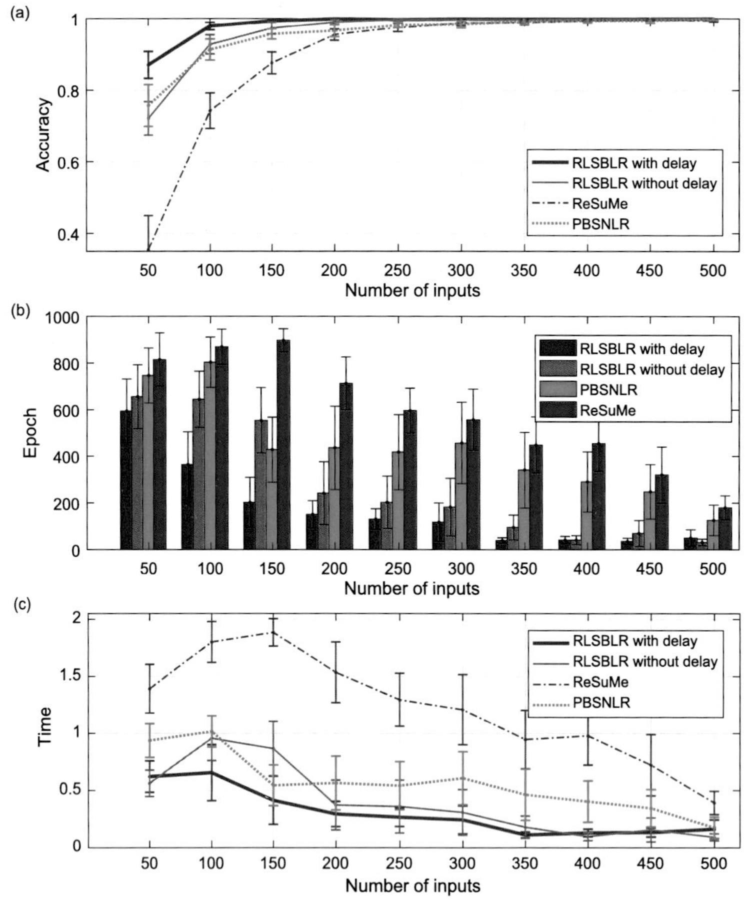

FIGURE 4.18 Effect of the number of inputs (ranges from 50 to 500) on learning performance in RLSBLR, PBSNLR, and ReSuMe. (a) The average maximum learning accuracy. (b) The average epoch required for the maximum learning accuracy. (c) The average training time required for the maximum learning accuracy.

epochs and time, and the RLSBLR method has a much higher learning performance than ReSuMe and PBSNLR.

C. Effect of the firing rate: The influence of the firing rate of spike trains is examined in this experiment. A Poisson distribution is used to randomly generate input and target output spike trains. The firing rate of the input spike trains (r_i) ranges from 1 to 5 Hz in intervals of 1 Hz. The firing rates of the desired output spike trains (r_d) are set from 20 to 80 Hz in intervals of 10 Hz, and $\tau_n = 5$ ms, $t_{len} = 5$ ms. The average maximum learning accuracy is shown in Fig. 4.19.

As shown in Fig. 4.19, the average learning accuracies of RLSBLR with delay and PBSNLR are higher than 0.9 regardless of the different firing rates, while ReSuMe has an accuracy of less than 0.9. The lower the r_i, the less information will be carried by the input neurons and the harder the output neuron learns. Similarly, the higher the r_d, more information will be carried by the output neuron and the more features the output neuron will need to learn. Therefore the learning accuracy grows with increasing r_i, while it falls with increasing r_d. In general, the accuracy of the RLSBLR method with delay exceeds that of ReSuMe and PBSNLR in any experimental firing rate, especially in lower r_i and higher r_d, which shows the effectiveness of the RLSBLR algorithm.

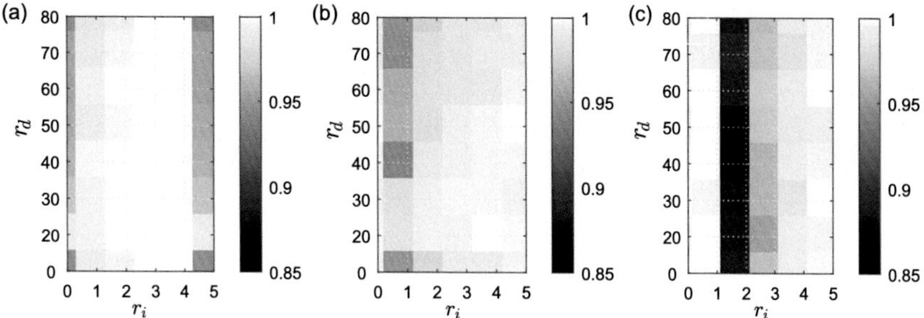

FIGURE 4.19 Effect of firing rates of the input spike trains and desired output spike train on the learning accuracy across all three methods. Figures (a), (b), and (c) show the results for RLSBLR with delay, PBSNLR, and ReSuMe, respectively.

4.4.3.2 Classification applications and results

In this section, the RLSBLR is applied to classification in the following experiments. The first experiment is speech recognition, the second is bearing fault diagnosis. The computation model used in these experiments is the same as that in [YTHT13], where each output neuron represents a category and emits its desired spike train.

A. Speech recognition: For machine learning algorithms, it is difficult to deal with speech recognition even with complex optimizing approaches [Rab89]. With the advantages of carrying spatiotemporal information, SNN is an effective tool to process speech recognition. Each sample is drawn from the TIDIGITS corpus datasets [LD93] that contain isolated speech digits from eleven words (zero, one, two, $\cdots$, nine, and oh) and over 300 speakers from 22 diverse dialectical regions. There are 2464 speech samples for training and 2486 for testing. There are many encoding methods [GS09,ZLJC15,DMJFDMJM16, WBK10,PKK19,Kas18,WCZ$^+$18] to encode speech samples to spike trains. The threshold encoding method [GS09] is used in this experiment, Fig. 4.20 shows the encoded processing.

In this experiment, there are 620 input neurons connected to 11 output neurons, and the input spike trains are added Gaussian white noises (input jitter) with 0 mean and 0.01 variance. The parameters $t_{len} = 10$, $\tau_n = 50$, $t_{length} = 100$, $t_{step} = 1$, and the delay learning is closed. The weights of all three methods are randomly initialized from a Gaussian distribution with 0.01 mean and 0.01 variance, and noises with 0 mean and 0.00001 variance are added when the weights are updated.

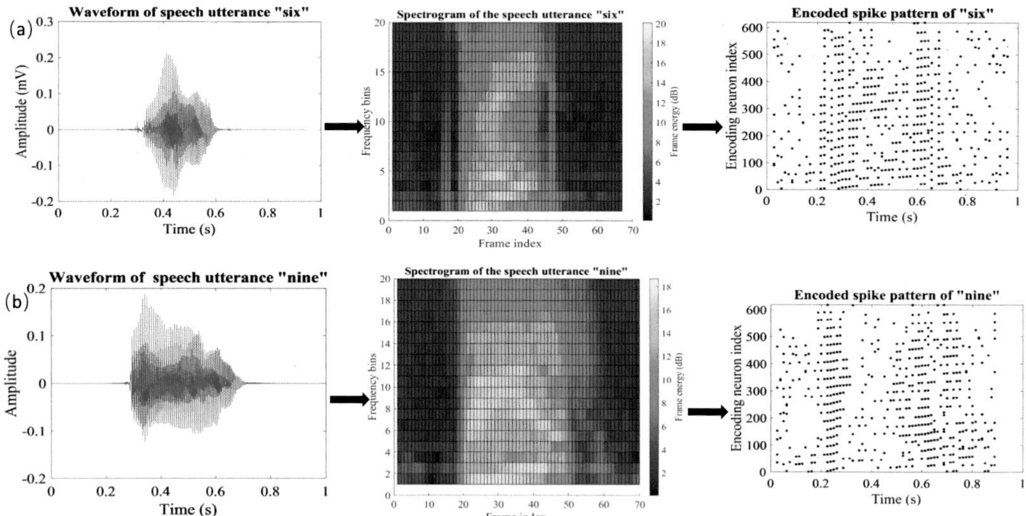

FIGURE 4.20 (a) and (b) show the process of encoding speech samples "nine" and "six" into spike trains. The left two pictures show the waveform of speech samples, the middle pictures show the corresponding spectrograms, and the right pictures show the encoded spike trains.

The output neurons are divided into two classes: a target neuron corresponding to the same category of input speech sample and non-target neurons. The target neuron is trained to emit the desired spike trains while the non-target neurons remain silent. The desired spike trains of the output neurons are dynamically generated as follows:

- Target neuron:
  - **a.** If the actual output spike train $\mathbf{T}_a$ is empty, then $\mathbf{T}_d$ is equivalent to the time arriving at the maximum membrane potential V_{max}, i.e., $\mathbf{T}_d = t_{(V_{max})}$.
  - **b.** If the actual output spike train $\mathbf{T}_a$ is not empty, then $\mathbf{T}_d = \mathbf{T}_a$. That is, there is no need to change weights.
- Non-target neuron:
  - **a.** If the actual output spike train $\mathbf{T}_a$ is empty, then $\mathbf{T}_d = \emptyset$. That is, there is no need to change weights.
  - **b.** If the actual output spikes train $\mathbf{T}_a$ is not empty, then $\mathbf{T}_d = 1 + t_{length}$, and $\mathbf{T}_a = t_a^l$, where t_a^l is the last output spike in $\mathbf{T}_a$.

In order to improve the accuracy, 10 independent groups of output neurons are chosen in the classification process. There are 11 output neurons in each group and every output neuron corresponds to its class. The output neuron in a group with the largest actual output spikes or the maximum membrane potential (when all the output neurons are impossible to emit a spike) wins. The group's output is the winning neuron's class, and the category voted by most groups is the final output. If the final output matches the actual category of the test sample, the sample is classified correctly. This experiment is finished after 100 epochs, the best test accuracy during 100 epochs is the test accuracy.

Table 4.6 shows the performance of speech recognition. The performances of the spiking convolution neural networks [TM17a], the deep recurrent network [NL16], and the multi-layer SNN Efficient Threshold-Driven Plasticity (ETDP) [ZLC+20] are relatively high (over 95.8%). Compared with the three complex multi-layered networks, the RLSBLR is rather simple with a single layer. However, it delivers the highest test accuracy (96.74%) among all the reported algorithms. In order to exclude the influence of other factors (e.g., the neuron model, the encoded scheme, the experimental parameters, and so on), ReSuMe and PBSNLR are chosen to be under the same environment as the RLSBLR. From the results in Table 4.6, the accuracy of ReSuMe and PBSNLR is at middle levels among these methods, therefore the RLSBLR method outperforms other methods depending on the algorithm itself. In addition, another method [WCZ+18] is used to encode speech data, and the test accuracy of the RLSBLR method is 94.61%, which means that different coding strategies will affect the learning of the algorithm.

Table 4.6 Performance of different methods on speech recognition task.

Model	Accuracy
Auditory Spectrogram and SVM [AL11]	78.73%
Single-layer SNN and SVM [TM17b]	91.00%
Liquid State Machine [ZLJC15]	92.30%
AER Silicon Cochlea and SVM [AL11]	95.58%
Spiking CNN and HMM [TM17a]	96.00%
AER Silicon Cochlea and Deep RNN [NL16]	96.10%
multi-layer SNN: ETDP [ZLC+20]	95.80%
Single-layer SNN: ReSuMe with encoding method [GS09]	93.32%
Single-layer SNN: PBSNLR with encoding method [GS09]	94.61%
Single-layer SNN: RLSBLR with encoding method [GS09]	**96.74**%
Single-layer SNN: RLSBLR with encoding method [WCZ+18]	94.61%

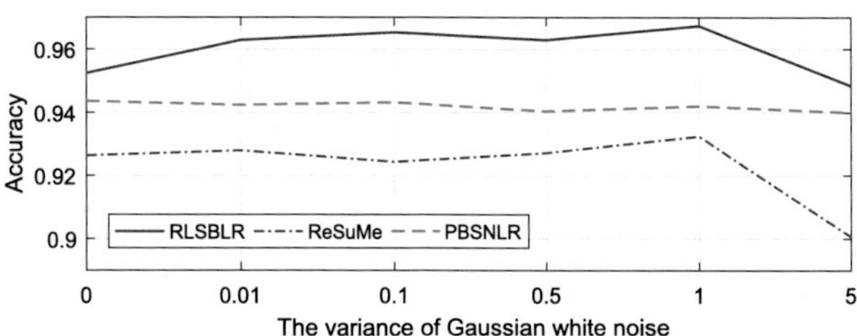

FIGURE 4.21 The variance of Gaussian input noise affects the speech recognition performance of RLSBLR, PBSNLR, and ReSuMe under the same experimental environment.

The variance of Gaussian white noise can alleviate the problem of over-fitting, which plays an important role in learning. With the increasing variances of the input noises, the results of speech recognition are shown in Fig. 4.21. For a smaller variance (below 1), the test accuracy shows an upward trend with small fluctuations. For a larger variance, Gaussian white noise destroys the features and structures of input spike trains, thus reducing the speech recognition performance.

B. Bearing fault diagnosis: To test the ability of the RLSBLR method to process streaming data, a typical streaming data processing scenario – fault diagnosis – is used. This experiment uses the bearing fault data set: the Machinery Failure Prevention Technology (MFPT) [Bec16]. MFPT includes 4 types of signal: 3 normal baseline signals, 7 inner race faults, and 2 kinds of outer race faults with a number of 3 and 7. Under-sampling is used to avoid unbalanced data distribution, each type is selected for 3 samples. Since the purpose of the experiment is to determine the location of the bearing fault, outer race faults are combined and treated as one class. Hence, there are three types of data in this experiment: 3 normal signals, 3 inner faults, and 6 outer faults. The data is preprocessed in the same way as in reference [LLZ+20]. First, the original signal S is divided into 60 segments (s_i), then s_i is decomposed into 30 features by using LMD [SJ05] method. Next, 30 features of s_i are encoded to 360 spikes by 12 overlapping Gaussian Receptive Fields neurons [YTTY14]. Finally, the RLSBLR is used to learn the features, i.e., the output neuron learns to fire when the corresponding input arrives. The diagnosis process of bearing fault is shown in Fig. 4.22.

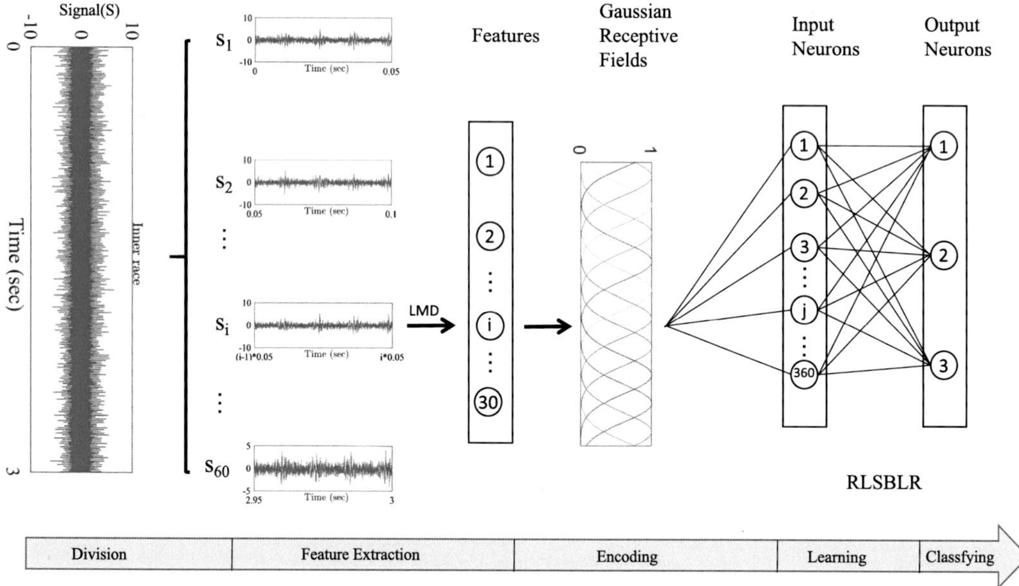

FIGURE 4.22 The diagnosis process of bearing fault. The parameters before learning are the same as those in reference [LLZ+20].

There are 720 ((3 + 3 + 6) × 60) samples (segments), and the network is trained with 80 percent of the samples and tested with the other 20 percent. The learning part consists of 360 input neurons fully connected to 3 output neurons. Using the RLSBLR learning rule, an output neuron responds only to the corresponding inputs, and remains silent with other types of inputs. The parameters of T_d and T_a are the same as in the speech recognition experiment. The delay learning is closed, and weights are randomly initialized from a Gaussian distribution with 0.02 mean and 0.02 variance. Other parameters are set as follows: $\tau_n = 10$, $t_{len} = 20$, $t_{step} = 1$, $\lambda^{-1} = 0.075$, $\tau_m = 20$, $\tau_s = 5$.

At the end of every epoch, the test samples are tested for accuracy. When a test sample is presented, the output neuron with the most spikes or the maximum membrane potential (if all output neurons remain silent) is regarded as the winner. If the label of the winning neuron matches the actual label of the test sample, the sample is classified correctly. The maximum test accuracy of the RLSBLR method after 200 epochs and the average test accuracies by repeating the experiments five times are shown in Table 4.7.

Table 4.7 Performance of different methods on the MFPT dataset.

Methods	# Training	# Test	Maximum (mean) accuracy (%)
Single-layer ANN [LLZ+20]	576	144	98.40 (–)
SNN with Tempotron [LLZ+20]	576	144	99.31 (–)
SNN with ReSuMe	576	144	97.92 (97.08)
SNN with PBSNLR	576	144	99.31 (98.47)
RLSBLR method	576	144	**100** (99.86)
RLSBLR method	1152	288	**100** (99.79)
RLSBLR method	1080	360	**100** (99.56)

The RLSBLR has been compared with other learning methods, it can be seen that RLSBLR is the best among these methods. This method is tested with different samples, for example, when the original signal S was divided into 120 segments (s_i) and there are 1440 samples. All the experimental results demonstrate that the accuracy of the RLSBLR method outperforms other algorithms.

4.5 Membrane potential driven aggregate-label learning

One of the long-standing questions in biology and machine learning is how neural networks may learn important features from the input activities with a delayed feedback, commonly known as the temporal credit-assignment problem. The aggregate-label learning is proposed to resolve this problem by matching the spike count of a neuron with the magnitude of a feedback signal. However, the existing threshold-driven aggregate-label learning algorithms are computationally intensive, resulting in relatively low learning efficiency, hence limiting their usability in practical applications. In order to address these limitations, a Membrane-Potential Driven Aggregate-Label (MPD-AL) learning algorithm was proposed [ZWC+19]. With this algorithm, the easiest modifiable time instant is identified from membrane potential traces of the neuron, and it guides the synaptic adaptation based on the presynaptic neurons' contribution at this time instant.

4.5.1 MPD-Al learning algorithm

The neuron model is shown in subsection 4.2.2. The goal of the MPD-AL learning algorithm is to modify the synaptic weights of the neuron so that the trained neuron fires the desired number of output spikes in response to a given input spike pattern. This goal is violated either when the actual output spike count N_o is less than the desired number N_d (i.e., $N_d > N_o$), or the neuron fires more spikes than the desired number (i.e., $N_o > N_d$). To address these two distinct scenarios, two different learning mechanisms were proposed, shown as follows.

4.5.1.1 *Firing less spikes than desired ($N_o < N_d$)*

When the desired output spike count is more than the actual output spike count, the synaptic weights should be strengthened to increase the current spike count iteratively till $N_d = N_o$. To achieve this goal, as shown in Fig. 4.23(a), the easiest modifiable time instant t^* is identified, at which the membrane potential $V(t^*)$ is the maximum among all peaks of the subthreshold membrane potential. Then, as shown in Eq. (4.30) and (4.31), the gradient descent method is applied to increase the membrane potential $V(t^*)$ towards the firing threshold ϑ with the aim of generating one more spike,

$$E = \frac{1}{2}\left(V\left(t^*\right) - \vartheta\right)^2, \tag{4.30}$$

$$\Delta w_i = -\lambda_1 \frac{\mathrm{d}E}{\mathrm{d}w_i} = -\lambda_1 \left(V\left(t^*\right) - \vartheta\right) \frac{\mathrm{d}V(t^*)}{\mathrm{d}w_i}, \tag{4.31}$$

where λ_1 is the learning rate that defines the magnitude of synaptic updates. Since $V(t^*)$ depends on the synaptic weight also through previous output spike times $t_s^j < t^*$, $j \in \{1, 2, \cdots, m\}$. Therefore $\mathrm{d}V(t^*)/\mathrm{d}w_i$ is given by

$$\frac{\mathrm{d}V(t^*)}{\mathrm{d}w_i} = \frac{\partial V(t^*)}{\partial w_i} + \sum_{j=1}^{m} \frac{\partial V(t^*)}{\partial t_s^j} \frac{\partial t_s^j}{\partial w_i} + \frac{\partial V(t^*)}{\partial t^*} \frac{\partial t^*}{\partial w_i}. \tag{4.32}$$

The last term in Eq. (4.32) makes no contribution to the synaptic update since $V(t^*)$ is either a local maximum with $\partial V(t^*)/\partial t^* = 0$ or t^* is the time of an inhibitory input spikes whose arrival time does not depend on w_i. According to the neuron model as shown in Eq. (4.2), the first term of Eq. (4.32) can be expressed as

$$\frac{\partial V(t^*)}{\partial w_i} = \sum_{t_i^j < t^*} K\left(t^* - t_i^j\right). \tag{4.33}$$

For the second term of Eq. (4.32), applying the chain rule, the following equation is obtained:

$$\frac{\partial V(t^*)}{\partial t_s^j} \frac{\partial t_s^j}{\partial w_i} = \frac{\partial V(t^*)}{\partial t_s^j} \frac{\partial t_s^j}{\partial V(t_s^j)} \frac{\partial V(t_s^j)}{\partial w_i}, \tag{4.34}$$

where $\partial V(t^*)/\partial t_s^j$ and $\partial t_s^j/\partial w_i$ are evaluated as below:

$$\frac{\partial V(t^*)}{\partial t_s^j} = -\frac{\vartheta}{\tau_m}\exp\left(-\frac{t^* - t_s^j}{\tau_m}\right), \tag{4.35}$$

$$\frac{\partial V(t_s^j)}{\partial w_i} = \sum_{t_i^j < t_s^j} K(t_s^j - t_i^j). \tag{4.36}$$

According to the linear assumption of threshold crossing [BKLP02,YLT18], the following formula is tenable:

$$\frac{\partial t_s^j}{\partial V(t_s^j)} = -\left(\frac{\partial V(t_s^j)}{\partial t_s^j}\right)^{-1}, \tag{4.37}$$

where

$$\begin{aligned}\frac{\partial V(t_s^j)}{\partial t_s^j} &= \left.\frac{\partial V(t)}{\partial t}\right|_{t=t_s^{j-}} \\ &= V_0 \sum_{i=1}^{N} w_i \left[\frac{1}{\tau_s}\sum_{t_i^j < t_s^j}\exp\left(-\frac{t_s^j - t_i^j}{\tau_s}\right) - \frac{1}{\tau_m}\sum_{t_i^j < t_s^j}\exp\left(-\frac{t_s^j - t_i^j}{\tau_m}\right)\right] \\ &\quad + \frac{\vartheta}{\tau_m}\sum_{t_s^m < t_s^j}\exp\left(-\frac{t_s^j - t_s^m}{\tau_m}\right).\end{aligned} \tag{4.38}$$

4.5.1.2 *Firing more spikes than desired ($N_o > N_d$)*

When the learning neuron fires more spikes than the desired spike count, the synaptic weights are weakened to reduce the output spike count. To minimize the changes to the membrane potential trace, as shown in Fig. 4.23(b), the modification is performed at the last output spike time with the aim of removing it. This choice is desirable as a modification to intermediate spikes could cause catastrophic effects to the spikes emitted immediately

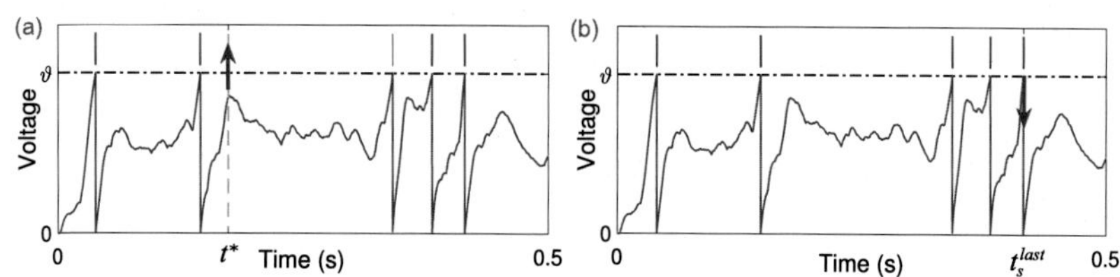

FIGURE 4.23 Demonstration of learning processes. (a) For $N_d > N_o$, the modification is performed at time t^* with the aim to generate one more spike. The subthreshold membrane potential $V(t^*)$ is the local maximum that is closest to the firing threshold ϑ. (b) For $N_d < N_o$, the modification is performed at the last output spike time $t_s^{last} \le t_s^j$, $j \in 1, 2$, with the aim to remove it.

after it. Assuming that the last output spike is emitted at t_s^{last}, the error function is constructed as

$$E = V(t_s^{last}) - \vartheta. \tag{4.39}$$

Likewise, applying the gradient descent leads to the following update rule

$$\Delta w_i = -\lambda_2 \frac{\mathrm{d}E}{\mathrm{d}w_i} = -\lambda_2 \frac{\mathrm{d}V(t_s^{last})}{\mathrm{d}w_i}, \tag{4.40}$$

where λ_2 is the learning rate. Since $V(t_s^{last})$ depends on the synaptic weight also through the previous spike times $t_s^j \le t_s^{last}$, $j \in \{1, 2, \cdots, m\}$; its derivative can be expressed as

$$\frac{\mathrm{d}V(t_s^{last})}{\mathrm{d}w_i} = \frac{\partial V(t_s^{last})}{\partial w_i} + \sum_{j=1}^{m} \frac{\partial V(t_s^{last})}{\partial t_s^j} \frac{\partial t_s^j}{\partial w_i}. \tag{4.41}$$

Eq. (4.41) is then solved using the same treatments as those for Eq. (4.32).

4.5.2 Comparison with other aggregate-label learning algorithms

The existing aggregate-label learning algorithms (MST [Güt16] and TDP [YLT18]) are all threshold driven. These algorithms modify the synaptic weights based on the error between the fixed firing threshold ϑ and the hypothetical threshold ϑ^*. Therefore it is necessary to determine the ϑ^* for each iteration of the synaptic update. For example, as shown in Fig. 4.24(a)(right), the neuron fires five spikes before learning, while the desired spike count is six. The threshold-driven algorithms will first numerically determine the critical threshold ϑ_6^*, with which the neuron fires exactly six spikes, as shown in Fig. 4.24(b) (right). However, the ϑ^* cannot be analytically obtained; therefore, ϑ^* is numerically obtained using interval halving, which is very time consuming. In contrast, the proposed MPD-AL adopts a more direct approach in which the membrane potential (instead of threshold) is considered as the relevant signal for synaptic updates. As shown in Fig. 4.24(b)(left), MPD-AL need not numerically determine ϑ^*. Instead, the learning is directly driven by the error between the firing threshold ϑ and the membrane potential, whose value is easily accessible.

In Fig. 4.24(c), the learning curves depict the spike-timing dependence of a synapse's contribution to the $\mathrm{d}V(t^*)/\mathrm{d}w$, which highlights the differences between the MPD-AL and the TDP1. In both sub-figures, the weight updates are governed by these learning curves with the aim to increase the membrane potential at t^*. According to the definition of t^* in the MPD-AL, $V(t^*)$ is the subthreshold membrane potential closest to the firing threshold, which makes the synaptic update a straight-forward process. In contrast, the TDP1 rule attempts to potentiate the synaptic weights at a different t^* that is typically further away from the threshold, hence requiring more changes. This is shown in Fig. 4.24(e), where MPD-AL requires fewer modifications to allow the neuron to generate a desired number of spikes.

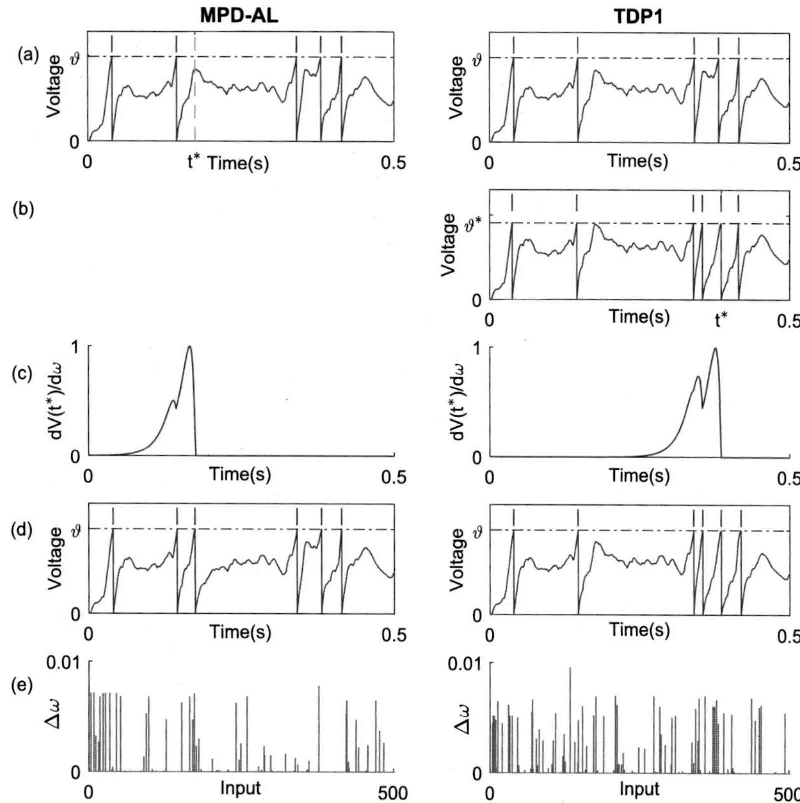

FIGURE 4.24 The comparison between MPD-AL and TDP1. (a) Membrane potential traces before learning. t^* denotes the time instant at which the subthreshold membrane potential is closest to the firing threshold. (b) The membrane potential trace of the neuron with spikes generated at the hypothetical threshold ϑ^*. Here, the t^* corresponds to the time instant at which the membrane potential reaches ϑ^*. (c) The shape of the learning curves, depicting the spike-timing dependence of a synapse's contribution to $\mathrm{d}V(t^*)/\mathrm{d}w$. (d) Membrane potential traces after learning. (e) The accumulated weight modifications during the learning process.

4.5.3 Applications and results

4.5.3.1 Learning to fire a desired number of spikes

In this section, a learning task is first introduced to demonstrate the ability of the proposed MPD-AL algorithm to teach a neuron to fire a desired number of spikes. Next, the learning efficiency of the MPD-AL against other competitive aggregate-label learning algorithms is compared.

In the first experiment, a single output neuron with $N = 500$ afferents is trained to fire 10 spikes under different input firing rates. The input spike patterns are generated over a time window of $T = 500$ ms and each presynaptic neuron fires at a Poisson firing rate $r_{in} = 5$ Hz (Fig. 4.25(a) and (b)) and 20 Hz (Fig. 4.25(c) and (d)). The initial synaptic weights are drawn

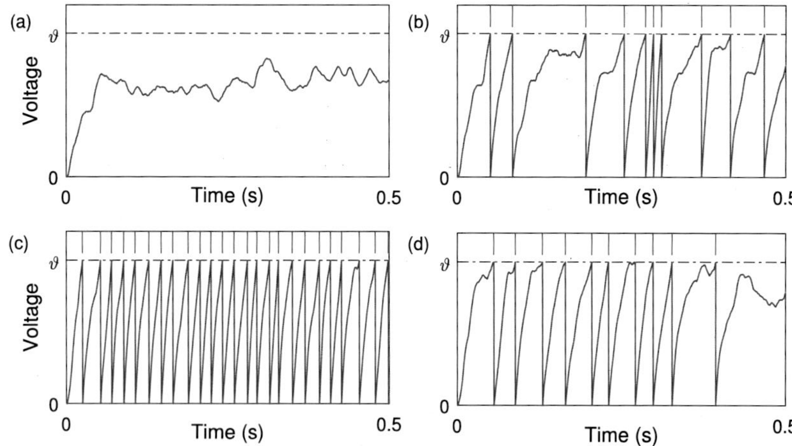

FIGURE 4.25 Neuron's membrane potential traces before (a and c) and after learning (b and d). The neuron is trained to emit 10 desired spikes under different initial firing rates, i.e., $r_{in} = 5$ Hz (a and b) and $r_{in} = 20$ Hz (c and d).

randomly from a Gaussian distribution with a mean of 0.01 and a standard deviation of 0.01.

Fig. 4.25(a) depicts the neuron's membrane potential trace before learning, in which there is no output spike initially. After training, the neuron successfully emits the desired number of spikes, distributed throughout the simulation, as shown in Fig. 4.25(b). In contrast, Fig. 4.25(c) depicts the responses of the neuron with an input firing rate of 20 Hz, in which the neuron exhibits a bursting behavior at the beginning. Likewise, as shown in Fig. 4.25(d), the MPD-AL algorithm adjusts the synaptic weights so that the trained neuron emits the desired number of spikes, many fewer than the initial bursting activities.

Furthermore, the learning efficiency of different algorithms with the desired spike counts varying from 2 to 20 in intervals of 2 is compared. The input firing rate for presynaptic neurons is set to 5 Hz. For each setup, 20 experiments are carried out with randomly generated input spike patterns and initial synaptic weights. The average number of learning epoch and CPU time used for each setup are calculated and reported in Fig. 4.26.

As shown in Fig. 4.26(a), due to the nature of the iterative optimization scheme employed, the required number of training epochs grows for all the algorithms with increasing spike count. The proposed MPD-AL algorithm consistently outperforms other algorithms and requires the lowest number of training epochs as well as CPU time. Specifically, when the desired spike count is 20, the proposed MPD-AL algorithm requires about 250 learning epochs, while the TDP1 and the MST require more than 600 and 800 learning epochs, respectively. As shown in Fig. 4.26(b), the average CPU time required for the MPD-AL algorithm is about 2 s for the desired spike count of 20, while the TDP1 and the MST algorithms require 6 s and 13 s, respectively. These results could be explained as follows: first, as illustrated in Fig. 4.26(a), the MPD-AL algorithm requires fewer learning epochs to reach the desired spike count due to the more direct adaptation strategy taken. On the other hand,

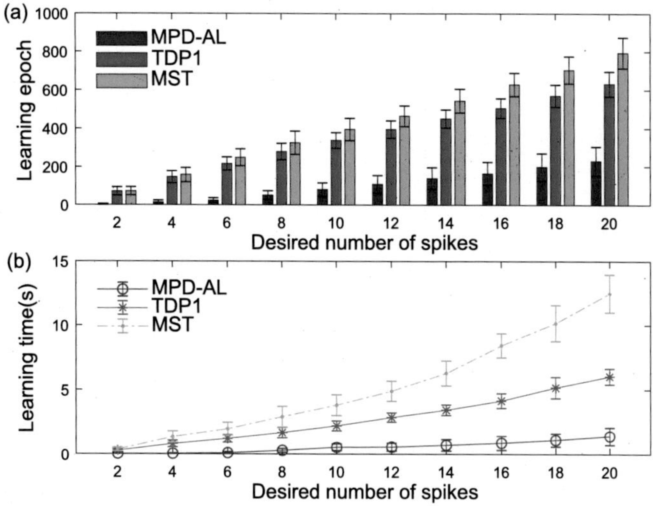

FIGURE 4.26 The comparison among MPD-AL, TDP1, and MST algorithms in terms of learning efficiency, i.e., the required number of learning epochs (a) and the required CPU time (b).

both the TDP1 and MST need to numerically determine the ϑ^*, which requires more computation times at each learning epoch. Consequently, the MPD-AL offers a better learning efficiency.

4.5.3.2 Learning predictive clues

To learn predictive sensory clues, an organism must bridge the gap between the time when a clue occurs and when the feedback arrives [Güt16]. The temporal credit-assignment problem is a core challenge in both cognition and machine learning. In this section, it can be demonstrated that the temporal credit-assignment problem can be solved using the proposed MPD-AL algorithm.

Similar to the tasks proposed in [Güt16], ten brief (50 ms) spiking patterns are constructed from 500 afferents with a firing rate of $r_f = 4$ Hz, which may represent spiking activities in response to perceived features from the environment. A certain number of these ten spike patterns will be designated as useful clues, while the rest are distractors. The single neuron connected to these sensory afferents is expected to signal all the useful features by firing a specific number of spikes. In contrast, the neuron should remain silent in the event of background activities or distractors. In each experimental trial, these ten spike patterns are sparsely embedded in background spike activity with duration T_b. The number of occurrences of each such pattern is drawn from a Poisson distribution with mean P_m. In order to better simulate non-stationarity of the environment, the background spike activities are generated according to a spontaneous firing rate varying from 0 to 4 Hz (with mean rate 2 Hz). During the training phase, they set the value of P_m and T_b to 0.1 and 500 ms, respectively. In the testing phase, these two values are set to 2 and 1000 ms corre-

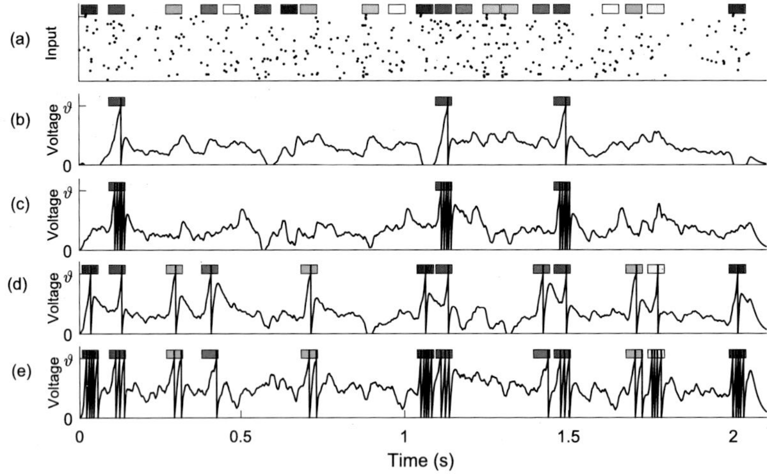

FIGURE 4.27 Learning predictive clues. (a) Input spike pattern, of which only 10% of the 500 synaptic afferents are shown. Colored rectangles represent 10 different sensory features (50 ms each) that are embedded within a stream of spontaneous background activities. (b) and (c) show the membrane potential traces after being trained to fire one or a burst of five spikes in response to a single clue (blue rectangle). (d) and (e) show the membrane potential traces after being trained to selectively respond to only five clues out of the total ten feature patterns. The neuron is expected to fire only a single spike (d) or distinct number of spikes {1, 2, 3, 4, 5} (e) in response to each clue.

spondingly to allow more exposure to both clues and distractors. For training, 100 samples based on the above described method are generated.

The authors first train the neuron to detect a single clue i among 9 distractors and background activities. In each trial, the desired spike count N_d is set to the number of clue event $i (N_d = c_i)$. Whenever the neuron fires greater or fewer spikes than the desired count N_d, the MPD-AL learning algorithm will weaken or potentiate the synaptic connections, respectively, so as to reach the desired spike count N_d. Fig. 4.27(b) illustrates the testing result, in which the neuron fires exactly one spike whenever the corresponding clue activity pattern (blue rectangle) occurs and remains silent otherwise. The N_d is not necessarily equal to the number of clue events since each clue may trigger more than one spike. To simulate this scenario, the authors design a task where the neuron is required to fire a burst of 5 spikes to the clue $i (N_d = 5c_i)$ and remain silent otherwise, as demonstrated in Fig. 4.27(c). Intriguingly, the proposed learning algorithm enables the trained neuron to decompose the feedback signal and associate each clue with a distinct desired spike count, such that $N_d = \sum_i c_i d_i$, where c_i is the number of clue events i within a trial and d_i is the corresponding desired spike count belonging to that clue i. Fig. 4.27(d) and 4.27(e) show the testing results of these challenging scenarios, where the d_i values for the five clues are set as {1, 1, 1, 1, 1} and {1, 2, 3, 4, 5}, respectively. The experimental results highlight the capabilities of the MPD-AL learning algorithm to decompose the delayed feedback signal.

4.5.3.3 Application to speech recognition

SNNs transform spatiotemporal spike patterns into desired output patterns, and are hence well suited for processing temporally rich signals, for instance, motion and speech recognition. However, the lack of efficient learning algorithms limits the application of SNN to mostly small toy problems that do not fundamentally involve spatiotemporal spike time computations [ZG18]. Although some promising learning algorithms [LDP16,NAPD17] have been proposed recently, they are applied to datasets of static images. Therefore the temporal pattern classification tasks remain a challenging topic warranting further investigation.

To demonstrate the capability of the MPD-AL learning algorithm in a temporal pattern classification task, the authors apply it to solve a speaker-independent spoken digit classification task. The TIDIGITS corpus [LD93] is investigated in this work, which is one of the most common datasets for benchmarking speech recognition algorithms [WCZ$^+$18, WCL18]. This dataset consists of isolated spoken digit strings from a vocabulary of 11 words (i.e., 'zero' to 'nine' and 'oh') and speakers from 22 different dialectical regions. This experiment uses the standard training and testing sets, consisting of 2464 and 2486 speech utterances, respectively. First, the raw speech waveform is filtered by a Constant-Q Transform (CQT) cochlear filter bank (20 cochlear filters ranging from 200 Hz to 8 kHz) to extract the spectral information [PLWC18]. Next, as shown in Fig. 4.28, the threshold-coding mechanism [GS09] has been applied to convert incoming speech signals into spike patterns.

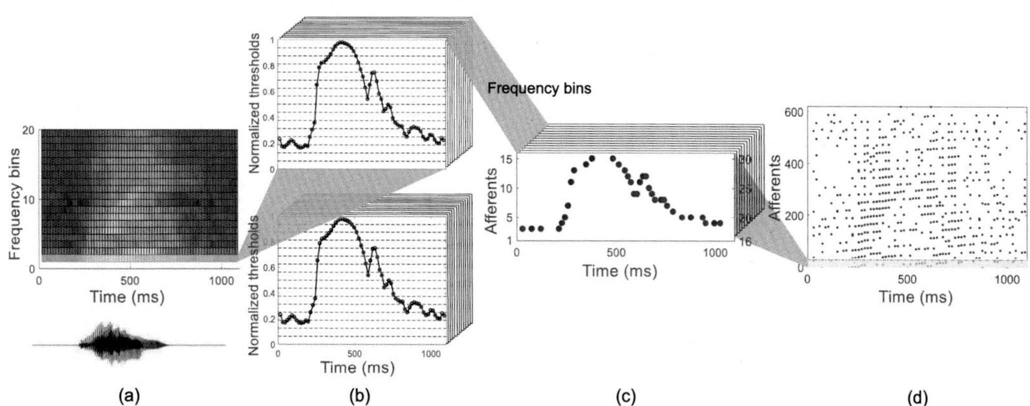

FIGURE 4.28 Illustration of the threshold coding mechanism. (a) The raw speech waveform and the spectrogram generated from the CQT cochlear filter bank. (b) The spectrogram is further encoded into spikes using the threshold coding. The top and bottom sub-figures depict the upward (red dots) and downward (blue dots) crossing events, respectively. For better visualization, only the output from the 1st cochlear filter is displayed. (c) The upward and downward events from (b) are merged to visualize the neuronal activation trajectory. The upward and downward crossing events for the 1st cochlear filter are represented by afferents 1–15 and 16–30, respectively. The threshold coding preserves temporal dynamics of the filtered spectral information. (d) The entire threshold-encoded spike pattern by concatenating the spike events from (c) vertically. The spike events that corresponds to the first filter in (c) is shaded in gray.

The encoded spike patterns are transmitted to the next layer for classification; there are eleven groups of output neurons in this layer with each group corresponding to one class. Each group consists of ten neurons. In order to discriminate between different spoken digits, neurons are trained to generate the desired number of spikes (N_d) only when a spike pattern from their assigned class is presented and remain silent otherwise. However, how the value of N_d is set remains an open question. On the one hand, each spoken digit is formed by the different number of sub-patterns and hence one common N_d for all classes is undesirable. On the other hand, a small value of N_d limits the use of available local temporal features, while a large N_d value is prone to the over-fitting problem. To resolve this problem, a data-driven dynamic decoding scheme is proposed.

When a training spike pattern is presented, the membrane potential trace of the corresponding output neuron is observed. The N_d is decided based on the following three cases:

- If the membrane potential $V(t)$ remains lower than the firing threshold ϑ and no spike is generated (as shown in Fig. 4.29(a)), then $N_d \leftarrow 1$.
- If the neuron generates N_o spikes and $V(t^*)$ is above the pre-defined encoding threshold ϑ_e (as shown in Fig. 4.29(b)), then $N_d \leftarrow N_o + 1$.
- If the neuron generates N_o spikes and $V(t^*)$ is below the pre-defined encoding threshold ϑ_e (as shown in Fig. 4.29(c)), then $N_d \leftarrow N_o$.

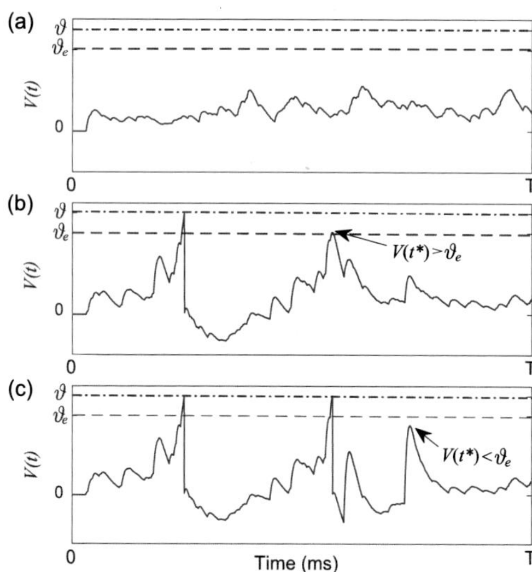

FIGURE 4.29 Illustration of the dynamic output decoding strategy.

As shown in Table 4.8, it is encouraging to note that the proposed MPD-AL algorithm with dynamic decoding achieves an accuracy of 97.52%, outperforming all other bio-inspired baseline systems. Moreover, to investigate the effectiveness of the proposed dynamic decoding strategy, experiments with fixed $N_d \in \{1, 2, 3, 4, 5, 6, 7, 8, 9, 10\}$ are performed and the best accuracy of 95.35% is achieved when $N_d = 3$. This result highlights

Table 4.8 Comparison of the proposed framework against other baseline frameworks.

Model	Accuracy (%)
Single-layer SNN and SVM [TM17b]	91.00
Spiking CNN and HMM [TM17a]	96.00
AER Silicon Cochlea and SVM [AL11]	95.58
Auditory Spectrogram and SVM [AL11]	78.73
AER Silicon Cochlea and Deep RNN [NL16]	96.10
Liquid State Machine [ZLJC15]	92.30
MPD-AL with $N_d = 3$	95.35
MPD-AL with Dynamic Decoding	**97.52**

the effectiveness of the dynamic decoding strategy, which could be applied for all temporal classification tasks. In this way, the classification performance is improved by training with margins and spike time noise [Güt16]. It is worth mentioning that the accuracy of this work can still be improved when the model is scaled up with hidden layers using techniques proposed in [LDP16,NAPD17].

4.6 Efficient threshold driven aggregate-label learning algorithm

The aggregate-label learning paradigm tackles the long-standing temporary credit-assignment (TCA) problem in neuroscience and machine learning, enabling spiking neural networks to learn multimodal sensory clues with delayed feedback signals. However, the existing aggregate-label learning algorithms only work for single-spiking neurons, and with low learning efficiency, which limits their real-world applicability. To address these limitations, an Efficient Threshold-Driven Plasticity (ETDP) algorithm for spiking neurons was proposed [ZLC+20]. It enables spiking neurons to generate the desired number of spikes that match the magnitude of delayed feedback signals and to learn useful multimodal sensory clues embedded within spontaneous spiking activities. Furthermore, the ETDP algorithm was extended to support multi-layer SNNs, which significantly improves the applicability of aggregate-label learning algorithms.

4.6.1 ETDP learning algorithm for single spiking neurons

The spiking neuron model in subsection 4.2.2 is also adopted in the ETDP algorithm. The ETDP algorithm learns to modify the synaptic weights so that the trained neuron fires the desired spike count. Due to the discrete nature of the spike count, its derivative with respect to synaptic weights cannot be obtained directly. To circumvent this problem, the Spike-Threshold-Surface (STS) is applied to map the discrete spike counts to continuous hypothetical firing thresholds [Güt16]. As shown in Fig. 4.30(b), the critical threshold ϑ_k^* denotes the threshold value at which the spike count jumps from $k-1$ to k. For example, given a particular input spike pattern and a set of synaptic weights, Fig. 4.30(a) shows that the neuron fires three spikes with the neuron's biological firing threshold $\vartheta = 1$ (red line). While the neuron fires four spikes (blue line) when the threshold decreases to ϑ_4^*. Based on the relationship between the STS and the number of output spikes, the problem of training a neuron to output the desired spike count d could be translated into adjusting the STS so that $\vartheta_{d+1}^* < \vartheta \leq \vartheta_d^*$. In other words, errors occur for either $\vartheta_{d+1}^* \geq \vartheta$ or $\vartheta_d^* < \vartheta$.

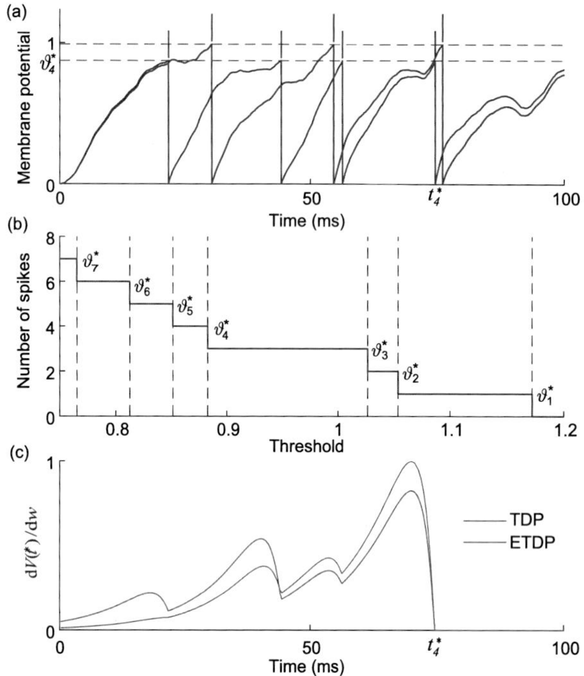

FIGURE 4.30 (a) Membrane potential traces with the fixed biological firing threshold ϑ (red line) and the hypothetical firing threshold ϑ_4^* (blue line). (b) Illustration of the Spike-Threshold-Surface (STS), which maps the neuron's hypothetical firing thresholds to the output spike counts. (c) The learning curve of different threshold-driven aggregate-label learning algorithms, which demonstrates the spike-timing dependence of synaptic contributions to $dV(t^*)/dw$.

In general, there are two strategies to optimize the STS. One is the "absolute" rule that directly uses ϑ_{d+1}^* and ϑ_d^* to calculate the synaptic updates; while the other one uses the actual output spike count o to determine the synaptic updates, namely the "relative" rule. The "absolute" and the "relative" rules are summarized in Eq. (4.42) and Eq. (4.43), respectively:

$$\Delta w = \begin{cases} -\lambda \dfrac{d\vartheta_{d+1}^*}{dw}, & \text{if} \quad \vartheta_{d+1}^* \geq \vartheta, \\ \lambda \dfrac{d\vartheta_d^*}{dw}, & \text{if} \quad \vartheta_d^* < \vartheta, \end{cases} \tag{4.42}$$

$$\Delta w = \begin{cases} -\lambda \frac{\mathrm{d}\vartheta_o^*}{\mathrm{d}w}, & \text{if} \quad o > d, \\ \lambda \frac{\mathrm{d}\vartheta_{o+1}^*}{\mathrm{d}w}, & \text{if} \quad d > o, \end{cases} \tag{4.43}$$

where λ is the learning rate. It is worth noting that the absolute learning rule requires the exact value of desired spike counts, while the relative learning rule is based on a binary feedback signal that only specifies whether the neuron should increase or decrease the spike count. It is easy to see that the relative learning rule is simpler and biologically more plausible [YLT18]. Therefore the ETDP learning algorithm is derived based on this relative learning rule.

According to the definition of the critical threshold ϑ^*, there exists a unique t^* that satisfies

$$\vartheta^* = V(t^*) = V_o(t^*) - \vartheta^* \sum_{j=1}^{m} \exp\left(-\frac{t^* - t_s^j}{\tau_m}\right), \tag{4.44}$$

with

$$V_o(t^*) = \sum_i^N w_i \sum_{t_i^j < t^*} K(t^* - t_i^j). \tag{4.45}$$

Here, m denotes the total number of output spikes fired before t^*, since ϑ^* depends on the synaptic weights also through previous output spikes $t_s^j < t^*$, $j \in \{1, 2, ..., m\}$. Thus $\mathrm{d}\vartheta^*/\mathrm{d}w_i$ can be determined as follows:

$$\frac{\mathrm{d}\vartheta^*}{\mathrm{d}w_i} = \frac{\mathrm{d}V(t^*)}{\mathrm{d}w_i} = \frac{\partial V(t^*)}{\partial w_i} + \sum_{j=1}^{m} \frac{\partial V(t^*)}{\partial t_s^j} \frac{\mathrm{d}t_s^j}{\mathrm{d}w_i} + \frac{\partial V(t^*)}{\partial t^*} \frac{\mathrm{d}t^*}{\mathrm{d}w_i}. \tag{4.46}$$

The last component of Eq. (4.46) makes no contribution to the synaptic update since $V(t^*)$ is either a local maximum with $\partial V(t^*)/\partial t^* = 0$ or t^* is the time of an inhibitory input spike whose arrival time does not depend on w_i. The difficulty in solving Eq. (4.46) lies in the $\mathrm{d}t_s^j/\mathrm{d}w_i$ term, and by applying the chain rule, it can be expressed as

$$\frac{\mathrm{d}t_s^j}{\mathrm{d}w_i} = \frac{\partial t_s^j}{\partial V(t_s^j)} \frac{\mathrm{d}V(t_s^j)}{\mathrm{d}w_i}, \tag{4.47}$$

with

$$\frac{\mathrm{d}V(t_s^j)}{\mathrm{d}w_i} = \frac{\partial V(t_s^j)}{\partial w_i} + \sum_{k=1}^{j} \frac{\partial V(t_s^j)}{\partial t_s^k} \frac{\mathrm{d}t_s^k}{\mathrm{d}w_i}. \tag{4.48}$$

According to the linear assumption of the firing threshold crossing [BKLP02], the following equation is obtained

$$\frac{\partial t_s^j}{\partial V(t_s^j)} = -\left[\frac{\partial V(t_s^j)}{\partial (t_s^j)}\right]^{-1} = -V'(t_s^j)^{-1}. \tag{4.49}$$

Then, Eq. (4.46) can be expressed as

$$\frac{\mathrm{d}\vartheta^*}{\mathrm{d}w_i} = \frac{\partial V(t^*)}{\partial w_i} - \sum_{j=1}^{m} \frac{\partial V(t^*)}{\partial t_s^j} \frac{1}{V'(t_s^j)} \frac{\mathrm{d}V(t_s^j)}{\mathrm{d}w_i}. \tag{4.50}$$

In order to solve the remaining components of Eq. (4.50), the set of output spike times is denoted as $t_x \in \{t_s^1, t_s^2, ..., t_s^m, t^*\}$. Eq. (4.44) thus can be evaluated as

$$V(t_x) = \frac{V_o(t_x)}{C_{t_x}}, \tag{4.51}$$

with

$$C_{t_x} = 1 + \sum_{t_s^j < t_x} \exp\left(-\frac{t_x - t_s^j}{\tau_m}\right). \tag{4.52}$$

Then, the remaining components of Eq. (4.50) can be determined as follows:

$$\frac{\partial V(t_x)}{\partial w_i} = \frac{1}{C_{t_x}} \sum_{t_i^j < t_x} K(t_x - t_i^j), \tag{4.53}$$

$$\frac{\partial V(t_x)}{\partial t_s^k} = \frac{-V_o(t_x)}{C_{t_x}^2} \frac{\exp\left(-\frac{t_x - t_s^k}{\tau_m}\right)}{\tau_m}, \quad \text{if} \quad t_s^k < t_x, \tag{4.54}$$

$$V'(t_x) = \frac{1}{C_{t_x}} \frac{\partial V_o(t_x)}{\partial t_x} + \frac{V_o(t_x)}{C_{t_x}^2 \tau_m} \sum_{t_s^j < t_x} \exp\left(-\frac{t_x - t_s^j}{\tau_m}\right). \tag{4.55}$$

Since the term $V'(t_x)$ is the denominator of Eq. (4.49), it gives rise to the gradient explosion problem when $V'(t_x)$ is close to 0. To solve this problem, an exploding gradient prevention strategy (EGPS) is proposed by setting a lower bound ϑ_b for $V'(t_x)$ as

$$V'(t_x) = \begin{cases} V'(t_x), & \text{if} \quad V'(t_x) > \vartheta_b, \\ \vartheta_b, & \text{otherwise.} \end{cases} \tag{4.56}$$

In the same vein of research, the threshold-driven aggregate-label learning algorithm TDP simplifies the recursive expression of the MST algorithm and demonstrated significantly improved learning efficiency in their experiments [YLT18]. Here, the focus is on the difference between the proposed ETDP and the TDP algorithms. The main difference between these two algorithms lies in the different solutions to the terms $\partial V(t_x)/\partial w_i$ and $\mathrm{d}V(t_s^j)/\mathrm{d}w_i$.

According to Eq. (4.44), $V(t_x)$ is defined as

$$V(t_x) = V_o(t_x) - \vartheta^* \sum_{j=1}^{m} \exp\left(-\frac{t_x - t_s^j}{\tau_m}\right). \tag{4.57}$$

TDP calculates $\partial V(t_x)/\partial w_i$ by simply considering the first term of Eq. (4.57) that leads to the following equation:

$$\frac{\partial V(t_x)}{\partial w_i} = \frac{\partial V_o(t_x)}{\partial w_i} = \sum_{t_i^j < t_x} K(t_x - t_i^j). \tag{4.58}$$

However, the membrane potential $V(t_x)$ depends on the synaptic weight w_i also through the second term of Eq. (4.57). To consider this dependency, the proposed ETDP rule first transforms Eq. (4.57) into Eq. (4.51) following the proposal in [Güt16], and then solves $\partial V(t_x)/\partial w_i$ according to Eq. (4.53), which is more mathematically rigorous.

On the other hand, TDP calculates the $\mathrm{d}V(t_s^j)/\mathrm{d}w_i$ as

$$\frac{\mathrm{d}V(t_s^j)}{\mathrm{d}w_i} = \frac{\partial t_s^j}{\partial V(t_s^j)} \frac{\partial V(t_s^j)}{\partial w_i}, \tag{4.59}$$

with

$$\frac{\partial V(t_s^j)}{\partial w_i} = \sum_{t_i^j < t_s^j} K(t_s^j - t_i^j), \tag{4.60}$$

which ignores the fact that the membrane potential $V(t_s^j)$ depends on the synaptic weights w_i also through the output spikes generated before t_s^j. This dependency is considered in the proposed ETDP rule, and $dV(t_s^j)/dw_i$ is determined as per Eq. (4.47) and Eq. (4.48). As shown in the learning curves in Fig. 4.30(c), the ETDP will allocate more credits to the earlier presynaptic spikes than TDP.

4.6.2 Extended ETDP learning algorithm for multi-layer SNNs

The existing aggregate-label learning algorithms are all designed for single-spiking neurons. It is noted that the powerful perceptual and cognitive capabilities of the human brain come from the huge number of neurons that are organized in a hierarchical manner. Therefore these algorithms certainly do not describe the learning process of biological neural networks [XZHY13,ZG18]. Furthermore, the applicability is limited by the computational capability of single-spiking neurons. Therefore in the following, the proposed ETDP algorithm is extended to multi-layer spiking neural networks.

The goal of the multi-layer ETDP learning algorithm is to update the synaptic weights in both the output layer and hidden layers, such that the neurons in the output layer can generate the desired number of spikes. As for the ETDP learning algorithm developed for single-spiking neurons, this goal can be accomplished by adapting the STS such that $\vartheta_{d+1}^* < \vartheta \leq \vartheta_d^*$. Considering spiking neural networks with a single hidden layer, since the synaptic weights w_{ih} between the input layer and hidden layer affect ϑ^* through both the spikes of hidden neurons (t_h^m) and output neurons (t_j^n), the weight update rule for w_{ih} can be expressed as

$$\frac{dV(t^*)}{dw_{ih}} = \sum_{t_h^m < t^*} \frac{\partial V(t^*)}{\partial t_h^m} \frac{dt_h^m}{dw_{ih}} + \sum_{t_j^n < t^*} \frac{\partial V(t^*)}{\partial t_j^n} \frac{dt_j^n}{dw_{ih}}, \tag{4.61}$$

with

$$\frac{dt_h^m}{dw_{ih}} = \frac{\partial t_h^m}{\partial V(t_h^m)} \left[\frac{\partial V(t_h^m)}{\partial w_{ih}} + \sum_{k=1}^{m} \frac{\partial V(t_h^m)}{\partial t_h^k} \frac{dt_h^k}{dw_{ih}} \right], \tag{4.62}$$

$$\frac{dt_j^n}{dw_{ih}} = \frac{\partial t_j^n}{\partial V(t_j^n)} \left[\sum_{t_h^m < t_j^n} \frac{\partial V(t_j^n)}{\partial t_h^m} \frac{dt_h^m}{dw_{ih}} + \sum_{k=1}^{n} \frac{\partial V(t_j^n)}{\partial t_j^k} \frac{dt_j^k}{dw_{ih}} \right], \tag{4.63}$$

where t_h^m is the mth spike of the hidden neuron h, and t_j^n is the nth spike of the output neuron j. All the components in Eq. (4.61)–(4.63) can be solved with a combination of Eq. (4.49), (4.54), (4.55), and the following equation:

$$\frac{\partial V(t_x)}{\partial t_h^m} = \frac{w_{ih} V_0}{C_{t_x}} \left[\frac{1}{\tau_m} \exp\left(-\frac{t_x - t_h^m}{\tau_m} \right) - \frac{1}{\tau_s} \exp\left(-\frac{t_x - t_h^m}{\tau_s} \right) \right]. \tag{4.64}$$

Furthermore, the SNNs with multiple hidden layers can be trained in a similar fashion by applying the chain rule.

4.6.3 Applications and results

In this section, extensive experiments are conducted to evaluate the performance of the ETDP learning algorithm for single-spiking neurons and multi-layer SNNs. First, the effectiveness and efficiency of the ETDP algorithm are evaluated by training a single-spiking neuron to generate the desired number of spikes. Then, it is demonstrated that the proposed ETDP algorithm can train spiking neurons to discover useful clues embedded within a long stream of multimodal sensory activities. Finally, the performance of the ETDP algorithm is evaluated by validating an SNN-based multimodal computational framework for audio-visual information processing.

4.6.3.1 Learning to fire a desired number of spikes

In this section, a learning example is first introduced to demonstrate the effectiveness of the proposed ETDP algorithm for single-spiking neurons. Additionally, the learning efficiency of this algorithm is compared with the threshold-driven aggregate-label learning algorithm TDP.

In the first set of experiments, a spiking neuron with $N = 500$ presynaptic neurons is trained to fire 10 spikes within a time window of $T = 500$ ms. The initial synaptic weights are drawn from a random Gaussian distribution with both mean and standard deviation equal to 0.01. The initial firing rate r_{pre} of presynaptic neurons is adjusted to 4 and 10 Hz

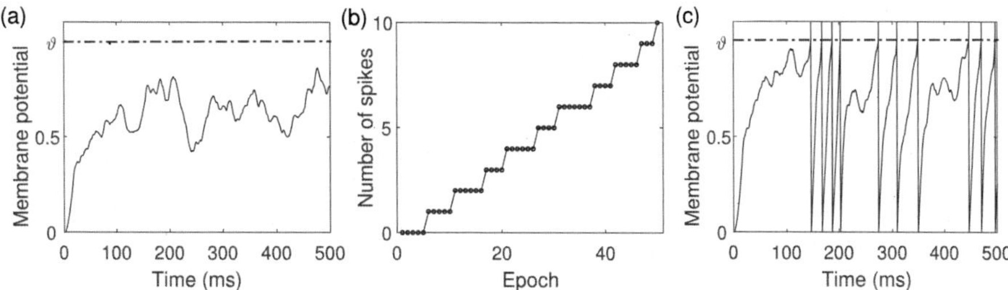

FIGURE 4.31 Learning a desired number of spikes with $r_{pre} = 4$ Hz (under-firing scenario). (a) Neuron's membrane potential trace before learning. (b) The number of output spikes at the end of each learning epoch. (c) Neuron's membrane potential trace after learning.

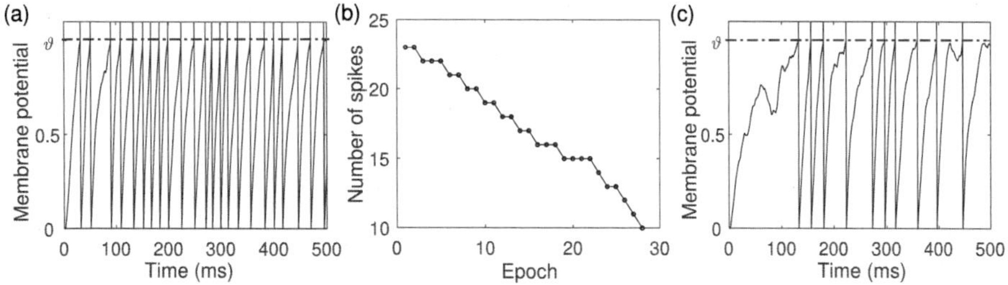

FIGURE 4.32 Learning a desired number of spikes with $r_{pre} = 10$ Hz (over-firing scenario). (a) Neuron's membrane potential trace before learning. (b) The number of output spikes at the end of each learning epoch. (c) Neuron's membrane potential trace after learning.

in order to cover both the under-firing and over-firing scenarios. The experimental results of these two scenarios are provided in Fig. 4.31 and Fig. 4.32, respectively.

Fig. 4.31 illustrates the learning process with an input firing rate of $r_{pre} = 4$ Hz. Due to the low input firing rate, the membrane potential of the output neuron cannot reach the firing threshold initially, and the output neuron thus remains quiescent. As shown in Fig. 4.31(b), when trained with the proposed ETDP learning algorithm, the output neuron gradually increases its number of output spikes and reaches the desired spike count after about 50 epochs. The membrane potential trace of a successful learning example is given in Fig. 4.31(c). Fig. 4.32 shows that the learning neuron exhibits a bursting behavior with a high input rate of $r_{pre} = 10$ Hz. As learning progresses, the number of output spikes decreases to the desired spike count after 28 learning epochs. These experimental results demonstrate that the proposed ETDP algorithm works effectively under different neuronal activity states.

Next, the learning efficiency between ETDP and TDP is compared. The experimental setup is the same as that in Fig. 4.31, while the desired number of spikes varies from 10 to 100 in steps of 10. For each desired spike count, 20 independent experiments are conducted, and the statistics of learning epochs and CPU time used are summarized in Fig. 4.33.

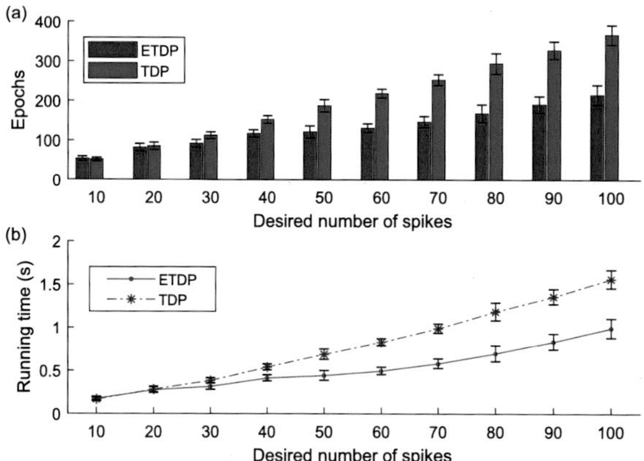

FIGURE 4.33 Comparison of learning efficiency between the proposed ETDP and TDP. (a) The required learning epochs of different algorithms. (b) The required CPU time of different algorithms.

As shown in Fig. 4.33, the required number of learning epochs and CPU times increase for both learning algorithms with an increasing number of the desired spike count. However, the proposed ETDP algorithm consistently outperforms TDP for all the tasks. For example, when the desired number of spikes is 100, the required number of learning epochs of the proposed algorithm is about 200, while it is about 370 for TDP. In addition, as shown in Fig. 4.33(b), the required average CPU time of the ETDP algorithm is also lower than that of the TDP. Specifically, for a desired spike count of 100, the CPU time needed for the ETDP and TDP is 0.9 s and 1.5 s, respectively. It is worth noting that despite the ETDP algorithm taking more CPU time per epoch to derive a higher quality gradient than TDP, it takes significantly shorter CPU time, which is due to savings in the required training epochs.

4.6.3.2 Learning multimodal sensory clues

Learning multimodal sensory clues can facilitate efficient identification and localization of external events, and hence enhance interactions with the environment. However, these useful clues are usually embedded within distracting streams of unrelated sensory activities, and the feedback signals may occur after long and varying delays. How to make effective use of the aggregated feedback signals to discover useful sensory clues, known as the Temporal Credit-Assignment (TCA) problem, remains a challenging research topic for both neuroscience and machine learning. In this section, the capability of the proposed ETDP algorithm to solve the TCA problem on both synthetic and real-world datasets is evaluated.

Similar to the tasks proposed in [Güt16], ten brief spike patterns are constructed to represent the spiking activities in response to different multimodal sensory clues. Each brief spike pattern consists of 500 spike trains of 50 ms, wherein each spike train is generated randomly at a firing rate of 5 Hz. In each trial, as shown in Fig. 4.33, a random number of these ten spike patterns are embedded within a long stream of background spiking activity generated at the same firing rate of 5 Hz. Each training cycle consists of 100 such trials generated with the set-up described above. Here, the task is to enable a single-spiking neuron to detect useful sensory clues by firing the specific number of spikes during their presence.

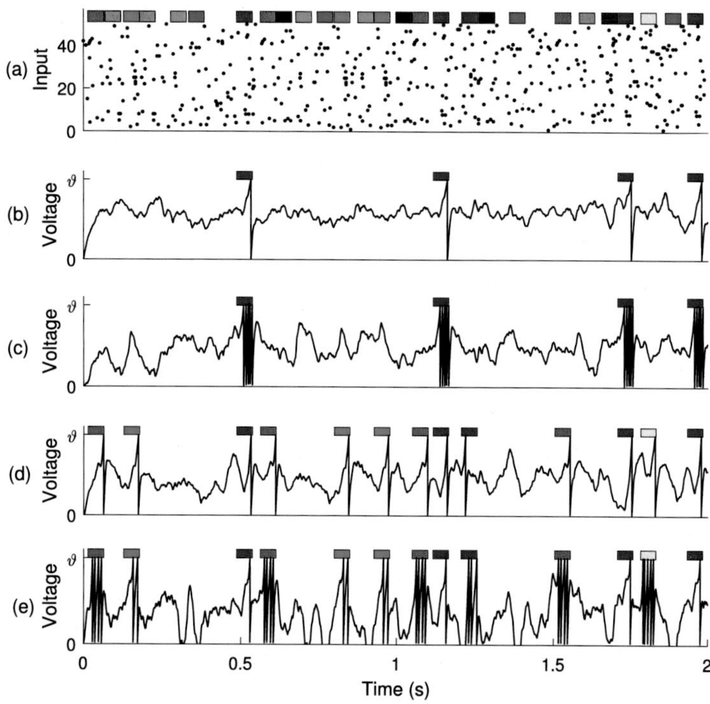

FIGURE 4.34 Learning useful multimodal sensory clues. (a) Input spike pattern. For better visualization, only the first 50 out of the 500 afferents are provided. Colored rectangles correspond to 10 different sensory clues. (b) The learning neuron is trained to generate one spike only during the presence of the ith clue (red rectangle). (c) The learning neuron is trained to generate a burst of five spikes only during the presence of the ith clue. (d) The learning neuron is trained to generate one spike only during the presence of the five different clues. (e) The learning neuron is trained to generate a distinct number of spikes {1, 2, 3, 4, 5} during the presence of the five different clues.

In Fig. 4.33(b), the neuron is trained to detect the clue i among the other 9 distractors and background activities. For each trial, the desired number of spikes N_d is set as the occurrences of clue i ($N_d = c_i$). If the learning neuron fires more or fewer spikes, the proposed learning algorithm will weaken or potentiate the synaptic weights to make the neuron fire the desired spike count. As shown in Fig. 4.33(b), the learning neuron can precisely fire one spike during the presence of the clue i. As shown in Fig. 4.33(c), when we set the desired spike count five times to the occurrences of the clue i ($N_d = 5c_i$), the neuron learns to generate a burst of 5 spikes in response to the clue i and remains silent otherwise. Moreover, by setting the desired spike count as $N_d = \sum_i c_i d_i$, where c_i denotes the number of clue i within a trial and d_i is the corresponding desired spike count to the clue i, the proposed

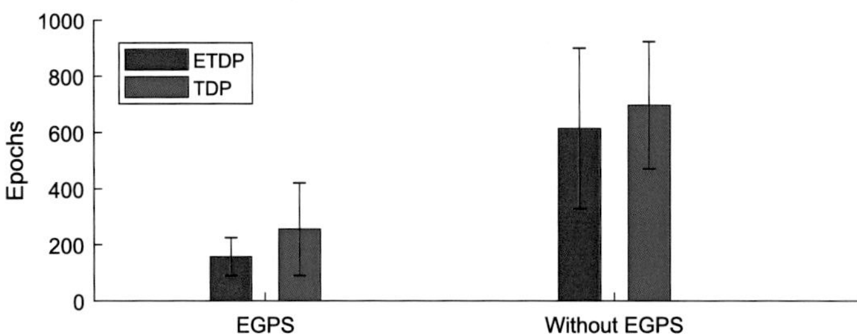

FIGURE 4.35 Learning efficiency of different learning algorithms to accomplish the task of Fig. 4.34(e). The left and right figures summarize the required learning epochs with and without EGPS, respectively.

learning algorithm enables the trained neuron to decompose the feedback signal and associate each clue with a distinct number of spikes. Fig. 4.33(d) and Fig. 4.33(e) show the testing results when d_i of the five useful sensory clues are set as $\{1,1,1,1,1\}$ and $\{1,2,3,4,5\}$, respectively. These experimental results demonstrate that the proposed learning algorithm can learn useful multimodal sensory clues with delayed feedback even when these clues are embedded within distracting streams of unrelated sensory and background activities.

As explained in Section 4.6.1, the derived error gradients are prone to the gradient explosion problem. Here, the effectiveness of the proposed EGPS method to overcome this problem is evaluated by comparing the required learning epochs, with and without the EGPS method, to solve the corresponding task in Fig. 4.33(e). As shown in Fig. 4.35, by combining the proposed EGPS method, the learning efficiency is improved for both the learning algorithms TDP and ETDP. Moreover, the learning efficiency of the proposed ETDP algorithm is higher than the TDP algorithm for this challenging multimodal sensory clues learning task. Specifically, when combined with the EGPS method, the required learning epochs of ETDP and TDP are about 150 and 250, respectively.

Next, the method is applied to a more challenging real-world task. In this task, 200 multimodal spiking streams are constructed by randomly embedding 10 spike patterns, encoded from five images and five speech signals, within a long stream of background activities. These five images are randomly selected from the MNIST dataset, and further encoded into spike patterns through the latency coding [Hop95][HTT+13], as illustrated in Fig. 4.36. These five speech signals are randomly selected from the TIDIGITS corpus and then encoded into spike patterns using the Biologically plausible Auditory Encoding scheme (BAE) [GS09][PCW+19] as shown in Fig. 4.37. There are two neurons in the output layer, which selectively respond to images and speech signals, respectively. The desired spike count of each output neuron is defined as $N_d = \sum_i c_i d_i$, where c_i denotes the number of clue i (ith image or ith speech signal) within a spiking stream, and d_i is the corresponding desired spike count of the clue i.

After training, a testing spike stream is generated to verify whether the two output neurons can separate and recognize different visual and auditory clues. Fig. 4.38(b) and Fig. 4.38(c) illustrate the membrane potential traces of the neurons that are trained to selectively respond to auditory (speech) and visual (image) information, respectively. After

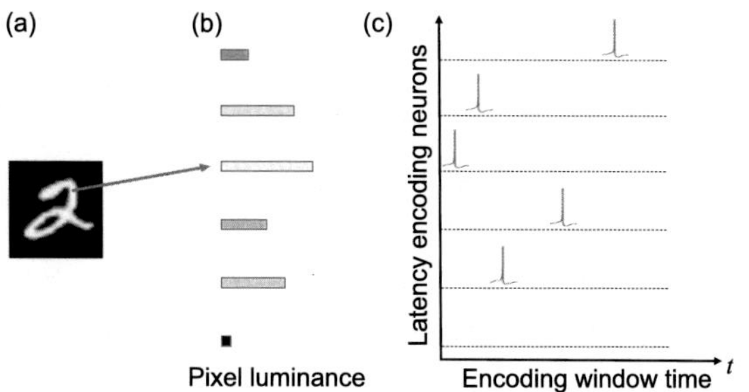

FIGURE 4.36 The illustration of the neural latency coding for images. The luminance or intensity value of each pixel is encoded into the spike time, whereby the earlier spike time corresponds to the larger intensity value. (a) An image of the hand-written digit "2". The horizontal bars in (b) depict the luminance or intensity value of 6 pixels, where a longer bar represents a brighter pixel. (c) The latency-encoded spike pattern, in which each pixel in (b) is encoded into a single spike (red pulse) in the corresponding row of (c).

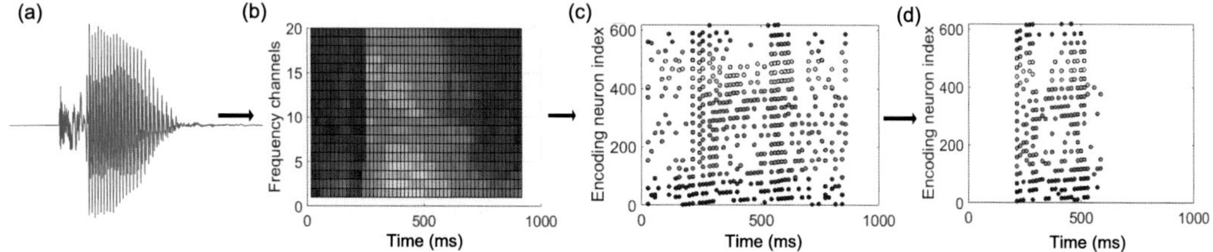

FIGURE 4.37 The illustration of the neural encoding for audio signals, using a biologically plausible Auditory Encoding scheme (BAE). A raw audio signal corresponding to the spoken digit "two" (a) is first filtered by a cochlear filter bank and decomposed into a 20-channel spectrogram (b). The spectrogram is further encoded with neural threshold coding (c), which effectively describes the moving trajectory of sub-band signals. Finally, an auditory masking scheme is applied to eliminate imperceptible spikes, resulting in a sparse yet effective spike pattern. (d) More details about the BAE scheme can be found in [PCW+19].

training with the proposed ETDP learning algorithm, these two output neurons can selectively respond to speech signals and images. Furthermore, they can recognize different clues by firing the corresponding number of spikes. For example, as shown in Fig. 4.38(c), this output neuron fires spikes whenever there is an image presented, while remaining silent during the presence of speech signals and background activities. In addition, the neuron fires a distinct number of spikes in response to different images.

4.6.3.3 Classification tasks

In order to demonstrate the effectiveness of the proposed ETDP learning algorithm for multi-layer SNNs, the researchers first validate the trained SNNs on the XOR classification task. Additionally, the authors put forth an SNN-based computational framework for multimodal pattern recognition tasks.

A. XOR classification task: In this experiment, the four training samples of the XOR task are encoded into spike time by associating the binary input '0' and '1' with spike times of 5 ms and 10 ms, respectively. The input spikes then project to a hidden layer consisting

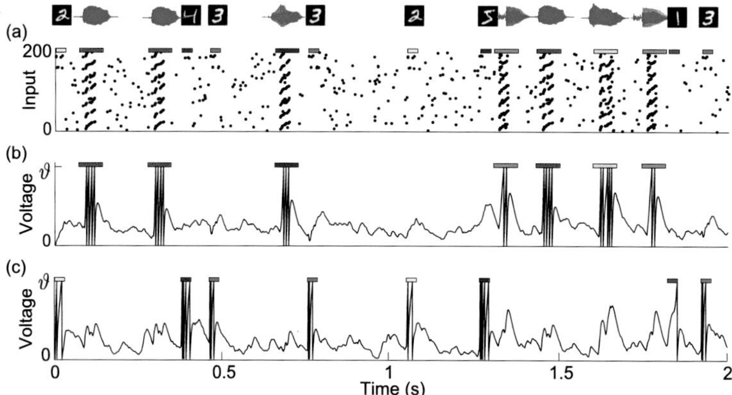

FIGURE 4.38 Illustration of the audio-visual pattern recognition with spiking neurons. (a) The input spiking stream corresponds to the audio-visual sensory stimuli on the top row, the random spontaneous spiking activities are added during the silence period. Only the first 200 synaptic afferents are given. (b) The membrane potential trace of the output neuron that is trained to selectively respond to speech signals. (c) The membrane potential trace of the output neuron that is trained to selectively respond to images.

of four neurons that are subsequently connected to a single output neuron. During the training process, the training samples of {5, 5} ms and {10, 10} ms are defined as the same class, and the output neuron is required to fire two spikes. When the samples of {5, 10} ms and {10, 5} ms are presented to the network, the output neuron is required to remain silent.

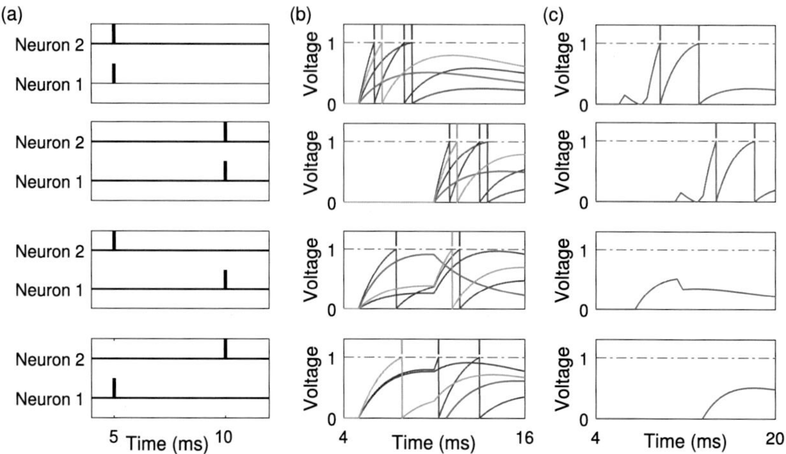

FIGURE 4.39 Illustration of the XOR classification task with the multi-layer SNN. (a) Four input spike patterns are constructed by associating the binary input '0' and '1' to spike times of 5 ms and 10 ms, respectively. (b) The membrane potential traces of the four hidden neurons after training. The membrane potential traces are color coded to denote different hidden neurons. (c) The membrane potential traces of the output neuron correspond to different input spike patterns.

As shown in Fig. 4.39(a), there are four different input spike patterns corresponding to the four training samples. Fig. 4.39(b) shows the membrane potential traces of the four hidden spiking neurons that are denoted in different colors. After training, the output neuron can precisely emit two spikes when the samples of {5, 5} ms and {10, 10} ms are presented, while remaining silent otherwise. This experimental result suggests that the proposed ETDP learning algorithm has the capability to train multi-layer SNNs to perform the nonlinear pattern classification task.

B. Multimodal pattern recognition: The studies in cognitive neuroscience suggest that the human brain can efficiently integrate sensory information of multiple modalities [Cal01,KKSG05,WBK10,RR18]. In addition, there is strong evidence showing that cross-modal coupling facilitates the influence of one modality on the areas of other modalities, and the integration occurs in the supramodal areas where neurons are sensitive to multimodal stimuli. Inspired by these findings, an SNN-based multimodal computational framework for audio-visual pattern recognition is proposed. As shown in Fig. 4.40, the proposed multimodal computational frame mainly consists of three parts, the unimodal processing part, the cross-modal coupling part, and the supramodal part. In the following, the working mechanism of each part will be introduced in sequence.

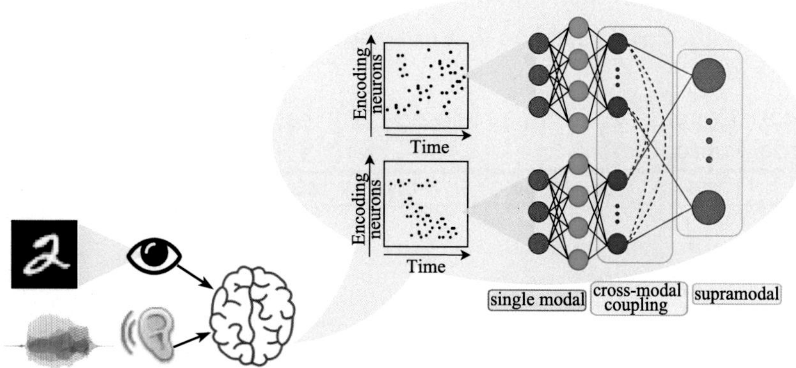

FIGURE 4.40 The proposed SNN-based computational framework for multimodal pattern recognition. This framework mainly consists of three parts, the single-modal processing part, the cross-modal coupling part, and the supramodal part.

In the unimodal processing part, two SNN-based computational models are working independently for visual and audio modalities. These two unimodal SNN models are trained following the proposed ETDP algorithm. The feedforward SNN architectures used for visual and audio signal processing are 784-800-10 and 620-800-10, respectively. The role of cross-modal coupling is to transmit the influence of one modality to the areas that intrinsically belong to other modalities. Hence, in the cross-modal coupling part, excitatory and inhibitory connections are constructed across two different modalities, such that when the output neurons of one modality fire spikes, the output neurons in the other modality will receive those spikes to facilitate synchronized behaviors across different modalities. For example, when both the image and speech patterns 'one' are presented to the unimodal SNNs, the output neuron representing image 'one' fires first. The generated spikes will excite the output neuron representing 'one' of the audio modalities, while inhibiting all other neurons to prevent them from firing.

There are ten neurons in the supramodal layer, which integrate the information from the corresponding output neurons of single modalities through excitatory connections. To facilitate a rapid response, the neurons in the supramodal layer will generate an output spike as soon as they receive an incoming spike from the cross-modal coupling layer.

The performance of the proposed multimodal computational framework is evaluated on the joint digit classification dataset. In this experiment, the training dataset consists of 60000 pairs of inputs (training samples in the TIDIGITS corpus are repeated to match the size of the MNIST dataset), and the testing dataset consists of 10000 samples, the same as the earlier experiments, the latency coding [Hop95][HTT+13] and the BAE scheme [PCW+19][GS09] are used to encode the image and speech signals into spike patterns, respectively. When the encoded spike pattern is presented to the unimodal SNN, the corresponding output neuron is trained with the proposed ETDP learning algorithm such that it fires the most number of spikes. The connections between different modalities are predefined so as to exert the desired influence on the other modality. In the supramodal part, the pattern is classified as the neuron that fires the most number of spikes.

Table 4.9 Comparison of the proposed ETDP learning algorithms with other unimodal approaches.

Model	Type	Layers	Modality	Dataset	Acc (%)
Diehl et al. [DM15]*	SNN	2	Uni	MNIST	95.0
Rathi et al. [RR18]*	SNN	3	Uni	MNIST	93.2
Kheradpisheh et al. [KGTM18]	SNN+SVM	6	Uni	MNIST	98.4
Hong et al. [HWW+19]	SNN	3	Uni	MNIST	97.2
Gu et al. [GXPT19]	SNN	3	Uni	MNIST	98.6
Tavanaei et al. [TM17b]	SNN+SVM	2	Uni	TIDIGITS	91.0
Tavanaei et al. [TM17a]	SNN+HMM	4	Uni	TIDIGITS	96.0
Neil et al. [NL16]	MFCC+RNN	4	Uni	TIDIGITS	96.1
ETDP	SNN	3	Uni	MNIST	96.8
ETDP	SNN	3	Uni	TIDIGITS	95.8
ETDP	SNN	3	Multi	MNIST&TIDIGITS	**98.9**

* The model is unsupervised, otherwise it is supervised.

As shown in Table 4.9, the multimodal classification framework equipped with the proposed ETDP learning algorithm outperforms many unimodal approaches. In addition, with the help of cross-modal coupling and the supramodal parts, the multimodal classification framework achieves a classification accuracy of 98.9%, which improves over single modalities by more than 2%.

4.7 Conclusions

Sequence learning and aggregate-label learning are two common tasks in SNNs. This chapter introduced the FE-Learn and RLSBLR algorithms for sequence learning, while the MPD-AL and ETDP algorithms were presented for aggregate-label learning. The FE-Learn algorithm adjusts parameters only for the first error spike time in each round of learning, whereas the RLSBLR algorithm learns at every error time point. Experimental results demonstrate that both algorithms exhibit higher accuracy and reduced computational resources compared to other conventional sequence learning methods. For aggregate-label learning, both MPD-AL and ETDP algorithms were introduced. MPD-AL is driven by membrane voltage and is designed to reduce the computational load of the aggregate-label learning algorithm, while ETDP is driven by thresholds and has excellent temporary credit-assignment capability. Experimental results show that these algorithms can effectively detect relevant information embedded within unrelated spiking activities and background noise with superior efficiency compared to state-of-the-art TDP1 and MST methods.

References

[AL11] Mohammad Abdollahi, Shih-Chii Liu, Speaker-independent isolated digit recognition using an AER silicon cochlea, in: Biomedical Circuits and Systems Conference (BIOCAS), 2011 IEEE, IEEE, 2011, pp. 269–272.

[AMS05] Peyman Adibi, Mohammad Reza Meybodi, Reza Safabakhsh, Unsupervised learning of synaptic delays based on learning automata in an rbf-like network of spiking neurons for data clustering, Neurocomputing 64 (2005) 335–357.

[AR15] Navin Anwani, Bipin Rajendran, NormAD – normalized approximate descent based supervised learning rule for spiking neurons, in: 2015 International Joint Conference on Neural Networks (IJCNN), IEEE, 2015, pp. 1–8.

[ASSN12] A. Mohemmed, S. Schliebs, S. Matsuda, N. Kasabov, Span: spike pattern association neuron for learning spatio-temporal spike patterns, International Journal of Neural Systems 22 (04) (2012) 1659–1685.

[Bec16] Eric Bechhoefer, Condition based maintenance fault database for testing of diagnostic and prognostics algorithms, https://www.mfpt.org/fault-data-sets/, 2016.

[BFMD11] Sami Boudkkazi, Laure Fronzaroli-Molinieres, Dominique Debanne, Presynaptic action potential waveform determines cortical synaptic latency, The Journal of Physiology 589 (5) (2011) 1117–1131.

[BKLP02] Sander M. Bohte, Joost N. Kok, Han La Poutre, Error-backpropagation in temporally encoded networks of spiking neurons, Neurocomputing 48 (1–4) (2002) 17–37.

[BNN21] F. Ball, A. Nentwich, T. Noesselt, Cross-modal perceptual enhancement of unisensory targets is uni-directional and does not affect temporal expectations, Vision Research 190 (107962) (2021).

[BP98] Guo-qiang Bi, Mu-ming Poo, Synaptic modifications in cultured hippocampal neurons: dependence on spike timing, synaptic strength, and postsynaptic cell type, Journal of Neuroscience 18 (24) (1998) 10464–10472.

[BSS+18] Guillaume Bellec, Darjan Salaj, Anand Subramoney, Robert Legenstein, Wolfgang Maass, Long short-term memory and learning-to-learn in networks of spiking neurons, Advances in Neural Information Processing Systems 31 (2018).

[BVDG11] Peter Bühlmann, Sara Van De Geer, Statistics for High-Dimensional Data: Methods, Theory and Applications, Springer Science & Business Media, 2011.

[Cal01] Gemma A. Calvert, Crossmodal processing in the human brain: insights from functional neuroimaging studies, Cerebral Cortex 11 (12) (2001) 1110–1123.

[CCB00] G.A. Calvert, R. Campbell, M.J. Brammer, Evidence from functional magnetic resonance imaging of crossmodal binding in the human heteromodal cortex, Current Biology 10 (11) (2000) 649–657.

[CT04] Gemma A. Calvert, Thomas Thesen, Multisensory integration: methodological approaches and emerging principles in the human brain, Journal of Physiology (Paris) 98 (1) (2004) 191–205.

[DG17] Dheeru Dua, Casey Graff, UCI machine learning repository, 2017.

[DM15] Peter U. Diehl, Cook Matthew, Unsupervised learning of digit recognition using spike-timing-dependent plasticity, Frontiers in Computational Neuroscience 9 (429) (2015) 99.

[DMJFDMJM16] Juan P. Dominguez-Morales, A. Jimenez-Fernandez, M. Dominguez-Morales, G. Jimenez-Moreno, Navis: neuromorphic auditory visualizer tool, Neurocomputing 237 (2016) 418–422.

[DSSS16] S. Dora, K. Subramanian, S. Suresh, N. Sundararajan, Development of a self regulating evolving spiking neural network for classification problem, Neurocomputing 171 (C) (2016) 1216–1229.

[FTB+18] Pierre Falez, Pierre Tirilly, Ioan Marius Bilasco, Philippe Devienne, Pierre Boulet, Mastering the output frequency in spiking neural networks, in: 2018 International Joint Conference on Neural Networks (IJCNN), 2018, pp. 1–8.

[GDA07] S. Ghosh-Dastidar, H. Adeli, Improved spiking neural networks for EEG classification and epilepsy and seizure detection, Integrated Computer-Aided Engineering 14 (3) (2007) 187–212.

[GDA09] Samanwoy Ghosh-Dastidar, Hojjat Adeli, A new supervised learning algorithm for multiple spiking neural networks with application in epilepsy and seizure detection, Neural Networks the Official Journal of the International Neural Network Society 22 (10) (2009) 1419–1431.

[GK02] Wulfram Gerstner, Werner M. Kistler, Spiking Neuron Models: Single Neurons, Populations, Plasticity, Cambridge University Press, Cambridge, 2002.

[GS09] Robert Gütig, Haim Sompolinsky, Time-warp–invariant neuronal processing, PLoS Biology 7 (7) (2009) e1000141.

[Güt16] Robert Gütig, Spiking neurons can discover predictive features by aggregate-label learning, Science 351 (6277) (2016) aab4113.

[GXPT19] Pengjie Gu, Rong Xiao, Gang Pan, Huajin Tang, STCA: spatio-temporal credit assignment with delayed feedback in deep spiking neural networks, in: Proceedings of the Twenty-Eighth International Joint Conference on Artificial Intelligence, IJCAI-19, International Joint Conferences on Artificial Intelligence Organization, 7 2019, pp. 1366–1372.

[Hay95] Simon Haykin, Adaptive Filter Theory, 3rd ed., Prentice Hall, 1995.

[HLB14] Shaista Hussain, Shih-Chii Liu, Arindam Basu, Improved margin multi-class classification using dendritic neurons with morphological learning, in: 2014 IEEE International Symposium on Circuits and Systems (ISCAS), 2014, pp. 2640–2643.

[Hop95] J.J. Hopfield, Pattern recognition computation using action potential timing for stimulus representation, Nature 376 (6535) (1995) 33–36.

[HTT+13] Jun Hu, Huajin Tang, Kay Chen Tan, Haizhou Li, Luping Shi, A spike-timing-based integrated model for pattern recognition, Neural Computation 25 (2) (2013) 450–472.

[HWW+19] Chaofei Hong, Xile Wei, Jiang Wang, Bin Deng, Haitao Yu, Yanqiu Che, Training spiking neural networks for cognitive tasks: a versatile framework compatible with various temporal codes, IEEE Transactions on Neural Networks and Learning Systems (2019).

[HWW+20] Chaofei Hong, Xile Wei, Jiang Wang, Bin Deng, Haitao Yu, Yanqiu Che, Training spiking neural networks for cognitive tasks: a versatile framework compatible to various temporal codes, IEEE Transactions on Neural Networks and Learning Systems 31 (4) (2020) 1285–1296.

[Kas18] Nikola K. Kasabov, Time-Space, Spiking Neural Networks and Brain-Inspired Artificial Intelligence, Springer, 2018.

[KGTM18] Saeed Reza Kheradpisheh, Mohammad Ganjtabesh, Simon J. Thorpe, Timothée Masquelier, Stdp-based spiking deep convolutional neural networks for object recognition, Neural Networks 99 (2018) 56–67.

[KKSG05] Katharina von Kriegstein, Andreas Kleinschmidt, Philipp Sterzer, Anne-Lise Giraud, Interaction of face and voice areas during speaker recognition, Journal of Cognitive Neuroscience 17 (3) (2005) 367–376.

[KM65] Bernard Katz, Ricardo Miledi, The measurement of synaptic delay, and the time course of acetylcholine release at the neuromuscular junction, Proceedings of the Royal Society of London. Series B, Biological Sciences 161 (985) (1965) 483–495.

[KM20] Saeed Reza Kheradpisheh, Timothée Masquelier, Temporal backpropagation for spiking neural networks with one spike per neuron, International Journal of Neural Systems 30 (6) (2020) 2050027.

[LBBH98] Yann LeCun, Léon Bottou, Yoshua Bengio, Patrick Haffner, Gradient-based learning applied to document recognition, Proceedings of the IEEE 86 (11) (1998) 2278–2324.

[LD93] R. Gary Leonard, George Doddington, Tidigits Speech Corpus, Texas Instruments, Inc, 1993.

[LDP16] Jun Haeng Lee, Tobi Delbruck, Michael Pfeiffer, Training deep spiking neural networks using backpropagation, Frontiers in Neuroscience 10 (2016) 508.

[LF02] Jen-Wei Lin, Donald S. Faber, Modulation of synaptic delay during synaptic plasticity, Trends in Neurosciences 25 (9) (2002) 449–455.

[LLZ+20] Zuo Lin, Zhang Lei, Zhang Zhehan, Luo Xiaoling, Yu Liu, A spiking neural network-based approach to bearing fault diagnosis, Journal of Manufacturing Systems (2020).

[LMMC18] Zhitao Lin, De Ma, Jianyi Meng, Linna Chen, Relative ordering learning in spiking neural network for pattern recognition, Neurocomputing 275 (2018) 94–106.

[LQZC19] Xiaoling Luo, Hong Qu, Yun Zhang, Yi Chen, First error-based supervised learning algorithm for spiking neural networks, Frontiers in Neuroscience 13 (2019) 559.

[Mat16] S. Matsuda Bpspike, A backpropagation learning for all parameters in spiking neural networks with multiple layers and multiple spikes, in: International Joint Conference on Neural Networks, 2016, pp. 293–298.

[MGT09] T. Masquelier, R. Guyonneau, S.J. Thorpe, Competitive STDP-based spike pattern learning, Neural Computation 21 (5) (2009) 1259.

[MKS12] Federico Minneci, Roby T. Kanichay, R. Angus Silver, Estimation of the time course of neurotransmitter release at central synapses from the first latency of postsynaptic currents, Journal of Neuroscience Methods 205 (1) (2012) 49–64.

[Mos17] H. Mostafa, Supervised learning based on temporal coding in spiking neural networks, IEEE Transactions on Neural Networks and Learning Systems 29 (7) (2017) 3227–3235.

[MROS14] R.M. Memmesheimer, R. Rubin, B.P. Olveczky, H. Sompolinsky, Learning precisely timed spikes, Neuron 82 (4) (2014) 925–938.

[NAPD17] Emre O. Neftci, Charles Augustine, Somnath Paul, Georgios Detorakis, Event-driven random back-propagation: enabling neuromorphic deep learning machines, Frontiers in Neuroscience 11 (2017) 324.

[NL16] Daniel Neil, Shih-Chii Liu, Effective sensor fusion with event-based sensors and deep network architectures, in: Circuits and Systems (ISCAS), 2016 IEEE International Symposium on, IEEE, 2016, pp. 2282–2285.

[PCW+19] Zihan Pan, Yansong Chua, Jibin Wu, Malu Zhang, Haizhou Li, Eliathamby Ambikairajah, An efficient and perceptually motivated auditory neural encoding and decoding algorithm for spiking neural networks, arXiv preprint, arXiv:1909.01302, 2019.

[PK10] Filip Ponulak, Andrzej Kasiński, Supervised learning in spiking neural networks with resume: sequence learning, classification, and spike shifting, Neural Computation 22 (22) (2010) 467–510.

[PKK19] Balint Petro, Nikola Kasabov, Rita M. Kiss, Selection and optimization of temporal spike encoding methods for spiking neural networks, IEEE Transactions on Neural Networks and Learning Systems 31 (2) (2019) 358–370.

[PLWC18] Zihan Pan, Haizhou Li, Jibin Wu, Yansong Chua, An event-based cochlear filter temporal encoding scheme for speech signals, in: 2018 International Joint Conference on Neural Networks (IJCNN), IEEE, 2018, pp. 1–8.

[PP10] Itzchak Parnas, Hanna Parnas, Control of neurotransmitter release: from ca 2+ to voltage dependent g-protein coupled receptors, Pflügers Archiv – European Journal of Physiology 460 (6) (2010) 975–990.

[PPC08] D.T. Pham, M.S. Packianather, E.Y.A. Charles, Control chart pattern clustering using a new self-organizing spiking neural network, Proceedings of the Institution of Mechanical Engineers. Part B, Journal of Engineering Manufacture 222 (B10) (2008) 1201–1211.

[Rab89] Lawrence R. Rabiner, A tutorial on hidden Markov models and selected applications in speech recognition, Proceedings of the IEEE 77 (2) (1989) 257–286.

[RR18] Nitin Rathi, Kaushik Roy, Stdp-based unsupervised multimodal learning with cross-modal processing in spiking neural network, IEEE Transactions on Emerging Topics in Computational Intelligence (2018) 1–11.

[SF13] Scarpetta Silvia, Giacco Ferdinando, Associative memory of phase-coded spatiotemporal patterns in leaky integrate and fire networks, The Journal of Neuroscience 34 (2) (2013) 319–336.

[SFW+03] S. Schreiber, J.M. Fellous, D. Whitmer, P. Tiesinga, T.J. Sejnowski, A new correlation-based measure of spike timing reliability, Neurocomputing 52 (3) (2003) 925–931.

[SJ05] Jonathan S. Smith, The local mean decomposition and its application to EEG perception data, Journal of the Royal Society Interface 2 (5) (2005) 443–454.

[SO18] Sumit Bam Shrestha, Garrick Orchard, SLAYER: spike layer error reassignment in time, in: Advances in Neural Information Processing Systems, Montréal, Canada, vol. 31, 2018, pp. 1412–1421.

[SS15] Sumit Bam Shrestha, Qing Song, Adaptive learning rate of spikeprop based on weight convergence analysis, Neural Networks 63 (63) (2015) 185–198.

[SS16] S.B. Shrestha, Q. Song, Adaptive delay learning in spikeprop based on delay convergence analysis, in: International Joint Conference on Neural Networks, 2016, pp. 277–284.

[TBLM15a] Aboozar Taherkhani, Ammar Belatreche, Yuhua Li, Liam P. Maguire, Dl-resume: a delay learning-based remote supervised method for spiking neurons, IEEE Transactions on Neural Networks and Learning Systems 26 (12) (2015) 3137–3149.

[TBLM15b] Aboozar Taherkhani, Ammar Belatreche, Yuhua Li, Liam P. Maguire, Edl: an extended delay learning based remote supervised method for spiking neurons, in: International Conference on Neural Information Processing, Springer, 2015, pp. 190–197.

[TBLM15c] Aboozar Taherkhani, Ammar Belatreche, Yuhua Li, Liam P. Maguire, Multi-dl-resume: multiple neurons delay learning remote supervised method, in: 2015 International Joint Conference on Neural Networks (IJCNN), IEEE, 2015, pp. 1–7.

[TBLM18] Aboozar Taherkhani, Ammar Belatreche, Yuhua Li, Liam P. Maguire, A supervised learning algorithm for learning precise timing of multiple spikes in multilayer spiking neural networks, IEEE Transactions on Neural Networks and Learning Systems 29 (11) (2018) 5394–5407.

[TM17a] Amirhossein Tavanaei, Anthony Maida, Bio-inspired multi-layer spiking neural network extracts discriminative features from speech signals, in: International Conference on Neural Information Processing, 2017, pp. 899–908.

[TM17b] Amirhossein Tavanaei, Anthony S. Maida, A spiking network that learns to extract spike signatures from speech signals, Neurocomputing 240 (2017) 191–199.

[TM18] Amirhossein Tavanaei, Anthony S. Maida, Bp-stdp: approximating backpropagation using spike timing dependent plasticity, Neurocomputing 330 (2018) 39–47.

[TRT08] Masquelier Timothée, Guyonneau Rudy, Simon J. Thorpe, Spike timing dependent plasticity finds the start of repeating patterns in continuous spike trains, PLoS ONE 3 (1) (2008) e1377.

[WBK10] Simei Gomes Wysoski, Lubica Benuskova, Nikola Kasabov, Evolving spiking neural networks for audiovisual information processing, Neural Networks 23 (7) (2010) 819–835.

[WBMM17] J. Wang, A. Belatreche, L.P. Maguire, T.M. Mcginnity, SpikeTemp: an enhanced rank-order-based learning approach for spiking neural networks with adaptive structure, IEEE Transactions on Neural Networks and Learning Systems 28 (1) (2017) 30–43.

[WCL18] Jibin Wu, Yansong Chua, Haizhou Li, A biologically plausible speech recognition framework based on spiking neural networks, in: 2018 International Joint Conference on Neural Networks (IJCNN), IEEE, 2018, pp. 1–8.

[WCZ+18] Jibin Wu, Yansong Chua, Malu Zhang, Haizhou Li, Kay Chen Tan, A spiking neural network framework for robust sound classification, Frontiers in Neuroscience 12 (2018) 836.

[WDL+18] Yu Jie Wu, Lei Deng, Guo Qi Li, Jun Zhu, Lu Ping Shi, Spatio-temporal backpropagation for training high-performance spiking neural networks, Frontiers in Neuroscience 12 (331) (2018) 1–12.

[WDL+19] Yujie Wu, Lei Deng, Guoqi Li, Jun Zhu, Yuan Xie, L.P. Shi, Direct training for spiking neural networks: faster, larger, better, in: Proceedings of the AAAI Conference on Artificial Intelligence, 2019, pp. 33:1311–1318, 07.

[Wer90] P.J. Werbos, Backpropagation through time: what it does and how to do it, Proceedings of the IEEE 78 (10) (1990) 1550–1560.

[WLD19] Xiangwen Wang, Xianghong Lin, Xiaochao Dang, A delay learning algorithm based on spike train kernels for spiking neurons, Frontiers in Neuroscience 13 (2019).

[WMSS10] John J. Wade, Liam J. Mcdaid, Jose A. Santos, Heather M. Sayers, Swat: a spiking neural network training algorithm for classification problems, IEEE Transactions on Neural Networks 21 (11) (2010) 1817–1830.

[XLC+18] Xiurui Xie, Guisong Liu, Qing Cai, Hong Qu, Malu Zhang, The maximum points-based supervised learning rule for spiking neural networks, Soft Computing 23 (11) (2018) 1–12.

[XZHY13] Yan Xu, Xiaoqin Zeng, Lixin Han, Jing Yang, A supervised multi-spike learning algorithm based on gradient descent for spiking neural networks, Neural Networks 43 (2013) 99–113.

[XZZ13] Yan Xu, Xiaoqin Zeng, Shuiming Zhong, A new supervised learning algorithm for spiking neurons, Neural Computation 25 (6) (2013) 1472–1511.

[YLT18] Qiang Yu, Haizhou Li, Kay Chen Tan, Spike timing or rate? Neurons learn to make decisions for both through threshold-driven plasticity, IEEE Transactions on Cybernetics 49 (6) (2018) 2178–2189.

[YTHT13] Qiang Yu, Huajin Tang, Jun Hu, Kay Chen Tan, Precise-spike-driven synaptic plasticity for hetero association of spatiotemporal spike patterns, PLoS ONE 8 (11) (2013) e78318.

[YTTL13] Qiang Yu, Hua Jin Tang, Kay Chen Tan, Hai Zhou Li, Precise-spike-driven synaptic plasticity: learning hetero-association of spatiotemporal spike patterns, PLoS ONE 8 (11) (2013) 65–87.

[YTTY14] Qiang Yu, Huajin Tang, Kay Chen Tan, Haoyong Yu, A brain-inspired spiking neural network model with temporal encoding and learning, Neurocomputing 138 (2014) 3–13.

[ZG18] Friedemann Zenke, Surya Ganguli, Superspike: supervised learning in multilayer spiking neural networks, Neural Computation 30 (6) (2018) 1514–1541.

[ZGZ+18] Yongqing Zhang, Tianyu Geng, Malu Zhang, Xi Wu, Jiliu Zhou, Hong Qu, Efficient and robust supervised learning algorithm for spiking neural networks, Sensing and Imaging 19 (1) (2018).

[ZLC+20] Malu Zhang, Xiaoling Luo, Yi Chen, Jibin Wu, Ammar Belatreche, Zihan Pan, Hong Qu, Haizhou Li, An efficient threshold-driven aggregate-label learning algorithm for multimodal information processing, IEEE Journal of Selected Topics in Signal Processing 14 (3) (2020) 592–602.

[ZLG+21] Yu Zhang, Yuntao Li, Yonghui Guo, Yonggang Li, Yonghua He, Tianyi Chai, Supervised learning algorithm tempotron based on pulse neural network, in: ICFEICT 2021: International Conference on Frontiers of Electronics, Information and Computation Technologies, vol. 110, 2021, pp. 1–4.

[ZLJC15] Yong Zhang, Peng Li, Yingyezhe Jin, Yoonsuck Choe, A digital liquid state machine with biologically inspired learning and its application to speech recognition, IEEE Transactions on Neural Networks and Learning Systems 26 (11) (2015) 2635–2649.

[ZQB+18] Malu Zhang, Hong Qu, Ammar Belatreche, Yi Chen, Zhang Yi, A highly effective and robust membrane potential-driven supervised learning method for spiking neurons, IEEE Transactions on Neural Networks and Learning Systems 30 (1) (2018) 123–137.

[ZQL+21] Yun Zhang, Hong Qu, Xiaoling Luo, Yi Chen, Yuchen Wang, Malu Zhang, Zefang Li, A new recursive least squares-based learning algorithm for spiking neurons, Neural Networks 138 (2021) 110–125.

[ZQX18] Malu Zhang, Hong Qu, Xiurui Xie, Empd: an efficient membrane potential driven supervised learning algorithm for spiking neurons, IEEE Transactions on Cognitive & Developmental Systems 10 (2) (2018) 151–162.

[ZWB+20] Malu Zhang, Jibin Wu, Ammar Belatreche, Zihan Pan, Xiurui Xie, Yansong Chua, Guoqi Li, Hong Qu, Haizhou Li, Supervised learning in spiking neural networks with synaptic delay-weight plasticity, Neurocomputing (2020) 103–118.

[ZWC+19] Malu Zhang, Jibin Wu, Yansong Chua, Xiaoling Luo, Zihan Pan, Dan Liu, Haizhou Li, Mpd-al: an efficient membrane potential driven aggregate-label learning algorithm for spiking neurons, in: Proceedings of the AAAI Conference on Artificial Intelligence, vol. 33, 2019, pp. 1327–1334.

[ZWW+21] Ma Lu Zhang, Jia Dong Wang, Ji Bin Wu, Ammar Belatreche, Burin Amornpaisannon, Zhi Xuan Zhang, Rectified linear postsynaptic potential function for backpropagation in deep spiking neural networks, IEEE Transactions on Neural Networks and Learning Systems 33 (5) (2021) 1947–1958.

5

Learning algorithms for deep spiking neural networks

5.1 Preface

Brain-inspired SNNs offer a low-power alternative for neural network implementation and provide great computing potential, equivalent to that of DNNs on ultra-low-power spike-driven neuromorphic hardware. However, due to the complex temporal dynamics of spiking neuronal models and the non-differentiable nature of their spiking activity, the well-known error backpropagation (BP) learning algorithm cannot be directly applied to deep SNNs. To address these problems, many solutions have been proposed, which can be grouped into two categories: ANN-to-SNN conversion methods and direct training methods. Direct training methods for SNNs can be divided into membrane potential-driven and spike-driven ones. Among the existing learning algorithms, only the spike-driven learning algorithms perform the SNNs training in a strictly event-driven manner and are compatible with the temporal coding in which the information is carried by the timing of individual spikes that has a high level of sparsity. Hence, spike-driven learning algorithms hold great potential to enable efficient training and inference on low-power neuromorphic devices.

Despite its energy efficiency, the existing spike-driven learning algorithm faces several problems, which restricts it to only shallow structures. As shown in Fig. 5.1, the dynamics of a typical artificial neuron used in DNNs differ greatly from their spiking neuron counterparts; therefore, the well-known BP algorithm cannot be directly applied to Deep SNNs (DSNNs) due to the non-differentiable nature of the neuron spiking activity, exploding gradients, and dead neurons problems. All these issues will be discussed in the following.

Consider a fully connected DSNN. In general, the membrane potential V_j^l of neuron j in layer l with N presynaptic connections can be expressed as:

$$V_j^l(t) = \sum_i^N w_{ij}^l K(t - t_i^{l-1}) - \eta(t - t_j^l), \tag{5.1}$$

where t_i^{l-1} is the spike of the ith neuron in layer $l-1$, and w_{ij}^l is the synaptic weight of the connection from neuron i (in layer $l-1$) to neuron j (in layer l). Each incoming spike from neuron i will induce a postsynaptic potential (PSP) at neuron j, and the kernel $K(t - t_i^{l-1})$ is used to describe the PSP generated by the spike t_i^{l-1}. Hence, each input spike makes a contribution to the membrane potential of the neuron as described by $w_{ij}^l K(t - t_i^{l-1})$ in Eq. (5.1). There are several PSP functions, Eq. (4.3) and (5.2) (alpha function) are the two

Towards Neuromorphic Machine Intelligence. https://doi.org/10.1016/B978-0-44-332820-6.00012-4

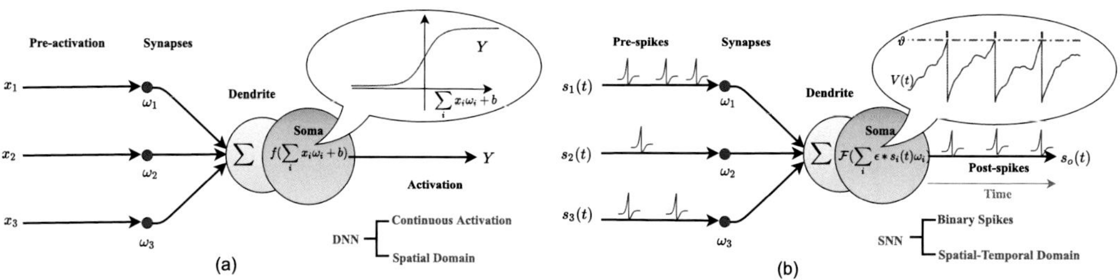

FIGURE 5.1 Neuron models in DNNs and SNNs. (a) A typical DNN neuron model, in which the information from the previous layer arrives in the form of real values in the spatial domain. x, w, b, and Y are input activation, synaptic weights, bias, and output activation, respectively. Output Y is produced by the differentiable activation function $f(\cdot)$. (b) A typical spiking neuron model, in which information from the previous layer arrives in the form of spatiotemporally distributed spike events. $s_i(t)$, w, and $s_o(t)$ are input spikes, synaptic weights, and output spikes, respectively. The non-differentiable function $\mathcal{F}(\cdot)$ generates output spikes $s_o(t)$ from the membrane potential $V(t)$.

common ones:

$$K(t) = \frac{t}{\tau}\exp\left(1 - \frac{t}{\tau}\right), \qquad t > 0. \tag{5.2}$$

Fig. 5.2(a) shows the alpha-PSP response function. As shown in Fig. 5.2(b), integrating the weighted PSPs gives the dynamics of the membrane potential $V_j^l(t)$. The neuron j will emit a spike when its membrane potential $V_j^l(t)$ reaches the firing threshold ϑ, as mathematically defined in the spike generation function $\mathcal{F}$:

$$t_j^l = \mathcal{F}\left\{t | V_j^l(t) = \vartheta, t \geq 0\right\}. \tag{5.3}$$

Once a spike is emitted, the refractory kernel $\eta(t - t_j^l)$ is used to reset the membrane potential to resting.

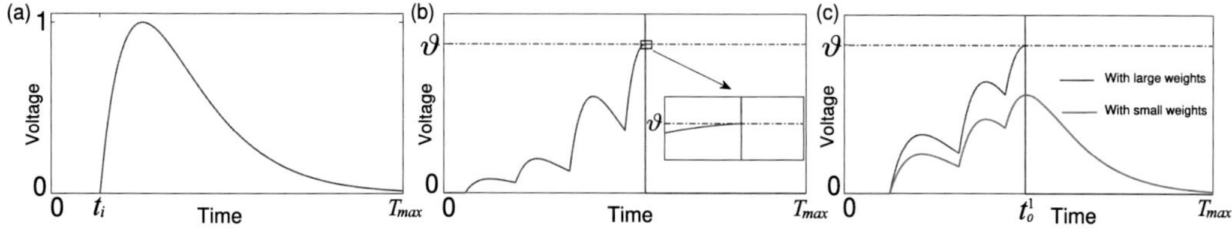

FIGURE 5.2 (a) Alpha shaped PSP function. (b) The membrane potential barely reaches the firing threshold, and an exploding gradient occurs. (c) The alpha-PSP neuron with weak synaptic weights is susceptible to being a dead neuron.

To train SNNs using BP, it needs to compute the derivative of the postsynaptic spike time t_j^l with respect to a presynaptic spike time t_i^{l-1} and synaptic weight w_{ij}^l of the corresponding connection:

$$\frac{\partial t_j^l}{\partial w_{ij}^l} = \frac{\partial t_j^l}{\partial V_j^l(t_j^l)} \frac{\partial V_j^l(t_j^l)}{\partial w_{ij}^l}, \qquad \text{if} \quad t_j^l > t_i^{l-1}, \tag{5.4}$$

$$\frac{\partial t_j^l}{\partial t_i^{l-1}} = \frac{\partial t_j^l}{\partial V_j^l(t_j^l)} \frac{\partial V_j^l(t_j^l)}{\partial t_i^{l-1}}, \qquad \text{if} \quad t_j^l > t_i^{l-1}. \tag{5.5}$$

5.1.1 Non-differentiable spike function

Due to the discrete nature of the spike generation function Eq. (5.3), a challenge arises in solving the partial derivative $\partial t_j^l / \partial V_j^l(t_j^l)$ in Eq. (5.4), which is referred to as the problem of a non-differentiable spike function. Existing spike-driven learning algorithms [BKLP02, YLT18] assume that the membrane potential $V_j^l(t)$ increases linearly in the infinitesimal time interval before spike time t_j. Then, as in Eq. (4.11) and (4.49), $\partial t_j / V_j(t)$ can be expressed as

$$\frac{\partial t_j^l}{\partial V_j^l(t_j^l)} = \frac{-1}{\partial V_j^l(t_j^l)/\partial t_j^l} = \frac{-1}{\sum_i^N w_{ij}^l \frac{\partial K(t_j^l - t_i^{l-1})}{\partial t_j^l}}. \tag{5.6}$$

5.1.2 Gradient explosion

The gradient explosion problem occurs when $\partial V_j^l(t_j^l)/\partial t_j^l \approx 0$, i.e., the membrane potential is reaching the firing threshold, emitting a spike (Fig. 5.2(b)). Since $\partial V_j(t_j)/\partial t_j$ is the denominator in Eq. (5.6), this causes Eq. (5.6) to explode with large weight updates. Despite the progress made to address this problem, such as adaptive learning rate [SS15] and dynamic firing threshold [HWW$^+$19], the problem has not been fully resolved.

5.1.3 Dead neuron

It is shown from Eq. (5.4) and Eq. (5.5) that when the presynaptic neuron does not emit a spike, the error cannot be backpropagated through $\partial V_j^l(t_j^l)/\partial t_i^{l-1}$, which then results in dead neurons. This problem also exists with analog neurons with the ReLU activation function in DNNs. However, due to the leaky nature of the PSP kernel and the spike generation mechanism, spiking neurons encounter a more serious dead neuron problem. As shown in Fig. 5.2(c), there are three input spikes, and the neuron emits a spike with large synaptic weights (blue curve). With slightly reduced synaptic weights, the membrane potential stays below the threshold, hence becoming a dead neuron (green curve). When the neuron does not spike, no errors can backpropagate through it. The dead neuron problem is fatal in spike-driven learning algorithms.

5.2 Learning algorithm with neural oscillation and phase information

Inspired by the findings from the biological neural networks, the above-mentioned problem was addressed by introducing neural oscillation and spike-phase information to

DSNNs [CQZW21]. Specifically, an Oscillation Postsynaptic Potential (Os-PSP) and phase-locking active function were proposed and a new spiking neuron model, namely the Resonate Spiking Neuron (RSN), was further put forward. Based on the RSN, a Spike-Level-Dependent Backpropagation (SLDBP) learning algorithm for DSNNs was proposed. Experimental results show that the proposed learning algorithm resolves the problems caused by the incompatibility between the BP learning algorithm and SNNs, and achieves state-of-the-art performance in single spike-based learning algorithms.

5.2.1 Solutions to three problems in learning of deep SNNs

The great success of DNNs in multiple fields is because of the BP algorithm, and this arouses the interest of applying the BP algorithm to DSNN. However, as described in section 5.1, the mechanisms of information encoding and processing between typical artificial neurons in DNNs and SNNs are different. Due to the non-differential spike function, dead neurons, and gradient explosion problems, BP cannot be applied to DSNNs directly. Next, how the DSNN formed with RSN (section 3.1) [CQZW21] solves these three problems will be discussed in depth.

For a DSNN with RSN, the binary spike trains are replaced by the number of ions, the outputs of DSNN are a_o, i.e., Eq. (5.1) to (5.3) are replaced by Eq. (3.1) to (3.3). When training this DSNN with BP, the derivative of ion number with respect to synaptic efficacy can be calculated as:

$$\frac{\partial a_j^l(t_j^l)}{\partial w_{ij}^l} = \frac{\partial a_j^l(t_j^l)}{\partial V_j^l(t_j^l)} \frac{\partial V_j^l(t_j)}{\partial w_{ij}^l}. \tag{5.7}$$

The calculation of the non-differential part in Eq. (5.3) is replaced by Eq. (3.3). The non-differential spike function is solved.

By introducing Eq. (3.3) with $F(V) = V$, the first factor on the right-hand side of Eq. (5.7) can be calculated as:

$$\frac{\partial a_j^l}{\partial V_j^l(t_j^l)} = 1. \tag{5.8}$$

From Eq. (3.1), the second factor is:

$$\frac{\partial V_j^l(t_j^l)}{\partial w_{ij}^l} = a_i^{l-1} \cos(t_j^l - (t_i^{l-1} + d_{ij}^l)). \tag{5.9}$$

The range of Eq. (5.8) is $[-\sum_i a_i^{l-1}, \ \sum_i a_i^{l-1}]$, rather than $(-\infty, \ +\infty)$. The gradient explosion problem caused by trigger neurons is solved.

As the phase-locking active function defined in Eq. (3.3), RSN always fires a spike when the membrane potential reaches its maximum in one cycle in the resonating phase. Information can be fed forward without losing and so does the required error in BP, which solves the dead neuron problem.

5.2.2 Algorithm description

The goal of the algorithm is to learn a set of target activity amounts, denoted a_d^l, at the output neurons for a given set of input patterns $P[a_1^1, \cdots, a_i^1]$. In order to be consistent with the following vision task experiments, the cross-entropy error function is adopted as the cost function. Given target class d and actual activity amounts a_d^l, the following loss function L is defined:

$$L = -\log\left(\frac{\exp(a_d^l)}{\sum_j \exp(a_j^l)}\right). \tag{5.10}$$

Combining Eq. (3.1) and Eq. (3.3), it can be seen that L is a function of w_{ij}^l and d_{ij}^l. Applying the BP algorithm:

$$\Delta w_{ij}^l = -\eta \frac{\partial L}{\partial w_{ij}^l}, \tag{5.11}$$

where η is the learning rate and w_{ij}^l the synaptic weight from neuron i to neuron j. According to the chain rule:

$$\frac{\partial L}{\partial w_{ij}^l} = \frac{\partial L}{\partial a_j^l}\frac{\partial a_j^l}{\partial w_{ij}^l}, \tag{5.12}$$

and from Eq. (5.8) and Eq. (5.9):

$$\frac{\partial a_j^l}{\partial w_{ij}^l} = 1 \cdot a_i^{l-1} \cos\left(t_j^l - (t_i^{l-1} + d_{ij}^l)\right) = a_i^{l-1} \cos\left(t_j^l - (t_i^{l-1} + d_{ij}^l)\right). \tag{5.13}$$

Similar to the traditional BP algorithm, the above weight adjustment rules can be extended to networks with multiple hidden layers. Combining Eq. (3.1) and Eq. (5.8):

$$\begin{aligned}\frac{\partial a_j^l}{\partial a_i^{l-1}} &= \frac{\partial a_j^l}{\partial V_j^l(t_j^l)}\frac{\partial V_j^l(t_j^l)}{\partial a_i^{l-1}} \\ &= 1 \cdot w_{ij}^l \cos\left(t_j^l - (t_i^{l-1} + d_{ij}^l)\right) \\ &= w_{ij}^l \cos\left(t_j^l - (t_i^{l-1} + d_{ij}^l)\right).\end{aligned} \tag{5.14}$$

The synaptic delays can also be adjusted by learning rules similar to weights, where the difference lies in the calculation of partial derivatives $\partial a_j^l / \partial d_{ij}^l$, which is:

$$\frac{\partial a_j^l}{\partial d_{ij}^l} = \frac{\partial a_j^l}{\partial V_j^l(t_j^l)}\frac{\partial V_j^l(t_j^l)}{\partial d_{ij}^l} = w_{ij}^l a_i^{l-1} \sin\left(t_j^l - (t_i^{l-1} + d_{ij}^l)\right). \tag{5.15}$$

5.2.3 Applications and results

In this section, the RSN model is first applied to the XOR problem. Then, the proposed learning algorithm is tested on multiple image data sets, and is compared with several recent results with the same or similar network sizes previously reported, including traditional ANNs, converted SNNs, and different SNN's BP methods.

5.2.3.1 XOR problem

In this part, the RSN model is applied to multiple XOR problems. As mentioned in the previous section, the information is encoded as the size and time of the spike. The size of the spike can be used to represent positive and negative classes, and the time of the spike can be used to represent the relationship between two inputs. The model is trained for 20 epochs and then tested for its ability to handle XOR problems from both absolute-oriented and relative-oriented ones.

First, *True* and *False* are encoded as the size of the spike $a^{True} = 0.9$ and $a^{False} = 0.1$, respectively, and the time of two corresponding spike events is the same. After that, we only adjust the weight of a single RSN with two input neurons, and the delay of each synapse is always 0. The results are shown in Fig. 5.3 upper. It can be seen when the input is *{True, False}* or *{False, True}*, the activity of RSN is significantly higher than other cases in Fig. 5.3(b). From the absolute-oriented case, RSN can handle the XOR problem.

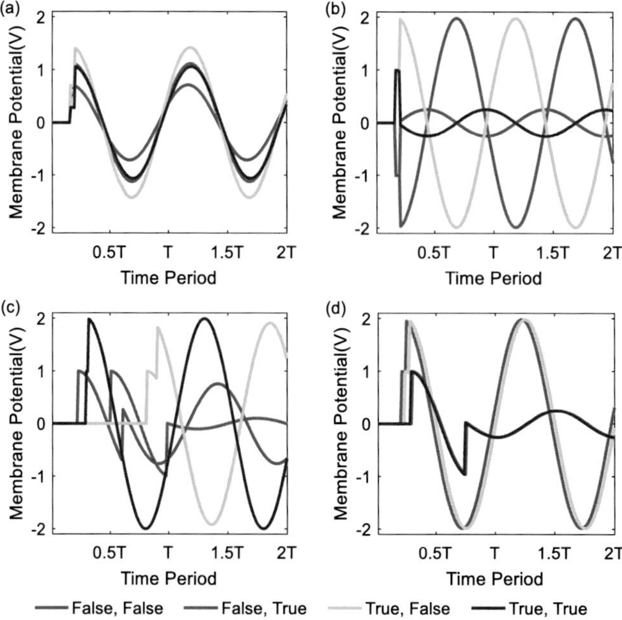

FIGURE 5.3 The XOR problems. (a) and (b) Membrane potential of RSN before and after learning in the absolute-oriented XOR problem. (c) and (d) Membrane potential of RSN before and after learning in the relative-oriented XOR problem.

Then, the XOR input pattern is encoded from the relative-oriented problem: the size of the spike $a^{True} = a^{False} = 1$, which means that both neurons have inputs, and the difference is the time of the spike. The time corresponding to the same input, such as *{False, False}* or *{True, True}*, is the same, and the time corresponding to different inputs differs by half a cycle T. A single RSN with two inputs is used for testing. The difference is that this time we only learn the synaptic delay, that is, the relationship between the two inputs, and do not care about their specific input size. Fig. 5.3(d) shows that when the input is *{True, False}* or *{False, True}*, the activity of RSN is significantly higher than other cases.

5.2.3.2 Vision task

To demonstrate the capability of the proposed model and learning algorithm, MNIST and CIFAR10 are chosen, which are two commonly used datasets for benchmarking vision classification algorithms. All the reported experiments below are conducted on an NVIDIA 1080 GPU within the Pytorch framework. The experimented SNNs are based on the RSN model described in the last section and all experiment results are obtained by repeating the experiments five times. For the MNIST dataset, adaptive moment estimation (Adam) is used as the optimizer and 150 epochs of training are performed. For the CIFAR10 dataset, Stochastic Gradient Descent (SGD) is used as the optimizer and 200 epochs of training are performed.

A. Network structure: The network models used for training or comparison is either a multi-layered perceptron (MLP) or convolutional neural networks (CNNs). These two network structures are shown in Table 5.1 where C stands for a convolutional layer, P stands for a pooling layer, and FC stands for a fully connected layer.

Table 5.1 Network structure used for vision task.

Dataset	Network structure
MNIST	784-400-10
MNIST	6C5-P2-16C5-P2-128FC-10
CIFAR10	64C3-P2-128C3-128C3-P2-256FC-10

In the spike-pooling layer, the spike with the largest amount of information is selected and its phase information is retained to achieve a winner-takes-all effect, while its temporal information with another spike is also retained.

B. Encoding: When SNNs are used to process real-world data, the data should be encoded into spike patterns. Here, each pixel value of the image is encoded into the spike's amount a^i directly and time t^i based on the latency coding method. It should be noted that the firing time is limited in $[0, 0.5T]$, T is the period of neural oscillation. For example, the input spike amount corresponding to the pixel value of $0.4I_{max}$ is $a^i = 0.4$, and the firing time is $t^i = 0.4 \times 0.5T$. In this way, the pixel with a higher value in the original image fires a larger spike, and the pixels with a similar value fire at the same time.

C. Accuracy: Table 5.2 compares the performance of different network architectures and algorithms on the MNIST dataset. It can be seen that the proposed algorithm achieves

Table 5.2 Comparison of the proposed algorithm against other baseline algorithms on MNIST.

Model	Structure	Method	Accuracy (%)
Hunsberger et al. [HE16]	MLP	Converted SNN	98.51
Hunsberger et al. [HE16]	CNN	Converted SNN	99.07
Diehl et al. [DM15]	CNN	STDP SNN	95.00
Zhang et al. [ZLC+20]	MLP	Surrogated SNN	96.80
Deng et al. [DWH+20]	MLP	Surrogated SNN	98.41
Deng et al. [DWH+20]	CNN	Surrogated SNN	99.22
This work	MLP	Resonate SNN	98.73
This work	CNN	Resonate SNN	**99.26**

Table 5.3 Comparison of the proposed model against other baseline models on CIFAR10.

Model	Method	Accuracy (%)
Nair et al. [NH10]	CNN with ReLU	84.15
Sengupta et al. [SYW+19]	Converted SNN	76.81
Deng et al. [DWH+20]	Surrogated SNN	74.23
This work	Resonate SNN	84.87

the best results without additional optimization strategies. The accuracy reported below is obtained by repeating the experiments five times.

Table 5.3 lists the results of the existing state-of-the-art SNNs-based learning methods on the CIFAR10 dataset. To ensure the fairness of the comparison, all the learning algorithms are compared with the same network structure, as shown in Table 5.1. The CNN with ReLU is used as the activation function as the baseline, which contains only the convolutional layer and the max-pooling layer. As shown in Table 5.3, both conversion and surrogate SNNs-based learning algorithms suffer from accuracy loss because of the approximation. However, this work achieves an accuracy of 84.87%, which is 8.06% higher than its counterparts.

5.3 Learning algorithms with rectified linear postsynaptic potential

In [ZWW+22], a simple yet efficient Rectified Linear PostSynaptic Potential function (ReL-PSP) for spiking neurons is proposed. Then, a Spike-Timing-Dependent BP (STDBP) learning algorithm for DSNNs is given, where the timing of individual spikes is used to convey information (temporal coding), and learning (BP) is performed based on spike timing in an event-driven manner. Furthermore, by utilizing the trained model parameters obtained from the proposed STDBP algorithm, the authors demonstrate ultra-low-power inference operations on a recently proposed neuromorphic inference accelerator.

5.3.1 Solutions to three problems in learning of deep SNNs

In this work, the adopted spiking neuron model is the ReL-PSP neuron model described in section 3.2, whose dynamics are defined by Eq. (3.4) and (3.5). Next, how the DSNN formed with ReL-PSP neuron [ZWW+22] solves these three problems will be discussed in depth.

5.3.1.1 Non-differentiable spike function

As shown in Fig. 5.2(b), due to the linearity of the ReL-PSP, the membrane potential $V_j^l(t)$ increases linearly prior to spike time t_j^l. The linearity is a much-desired property of a postsynaptic potential function. Hence, it can now directly use Eq. (5.16) to compute $\partial t_j^l/\partial V_j^l(t_j^l)$. This resolves the issue of non-differentiable spike generation:

$$\frac{\partial t_j^l}{\partial V_j^l(t_j^l)} = -\frac{1}{\partial V_j^l(t_j^l)/\partial t_j^l} = \frac{-1}{\sum_i^N w_{ij}^l \frac{\partial K(t_j^l - t_i^{l-1})}{\partial t_j^l}} = \frac{-1}{\sum_i^N w_{ij}^l}, \qquad \text{if} \quad t_j^l > t_i^{l-1}. \tag{5.16}$$

The precise gradients in BP provide the necessary information for network optimization, which is the key to the performance of DNNs. By avoiding the need to make assumptions about linearity, the precise value of $\partial t_j^l/\partial V_j^l(t_j^l)$ is utilized instead of relying on approximations. This approach helps to prevent the accumulation of errors across multiple layers.

5.3.1.2 Gradient explosion

An exploding gradient occurs when the denominator in Eq. (5.6) approaches 0. In this case, the membrane potential just reaches the firing threshold at spike time, and is caused by the combined effect of w_{ij}^l and partial derivative of the PSP function. As $\sum_i^N w_{ij}^l$ may still be close to 0, the exploding gradient problem may not be completely solved. However, from Eq. (5.3) and (3.4), the spike time t_j^l is determined as a function of the input spikes and synaptic weights w_{ij}^l, and the spike time t_j^l can be calculated as:

$$t_j^l = \frac{\vartheta + \sum_i^N w_{ij}^l t_i^{l-1}}{\sum_i^N w_{ij}^l}, \qquad \text{if} \quad t_j^l > t_i^{l-1}. \tag{5.17}$$

Should the $\sum_i^N w_{ij}^l$ be close to 0, the spike t_j^l will be emitted late, and may not contribute to the spike t_j^{l+1} in the next layer. Therefore the neuron j in the layer l does not participate in error BP, and does not result in an exploding gradient.

5.3.1.3 Dead neuron

In neural networks, sparse representation (few activated neurons) has many advantages, such as information disentangling, efficient variable-size representation, linear separability, etc. However, sparsity may also adversely affect predictive performance. Given the same number of neurons, sparsity reduces the effective capacity of the model [GBB11].

Unfortunately, as shown in Fig. 5.2(c), due to the leaky nature of the alpha-PSP and the spike generation mechanism, such a spiking neuron is more likely to suffer from the dead neuron problem.

As shown in Fig. 5.2(c), with the ReL-PSP kernel, the PSP increases over time within the simulation window T_{max} until the postsynaptic neuron fires a spike. Hence, the neuron with a more positive sum of weights fires earlier than one with a less positive sum, with a lower probability of becoming a dead neuron. Overall, the ReL-PSP greatly alleviates the dead neuron problem as the PSP does not decay over time while maintaining a sparse representation to the same extent as the ReLU activation function.

5.3.2 Algorithm description

Given a classification task with n categories, each neuron in the output layer is assigned to a category. When a training sample is presented to the neural network, the corresponding output neuron should fire the earliest. Several loss functions can be constructed to achieve this goal [Mos17,KM19,CPV+19]. In this study, the cross-entropy loss function is used. To minimize the spike time of the target neuron, at the same time to maximize the spike time of non-target neurons, the softmax function on the negative values of the spike times in the output layer is adopted: $p_j = \exp(-t_j)/\sum_i^n \exp(-t_i)$. The loss function is given by

$$L(g, \mathbf{t^o}) = -\ln \frac{\exp(-\mathbf{t^o}[g]))}{\sum_i^n \exp(-\mathbf{t^o}[i])}, \tag{5.18}$$

where $\mathbf{t^o}$ is the vector of the spike times in the output layer and g is the target class index [Mos17].

The loss function is minimized by updating the synaptic weights across the network. This has the effect of delaying or advancing spike times across the network. The derivatives of the first spike time t_j^l with respect to synaptic weights w_{ij}^l and input spike times t_i^{l-1} are given by

$$\frac{\partial t_j^l}{\partial w_{ij}^l} = \frac{\partial t_j^l}{\partial V_j^l(t_j^l)} \frac{\partial V_j^l(t_j^l)}{\partial w_{ij}^l} = \frac{t_i^{l-1} - t_j^l}{\sum_i^N w_{ij}^l}, \quad \text{if} \quad t_j^l > t_i^{l-1}, \tag{5.19}$$

$$\frac{\partial t_j^l}{\partial t_i^{l-1}} = \frac{\partial t_j^l}{\partial V_j^l(t_j^l)} \frac{\partial V_j^l(t_j^l)}{\partial t_i^{l-1}} = \frac{w_{ij}^l}{\sum_i^N w_{ij}^l}, \quad \text{if} \quad t_j^l > t_i^{l-1}. \tag{5.20}$$

Following Eq. (5.19) and Eq. (5.20), a standard BP can be applied for DSNNs training.

5.3.3 Hardware simulation methodology

To put the STDBP learning algorithm into action, the authors evaluate the deployment of STDBP on a hardware architecture for pattern classification tasks. The implementation of these methods in spiking neural networks for inference operations is carried out on the YOSO platform [SKY+20] first, which is specifically designed for accelerating temporal coding-based SNN models with sparse spiking activity. It was shown that YOSO facilitates ultra-low-power inference operations (< 1 mW) as a neuromorphic accelerator with state-of-the-art performance.

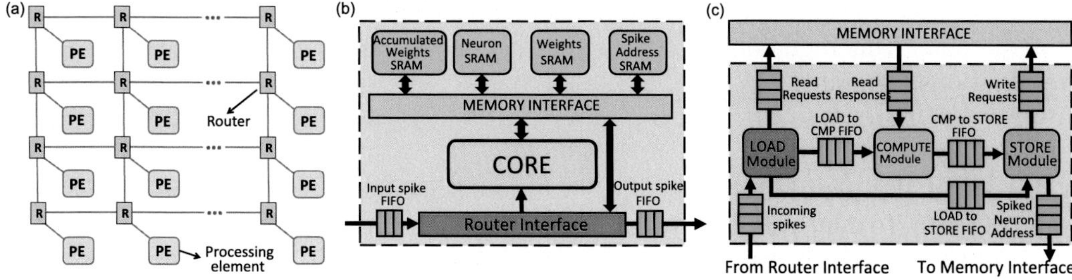

FIGURE 5.4 (a) The YOSO accelerator with network-on-chip (NoC) architecture, (b) the architecture of each processing element (PE) in YOSO, and (c) the computational core in each PE [SKY+20].

5.3.3.1 Hardware architecture

As shown in Fig. 5.4(a), YOSO is a Network-On-Chip (NoC) architecture with multiple processing elements (PEs) connected in a mesh topology. Each PE has a router, which facilitates the propagation of spikes from one PE to another. As shown in Fig. 5.4(b), each PE in the NoC consists of four static random-access memories (SRAMs), a memory interface, a core, a router interface, first-in-first-out (FIFO) buffers to facilitate communication between the router and router interface. The router sends or receives the spikes to or from other PEs in the NoC. During the initialization phase, i.e., when the accelerator is downloading the model to be run, the router sends the spikes to SRAMs directly via the router and memory interfaces. During the inference phase, the router sends the spikes to the core, where all the computations take place. Note that YOSO [SKY+20] can only accelerate inference operations and training needs to be performed offline.

The SRAMs are used to store all the information required for processing the incoming spikes and for generating the output spikes. As shown in Fig. 5.4(b), the SRAMs can communicate with the core and router interface via a memory interface. The accumulated weight, neuron, weight, and spike address SRAMs store accumulated weights, neuron potentials, weights between two layers, and the spike addresses of the neurons allocated for that PE, respectively.

As shown in Fig. 5.4(c), the core consists of three modules – load, compute, and store. The load module is responsible for decoding the information encoded in incoming spikes. A spike processing algorithm introduced in [SKY+20] is used to encode the information in spike packets that can be read by the load module. After decoding the information in incoming spikes, the load module generates read requests to different SRAM blocks. After sending the read requests generated by one incoming spike, it transits to the idle state and waits for the next input spike. The compute module receives the data requested by the load module from the SRAMs, updates the data using the saturated adder, and sends the results to the FIFO connected to the store module. The store module receives the addresses of the loaded data from the load module and the results from the compute module. Using the data and addresses received, it writes the data back to the SRAMs. It also generates spikes when a condition, depending on the chosen techniques, TTFS or softmax, is met to be sent to the next layer. In addition, the core is designed based on the decoupled access-execute model [Smi82], which enables it to hide memory access latency by performing different computations in parallel.

5.3.3.2 Mapping

In this study, the plan is to accelerate the trained SNN models using the YOSO platform [SKY+20]. To map a $m \times n$ fully connected SNN layer on YOSO [SKY+20], a minimum of $C = MAX(\frac{n}{N}, \frac{m \times n}{W})$ PEs are needed, where N is the maximum number of neurons that can be mapped to a single core and W is the maximum number of weights that the core can contain. The PEs are placed within a $\sqrt{C}$ by $\sqrt{C}$ grid. Each PE in the grid will be allocated to a layer or a part of a layer for processing received by that layer.

5.3.3.3 Hardware simulation methodology

The implementation of the YOSO platform's Network-on-Chip (NoC) architecture was carried out using the OpenSMART NoC generator [KK17]. The X-Y routing mechanism is used to send the spike packets from one PE to another. In addition, the design of the processing elements (PEs) was carried out in a manner that ensures each PE is capable of fulfilling the memory and computational demands of a minimum of 256 neurons [SKY+20]. To assess the performance of YOSO [SKY+20], the hardware architecture depicted in Fig. 5.4 was synthesized using the Synopsys Design Compiler version P-2019.03-SP5 targeting a 22 nm technology node with a 6×7 PE configuration. Gate-level simulations are performed using the Synopsys VCS-MX K-2015.09-SP2-9 and power analysis is performed using the Synopsys PrimePower version P-2019.03-SP5.

5.3.4 Applications and results

In this section, an evaluation is conducted on both fully connected SNNs and convolutional SNNs for the task of image classification. The evaluation is performed using the MNIST [LBBH98], Fashion-MNIST [XRV17], and Caltech 101 face/motorbike datasets, which can be obtained from the Caltech Vision website (http://www.vision.caltech.edu). The learning capabilities of the fully connected SNNs and convolutional SNNs are assessed by benchmarking them against existing spike-driven learning algorithms. Furthermore, the inference speed and energy efficiency of the fully connected SNN on the YOSO neuromorphic accelerator are evaluated.

5.3.4.1 Temporal coding

An efficient temporal coding scheme is employed, which encodes information into spike timing based on the assumption that highly activated neurons tend to exhibit early firing patterns [TDVR01]. In practice, the input pixel intensity value is encoded into spike tim-

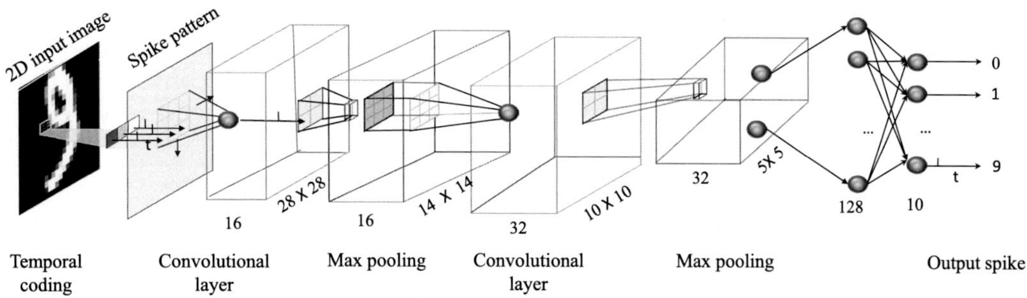

FIGURE 5.5 The convolutional spiking neural network used in this study.

ing according to $t_i = \alpha(-s_i + 255)/255$, where t_i is the firing time of the ith neuron, s_i is the intensity value of the ith pixel with $s_i \in [0, 255]$, and α is a scaling factor. In this way, more salient information is encoded into an earlier spike by the corresponding input neuron. These encoded spikes are propagated to subsequent layers following the dynamics of the SNN. Similar to the input layer, the neurons in the hidden and output layers that are strongly activated will fire first. As such, the temporal coding is maintained throughout the DSNN, and the output neuron that fires first categorizes the input sample.

5.3.4.2 MNIST dataset

Initially, an ANN model is trained to serve as the basis for initializing the corresponding SNN. Employing the temporal coding approach, the images are encoded into spike patterns, which are subsequently utilized to train both a fully connected and convolutional SNN using the STDBP algorithm. A complete convolutional SNN network structure is provided in Fig. 5.5. During the training process, jittering noise is introduced to the input spike patterns, aiming to enhance the performance of the trained model. The jitter intervals are randomly drawn from a Gaussian distribution with zero mean and variance $\sigma_j = 0.14$. The SNN is trained for 150 epochs using the Adam optimizer, with a batch size of 128. The hyperparameters β_1 and β_2 of the Adam optimizer are set to 0.9 and 0.999, respectively. The learning rate starts at 0.0002 and gradually decreases to 0.00005 by the end of the training.

As the experimental results summarized in Table 5.4 show, the STDBP learning algorithm could reach accuracies of 98.1% and 98.5% with the network structures of 784-400-10 and 784-800-10, respectively. They outperform previously reported results of SNNs with the same network structures. For example, with the structure of 784-400-10, the classification accuracy of STDBP is 98.1%, while the accuracy achieved by Mostafa [Mos17] is 97.5%. Another advantage of STDBP is that it does not need additional training strategies, such as constraints on weights and gradient normalization, which were widely used in previous works to improve their performance [Mos17,CPV+19,KM19]. This facilitates large-scale implementation of STDBP, and makes it possible to train more complex CNN structures. The convolutional SNN with STDBP achieves an accuracy of 99.4%, which is much higher

Table 5.4 The classification accuracies of existing spike-driven learning algorithms on the MNIST dataset. The SNN architecture is denoted using the following notation. Layers are separated by - and spatial dimensions are separated by ×. The convolution layer and pooling layer are represented by C and P, respectively. W and G represent weights and gradients, respectively.

Model	Coding	Network architecture	Additional strategy	Acc. (%)
[TM18]	Rate	784-1000-10	None	96.6
[KM19]	Temporal	784-400-10	Weight Constraint	97.4
[Mos17]	Temporal	784-800-10	W & G Constraint	97.5
[CPV+19]	Temporal	784-340-10	W & G Constraint	97.9
ANN	Rate	784-800-10	None	98.6
STDBP	Temporal	784-340-10	None	**98.0**
STDBP	Temporal	784-400-10	None	**98.1**
STDBP	Temporal	784-800-10	None	**98.5**
STDBP	Temporal	784-1000-10	None	**98.5**
CNN	Rate	28×28-16C5-P2-32C5-P2-800-128-10	None	99.5
STDBP	Temporal	28×28-16C5-P2-32C5-P2-800-128-10	None	**99.4**

than all the results obtained by the fully connected SNNs. To the best of our knowledge, this is the first implementation of a convolutional SNN structure with the single-spike-timing-based supervised learning algorithm.

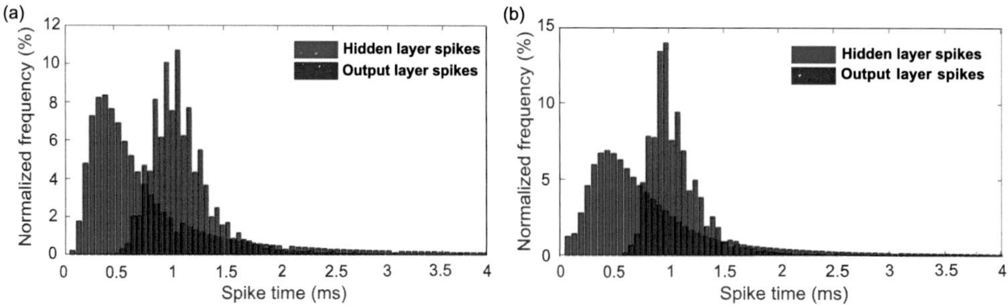

FIGURE 5.6 Histograms of spike times in the hidden layers and the output layer across 10 000 test images for the two SNNs: (a) 784-400-10 and (b) 784-800-10.

Fig. 5.6 shows the distribution of spike timing in the hidden layers and of the earliest spike time in the output layer across 10 000 test images for two SNNs, namely 784-400-10 and 784-800-10. In both cases, the SNN makes a decision after only a fraction of the hidden layer neurons are activated. For the 784-400-10 topology, an output neuron spikes (a class is selected) after only 48.6% of the hidden neurons have spiked. The network is thus able to make rapid decisions about the input class. In addition, during the simulation time, only 66.3% of the hidden neurons spiked. Therefore the experimental results suggest that the STDBP learning algorithm works in an accurate, fast, and sparse manner.

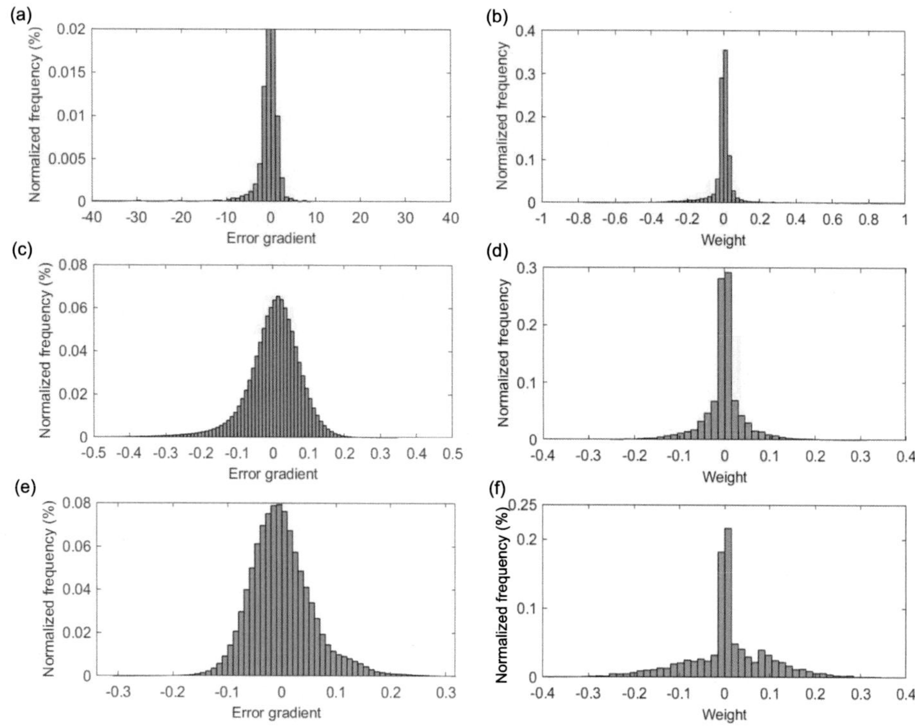

FIGURE 5.7 Distribution of error gradients (left column) and learned weights (right column) of different methods. (a) and (b) SNN with alpha-PSP function. (c) and (d) SNN with ReL-PSP function. (e) and (f) ANN.

To explore the effectiveness of the ReL-PSP in addressing the issues of exploding gradients and dead neurons, a set of fully connected SNNs is selected as an example. In order to ensure the robustness and reliability of the results, 20 independent experiments are performed, each with different initial synaptic weights. The data distribution of error gradients, learned synaptic weights, and dead neuron counts are reported in Fig. 5.7 and 5.8, respectively.

Fig. 5.7(a) shows the error gradients of the SNN with an alpha-PSP function, where gradients generally take values that are much larger than those in ReL-PSP (Fig. 5.7(c)) and ANNs (Fig. 5.7(e)). The results confirm findings in the problem analysis, that is, the alpha-PSP function is prone to the gradient exploding problem. It is worth mentioning that previous studies have only provided partial solutions to this problem. For instance, methods such as adaptive learning rate [SS15] and dynamic firing threshold [HWW+19] have been proposed, but they only partially alleviate the issue. The observation of the ReL-PSP function's gradients closely resembling a normal distribution, similar to those observed in ANNs, is promising. This indicates a stable propagation of gradients in DSNNs, which is an encouraging finding. In addition, as shown in Fig. 5.7(b), the gradient exploding problem also leads to skewed weights, which may adversely affect the performance of the trained model, and is now addressed by the ReL-PSP function.

For ANNs, typically only a subset of neurons are activated at the same time [GBB11]. It should be noted that excessive inactivation can result in the issue of dead neurons, which diminishes the effective capacity of the network and consequently impairs its predictive capability. In order to evaluate the extent of the dead neuron problem, the percentage of dead neurons is recorded throughout the training process. The mean and standard deviations across 20 independent runs are reported in Fig. 5.8. As the training progresses, the percentage of dead neurons increases across both SNNs and ANN. After 100 training epochs, the SNN with ReL-PSP has 30% active neurons and achieves a test accuracy of 98.5%. In contrast, the SNN with alpha-PSP only has 5% active neurons with a test accuracy of 92.5%. Due to the leaky nature of the traditional alpha-PSP function and the spike generation mechanism, SNNs with the alpha-PSP function are more likely to suffer from the dead neuron problem. The experimental results corroborate the hypothesis and suggest that the ReL-PSP function effectively addresses this problem. After 100 training epochs, the ANN has about 40% active neurons with an accuracy of 98.6%. Overall, the results show that the SNN model with ReL-PSP achieves competitive results with sparse neuronal activities.

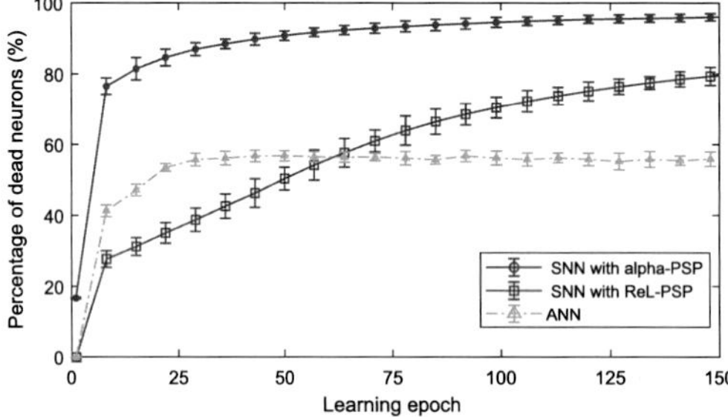

FIGURE 5.8 The percentage of dead neurons during the training process. The error bars denote the standard deviations across 20 independent experiments.

5.3.4.3 Fashion-MNIST dataset

The Fashion-MNIST dataset [XRV17] has the same number of training/testing samples as MNIST, but is more challenging than MNIST. The samples are associated with 10 different classes like T-shirt/top, Pullover, Trouser, Dress, Sandal, Coat, Shirt, Bag, Sneaker, and Ankle boot. In this comparison, the Fashion-MNIST dataset is utilized to evaluate and compare the STDBP with existing fully connected feedforward SNNs and convolutional SNNs.

Table 5.5 shows the classification accuracies and characteristics of different methods on the Fashion-MNIST dataset. The STDBP still delivers the best test accuracy in temporal coding-based SNN methods. For example, the STDBP can achieve accuracies of 88.1% and 90.1% with the fully connected SNN and convolutional SNN, respectively. These re-

Table 5.5 The classification accuracy (Acc.) of the existing SNN-based computational models on the Fashion-MNIST dataset.

Model	Coding	Network architecture	Acc. (%)
S4NN [KM19]	Temporal	784-1000-10	88.0
BS4NN [KMM20]	Temporal	784-1000-10	87.3
Hao et al. [HHDX20]	Rate	784-6000-10	85.3
Zhang et al. [ZL20]	Rate	784-400-400-10	89.5
STDBP	Temporal	784-1000-10	88.1
Ranjan et al. [RSB19]	Rate	28×28-32C3-32C3-P2-128-10	89.0
STDBP	Temporal	28×28-16C5-P2-32C5-P2-800-128-10	90.1

sults outperform the best-reported result of 88.0% [KM19] in temporal coding-based SNN models.

5.3.4.4 Caltech face/motorbike dataset

In this experiment, the performance of the STDBP is evaluated on the face/motobike categories of the Caltech 101 dataset (http://www.vision.caltech.edu). For each category, the training and validation set consists of 200 and 50 randomly selected samples, respectively, and the others are regarded as testing samples. Before training, all images are rescaled and converted to 160 × 250 grayscale images. Fig. 5.9 shows some samples of the converted images. The converted images are then encoded into spike patterns by temporal coding.

FIGURE 5.9 Some samples of the converted images from the Caltech 101 face/motorbike dataset.

Table 5.6 The classification accuracy (Acc.) of existing SNN-based computational models on the Caltech face/motorbike dataset.

Model	Learning method	Network architecture	Classifier	Acc. (%)
Masquelier et al. [MT07]	Unsupervised STDP	HMAX [RP99]	RBF	99.2
Kheradpisheh et al. [KGTM18]	Unsupervised STDP	28×28-4C5-P7-20C16-P2-10C5	SVM	99.1
Mozafari et al. [MKM+18]	Reward STDP	HMAX [RP99]	Spike-based	98.2
Kheradpisheh et al. [KM19]	Spike-based BP	160×250-4-2	Spike-based	99.2
STDBP	Spike-based BP	160×250-4-2	Spike-based	**99.2**
STDBP	Spike-based BP	28×28-16C5-P2-32C5-P2-800-128-10	Spike-based	**99.5**

The classification accuracies of different SNN-based computational models are shown in Table 5.6. The STDBP learning algorithm achieves an accuracy of 99.2% with the fully connected SNN structure and an accuracy of 99.5% with the convolutional SNN structure. The accuracy obtained by STDBP outperforms the previously reported SNN-based methods on this dataset. For example, In Kheradpisheh et al. [KGTM18], a convolutional SNN structure with an SVM classifier achieves an accuracy of 99.1% on the same dataset. Moreover, it is not a fully spike-based computational model that the membrane potential used as the classification signal. Recently, a spike-based fully connected SNNs model achieved an accuracy of 99.2%. However, the convolutional SNN structure with STDBP reaches an accuracy of 99.5%, which is state-of-the-art performance on this benchmark.

5.3.4.5 Hardware simulation results

The focus now shifts toward the evaluation of the power and energy efficiency of the SNN models. This evaluation entails accelerating the inference operations of the models on the YOSO platform. A fully connected SNN with a network architecture of 784-800-10 was selected as the baseline for comparison with other neuromorphic accelerators. The SNN model was trained on MNIST data using the STDBP learning algorithm. The learned weights are then transferred to YOSO for accelerating the inference operations. As shown in Table 5.7, YOSO consumes 0.751 mW of total power consumption and 47.71 ms of latency to classify an image from MNIST dataset. In addition, YOSO achieves 399×, 159.8×, 143.8×, and 1.67× power savings as compared to Spinnaker [KLP+08], Tianji [JZCX18], TrueNorth-b [EAM+15], and Shenjing [WZWP20], respectively. Although TrueNorth-a consumes less power than YOSO, there is a significant difference between the classification accuracies of TrueNorth-a and YOSO (see Table 5.7). Moreover, YOSO provides 108.7×, 6×, and 3× energy efficiency as compared to Spinnaker [KLP+08], SNNwt [DBDRC+15], and TrueNorth-b [EAM+15], respectively.

Table 5.7 Comparison of a fully connected SNN with various neuromorphic accelerators on the MNIST dataset sorted by accuracy. Acc. denotes Top-1 accuracy, the frame rate is reported as frames per second (fps), Tech is CMOS technology node in nm, power in mW.

Accelerator	Coding	Acc. (%)	fps	Tech	Power	uJ/frame
SNNwt [DBDRC+15]	Rate	91.82	–	65	–	214.700
TrueNorth-a [EAM+15]	Rate	92.70	1000	28	0.268	0.268
TrueNorth-b [EAM+15]	Rate	99.42	1000	28	108.000	108.000
Loihi-a [MMMS20]	Rate	98.79	120	14	–	–
Loihi-b [RBG+22]	Rate	99.21	150	14	99.248	660.000
Spinnaker [KLP+08]	Rate	95.01	77	130	300.000	3896.000
Tianji [JZCX18]	Rate	96.59	–	120	120.000	–
Shenjing [WZWP20]	Rate	96.11	40	28	1.260	38.000
STDBP+YOSO	Temp.	98.45	21	22	**(0.878*) 0.751**	**(41.93*) 35.839**

* Scaled for 28 nm process (×1.17 for half a generation).

5.4 Conclusion

In this chapter, two learning algorithms for training DSNNs were introduced. In SLDBP, the authors investigated the contribution of introducing biologically inspired mechanisms, such as neural oscillation and spike-phase information to DSNNs. It was shown that DSNNs trained with the SLDBP learning algorithm could achieve high classification accuracy at the time. In STDBP, the authors investigated the contribution of spike timing dynamics for information encoding, synaptic plasticity, and decision making. The experimental results demonstrated its superior performance on hardware architecture with low power consumption and low latency. Both of these algorithms provide new perspectives into the design of future DSNNs and neuromorphic hardware.

References

[BKLP02] Sander M. Bohte, Joost N. Kok, Han La Poutre, Error-backpropagation in temporally encoded networks of spiking neurons, Neurocomputing 48 (1–4) (2002) 17–37.

[CPV+19] Iulia M. Comsa, Krzysztof Potempa, Luca Versari, Thomas Fischbacher, Andrea Gesmundo, Jyrki Alakuijala, Temporal coding in spiking neural networks with alpha synaptic function, arXiv preprint, arXiv:1907.13223, 2019.

[CQZW21] Yi Chen, Hong Qu, Malu Zhang, Yuchen Wang, Deep spiking neural network with neural oscillation and spike-phase information, in: Proceedings of the AAAI Conference on Artificial Intelligence, vol. 35, 05 2021, pp. 7073–7080.

[DBDRC+15] Zidong Du, Daniel D. Ben-Dayan Rubin, Yunji Chen, Liqiang He, Tianshi Chen, Lei Zhang, Chengyong Wu, Olivier Temam, Neuromorphic accelerators: a comparison between neuroscience and machine-learning approaches, in: Proceedings of the 48th International Symposium on Microarchitecture, 2015, pp. 494–507.

[DM15] Peter U. Diehl, Cook Matthew, Unsupervised learning of digit recognition using spike-timing-dependent plasticity, Frontiers in Computational Neuroscience 9 (429) (2015) 99.

[DWH+20] Lei Deng, Yujie Wu, Xing Hu, Ling Liang, Yufei Ding, Guoqi Li, Guangshe Zhao, Peng Li, Yuan Xie, Rethinking the performance comparison between snns and anns, Neural Networks 121 (2020) 294–307.

[EAM+15] Steve K. Esser, Rathinakumar Appuswamy, Paul Merolla, John V. Arthur, Dharmendra S. Modha, Backpropagation for energy-efficient neuromorphic computing, in: Advances in Neural Information Processing Systems, 2015, pp. 1117–1125.

[GBB11] Xavier Glorot, Antoine Bordes, Yoshua Bengio, Deep sparse rectifier neural networks, in: Proceedings of the Fourteenth International Conference on Artificial Intelligence and Statistics, 2011, pp. 315–323.

[HE16] Eric Hunsberger, C. Eliasmith, Training spiking deep networks for neuromorphic hardware, arXiv preprint, arXiv:1611.05141 [abs], 2016.

[HHDX20] Yunzhe Hao, Xuhui Huang, Meng Dong, Bo Xu, A biologically plausible supervised learning method for spiking neural networks using the symmetric stdp rule, Neural Networks 121 (2020) 387–395.

[HWW+19] Chaofei Hong, Xile Wei, Jiang Wang, Bin Deng, Haitao Yu, Yanqiu Che, Training spiking neural networks for cognitive tasks: a versatile framework compatible with various temporal codes, in: IEEE Transactions on Neural Networks and Learning Systems, 2019.

[JZCX18] Yu Ji, Youhui Zhang, Wenguang Chen, Yuan Xie, Bridge the gap between neural networks and neuromorphic hardware with a neural network compiler, in: Proceedings of the Twenty-Third International Conference on Architectural Support for Programming Languages and Operating Systems, 2018, pp. 448–460.

[KGTM18] Saeed Reza Kheradpisheh, Mohammad Ganjtabesh, Simon J. Thorpe, Timothée Masquelier, Stdp-based spiking deep convolutional neural networks for object recognition, Neural Networks 99 (2018) 56–67.

[KK17] Hyoukjun Kwon, Tushar Krishna, OpenSMART: single-cycle multi-hop noc generator in BSV and Chisel, in: 2017 IEEE International Symposium on Performance Analysis of Systems and Software (ISPASS), April 2017, pp. 195–204.

[KLP+08] Muhammad Mukaram Khan, David R. Lester, Luis A. Plana, A. Rast, Xin Jin, Eustace Painkras, Stephen B. Furber, Spinnaker: mapping neural networks onto a massively-parallel chip multiprocessor, in: 2008 IEEE International Joint Conference on Neural Networks (IEEE World Congress on Computational Intelligence), IEEE, 2008, pp. 2849–2856.

[KM19] Saeed Reza Kheradpisheh, Timothée Masquelier, S4nn: temporal backpropagation for spiking neural networks with one spike per neuron, arXiv preprint, arXiv:1910.09495, 2019.

[KMM20] Saeed Reza Kheradpisheh, Maryam Mirsadeghi, Timothée Masquelier, Bs4nn: binarized spiking neural networks with temporal coding and learning, arXiv preprint, arXiv:2007.04039, 2020.

[LBBH98] Yann LeCun, Léon Bottou, Yoshua Bengio, Patrick Haffner, Gradient-based learning applied to document recognition, Proceedings of the IEEE 86 (11) (1998) 2278–2324.

[MKM+18] Milad Mozafari, Saeed Reza Kheradpisheh, Timothée Masquelier, Abbas Nowzari-Dalini, Mohammad Ganjtabesh, First-spike-based visual categorization using reward-modulated stdp, IEEE Transactions on Neural Networks and Learning Systems 29 (12) (2018) 6178–6190.

[MMMS20] Riccardo Massa, Alberto Marchisio, Maurizio Martina, Muhammad Shafique, An efficient spiking neural network for recognizing gestures with a dvs camera on the loihi neuromorphic processor, in: 2020 International Joint Conference on Neural Networks (IJCNN), IEEE, 2020, pp. 1–9.

[Mos17] H. Mostafa, Supervised learning based on temporal coding in spiking neural networks, IEEE Transactions on Neural Networks and Learning Systems 29 (7) (2017) 3227–3235.

[MT07] Timothée Masquelier, Simon J. Thorpe, Unsupervised learning of visual features through spike timing dependent plasticity, PLoS Computational Biology 3 (2) (2007).

[NH10] Vinod Nair, Geoffrey E. Hinton, Rectified linear units improve restricted Boltzmann machines, in: ICML, 2010.

[RBG+22] Bodo Rueckauer, Connor Bybee, Ralf Goettsche, Yashwardhan Singh, Joyesh Mishra, Andreas Wild Nxtf, An api and compiler for deep spiking neural networks on Intel loihi, ACM Journal on Emerging Technologies in Computing Systems (JETC) 18 (3) (2022) 1–22.

[RP99] Maximilian Riesenhuber, Tomaso Poggio, Hierarchical models of object recognition in cortex, Nature Neuroscience 2 (11) (1999) 1019–1025.

[RSB19] Joshua Arul Kumar Ranjan, Titus Sigamani, Janet Barnabas, A novel and efficient classifier using spiking neural network, Journal of Supercomputing (2019) 1–16.

[SKY+20] P. Srivatsa, Timothy Ng Chu Kyle, Tavva Yaswanth, Wu Jibin, Zhang Malu, Li Haizhou, T.E. Carlson, You only spike once: improving energy-efficient neuromorphic inference to ann-level accuracy, in: 2nd Workshop on Accelerated Machine Learning (AccML), Valencia, Spain, 2020, pp. 1–8.

[Smi82] James E. Smith, Decoupled access/execute computer architectures, in: Proceedings of the 9th Annual Symposium on Computer Architecture (ISCA), April 1982, pp. 112–119.

[SS15] Sumit Bam Shrestha, Qing Song, Adaptive learning rate of spikeprop based on weight convergence analysis, Neural Networks 63 (63) (2015) 185–198.

[SYW+19] Abhronil Sengupta, Yuting Ye, Robert Wang, Chiao Liu, Kaushik Roy, Going deeper in spiking neural networks: Vgg and residual architectures, Frontiers in Neuroscience 13 (2019) 95.

[TDVR01] Simon Thorpe, Arnaud Delorme, Rufin Van Rullen, Spike-based strategies for rapid processing, Neural Networks 14 (6–7) (2001) 715–725.

[TM18] Amirhossein Tavanaei, Anthony S. Maida, Bp-stdp: approximating backpropagation using spike timing dependent plasticity, Neurocomputing 330 (2018) 39–47.

[WZWP20] Bo Wang, Jun Zhou, Weng-Fai Wong, Li-Shiuan Peh, Shenjing: a low power reconfigurable neuromorphic accelerator with partial-sum and spike networks-on-chip, in: 2020 Design, Automation & Test in Europe Conference & Exhibition (DATE), IEEE, 2020, pp. 240–245.

[XRV17] Han Xiao, Kashif Rasul, Roland Vollgraf, Fashion-mnist: a novel image dataset for benchmarking machine learning algorithms, arXiv preprint, arXiv:1708.07747, 2017.

[YLT18] Qiang Yu, Haizhou Li, Kay Chen Tan, Spike timing or rate? Neurons learn to make decisions for both through threshold-driven plasticity, IEEE Transactions on Cybernetics 49 (6) (2018) 2178–2189.

[ZL20] Wenrui Zhang, Peng Li, Temporal spike sequence learning via backpropagation for deep spiking neural networks, arXiv preprint, arXiv:2002.10085, 2020.

[ZLC+20] Malu Zhang, Xiaoling Luo, Yi Chen, Jibin Wu, Ammar Belatreche, Zihan Pan, Hong Qu, Haizhou Li, An efficient threshold-driven aggregate-label learning algorithm for multimodal information processing, IEEE Journal of Selected Topics in Signal Processing 14 (3) (2020) 592–602.

[ZWW+22] Malu Zhang, Jiadong Wang, Jibin Wu, Ammar Belatreche, Burin Amornpaisannon, Zhixuan Zhang, Venkata Pavan Kumar Miriyala, Hong Qu, Yansong Chua, Trevor E. Carlson, Haizhou Li, Rectified linear postsynaptic potential function for backpropagation in deep spiking neural networks, IEEE Transactions on Neural Networks and Learning Systems 33 (5) (2022) 1947–1958.

6

Neural column-inspired spiking neural networks for episodic memory

6.1 Preface

The cerebral cortex is made up of about 150 000 neural columns, which some scholars believe are the units of intelligence [Haw21]. The neural columns are not visible under the microscope because there is no clear boundary between the columns. However, experiments have shown that neurons in one column respond to the same area in the skin (or the same part of the retina), and this property becomes the basis for the division of neural columns. The neural column is composed of smaller minicolumns, each one contains hundreds of minicolumns, which are physically clearly visible [Haw21]. In this chapter, SNN models that simulate the property of neural columns/minicolumns are introduced. In these models, the structure of the columns/minicolumns does not correspond to the structure of biological neural columns, but is simplified to a collection of identical neurons. These neurons are sensitive to the same specific input stimulus, and are formally arranged into a column, but their position in the column is meaningless, and there is no division of "layers" as in the biological neural columns.

The pyramidal cells [SL18] were the main projective neurons of the cerebral cortex, with a cone shape. As shown on the left of Fig. 6.1(a), a large protrusion from the tip of the cell is called an apical dendrite, which extends to the surface of the cortex. The basal dendrites emanating from the base of the cell body are mostly horizontal, making synaptic connections with the axons of other neurons around them. The axons originate from the center of the base of the cell body opposite the apical dendrites, and their lateral branches establish connections with the dendrites of other neurons in the same or adjacent layers. Recent studies have found that dendrites are not only simple conduits for transmitting inputs, but also complex nonlinear processing units. Inspired by this, the authors of [HAD+11] constructed a kind of neuron with a dendrite structure, which is referred to as a HTM (Hierarchical Temporal Memory) neuron.

HTM neurons omit the apical dendrites of pyramidal cells and divide the basal dendrites of pyramidal cells into proximal dendrites and distal dendrites. There is only one proximal dendrite with multiple synapses on it for receiving feedforward inputs (external inputs). These inputs directly cause reactions in the cell body, and these reactions can be summed linearly. Distal dendrites have multiple synapses that form connections with other nearby cells. When a synapse on the distal dendrite is activated, there is no effect on

Towards Neuromorphic Machine Intelligence. https://doi.org/10.1016/B978-0-44-332820-6.00013-6

the cell body, but if enough synapses are activated in a short period of time, the dendrite will produce a dendrite spike and pass it to the cell body.

In this chapter, we introduce novel neuron models based on the properties of pyramidal cells and HTM neurons, as well as the columnar-structured network models built on these neurons, which are used to realize episodic memory tasks.

6.2 Minicolumn-based model for episodic memory

Combining hippocampus structure with a SNN, a Bionic Spiking Temporal Memory (BSTM) model is shown in [ZCZ+22] to explore the encoding, formation, and retrieval of episodic memory. For encoding episodic memory, the Spike-Timing-Dependent-Plasticity (STDP) learning algorithm and a new minicolumn selection algorithm are used to encode each input item into several active minicolumns. For the formation of episodic memory, a sequential memory algorithm is shown to store the contexts between items. For retrieval of episodic memory, the authors proposed the local retrieval algorithm and the global retrieval algorithm to retrieve sequence information, achieving multi-sentence prediction and multi-time step prediction. All functions of BSTM are based on bionic spiking neurons, which have biological characteristics including columnar and dendritic structures, firing and receiving spikes, and delaying transmission.

6.2.1 Model architecture

Referring to the biological structure of pyramidal neurons and the information processing structure of the hippocampus, the neuron structure, the minicolumn organization, and the network structure of the BSTM model are described successively.

6.2.1.1 The neuron structure

There are a large number of pyramidal neurons in both the CA3 and CA1 regions of the hippocampus [MHCJ98,SSC+17,MEFG01], and the biological structure of a pyramidal neuron is shown in Fig. 6.1(a). The pyramidal neuron receives the feedforward inputs from the lower layer by the proximal dendrite (red rectangle), lateral inputs from the same layer by the distal dendrite, and the feedback inputs from the higher layer by the apical dendrite. When the neuron receives enough inputs, it generates a spike that transmits to neurons through the axon.

Inspired by the pyramidal neuron, the BSTM neuron has one proximal dendrite and multiple (sometimes zero) distal dendrites, as shown in Fig. 6.1(b). Similarly, the BSTM neuron receives feedforward input spikes by the proximal dendrite and receives lateral inputs by distal dendrites. When a neuron receives enough feedforward input spikes, it generates an output spike that is transmitted from the axon to the neurons of higher layers and the same layer.

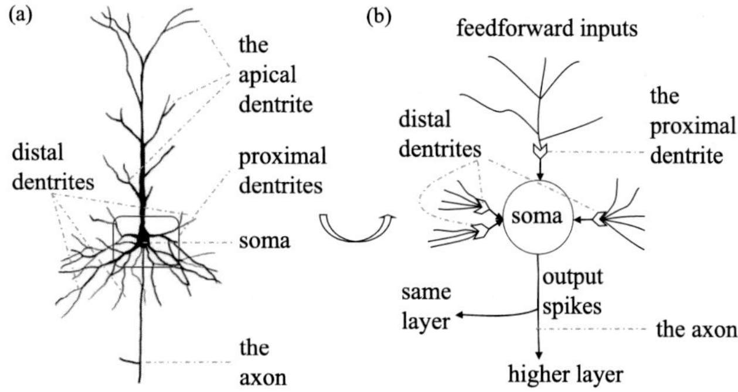

FIGURE 6.1 (a) The structure of a biological pyramidal neuron. (b) The structure of a BSTM neuron.

6.2.1.2 The minicolumn organization

The minicolumn structure is designed by referring to the one in HTM [HAD+11]. There are $M = 512$ minicolumns, and a minicolumn includes $N = 64$ neurons that share the same proximal dendrite. After receiving one input item from the proximal dendrite, each minicolumn is in one of two states, active or inactive, as shown in Fig. 6.2(a). When learning the information representation of an item, all neurons in active and inactive minicolumns are active and inactive, respectively. An input item is encoded by B active minicolumns, where in the computations $B = 10$ (2% of the active minicolumns), and in figures and the example $B = 4$. For a minicolumn, it may be a component of multiple item representations, as shown in Fig. 6.2(a).

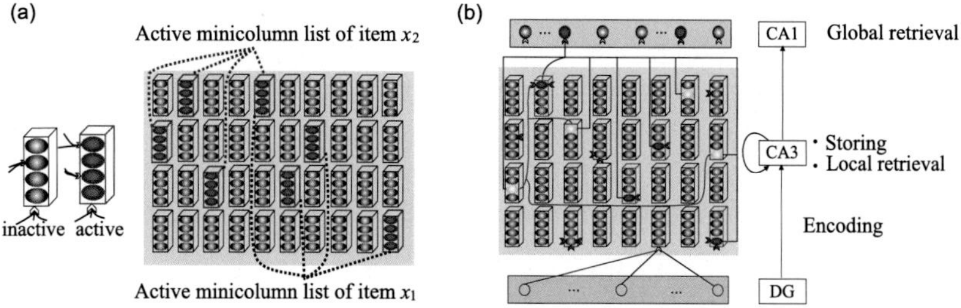

FIGURE 6.2 The schematic diagram of a minicolumn. A minicolumn includes 4 neurons that are either active (red) or inactive (gray). 4 active minicolumns represent an item, where the top 5th minicolumn is both in 'x_1' and 'x_2'.

6.2.1.3 The neural networks organization

The hippocampus of the brain is the region where episodic memory resides, and its main areas include the dentate gyrus (DG), CA3, and CA1. The typical view [BBS+11] is that the inputs of DG flow unidirectionally to CA3 and then unidirectionally to CA1, where CA3 is endowed with recurrent connections. There are time cells in CA3, which can encode temporal information, form the contextual information of memory, and retrieve information

[UKJ+20]. Inspired by all of these results, the authors proposed the BSTM network to simulate episodic memory in the hippocampus, which includes three layers: the DG layer, the CA3 layer, and the CA1 layer. Among them, only the CA3 layer is a columnar structure.

Fig. 6.2(b) shows the organization of the BSTM networks. The DG neurons are fully connected to all CA3 minicolumns by the proximal dendrite (white). The red, gray, and pink CA3 neurons are active neurons of the current item, inactive neurons of the current item, and active neurons of the previous item, respectively. Only one active neuron is in an active (red) minicolumn, it creates distal connections with pink CA3 neurons to store the new context by its winner (red) distal dendrite. The inactive (dark blue) distal dendrites store other irrelevant contexts. A new (red) CA1 neuron stores the current sequence, it connects all active CA3 neurons of its sequence by the proximal dendrite.

6.2.2 How does the BSTM simulate episodic memory?

This section describes how the BSTM model can encode, store, and retrieve episodic memory. For encoding, the DG inputs are encoded into $B = 10$ CA3 active minicolumns by the proximal dendrites, which are learned by the STDP method and the new minicolumn selection and determination algorithms. For storing, the distal dendrites of the CA3 neurons are established to store short-term information (the contexts between items), and the proximal dendrite of a new CA1 neuron is established to store the long-term information of each sequence. For retrieval, the distal dendrites of the CA3 layer are used for local retrieval, and the proximal dendrites of the CA1 layer are used for global retrieval, which corresponds to the two new retrieval algorithms.

6.2.2.1 The encoding process

The encoding process of episodic memory is the learning process from the DG layer to the CA3 layer. Before this encoding process, an input word is first converted into a spike representation of 1000 DG neurons, which is called an input term. The conversion process is divided into two steps: For a word, the Poisson distribution with $\lambda = \frac{20*T}{1000}$ is first used to generate the number of spikes of each DG neuron within a period $T = 10$ ms. Then, the times of each spike are randomly generated in $[0, T]$. Thus the word is randomly transformed into an input item $x = [S_1, S_2, \cdots, S_{1000}]$, where S_i $(i = 1, 2, \cdots, 1000)$ is the spike train of the ith DG neuron.

Then, the input items of the DG layer are encoded into the active minicolumns of the CA3 layer in three steps. First, the membrane potential dynamics of the minicolumns are calculated, then ten active minicolumns are selected and determined to represent an input term, and finally, the weights on the proximal dendrites are learned. Note that during encoding, a minicolumn is treated as a whole, and all operations are based on the minicolumns rather than the neurons.

1) Calculation model of the minicolumns: The spike response model (SRM) [JTG03] is used to compute the membrane potential dynamics of each minicolumn. The minicolumn j receives an item $x = [S_1, S_2, \cdots, S_{1000}]$ from the DG neurons, where $S_i = [t_i^1, t_i^2, \cdots, t_i^f, \cdots]$ $(i = 1, 2, \cdots, 1000)$, and its membrane potential $V_j(t)$ is the weighted sum of postsynaptic potentials induced by these input spikes, which is defined as:

$$V_j(t) = \sum_{i=1}^{1000} w_{ji} \sum_{t_i^f} PSP\left(t - t_i^f\right) - \theta_1 \cdot \exp\left(-\frac{t - t_j}{\tau_m}\right), \tag{6.1}$$

where w_{ji} is the synaptic weight from the DG neuron i to the minicolumn j, t_i^f is the time of the fth spike in S_i. $PSP\left(t - t_i^f\right)$ is the postsynaptic potential (PSP) induced by t_i^f, which is defined as:

$$PSP(x) = V_0\left[\exp\left(\frac{-x}{\tau_m}\right) - \exp\left(\frac{-x}{\tau_s}\right)\right] \quad \text{if } x > 0, \tag{6.2}$$

where $x = t - t_i^f$, and PSP is greater than 0 if $x > 0$, otherwise, it remains at 0; $\tau_m = 5$ is the integration time constant of PSP and $\tau_s = 1.25$ is the decay time constant of synaptic current (τ_s is usually set to a quarter of τ_m), they are used to control the PSP shape; $V_0 = \frac{\alpha^{\alpha/(\alpha-1)}}{\alpha-1}$ is used to scale the maximal PSP to 1 and $\alpha = \tau_m/\tau_s$. The minicolumn j emits (fires) an output spike $t_j = t$, when $V_j(t)$ surpasses the firing threshold $\theta_1 = 1$ from below, and then it enters the refractory period, no longer responding to the input spikes. That is, each minicolumn at most emits a spike at one period.

2) Active minicolumn selection algorithm: When an item x_j is fed into the CA3 layer, the membrane potential of each minicolumn is calculated. The membrane voltage reflects the response of the minicolumn to the input item x_j, and the 2% minicolumns (10 minicolumns) with the strongest response are selected to form the active minicolumn list A_j, and the corresponding output spike times are recorded in the output list O_j. To avoid the fact that some minicolumns are never selected and others are frequently selected, the authors enforce that each minicolumn can only be selected by $K = 100$ items at most (it is proved to be reasonable by experiments and suitable for retrieval from 1000 to 10 000 sentences, as shown in Table 6.5).

The selection algorithm is defined as follows:

a. Create a blacklist, the minicolumns that have been selected for 100 items are added to this blacklist, then can no longer be selected.

b. Find all firing minicolumns that are not in the blacklist, the number of which is N_{fire}. Then,

- if $N_{fire} \geq 10$, the earlier firing minicolumn is preferentially added to A_j. For the same output spiking time t_k, the minicolumn with higher membrane potential at t_k is preferentially added to A_j. The output times of these active minicolumns are added to O_j.
- if $N_{fire} < 10$, all firing minicolumns and their output times are added to A_j and O_j, respectively. For the unfired minicolumns, any minicolumn m has a maximum membrane potential $V_m^{\max} = \max_{t \in [(j-1)\mathrm{T}, j\mathrm{T}]} \{V_m(t)\}$. The minicolumns with $10 - N_{fire}$ largest $V_m^{\max}$ are added to A_j, and their times $t_m = t_{V_m^{\max}}$ (time at $V_m^{\max}$) are added to O_j.

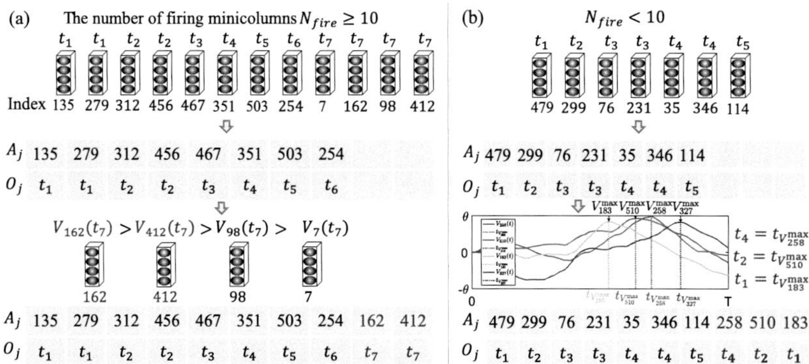

FIGURE 6.3 The process of selecting 10 active minicolumns. The t_k on the top is its output spike time ($t_1 < t_2 < \cdots < t_7$). (a) The $V_m(t_k)$ is the membrane potential of minicolumn m at time t_k, preferentially select the one with higher membrane potential when t_k is the same. (b) The $10 - N_{fire}$ minicolumns with $10 - N_{fire}$ largest $V_m^{\max}$ are added to A_j.

Fig. 6.3 shows the process in step b of the selection algorithm.

3) Active minicolumns determination algorithm: A_j should be determined by comparing the similarity with the previous learned active minicolumn lists (A_i, $0 < i < j$). The similarity $C(j,i)$ between A_j and A_i is defined as:

$$C(j,i) = \frac{|A_j \bigcap A_i|}{10}, \tag{6.3}$$

where $|C|$ is the cardinality of C, and $0 < i < j$. The minicolumn lists of any two items share at most $C^{\max} = 30\%$ minicolumns; otherwise, the active minicolumns must be reselected by the selection algorithm until the requirement is met. The process for determining A_j and O_j is as follows:

a. Calculate the similarity $C(i,j)$. If $D(i,j) > C^{\max}$: $h = |A_j \bigcap A_i|$, $\frac{h}{2}$ (h is even) or $\frac{h+1}{2}$ (h is odd) minicolumns are randomly removed from $A_j \bigcap A_i$, then added to the blacklist and remove their output times from O_j.

b. Assume that the number of active minicolumns in A_j after traversing the whole learned A_i ($0 < i < j$) is b,

- if $b < 10$, select $10 - b$ minicolumns to fill A_j and O_j according to the selection algorithm in the previous section. Then, go to step a to re-determine A_j.
- if $b = 10$, A_j and O_j represent the current item x_j.

4) Minicolumns learning algorithm – STDP: Spike-timing-dependent-plasticity (STDP [BP98]) is considered to be the underlying mechanism of information learning and memory in the brain. It is used to adjust the synaptic weight on the proximal dendrites of the CA3 layer. STDP is divided into long-term potentiation (LTP) and long-term depression (LTD). When the presynaptic spike time precedes the postsynaptic time, LTP will increase the connected synaptic weight; on the contrary, LTD will reduce the synaptic weight. The weight update of STDP is defined as:

$$\Delta w(x) = \begin{cases} \alpha^{+} \exp\left(\frac{x}{\tau^{+}}\right), & \text{if} \quad x < 0, \\ -\alpha^{-} \exp\left(\frac{-x}{\tau^{-}}\right), & \text{if} \quad x > 0, \end{cases} \tag{6.4}$$

where $\alpha^{+} = 0.005$ and $\alpha^{-} = 0.0005$ are the learning rates for LTP and LTD, respectively, $\tau^{+} = 20$ and $\tau^{-} = 20$ are time-constant parameters, and $x = t_i^f - t_j$ is the spike time difference between the presynaptic neuron i and the postsynaptic minicolumn j. Fig. 6.4(a) shows the weight update of STDP.

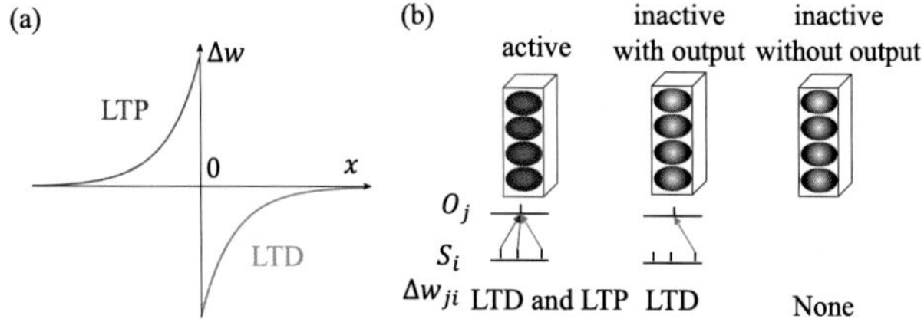

FIGURE 6.4 The weight update of STDP (a) and a minicolumn (b). (a) The red line represents the increased weight of LTP, while the green one represents the LTD with decreased weight. (b) The weight update of different minicolumns.

The input spike train of neuron i is $S_i = [t_i^1, t_i^2, \cdots, t_i^f, \cdots]$, and the output spike time of minicolumn j is t_j. The synaptic weight w_{ji} from DG neuron i to the minicolumn j is divided into three cases. For each active minicolumn j, w_{ji} is increased by LTP ($t_i^f < t_j$) and suppressed by LTD ($t_i^f > t_j$). For each inactive minicolumn j with generating output spike, w_{ji} is suppressed by LTD ($t_i^f > t_j$). For inactive minicolumns without output spikes, which do not fire spikes, the weight remains the same. Hence, w_{ji} is defined as:

$$\Delta w_{ji} = \begin{cases} \sum\limits_{t_i^f} \Delta w\left(t_i^f - t_j\right), & \text{if} \quad j \text{ is active,} \\ \sum\limits_{t_i^f > t_j} \Delta w\left(t_i^f - t_j\right), & \text{if} \quad j \text{ is inactive but fires,} \\ 0, & \text{otherwise.} \end{cases} \tag{6.5}$$

A clipping operation is used to restrict w_{ji} to be in $[-1,1]$. Fig. 6.4(b) shows the weight update the proximal dendrite.

The synaptic weight adjustment on the proximal dendrites of the CA3 layer needs to be performed for many epochs (100) so that the CA3 layer can learn the minicolumn representation of all items in the dataset. Assuming that the item x_j in the eth epoch is encoded as A_j^e, then the similarity between A_j^e and A_j^{e-1} is calculated by Eq. (6.3). The encoding process ends prematurely when the average similarity of all items is greater than 99% (a suitable value obtained from the preliminary experiments, which ensures that STDP is almost converged and requires fewer than 100 epochs). Fig. 6.5 shows the weights from 200

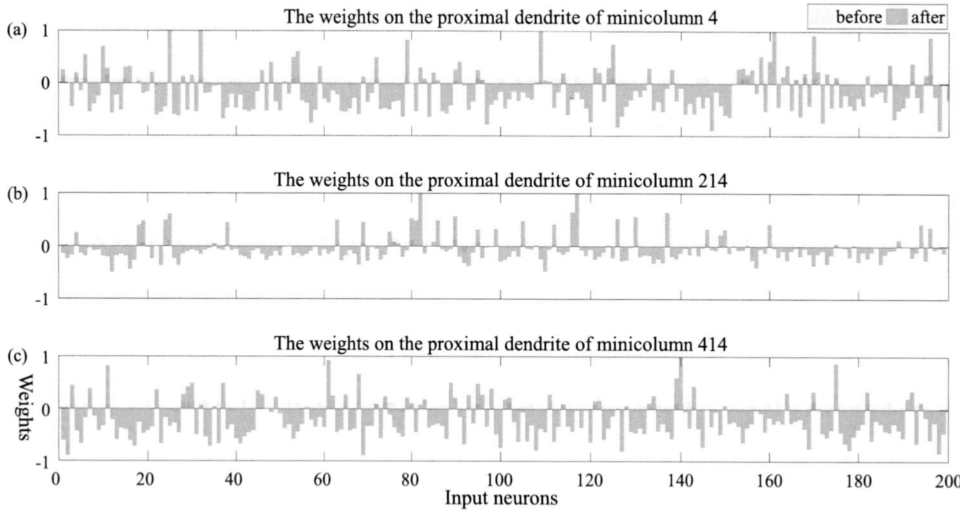

FIGURE 6.5 The weights from 200 DG neurons to three minicolumns before and after learning. The weights before learning were relatively small (yellow), while some weights are significantly increased after learning, indicating that the connections between these input neurons and the corresponding minicolumns are enhanced.

input neurons to three minicolumns before (yellow) and after (blue) learning. Then, the weights of the proximal dendrites no longer change and an item is encoded as a fixed set of active minicolumns.

6.2.2.2 The storing process

The training sequence set is $\mathbf{X} = [X_1, X_2, \cdots, X_n]$ with the kth ($k = 1, 2, \cdots, n$) training sequence $X_k = [x_k^1, x_k^2, \cdots, x_k^j, \cdots]$. The jth item x_k^j is fed at the jth period $[(j-1)\mathrm{T}, j\mathrm{T}]$ (Fig. 6.6(a)), and minicolumns in the active minicolumn list A_k^j become active (Fig. 6.6(b)). Next, the storing process for short-term information and long-term information are described in detail.

1) Storing the short-term information: The short-term information (contexts between adjacent items $[x_k^{j-1}, x_k^j]$) are stored in the distal dendrites of the active neurons.

First, select the active neurons on active minicolumns. Neuron a_{lm} is the lth neuron in minicolumn m with output time $t_{lm} = t_m$. For neuron a_{lm}, the more outgoing connections it has, the more post-test information it indicates; the more distal dendrites it has, the more pre-test information it represents. Only select one active neuron in an active minicolumn, and 10 active neurons for item x_k^j are formed in the active neuron list $\mathscr{A}_k^j$. The active neuron selection strategy is shown as follows:

- For each active minicolumn of the first item x_k^1, the active neuron is the neuron with the fewest outward connections. Randomly select one if there are multiple such neurons.
- For each active minicolumn of the other items x_k^j $(j > 1)$, the active neuron is the neuron with the fewest dendrites. Randomly select one if there are multiple such neurons.

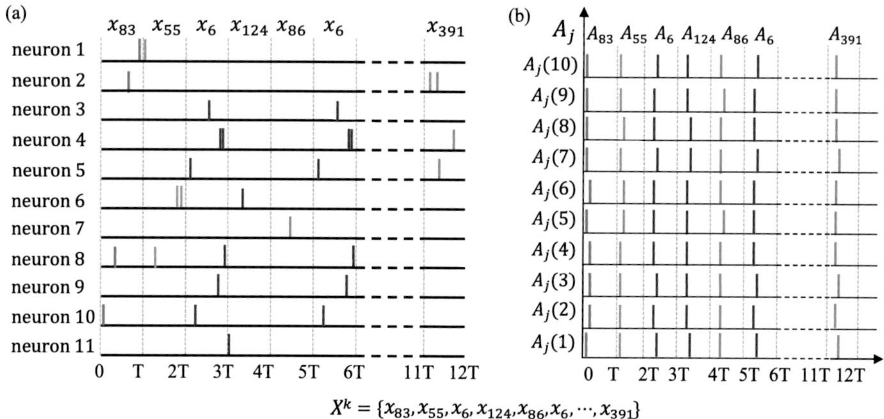

FIGURE 6.6 (a) The spike trains of the first 11 DG neurons for the kth sequence X_k. (b) The input item x_j is encoded as 10 active minicolumns in A_j with their outputs O_j. $A_j(k)$ is the kth element in A_j, and the same item at different positions in a sequence activates the same A_j at different periods, e.g., x_6.

Secondly, a new context Con_{lm} between adjacent items $[x_k^{j-1}, x_k^j]$ is created on each active neuron $a_{lm} \in \mathscr{A}_k^j$. There are 10 previous active neurons $a_{ef} \in \mathscr{A}_k^{j-1}$, randomly select 7 previous neurons in Con_{lm} (sub-sampling) to improve the memory capacity and robustness, which can be found in [HAD+11,CAH16]. Con_{lm} store 7 connections from previous active neurons, including four elements: the previous active neurons a_{ef}, the synaptic weights $w_{ef,lm}$ and delays $d_{ef,lm}$, and the label of current item x_k^j. To make each previous active neuron a_{ef} have the same effect on neuron a_{lm}, the weight $w_{ef,lm} = \frac{1}{7}$ and the delay $d_{ef,lm}$ [ZQL+21] from a_{ef} to a_{lm} is defined as:

$$d_{ef,lm} = t_{lm} - t_{ef} - t_{max}, \tag{6.6}$$

where t_{lm} and t_{ef} are the times of output spikes of neurons a_{lm} and a_{ef}, respectively; $t_{max} = \frac{\tau_m \tau_s[\ln(\tau_m) - \ln(\tau_s)]}{\tau_m - \tau_s}$ is the time required for the PSP to reach its maximum value. Hence, after the delays, neuron a_{lm} receives lateral inputs from the previous neurons in Con_{lm} at time $t_{lm} - t_{max}$ with the same effects, and the neuron a_{lm} receives the maximum weighted PSPs at t_{lm}. Fig. 6.7 shows the delay learning.

Finally, the new context Con_{lm} is stored on a distal dendrite of neuron a_{lm}. D_{lm}^d is the dth ($d \geq 0$) distal segment of the active neuron a_{lm}. Each D_{lm}^d stores at most $Con^{\max} = 4$ contexts [HAD+11,CAH16], and its different contexts connect to different neurons. The selected D_{lm}^d is the one that contains fewer than 4 contexts and has no connections to the neurons in the new context Con_{lm}. If no such D_{lm}^d exists, a new distal dendrite for neuron a_{lm} is created and selected.

Fig. 6.8 show the contexts establishment process. In Fig. 6.8, the model receives an input item every period with the active (red) minicolumns and the output spikes (top). An active (red) neuron is selected for each active minicolumn and stores the context by making connections with previous active neurons. For the active minicolumns of the first item

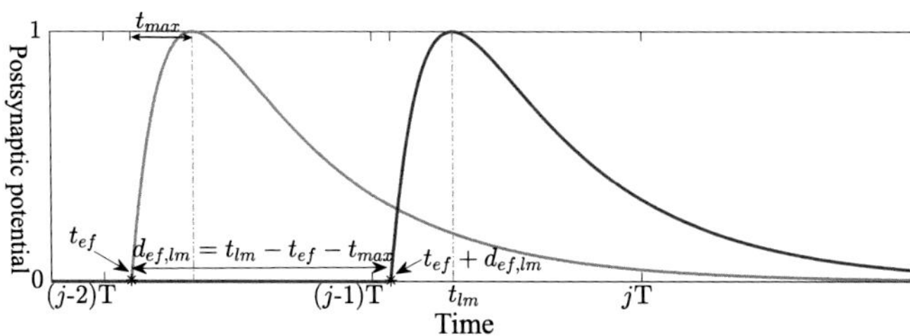

FIGURE 6.7 Schematic diagram of the delay learning. The gray line is the PSP induced by the time t_{ef}. After transmission delay $d_{ef,lm}$, the neuron a_{lm} receives the maximum PSP at t_{lm}, as shown in the red line.

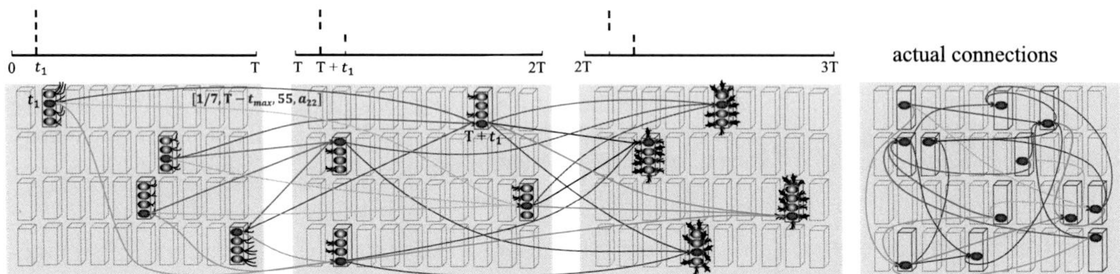

FIGURE 6.8 The context establishment process in the CA3 layer. Only one active neuron is in each active minicolumn, which selects a distal dendrite (red) to store a context between two adjacent items. To show the connections (context) more clearly, the connections on segments corresponding to the three input items are shown separately in the first three pictures, and the actual (recurrent) connections between them are in the fourth figure.

x_k^1, active neurons are those with the fewest outward connections; otherwise, for the other items x_k^j $(j > 1)$, active neurons are those with the fewest dendrites. Every active neuron randomly selects 7 previous active neurons to establish new connections on its selected dendrite (red).

2) Storing the long-term information: Long-term information of a new sequence is stored by establishing connections of the proximal dendrite on the newly created CA1 neuron. Each CA1 neuron represents a sequence, and CA1 neurons are not connected to each other, nor do they have distal dendrites. The long-term information of a new sequence X_k is as follows:

a. When the final input item x_k^l in X_k is completed, the CA1 layer creates a new neuron k.

b. The CA3 active neurons of the item x_k^j $(j = 1, 2, \cdots, l)$ connect to the proximal dendrite D_k^{ca1} of the kth CA1 neuron with the weight 0.025 and the delay $(l + 1 - j)$ T.

The delays make this CA1 neuron receive the CA3 input spikes at $[l\text{T}, (l+1)\text{T}]$ and reach the maximum membrane potential at this period. Fig. 6.9 shows the long-term information of a new sequence. The newly created CA1 neuron with its proximal dendrite is shown in red.

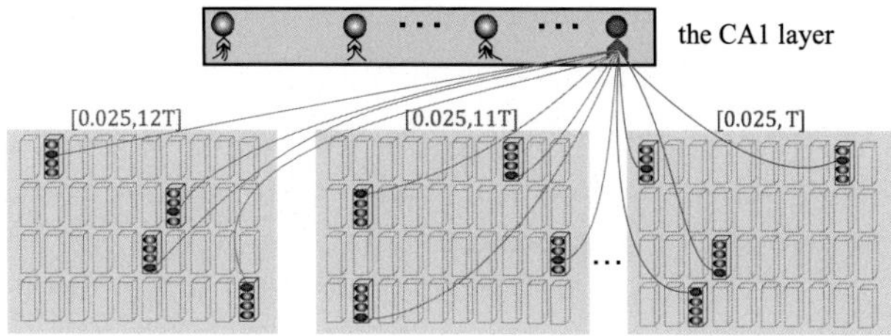

FIGURE 6.9 The long-term information of a new sequence. The values in $[0.025, a\mathrm{T}]$ are the weight and delay of the connection.

6.2.2.3 The retrieval process

After all sequences have been learned once, the training ends and the network structure remains unchanged. Then, test the retrieval capability of the BSTM model. The retrieval process includes: 1) neuron state change process; 2) two new retrieval algorithms; 3) criterion of retrieval quality.

1) Neuron state: The CA3 neurons during retrieval are in three states: active, predictive, and inactive, and these states can be dynamically switched, as shown in Fig. 6.10. The default state of neurons for each period is inactive. The neuron becomes active after receiving enough feedforward inputs. While enough active synapses on its distal dendrite from other active neurons will depolarize it into a predictive state. The predictive neurons become active (inactive) in the next period with enough (insufficient) feedforward inputs. However, if there are no feedforward inputs in the next period, the predictive neurons will become active to make further predictions.

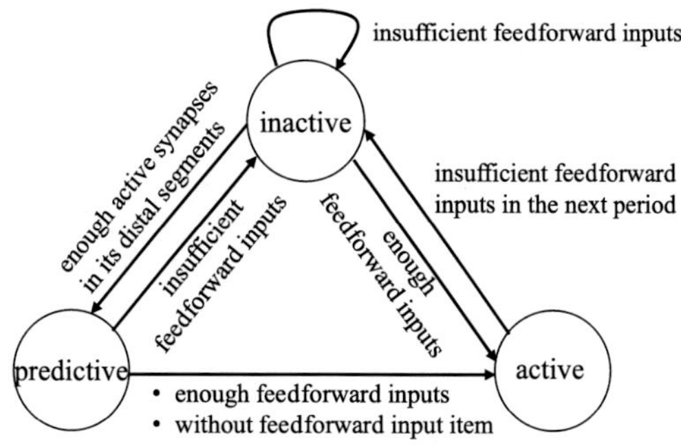

FIGURE 6.10 The state transition between the BSTM neurons.

In detail, an item x_k^j feeds at the jth period, the minicolumns in A_k^j become active. The predictive neurons a_{lm} ($\mathbb{P}_{lm}^{j-1} = 1$) in an active minicolumn ($m \in A_k^j$) become active ($\mathbb{A}_{lm}^j = 1$), where $\mathbb{P}^j$ and $\mathbb{A}^j$ are a binary predictive matrix and an active matrix of all CA3 neurons at period j, respectively. If there are no predictive neurons in the active minicolumn m, all neurons in minicolumn m become active ($\mathbb{A}_{.m}^j = 1$). If there is no feedforward input, the predictive neurons ($\mathbb{P}_{lm}^{j-1} = 1$) become active ($\mathbb{A}_{lm}^j = 1$). D_{gh}^d is the dth distal dendritic matrix of neuron a_{gh}, and it becomes active ($\mathbb{D}^d_{gh} = 1$) if the number of connected active neurons exceeds the threshold θ_2 and makes neuron a_{gh} become predictive ($\mathbb{P}^j_{gh} = 1$).

The neurons can become active in three ways. i) When x^j_k is fed into the network, the predictive neurons on any active minicolumn m will become active, indicating that the prediction is correct; ii) or all neurons become active if its minicolumn m is without predictive neurons, indicating that minicolumn m is unpredicted; iii) When there is no feedforward item ($x^j_k = \emptyset$), the predictive neurons become active to make further predictions. Hence, the active neuron at the jth period is defined as:

$$\mathbb{A}^j_{lm} = \begin{cases} 1, & \text{if } \mathbb{P}^{j-1}_{lm} = 1 \ \& \ m \in A^j_k, \\ 1, & \text{if } \sum_l \mathbb{P}^{j-1}_{lm} = 0 \ \& \ m \in A^j_k, \\ 1, & \text{if } \mathbb{P}^{j-1}_{lm} = 1 \ \& \ x^j_k = \emptyset, \\ 0, & \text{otherwise.} \end{cases} \tag{6.7}$$

The active neurons in the jth period can be used to predict the contexts in the $(j+1)$th period by lateral connections on the distal dendrites. The state of D^d_{gh} at the jth period is defined as:

$$\mathbb{D}^d_{gh} = \begin{cases} 1, & \text{if } \sum\limits_{\substack{l,m \\ a_{lm} \in D^d_{gh}}} \mathbb{A}^j_{lm} \geq \theta_2, \\ 0, & \text{otherwise,} \end{cases} \tag{6.8}$$

where the neuron a_{lm} is connected to the neuron a_{gh} by D^d_{gh}, and θ_2 is the threshold of an active distal dendrite. The neuron a_{gh} at the jth period becomes predictive ($\mathbb{P}^j_{gh} = 1$) if it has an active distal dendrite, which is defined as:

$$\mathbb{P}^j_{gh} = \begin{cases} 1, & \text{if } \exists_d \, \mathbb{D}^d_{gh} = 1, \\ 0, & \text{otherwise.} \end{cases} \tag{6.9}$$

Since the neurons are predicted by the contexts from lateral connections before being activated by the current item, the active neurons also include contexts generated by the previous input items. The memory is stored among these active and predictive neurons rather than input patterns by central storage.

Fig. 6.11 shows the neuron state change process when predicting a sentence at multi-time steps. The number near a neuron is its label. In (a), the first item x_{83} activates all the neurons on its corresponding active minicolumns, and these active neurons predicted eight neurons by activating their distal dendrites (draw by 2). The items x_{55} and x_6 only activate the predictive neurons on the active minicolumns. There is no feedforward input after the fourth period, and the predictive neurons become active. In (b), there are no predictive neurons in the active minicolumns of items x_{258} and x_6, and all neurons on the active minicolumns become active.

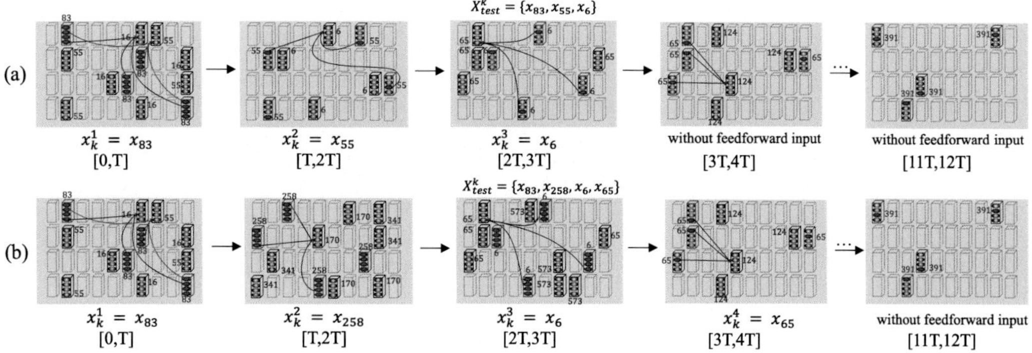

FIGURE 6.11 The neuron state changes process when three (a) and four (b) input items are provided, respectively. The second input item x_{258} in (b) is noise.

2) Local retrieval algorithm: Context information is stored in the distal dendrites of CA3 neurons, and local retrieval uses these distal dendrites to retrieve contextual information related to the input items. Choose some items from a training sequence ($X^k = [x_k^1, x_k^2, \ldots, x_k^l, \cdots]$) to form a test sequence $X_{test}^k = [x_k^j, \ldots, x_k^l]$ $(j > 0)$, the local retrieval algorithm starts working at the period of the last input item x_k^l of X_{test}^k. These are active neurons a_{ef} in the jth $(j \geq l)$ period, and they make the neurons a_{lm} with corresponding contexts become predictive in this jth period. The membrane potential $V_{lm}(t)$ of each predictive neuron a_{lm} is calculated as:

$$V_{lm}(t) = \sum_{a_{ef} \in D_{lm}^d} w_{ef,lm} PSP\left(t - t_{ef} - d_{ef,lm}\right), \tag{6.10}$$

where $t \in [j\text{T}, (j+1)\text{T}]$ is in the $(j+1)$th period, a_{ef} is an active neuron connected with a_{lm} by D_{lm}^d and its output time t_{ef} is in the jth period. The D_{lm}^d has 4 types of information: all connected neurons a_{ef}, connected delays $d_{ef,lm}$, labels of neuron a_{lm}, and connected weights $w_{ef,lm}$. The output time $t_{lm} = t_{V_{lm}^{\max}}$ is the time when $V_{lm}(t)$ reaches $V_{lm}^{\max} = \max_{t \in [0,\text{T}]} \{V_{lm}(t)\}$.

A dendrite matrix D_{lm}^d contains multiple contexts with different combinations of connections. Connections to active neurons are active connections, otherwise they are inactive connections. The label of its predictive neuron a_{lm} is the label of active connections on D_{lm}^d, or the one on most active connections if there are many labels. The predictive neurons with the same label form one predictive population, as shown in Fig. 6.12. If a predictive population has more than θ_2 predictive neurons, this population is added to the population stack. After adding all predictive populations of this period, read a predictive population from the top of the stack and its neurons become active for subsequent predictions. If there is no predictive population in a period or the number of active neurons minus the number of predictive neurons is $\geq \theta_2$, meaning that existing active neurons have no contexts, then a multi-time step prediction for a sentence ends (shown in Fig. 6.11), and

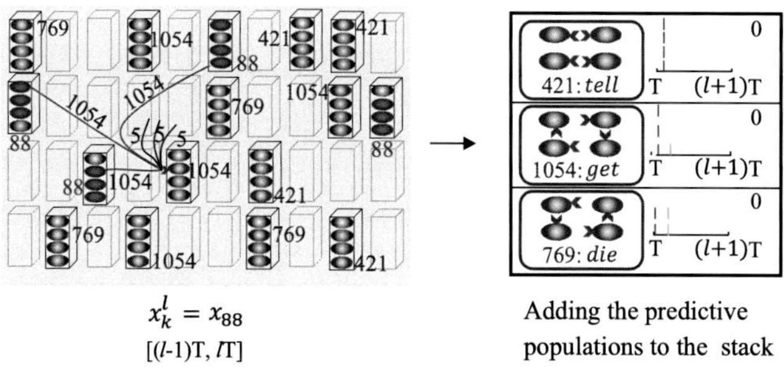

FIGURE 6.12 The formation of a predictive population of the last item x_k^l. The active neurons predict 12 predictive neurons with three different labels, forming three different predictive populations. For the distal dendrite shown here, it has three active connections labeled 1054 and inactive connections labeled 5, so its neurons have a predictive label of 1054.

it is a predictive sentence. Different predictive populations make their independent subsequent prediction, and the multi-sentence prediction ends when the stack becomes empty.

The local retrieval algorithm is shown below:

a. Find the active distal dendrites and make their neurons predictive in the current jth period with the corresponding predictive labels.

b. Calculate the membrane potential of each predictive neuron by Eq. (6.10), and then get its predictive output in the next $(j+1)$th period.

c. The predictive neurons with the same label form a predictive population.

- If there are predictive populations with more than θ_2 neurons, add them to the prediction stack with initial state 0.
- If the number of active neurons minus the number of predictive neurons is $\geq \theta_2$, the population with state 1 is added to the local predictive sentence list.
- If there is no predictive population, the population information with state 1 is added to the local predictive sentence list. Then, delete the populations with state 1 from the top of the stack until the state of a top population is 0. If the stack is empty, the local retrieval is finished.

d. Read a predictive population from the top of the stack and set its state to 1, and all neurons in this population become active. Then, repeat steps a–c to determine new predictive populations and add them to the stack.

Fig. 6.13 shows the process of local retrieval.

3) Global retrieval algorithm: Local retrieval can only predict from the first item x_k^j of the test sentence to the last item of its original sequence. If the input item $x_k^j\,(j > 1)$ starts in the middle of the sentence, the previous items x_k^i $(i = 1, \cdots, j-1)$ cannot be retrieved. The global retrieval algorithm is used to predict the complete sequence. Global retrieval can work with local retrieval or alone. When they work together, the global retrieval begins after the local retrieval. Each local predictive sentence corresponds to a global predictive

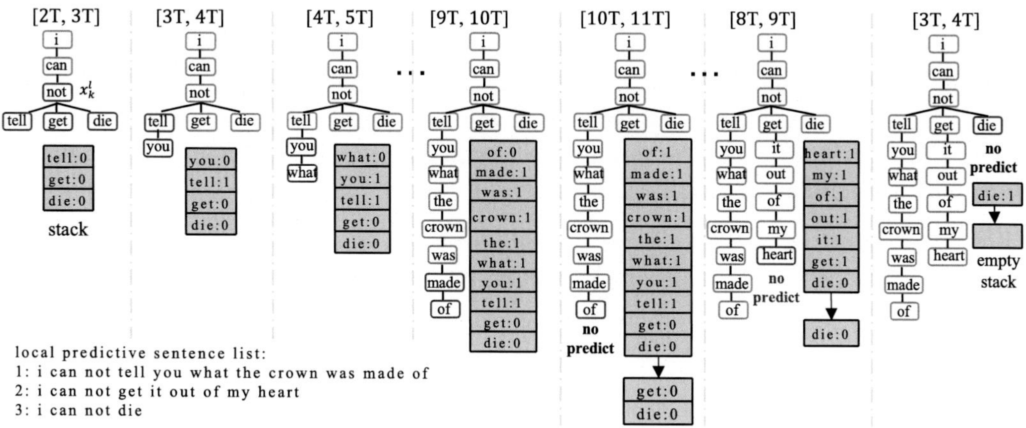

FIGURE 6.13 The process of local retrieval. A population only displays the word corresponding to its label. The gray, red, and purple rectangles represent the inactive neurons, the active neurons, and the predictive population, respectively.

sentence that can supplement the information not obtained by the local retrieval. When global retrieval works alone, global retrieval begins when the last item of a test sequence ends, and there is only one global predictive sentence.

For global retrieval, the CA1 neurons through proximal dendrites receive input spikes from all active CA3 neurons of a sequence. If the number of connected active CA3 neurons in a proximal dendrite D_i^{ca1} is not less than θ_3, this CA1 neuron i is active ($\mathbb{A}_i^{ca1} = 1$) and is defined as:

$$\mathbb{A}_i^{ca1} = \begin{cases} 1, & \text{if } \sum_{j} \sum_{\substack{l,m \\ a_{lm} \in D_i^{ca1}}} \mathbb{A}_{lm}^{j} \geq \theta_3, \\ 0, & \text{otherwise,} \end{cases} \tag{6.11}$$

where a_{lm} is the CA3 neuron connected to CA1 neuron i by D_i^{ca1}, and an active a_{lm} with $\mathbb{A}_{lm}^{j} = 1$. Since an input item activates 10 minicolumns, and each minicolumn has at least one active neuron, each item activates at least 10 CA3 neurons, which is why θ_3 is set to 10 to make an active CA3 neuron have at least one input item. Only active CA1 neurons will calculate the membrane voltage $V^{ca1}(t)$, and the active CA1 neuron with the largest membrane voltage is the predicted output neuron. The corresponding sentence for this predicted neuron is added to the global predictive sentence list. $V_i^{ca1}(t)$ of an active CA1 neuron i is defined as:

$$V_i^{ca1}(t) = \sum_{a_{lm} \in D_i^{ca1}} w_{lm,i}^{ca1} PSP\left(t - t_{lm} - d_{lm,i}^{ca1}\right), \tag{6.12}$$

where t_{lm} is the output of active CA3 neuron a_{lm}, $w_{lm,i}^{ca1}$ and $d_{lm,i}^{ca1}$ are the weight and delay from a_{lm} to CA1 neuron i.

Fig. 6.14 shows the process of the global retrieval. The delays to neuron 2 are chaotic, while those to neuron 6 decrease sequentially. As a result, neuron 2 receives input spikes scattered over multiple periods, while neuron 6 receives spikes concentrated in the 10th period ([9T, 10T]). The maximum membrane voltage is on the top of a neuron. The predicted output neuron is neuron 6 with the largest membrane voltage (2.4340), and the corresponding sentence is the global predictive sentence.

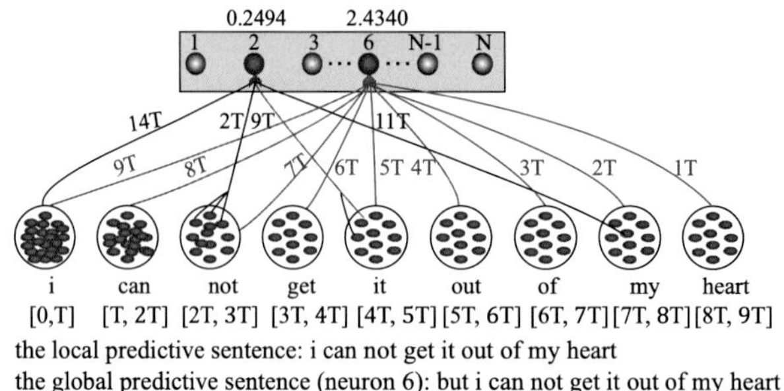

FIGURE 6.14 The process of global retrieval. The kT directly related to the population is the delay of the 10 active neurons in the population, and the kT related to the neurons is the delay of these neurons.

4) Retrieval quality: The kth test sequence X^k_{test}, predicted by i sentences in the global predictive sentence list $H_g = [h_g(1), h_g(2), \cdots, h_g(i)]$, has j actual target sentences in list $H_a = [h_a(1), h_a(2), \cdots, h_a(j)]$. The test accuracy C of the sequence X^k_{test} is defined as follows:

$$C = \frac{|H_g \bigcap H_a|}{|H_g \bigcup H_a|}. \tag{6.13}$$

6.2.3 Applications and results

In this section, several experiments are conducted to demonstrate the retrieval accuracy, context-based prediction, robustness, and memory capacity of the BSTM. These experiments were conducted in the retrieval stage by truncating and modifying sequences after one-trial sequence learning. Compared with the other methods, the performance of BSTM is better.

Table 6.1 shows the default parameters for learning and retrieval of the BSTM. The number of input neurons (1000), minicolumns (M), neurons (N), active minicolumns (B), and contexts ($Con^{\max}$) are set, refer to papers [HAD+11,CAH16,SMH20]. Any parameter that is different from the default one is declared in the corresponding experiments, and we have verified the effect of some parameters on performance with experiments.

All the training sentences are extracted from the Children's Books Test (CBT), including 10 or more words. Each word corresponds to the spike trains of 1000 DG neurons by the Poisson distribution, and a word is fed into the network every period until the end of the sentence. Each experiment is repeated 5 times, and the results are the average test accuracy.

Table 6.1 The parameters for BSTM.

DG	Number of DG neurons	1000
	Mean / variance of input weights	0.05
CA3	Number of minicolumns (N)	512
	Number of neurons in a minicolumn (M)	64
	Number of active minicolumns for an item (B)	10
	Maximum number of contexts per dendrite ($Con^{\max}$)	4
	Threshold of a firing minicolumn (θ_1)	1
	Threshold of an active distal dendrite (θ_2)	6
CA1	Threshold of an active CA1 dendrite (θ_3)	10

6.2.3.1 The impact of corrupted training sequences on retrieval performance

The test sequences are modified 1–9 items from the training sequences to test the retrieval performance of the network. The local and global retrieval algorithms are used to predict the test sequences consisting of the part items, and only the global retrieval algorithm is used to predict the other test sequences. These experiments use the first 1000 sentences to train the network, which contains 1978 words. The results of different test sequences are shown in Table 6.2.

Table 6.2 Retrieval accuracy of BSTM with various test sequences.

C(%) \ *Num*	1	2	3	4	5	6	7	8	9
Part items	90.4	96.6	99.4	99.7	99.9	100	100	100	100
Space delete	100	100	99.9	99.9	99.9	99.9	99.5	95.5	80.9
Direct delete	99.8	99.5	97.9	92.9	85.2	76.4	65.5	55.4	46.4
Add items	99.9	99.7	99.6	99.1	98.3	97.4	96.2	94.9	92.9
Replace items	100	100	99.9	99.9	99.8	99.7	98.5	92.7	76.1

For the test sequences consisting of consecutive 1–9 items (part items) of training sequences: In principle, input items can start anywhere in a training sequence, while the words at the beginning of a sentence may have more related sentences, making it harder to retrieve. For example, taking two consecutive items from X_k "It is $\cdots$ to honor $\cdots$", there are more sentences associated with 'it is' than with 'to honor'. From Table 6.2, the test accuracy grows with the number of input items. Table 6.3 shows the partial results of X^6_{test}, and X^{26}_{test}. The local retrieval algorithm predicts the sentence from the input word to the end, while the global one predicts the entire sentence. Notably, it can predict the sentences in which the input words are in the middle of the sentence.

For the test sequences by destroying items from training sequences: Randomly adding, deleting or replacing 1–9 words to anywhere in a training sequence as a test sequence. Among them, space delete and direct delete are used to delete items, e.g., $X_k = \{x_1, x_2, x_3, \cdots, \}$, space delete '$x_2$': $X^k_{test} = \{x_1, \ , x_3, \cdots, \}$, and direct delete '$x_2$': $X^k_{test} = \{x_1, x_3, \cdots, \}$. Table 6.2 shows that the more items destroyed, the lower the test accuracy. For these four kinds of test sequences, the retrieval accuracy of 'space delete' is the highest, and that of 'direct delete' is the lowest. Next, we give a detailed description of these four types of test sequences.

For 'space delete', the input items activate all neurons or the neurons with the corresponding contexts in the active minicolumns. After adding the delays, the target CA1 neuron received the most spikes in one period, resulting in its membrane potential being the largest. For 'direct delete', it greatly destroys the periods of the active CA3 neurons so that their spikes reach the CA1 neurons at different periods, hence its accuracy falls fastest. For 'replace items', it introduces some noisy items with some unrelated contexts. For 'add items', even if 9 words are added, the accuracy is still high since the randomly added words cannot completely separate all the words of one sentence. For example, if $X_k = \{x_i, i = 1{:}10\}$ is added to 9 items x_j $(j = 11{:}19)$. Unless the added items are added exactly between two consecutive items $[x_{i-1}, x_i]$, completely destroying the training sequence: $X^k_{test} = \{x_1, x_{11}, x_2, \cdots, x_i, x_{i+10}, x_{i+1}, \cdots, x_9, x_{19}, x_{10}\}$, otherwise, there are at least two consecutive items in X^k_{test}, which are enough to retrieve. In addition, most of the training sequences have more than ten items, most test sequences have at least two consecutive items, and the test C is high.

Table 6.3 The results of the local and global retrieval algorithm when inputting partial words.

Inputs	Retrieval results
X^6_{test}: no one	**1st predict sentence**: no one in the whole world could do (**local**)
	Full sentence (965): for i have been set to do a task which no one in the whole world could do (**global**)
	10th predict sentence: no one will trouble to take it away from there (**local**)
	Full sentence (6): no one will trouble to take it away from there (**global**)
X^{26}_{test}: i do not	**1st predict sentence**: i do not think it possible that the ring can have all the power you say it has (**local**)
	Full sentence (206): i do not think it possible that the ring can have all the power you say it has (**global**)
	5th predict sentence: i do not decide immediately on this important matter (**local**)
	Full sentence (174): if i do not decide immediately on this important matter (**global**)

6.2.3.2 The effect of network parameters on retrieval performance

In this section, the effect of network parameters on memory was tested, as shown in Table 6.4. Test sequences only provide the first three items of each training sequence. Only the test parameter changes, and the remaining parameters are default. For some parameters, e.g., $N = 4$, many populations repeatedly add the stack making the prediction impossible to end, so limiting each test sequence to predict 50 sentences at most.

For the number of minicolumns (M): The results show that the retrieval accuracy increases with the increase of M when $M \leq 512$, since the smaller M is, the more shared minicolumns between different items there are. These common minicolumns will intro-

Table 6.4 Retrieval accuracy of BSTM on the various parameters.

Column number M	256	300	400	512	768	1024
C (%)	98.4	98.8	99.1	99.8	99.7	99.8
Neuron number N	4	8	16	32	64	128
C (%)	55.4	80.0	92.3	97.6	99.8	99.9
Segment number D^{max}	1	5	10	20	30	40
C (%)	58.2	89.6	99.7	99.8	99.8	99.7
Context number Con^{max}	1	2	4	8	16	32
C (%)	99.9	99.8	99.8	98.5	95.5	87.9
Items' similarity C^{max}	0.2	0.3	0.4	**0.5**	0.7	1
C(%)	99.7	99.7	94.0	88.8	86.7	88.7

duce some noisy contexts during retrieval, resulting in decreased accuracy. For 1000 sequences with 1978 items, 512 minicolumns were enough to represent them.

For the number of neurons (N) on a minicolumn: Test accuracy improves as N increases, since storing the same sequences, fewer neurons will lead to more contexts associated with a neuron, more irrelevant contexts appear during retrieval, thus increasing the difficulty of retrieval and decreasing C.

For the maximum number of distal segments of a CA3 neuron (D^{max}): In previous experiments, there was no upper limit on the number of distal dendrites. In this experiment, D^{max} changes and the contexts without a distal segment to store are ignored. The results show that the accuracy increased as D^{max} increased when $D^{max} \leq 20$, since the smaller D^{max} is, the fewer contexts can be stored, and the lower C. When $D^{max} \geq 20$, the memory capacity is more than 1000 sentences, so the retrieval accuracy is not affected by D^{max}.

For the maximum number of contexts of a distal segment Con^{max}: The results show that C decreases as Con^{max} increases. Since a larger Con^{max} means more connections in a segment, this may cause more unexpected segments to become active and decrease the accuracy.

For the maximum similarity between two items C^{max}: The results show that the accuracy decreases as the C^{max} increases. The maximum similarity of the encoding combinations improves the accuracy but limits memory capacity.

6.2.3.3 Test memory capacity

The CBT has a total of 10 139 sentences with the number of words $\geqslant 10$. To test the memory capacity, the retrieval performance is explored by learning more sentences, from 1000 (1k) to 10 000 (10k) sentences in 1000 (1k) intervals. The number of minicolumns is 1024 with 128 neurons per minicolumn, and the other parameters are default values. Replace 0 to 9 words with 3 intervals from the training sentence to form a test sentence, and the results are shown in Table 6.5. Under the same network settings with different sentence lengths, the retrieval accuracy decreases slightly ($\leq$0.2%) with the increase in sentence number when replacing 0 to 6 words. However, after most of the items in a sequence were destroyed (replace 9 words), the accuracy of 10 000 sentences was significantly lower (6.2%) than that of 1000 sentences. As the number of sentences increases, so does the number of contexts. The more noisy items are added, the more noise contexts are in the following prediction, which leads to a decrease in accuracy. Notably, only 1024 minicolumns can express the information of 10 000 sentences and have good robustness.

Table 6.5 Retrieval accuracy of BSTM for various sentence numbers.

Sentence	1k	2k	3k	4k	5k	6k	7k	8k	9k	10k
replace 0	100	100	100	100	100	100	100	100	100	100
replace 3	100	100	99.9	100	99.9	100	100	100	100	100
replace 6	99.8	99.8	99.7	99.6	99.6	99.6	99.7	99.7	99.6	99.6
replace 9	80.0	78.8	77.1	76.3	75.6	75.1	74.9	74.6	74.0	73.8

6.2.3.4 Comparison with other algorithms

In this section, the BSTM is compared with other sequential memory algorithms LSTM [HS97], HTM [HAD+11], LUMAKG [BSH19], LSNN [BSS+18], and RNN+LIF [BSS+18]. 100 sequences drawn from CBT are used for training and testing, each of which contains 10 items. Replace 0–9 words of the training sentence to form a test sentence. The BSTM includes 512 minicolumns with 32 neurons in each minicolumn, as does the HTM. The LSTM and HTM settings are based on paper [SMH20], and the LSNN and RNN+LIF settings are based on paper [BSS+18]. There are three methods [Num16] to calculate the test accuracy of HTM: Cell Dist (method 1), Pred-Active FreqDist (method 2), and Active FreqDist (method 3).

Table 6.6 Results vary with the number of replacement words.

Method	Architecture	Epoch	Parameters	1	2	3	4	5	6	7	8	9
LSTM	32-800-100	1000	2 745 700	99.9	99.5	98.1	88.6	73.7	49.4	30.1	13.4	4.1
LUMAKG	425(32)	/	16 888	96.3	88.6	84.8	80.2	70.6	51.0	36.6	13.2	2.6
HTM^1	1000-512(32)	50	1 916 148	**100**	94.4	63.2	47.3	27.8	19.5	7.0	4.0	3.0
HTM^2	1000-512(32)	50	1 916 148	96.2	76.0	52.6	37.6	18.2	16.3	6.4	4.1	3.2
HTM^3	1000-512(32)	50	1 916 148	**100**	95.2	66.4	45.3	27.0	17.1	7.2	5.2	2.8
RNN+LIF	1000-620-100	1000	1 066 500	98.3	92.0	83.3	77.7	59.8	39.0	21.3	11.7	3.7
LSNN	1000-200^A+420^R-100	1000	127 980	98.7	98.3	93.5	86.8	66.3	54.0	30.7	15.7	4.0
BSTM	1000-512(32)-100	100+1	815 200	**100**	**100**	**100**	**100**	**100**	**100**	**98.2**	**88.2**	**9.6**

$M(N)$: M minicolumns, each of which contains N neurons; A: adaptive neurons; R: regular neurons; HTM^k: HTM with method k, $k = 1, 2, 3$.

The results in Table 6.6 show that the retrieval performance of the BSTM is obviously higher than other algorithms, although the BSTM model only learns the contexts once (1 epoch for the learning and 100 epochs for the encoding). Especially when replacing more than 4 words, the accuracy of the BSTM model is still very high and robust. However, the BSTM method uses more parameters than LUMAKG and LSNN. LUMAKG has the fewest parameters, since it only has one layer, just consisting of minicolumns and neurons on them. Each item is represented by a minicolumn, and there is no encoding layer to learn the representation of items, and no output layer. It only learns the connections between the minicolumns (items), similar to the learning of the distal dendrites of the CA3 layer. The LSNN is a sparse network connectivity structure with a global connectivity level of 12%, while the connections from the DG layer to the CA3 layer and from the CA3 layer to the CA1 layer in the BSTM model are all fully connected.

6.3 Columnar-structured model for temporal-sequential learning

Humans can memorize complex temporal sequences, such as music, indicating that the brain has a mechanism for storing time intervals between elements. However, most of the existing sequential memory models can only handle sequences that lack temporal information between elements, such as sentences. In [LLC+22], the authors proposed a Column-based Spatial-Temporal Memory (CSTM) model that can memorize sequences with variable time intervals. In the model, each column is composed of several spiking neurons that have the dendritic structure and the synaptic delays. Dendrites allow a neuron to represent the same element belonging to different contexts, while transmission delays between two spiking neurons preserve the time intervals between sequence elements. Moreover, the model can remember sequence information even after a single presentation of a new input sample, i.e., it is capable of one-shot learning.

6.3.1 Network design

The model consists of a spatiotemporal subnetwork and a goal cluster. The former can store both sequence elements and time intervals, avoiding the creation of additional subnets dedicated to memory time intervals like the Temporal-Sequential Learning (TSL) [LZX20]. The goal cluster contains a group of goal neurons, which makes sense just as the human brain stores title information.

6.3.1.1 Spatiotemporal subnetwork

Studies have shown that in different regions of the cerebral cortex neurons almost have the same arrangements – columnar structure, and neurons in a column share similar response properties [Shi07]. Simply, a complex biological column is abstracted into a column containing M identical neurons (Fig. 6.15(a)) that are sensitive to the same elements. Such N columns form the spatiotemporal subnetwork, as shown in the bottom of Fig. 6.15(d). Then, sequence memory is formed by establishing synaptic connections between these neurons. The concatenation of neurons represents the order of sequence elements, while the delay property of the connections represents the time intervals.

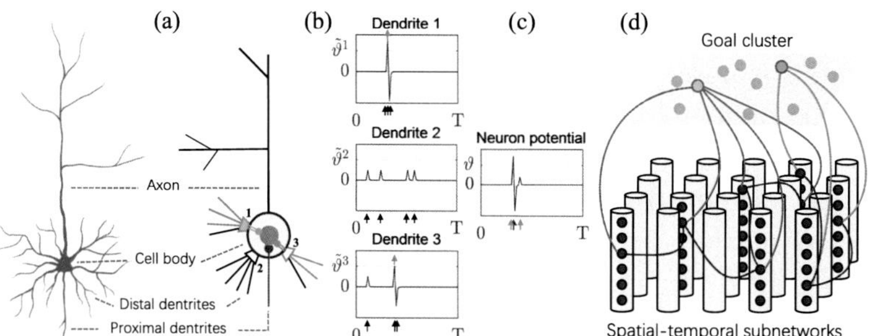

FIGURE 6.15 (a) Pyramidal cell (left) and the applied neuron model (right). The green lines represent synapses that are directly responsible for dendrite firing. (b) Dendritic potentials of the three distal dendrites in (a). (c) Neuronal Potential. The cell body of the neuron receives inputs from the proximal (red arrow) and distal dendrites (green arrow). (d) Schematic of network structure.

6.3.1.2 Goal cluster

The goal cluster contains many neurons, each representing the "title" or "label" of a specific sequence. During learning, bidirectional connections are established between the neurons in the spatiotemporal subnetwork and a goal neuron. A goal neuron can fire at the excitation of several (usually K) consecutively firing neurons of spatiotemporal subnetworks. Note that there is a mutual inhibition mechanism during a sequence retrieval to ensure that only one goal neuron fires. In turn, the firing goal neuron can activate the neurons in the spatiotemporal subnetwork to assist the sequence retrieval.

6.3.1.3 Spiking neuron model inspired by pyramidal cell

The spiking neuron model employed in the spatiotemporal subnetwork is inspired by the HTM cells [HAD$^+$11] and pyramidal cells that are widely present in the cerebral cortex [SL18], while the goal neuron is a simple non-leaky integrate-and-fire neuron, and for its calculation process we can refer to [WZCQ22,ZWW$^+$22]. Only the neurons in the spatiotemporal subnetwork are described here. As shown in Fig. 6.15(a), input from the lower layer is received through the proximal dendrite, which is usually strong enough to make the neuron fire. Lateral input from the same layer is transferred to the cell body through the integration of distal dendrites. The cell body, which receives input from both proximal and distal dendrites, fires when its potential reaches the threshold, and the neuron is considered to be truly activated. An activated neuron will send a spike through its axon, with horizontal branches going to neurons in the same layer and vertical branches going to neurons in a goal cluster.

Distal dendrites, as semi-independent information processing units, are dynamically established during learning. They receive spikes from other neurons in the same layer, and transmit a current to the cell body when their potentials cross the dendritic threshold, as shown in Fig. 6.15(a) and (b). The set of presynaptic neurons connected to the distal dendrite k is defined as $\Gamma_k = \{j | j \text{ presynaptic to } k\}$. s_j is the jth presynaptic spike, and d_j is the delay required for it to reach the dendrite (for ease of representation, the black arrow in Fig. 6.15(b) represents the delayed presynaptic spike). Then, the potential of the dendrite $\tilde{U}^k$ is:

$$\tilde{U}^k(t) = \tilde{\gamma} \cdot \tilde{U}^k(t - \Delta t) + \sum_{j \in \Gamma_k} \text{sign}(s_j(t - d_j)) - \tilde{\vartheta} \cdot \tilde{s}^k(t - \Delta t),$$
$$\tilde{s}^k(t) = \begin{cases} 1, & \text{if } \tilde{U}^k(t) \geq \tilde{\vartheta}, \\ 0, & \text{otherwise}, \end{cases} \tag{6.14}$$

where $\tilde{s}^k$ indicates whether the dendrite is activated. $\tilde{\gamma}$ $(= 0.3)$ is an attenuation coefficient of dendrite potentials and $\tilde{\vartheta}$ is the dendritic threshold.

The cell body receives input currents from its proximal dendrite ($\bar{I}$), distal dendrites ($\tilde{I}$), and goal cluster ($\hat{I}$). Suppose the set of distal dendrites is D, the set of goal neurons is G, then the potential of the cell body U is:

$$U(t) = \gamma U(t - \Delta t) + W_p \bar{I}(t) + W_d \sum_{k \in D} w^k \tilde{I}^k(t) + W_g \sum_{k \in G} \hat{I}^k(t) - \vartheta s(t - \Delta t),$$
$$s(t) = \begin{cases} U(t)/\vartheta, & \text{if } U(t) \geq \vartheta, \\ 0, & \text{otherwise}, \end{cases} \tag{6.15}$$

where $W_p > W_g > W_d$ shows the contribution of the three inputs to neuron firing. w^k is the weight of the kth distal dendrite. ϑ is the firing threshold of the cell body. s indicates whether the neuron is activated, and is different from the general spiking neuron that is either 0 or 1, it can represent the activation level of the neuron. γ $(= 0.3)$ is the potential attenuation coefficient. The current from the kth distal dendrite is positively related to its potential at the moment of excitation, i.e., $\tilde{I}^k(t) \propto \tilde{U}^k(t)$ $(\tilde{s}^k(t) = 1)$. For convenience of calculation, it is actually taken as equal to the potential. The cell body emits at most one spike in the time duration T (maximum time interval between adjacent elements).

6.3.2 Learning and retrieval

In the process of learning, the model learns the sequence elements one by one. Under the co-excitation of the proximal input and the distal input, within period T, a certain neuron is fired by competing to become the winner. Then, lateral connections are established between the winner and other historical winners, bidirectional connections with the corresponding goal neuron are also created.

6.3.2.1 Choice of winner

When an element is injected as the proximal input into all neurons of the column that favors it, the one with the strongest activation becomes the winner, thereby inhibiting other neurons from firing. The key to winning is that there is a distal dendrite that receives spikes from the historically winning neuron, then emits a dendritic spike just as the proximal input arrives. Therefore according to Eq. (6.15), the firing potential of this neuron will be larger than other neurons without a dendritic spike, thus it fires a larger spike. If there is more than one neuron firing with the largest spike (including the case where all the neurons in the column have no distal dendrites, for example, when the network has just been initialized), then a random one among these neurons with the fewest distal dendrites wins. W is a dynamic set of historically winning neurons, containing up to K neurons that fired recently. The neurons with the earliest firing time will be removed from the set when a new winner joins.

6.3.2.2 Establishment of connections

Lateral connections on distal dendrites link sequence elements, i.e., the keys to forming memories. Initially, the network is empty and no lateral connections exist, which means that each neuron in the spatiotemporal subnetwork has only one proximal dendrite. As learning progresses, the winning neurons form/update distal dendrites, on which they make lateral connections with other neurons.

- When a distal dendrite of the winner contributes directly to its firing, that is, the timing of the dendritic spike coincides with the timing of the proximal dendrite input, the distal dendrite is "selected" (dendrite 1 in Fig. 6.15(a), (b)). If its number of valid synapses (that contribute directly to its firing) is less than K, new connections are created on it from neurons in W that have not been connected before.
- When the neuron has no distal dendrites, or its distal dendrites do not transmit any valid spikes (an invalid spike is like the spike of dendrite 3 in Fig. 6.15), it fires only through the stimulation of its proximal dendrite. Then, a new distal dendrite is established, on which K synaptic connections are created with the historical winner neurons in W.

A synapse on a distal dendrite has two properties: permanence p and delay d. For newly established synapses, $p = 0.5$ and $d = t_{post} - t_{pre}$, where t_{post} and t_{pre} are the firing times of the pre- and postsynaptic neurons, respectively. For selected dendrites, the valid synapses (green synapses in dendrite 1) will be enhanced: $p \leftarrow p + 0.02$, and other synapses (black synapse in dendrite 1) will be weakened: $p \leftarrow p - 0.02$. When $p = 0$, the synapse disappears. In addition, the dendrite's weight w^k is equal to $1/n^k$, where n^k is the number of synapses on this dendrite, but when $n^k > K$, $w^k = 1/K$.

Bidirectional connections with the goal neurons are divided into the feedforward connections to it and the feedback connections from it. All feedforward connections are fixed with a weight of $1/K$ and no delay. All feedback connections have a weight of 1, and the delay is equal to the difference in firing time between the winner and the goal neuron.

6.3.2.3 Learning process of a sequence

A simple sequence is used to describe the learning process from an empty network: *G1: {B, 270 ms, A, 330 ms, D, 230 ms, C}*, where *G1* is the goal, as shown in Fig. 6.16. During learning, the threshold ϑ is equal to W_p, which ensures that neurons can fire even with only proximal input stimuli.

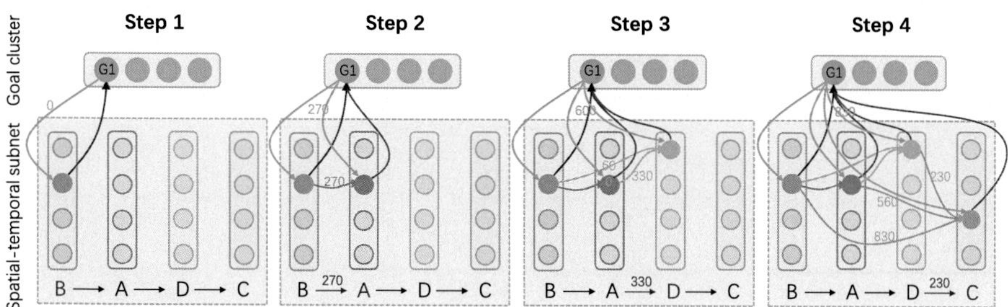

FIGURE 6.16 The process of storing sequence *G1: {B, 270 ms, A, 330 ms, D, 230 ms, C}* begins with an empty network. Lines represent synaptic connections, and numbers on them represent synaptic delays.

- **Step 1:** The neuron *G1* in the goal cluster is first stimulated and fired immediately at time 0. At the same time, neurons in the column preferring *B* in the spatiotemporal subnetwork are excited by the proximal input, one of which wins by competing. Next, this neuron extends a feedforward connection to the goal neuron *G1*, which can be regarded as a synapse on the vertical branch of the neuron's axon. *G1* also extends a feedback connection to this neuron.
- **Step 2:** After 270 ms, a neuron in the column preferring *A* fires upon stimulation of *A*, becoming the winner. This winner not only connects with *G1*, but also generates a distal dendrite, on which a synapse is established with the previous winner. As stated above, the newly created synapse on the distal dendrite has an initial permanence of 0.5, and the delay is equal to the difference between the firing time of the presynaptic neuron and the postsynaptic neuron, i.e., 270 ms.
- **Step 3:** Likewise, after another 330 ms, one neuron in the *D*-preferring column fires at 600 ms and becomes the new winner. Connections with *G1* are established, and a distal dendrite is generated, on which synaptic connections to the previous two winners are built.
- **Step 4:** At 830 ms, one neuron in the *C*-preferring column fires. The same connections are generated, but there are 3 connections on its newly generated distal dendrites. In fact, connections will be established with all neurons in W, i.e., the most recent K winners.

The operation of storing a new sequence in a non-empty network is similar to the above procedure, the difference is that some synapses will be created on the existing dendrites instead of creating a new dendrite each time.

6.3.2.4 Retrieval

When we hear a short piece of music we have heard before, even if we do not know the name, it is still possible to recall what followed (without the guidance of the goal). If we recall the music's name, then we are likely to recall the full piece from beginning to end (with the guidance of the goal). In TSL, the latter is called context-based retrieval, while the goal-based retrieval is retrieval based on a given target information. However, both actually

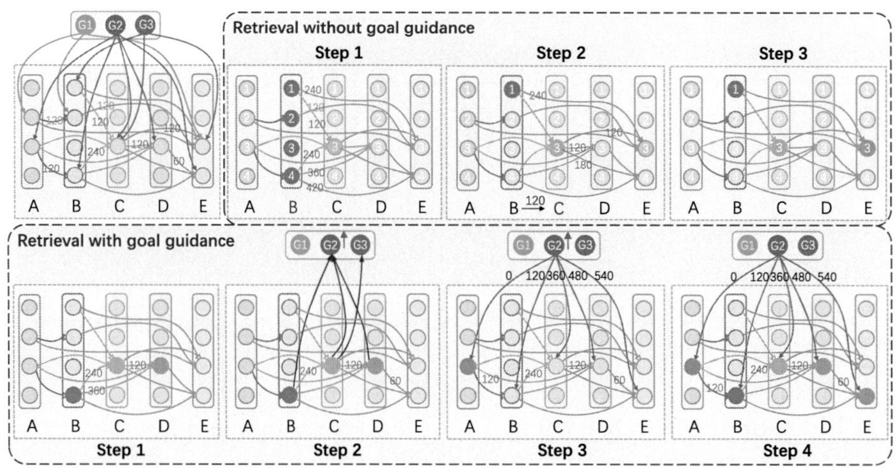

FIGURE 6.17 Retrieval (without the goal) with input *{B, 120 ms, C}*, and retrieval (with the goal) with input *{B, 240 ms, C, 120 ms}* in a network that stores three sequences (upper left). Some connections are not drawn.

depend on the goal. Here, we describe how to retrieve with or without goal information, simulating the way the human brain recalls.

It was mentioned earlier that when there are proximal inputs in the network, the threshold is equal to W_p. However, when there is no proximal input, neurons cannot reach this threshold. Hence, an adaptive threshold is needed. That is, if there is a goal information, the threshold drops below W_g to ensure that the goal information can make the neurons fire. If the network contains neither proximal input nor goal information, the threshold drops below W_d so that neurons can fire when they get enough distal input. Three sequences are stored in a network: *G1: {A, 120 ms, B, 120 ms, E}*, *G2: {A, 120 ms, B, 240 ms, C, 120 ms, D, 60 ms, E}*, *G3: {B, 120 ms, C, 120 ms, E}*, as shown in the upper-left corner of Fig. 6.17. Then, two retrieval processes are described based on the network.

A. Retrieval without the guidance of the goal: In this case, except for the initial few hints (in this example, there are *{B, 120 ms, C}*), there is no proximal input and feedback input in the subsequent retrieval process.

- **Step 1:** Upon input of element *B*, all neurons in the column favoring *B* fire at 0 ms on the stimulus of the proximal input. Unlike when learning, these neurons are all winners, they transmit their spikes to other neurons (C3, D3, E3, E4).
- **Step 2:** After 120 ms, *C* is input. The temporal coupling of proximal and distal inputs prompts C3 to fire a large spike at 120 ms. In contrast, D3, E3, and E4 have no proximal inputs, and inputs from distal dendrites are either not yet reached or insufficient to fire them. C3 becomes the winner. Its direct contributor B1 is the historical winner, and the other neurons in B are no longer winners because they have no firing postsynaptic neurons.

- **Step 3:** With no proximal input, one of the distal dendrites of E3, receives spikes from B1 and C3 at the same time and fires at 240 ms, thereby activating E3 (winner), while neither D3 nor E4 received enough spikes to fire. Then, the retrieval is terminated because E3 has no postsynaptic neuron.

When there is no proximal input, the detection of the next element is completely dependent on the history element. If multiple neurons fire due to the distal input, the one with the largest spike wins. If there is more than one such neuron, they all transmit spikes down, resulting in more than one sequence being detected.

B. Retrieval with the guidance of the goal: Retrieval without target guidance can only recall the following elements. Goal information is necessary if we want to recall elements prior to the given hints (here, there are *{B, 240 ms, C, 120 ms}*):

- **Step 1:** When these cues are input, context-based retrieval is conducted first, and neurons B4, C3, and D3 fire in sequence, and they transmit their own spikes to the goal neurons connected to them.
- **Step 2:** G2 fires after receiving three spikes from the spatiotemporal subnetwork, while G3 fails to fire due to insufficient excitation. Then, G2 inhibits all other goal neurons, and dominates the subsequent retrieval.
- **Step 3:** After G2 fires, A3 fires immediately via the delay-free connection from G2.
- **Step 4:** B4 fires under the combined excitation of the goal and A3. Similarly, C3, D3, and E4 are also excited successively.

6.3.3 Applications and results

The model performance is validated on a MIDI dataset containing 331 classic piano pieces [Kru]. Each piece consists of two tracks, each containing hundreds to thousands of notes. One spatiotemporal subnetwork is built for each track, and each subnetwork contains 89 columns (50 neurons per column), corresponding to the 88 standard pitches of piano keys (MIDI numbers $21-108$) and 1 terminator. The extra terminator is to make sure the duration of the last note of the piece is remembered, whereas TSL only has 88 columns because its duration is remembered with another subnet. Note that durations are mapped to $0-64$ ms (i.e., $T=64$), corresponding to the tick number in MIDI from a demisemiquaver to two semibreves. In the following two retrieval experiments, the number of historically winning neurons $K=15$, the dendrite firing threshold $\tilde{\vartheta}=1.0$.

6.3.3.1 Goal-based retrieval

25 pieces randomly selected from the dataset and another 25 pieces identical to those in TSL, totaling 50 pieces, are used for goal-based retrieval. The task is to retrieve the first 100 notes given a melody name. A note is considered to be correctly detected when both the note and its duration are correctly detected. Fig. 6.18(a) shows the retrieval accuracy. It can be seen that the proposed method can completely retrieve the first 100 notes of each melody, which outperforms TSL. In fact, instead of recalling the first 100 elements, the model executed freely until a terminator was encountered, and it turned out that the

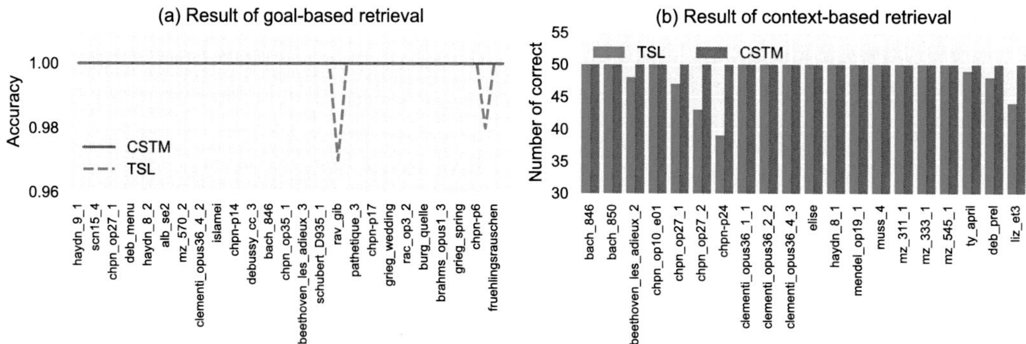

FIGURE 6.18 The retrieval accuracy of goal-based retrieval (a) and the correct number of notes in context-based retrieval (b). The results of TSL are derived from [LZX20].

model can recall all elements of the test set with 100% accuracy. Fig. 6.19 shows the retrieval results of a sequence.

6.3.3.2 *Context-based retrieval*

The same 20 pieces as in TSL are selected for context-based retrieval. The task is to retrieve the remaining 50 notes and the name of the piece from the given short episode (10 consecutive notes with duration). Both this model and TSL can retrieve the names of all the melodies. Fig. 6.18(b) shows the number of correctly retrieved notes for each piece. This model can detect all the 50 notes of each test piece, which is significantly better than TSL.

6.3.3.3 *Parameter influence*

It is natural that the retrieval accuracy will decrease as the number of input elements increases. However, how do different parameters that affect this descent process need to be verified? The influence of the dendritic activation threshold $\tilde{\vartheta}$ and the number of historical winning neurons K is analyzed experimentally. The former determines the condition under which dendrites may be reused, and the latter determines how dependent an el-

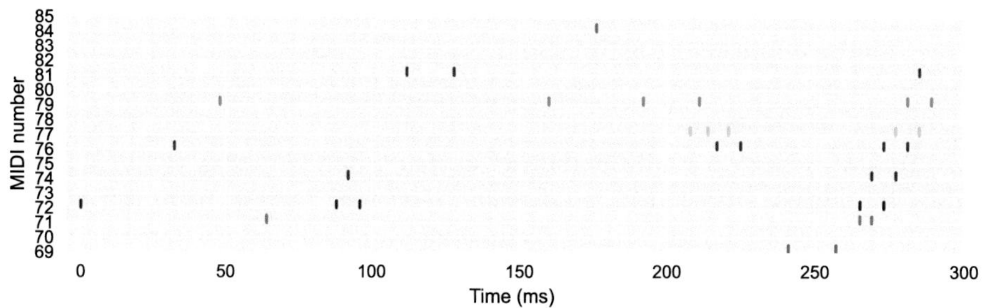

FIGURE 6.19 The retrieval result of the track 1 of Mozart's Sonata No. 16 in C Maior, KV 545 (a segment). Vertical bars represent spikes fired by neurons in the corresponding columns.

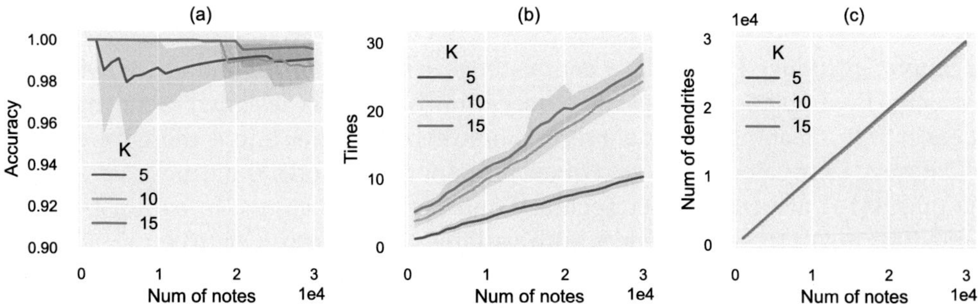

FIGURE 6.20 The retrieval accuracy, the retrieval time (s) per 1000 elements and the number of dendrites with the increase of the input number when $\tilde{\vartheta} = 2.0$.

ement is on its context. In this section, experiments are conducted under more difficult conditions, relying solely on context and not guided by the goal. Tests were performed every 1000 elements presented. 10 independent trials were repeated for each experimental condition, and the mean and standard deviation were reported.

A larger dendritic threshold means that dendrites are less likely to be activated in another sequence and thus be reused. This makes almost all dendrites dedicated to only one particular sequence. Therefore extremely high accuracy is achieved at the cost of a huge number of dendrites, as shown in Fig. 6.20.

A smaller dendrite threshold leads to increased dendrite reuse, but it also leads to lower retrieval accuracy. However, the increase of K will weaken this decline in retrieval accuracy, as shown in Fig. 6.21, because each element depends on more contextual information. The increase of K does not necessarily mean longer computing time, sometimes a smaller K will consume more time due to failed retrieval (Fig. 6.21(b)). Then, it was found that $\tilde{\vartheta} = 1.0$, $K = 15$ is a good choice for balancing retrieval accuracy and computation time.

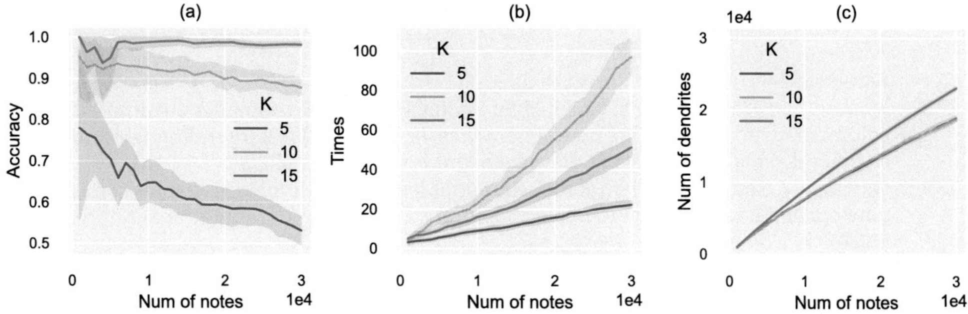

FIGURE 6.21 The retrieval accuracy, the retrieval time (s) per 1000 elements and the number of dendrites with the increase of the input number when $\tilde{\vartheta} = 1.0$.

6.4 Conclusion

This chapter introduced two spiking neural network models, BSTM and CSTM, which were constructed by simulating biological neural columns. BSTM is designed for the memory of sequences with meaningless time intervals between elements, and is therefore tested on CBT datasets. Compared to other sequence memory methods, the experimental results show that BSTM achieves higher accuracy and better robustness. In contrast, CSTM is designed for memorizing sequences with variable time intervals between elements. Experimental results demonstrate that it can memorize complex temporal sequences like musical pieces, and recall the entire sequence with high accuracy, given an extremely short sub-sequence. The significance of these two models is not only in their superiority to comparable methods, but also in providing reference for the development of neuromorphic memory systems.

References

[BBS+11] Francesco P. Battaglia, Karim Benchenane, Anton Sirota, Cyriel M.A. Pennartz, Sidney I. Wiener, The hippocampus: hub of brain network communication for memory, Trends in Cognitive Sciences 15 (7) (2011) 310–318.

[BP98] Guo-qiang Bi, Mu-ming Poo, Synaptic modifications in cultured hippocampal neurons: dependence on spike timing, synaptic strength, and postsynaptic cell type, Journal of Neuroscience 18 (24) (1998) 10464–10472.

[BSH19] Basawaraj, Janusz A. Starzyk, Adrian Horzyk, Episodic memory in minicolumn associative knowledge graphs, IEEE Transactions on Neural Networks and Learning Systems 30 (11) (2019) 3505–3516.

[BSS+18] Guillaume Bellec, Darjan Salaj, Anand Subramoney, Robert Legenstein, Wolfgang Maass, Long short-term memory and learning-to-learn in networks of spiking neurons, Advances in Neural Information Processing Systems 31 (2018).

[CAH16] Yuwei Cui, Subutai Ahmad, Jeff Hawkins, Continuous online sequence learning with an unsupervised neural network model, Neural Computation 28 (11) (2016) 2474–2504.

[HAD+11] Jeff Hawkins, Subutai Ahmad, Donna Dubinsky, et al., Cortical learning algorithm and hierarchical temporal memory, Numenta Whitepaper 1 (2011) 68.

[Haw21] Jeff Hawkins, A Thousand Brains: a New Theory of Intelligence, Basic Books, New York, 2021.

[HS97] Sepp Hochreiter, Jürgen Schmidhuber, Long short-term memory, Neural Computation 9 (8) (1997) 1735–1780.

[JTG03] Renaud Jolivet, J. Timothy, Wulfram Gerstner, The spike response model: a framework to predict neuronal spike trains, in: ICONIP2003: Artificial Neural Networks & Neural Information Processing, vol. 2714, 2003.

[Kru] Bernd Krueger, Classical piano midi page.

[LLC+22] Xiaoling Luo, Hanwen Liu, Yi Chen, Malu Zhang, Hong Qu, Temporal-sequential learning with columnar-structured spiking neural networks, in: ICONIP 2022: International Conference on Neural Information Processing, New Delhi, India, vol. 1791, 2022, pp. 153–164.

[LZX20] Q. Liang, Y. Zeng, B. Xu, Temporal-sequential learning with a brain-inspired spiking neural network and its application to musical memory, Frontiers in Computational Neuroscience 14 (2020).

[MEFG01] M. Megıas, Z.S. Emri, T.F. Freund, A.I. Gulyas, Total number and distribution of inhibitory and excitatory synapses on hippocampal ca1 pyramidal cells, Neuroscience 102 (3) (2001) 527–540.

[MHCJ98] Jeffrey Magee, Dax Hoffman, Costa Colbert, Daniel Johnston, Electrical and calcium signaling in dendrites of hippocampal pyramidal neurons, Annual Review of Physiology 60 (1) (1998) 327–346.

[Num16] Numenta, Inc., Numenta platform for intelligent computing, https://programtalk.com/vs2/?source=python/9411/nupic.research/projects/sequence_classification/run_sequence_classifcation_experiment.py, 2016.

[Shi07] S. Shipp, Structure and function of the cerebral cortex, Current Biology 17 (12) (2007) R443–R449.

[SL18] I. Soltesz, A. Losonczy, Ca1 pyramidal cell diversity enabling parallel information processing in the hippocampus, Nature Neuroscience 21 (4) (2018) 484–493.

[SMH20] Janusz A. Starzyk, Lukasz Maciura, Adrian Horzyk, Associative memories with synaptic delays, IEEE Transactions on Neural Networks and Learning Systems 31 (1) (2020) 331–344.

[SSC+17] Qian Sun, Alaba Sotayo, Alejandro S. Cazzulino, Anna M. Snyder, Christine A. Denny, Steven A. Siegelbaum, Proximodistal heterogeneity of hippocampal ca3 pyramidal neuron intrinsic properties, connectivity, and reactivation during memory recall, Neuron 95 (3) (2017) 656–672.

[UKJ+20] Gray Umbach, Pranish Kantak, Joshua Jacobs, Michael Kahana, Brad E. Pfeiffer, Michael Sperling, Bradley Lega, Time cells in the human hippocampus and entorhinal cortex support episodic memory, Proceedings of the National Academy of Sciences 117 (45) (2020) 28463–28474.

[WZCQ22] Yuchen Wang, Malu Zhang, Yi Chen, Hong Qu, Signed neuron with memory: towards simple, accurate and high-efficient ann-snn conversion, in: Proceedings of the Thirty-First International Joint Conference on Artificial Intelligence, 2022, pp. 2501–2508.

[ZCZ+22] Yun Zhang, Yi Chen, Jilun Zhang, Xiaoling Luo, Malu Zhang, Hong Qu, Zhang Yi, Minicolumn-based episodic memory model with spiking neurons, dendrites and delays, IEEE Transactions on Neural Networks and Learning Systems (2022) 1–15.

[ZQL+21] Yun Zhang, Hong Qu, Xiaoling Luo, Yi Chen, Yuchen Wang, Malu Zhang, Zefang Li, A new recursive least squares-based learning algorithm for spiking neurons, Neural Networks 138 (2021) 110–125.

[ZWW+22] Malu Zhang, Jiadong Wang, Jibin Wu, Ammar Belatreche, Burin Amornpaisannon, Zhixuan Zhang, Venkata Pavan Kumar Miriyala, Hong Qu, Yansong Chua, Trevor E. Carlson, Haizhou Li, Rectified linear postsynaptic potential function for backpropagation in deep spiking neural networks, IEEE Transactions on Neural Networks and Learning Systems 33 (5) (2022) 1947–1958.

7

An ANN–SNN algorithm suitable for ultra energy efficient image classification

7.1 Preface

At present, there are two promising SNN training approaches, which are direct training SNNs from scratch and ANN–SNN conversion. Direct training SNNs need to tackle the problem of non-differentiable binary activation function; popular methods are training SNNs with the surrogate gradient [WDL$^+$18,NMZ19] and synaptic plasticity [KGTM18]. However, their training procedure requires tremendous resources and suffers from unsatisfactory accuracy. ANN–SNN conversion methods directly map the parameters of a pre-trained ANN to SNN with the same structure [DNB$^+$15,RLH$^+$17]. These methods not only bypass the non-differentiable issue of the spike activity but also save training time and resources compared with the direct training rules. Therefore ANN–SNN conversion methods are promising to train large-scale SNNs. Although ANN–SNN conversion has made some progress, all the up-to-date methods are still much less mature, and the limited time steps (<256) will result in a marked accuracy drop. As a consequence, the existing converted SNNs need thousands of inference time steps to reach the level of ANNs in terms of accuracy, leading to the power consumption and latency of SNNs being higher than ANNs in applications. We believe that there are still covert errors in the conversion process that have not been discovered.

In this chapter, we explore two intractable problems to achieve near-loss-less ultra-low-latency ANN–SNN conversion. In particular, we meticulously analyze the difference between SNNs and ANNs, then find that the asynchronous transmission characteristic of SNNs causes conversion error, and the information loss after parameter normalization results in long SNN inference latency. We introduce optimal solutions and yield a conversion model that enables high accuracy and low latency. Experimental results on benchmark datasets show that the model is better than existing state-of-the-art models in terms of accuracy and latency.

7.2 Convert pre-trained ANNs to SNNs

As a basic background, we first introduce the forward propagation process of ANNs and SNNs, and then briefly explain how ANNs are converted to SNNs in general.

7.2.1 Forward propagation of ANN

For an ANN of L layers, we can describe the activation values in layer $l(1 \leqslant l \leqslant L)$ as

$$\mathbf{a}^l = f(W^l \mathbf{a}^{l-1} + b^l), \tag{7.1}$$

where $f(x)$ is the activation function. W^l and b^l denote the weight parameters and bias parameters in layer l. The most commonly used activation function is Rectified Linear Unit (ReLU) activation, i.e., $f(x) = \max(0, x)$.

7.2.2 Forward propagation of SNN

The ReLU activation function is typically used in a large number of deep neural networks at present. Fortunately, the functional relationship between Integrate-Fire (IF) neurons input and output is similar to ReLU. The membrane potential $v_j^l(t)$ of IF neuron j in layer l at time step t is described by:

$$\tilde{v}_j^l(t) = v_j^l(t-1) + \sum_i w_{ij} s_i^{l-1}(t) + b_j, \tag{7.2}$$

$$s_j^l(t) = \begin{cases} 1 & \tilde{v}_j^l(t) \geq \theta_j^l \\ 0 & \text{otherwise} \end{cases}, \tag{7.3}$$

$$v_j^l(t) = (1 - s_j^l(t))\tilde{v}_j^l(t) + s_j^l(t) v_{\text{rest}}, \tag{7.4}$$

where s_i^{l-1} is the spike from presynaptic neuron i and v_{rest} donates the resting potential. When $\tilde{v}_j^l(t)$ exceeds the firing threshold θ_j^l, neuron j will send a spike $s_j^l(t)$ to its postsynaptic neuron. In terms of the hard-reset neuron, the membrane potential will immediately return to the resting potential after firing a spike. Therefore hard-reset neurons ignore residual potential at firing instants, resulting in an accuracy drop for the converted SNN. Soft-reset neurons avoid the above problem and are widely used in various models. For soft-reset neurons, Eq. (7.4) is described as:

$$v_j^l(t) = \tilde{v}_j^l(t) - s_j^l(t). \tag{7.5}$$

In this case, the soft-reset neuron will not return to the resting potential after firing a spike, but maintains the residual potential above the firing threshold.

7.2.3 Converting ANNs to SNNs

According to the calculation of spiking neuron output rate, an SNN can meet the accuracy of an ANN only if there are plenty of time steps [LDD+21]. However, this will cause the converted SNN to have more power consumption than the ANN. Since the output rate of IF neurons cannot exceed 1, which requires the output range of ReLU function to be [0, 1], it is required to transform the parameters of an ANN. To address this problem, the well-known layer-wise parameter normalization (called LayerNorm for convenience) [RLH+17] rescales all parameters by the maximum output value λ^l of layer l as follows:

$$W^l = W^l \frac{\lambda^{l-1}}{\lambda^l}, \quad b^l = \frac{b^l}{\lambda^l}. \tag{7.6}$$

Parameter normalization is equivalent to transmitting the threshold value in SNN [LDD+21]. Since the firing rate of neurons in SNN cannot exceed 1, the firing threshold can be set to the maximum activation value of ANN. Hence, Eq. (7.6) is also equivalent to directly modifying the firing threshold and spike value; take the soft-reset neuron as an example:

$$\theta_j^l = \lambda^l, \quad s_j^l(t) = \begin{cases} \theta_j^l, & v_j^l(t) \geq \theta_j^l, \\ 0, & \text{otherwise}. \end{cases} \tag{7.7}$$

After replacing the neurons of ANN with soft-reset neurons, and setting the firing threshold of soft-reset neurons to the maximum activation value of their corresponding layer, a pre-trained ANN is transformed into an SNN that can be used directly. As for the input of an SNN, it can be regarded as the input current of the spiking neurons, so no additional encoding is performed.

7.3 ANN–SNN conversion with signed neuron with memory

In this section, we first analyze the covert conversion error caused by asynchronous spikes. Then, we introduce the new model named *Signed Neuron with Memory (SNM)*, which can solve this problem.

7.3.1 Error analysis

In an ANN, one neuron will add the input simultaneously to get an activation value. However, in an SNN, since spikes may be scattered at any time steps along the time axis, the output rate of neurons may have unexpected variation. This problem can be summarized as: improper handling of the late arrival of spikes transmitted by negative weights leads to a higher output rate of spiking neurons, which makes ANNs and converted SNNs unable to correspond. Let us explain through the examples in Fig. 7.1.

Assuming that input data are $x_1 = 3$ and $x_2 = 2$, the example in the first row is that when corresponding weights $w_1 = 1$, $w_2 = -1$, the output of the ANN neuron is 1. The example in the second row is that when corresponding weights $w_1 = -1$, $w_2 = 1$, the output of the ANN neuron is 0. According to rate-based encoding, which encodes the data into a proportional number of spikes, we can assume that x_1 corresponds to three spikes and x_2 corresponds to two spikes. In addition, the resting potential of the IF neuron is 0, and the firing threshold is 1.

Output spikes of neurons in a deep SNN may show various distributions on the time axis. We analyze two special cases, i.e., the early arrival or late arrival of spikes transmitted by the negative weight, which correspond to column two and column three in Fig. 7.1. For

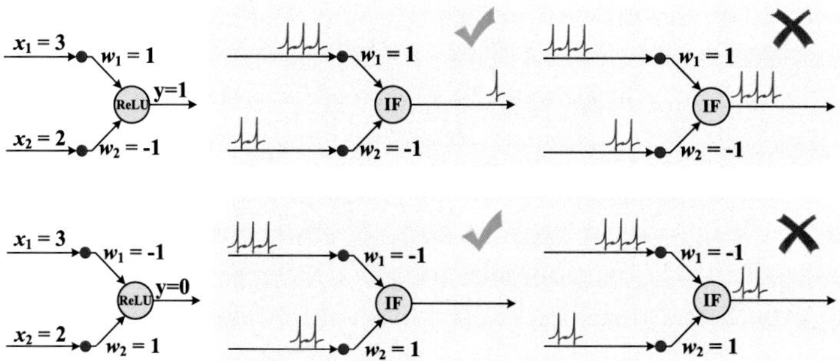

FIGURE 7.1 Explanation of an SNN asynchronous transmission information error. This occurs when spikes input from the negative synapses arrive too late, which leads to a higher neuron output rate.

column two, when spikes transmitted by the negative weight arrive first, the neuron output rate can correspond to the output of the ANN neuron. However, when spikes transmitted by the positive weight arrive first, the neuron will fire immediately, causing a high output rate. For the SNN using rate-based encoding, although we can control the distribution of input spikes, the distribution of output spikes in hidden layers cannot be controlled, making the above error unavoidable.

7.3.2 The solution: signed neuron with memory

If all spikes are evenly distributed on the time axis, or the spikes transmitted by the negative synapse always reach the postsynaptic neurons earlier, then the above problem can be avoided. From this, it is easy to see that in hidden layers, we can shift all spikes to the first few time steps, or place spikes on equidistant time steps to make them evenly distributed. However, the consequence is that we have to wait to ensure that all possible spikes of layer l are triggered before sending the spike trains to layer $l+1$. In other words, the network only has the synchronous transmission ability.

The neuron model SNM (Section 3.4) was designed to address the above problem. The negative spike of an SNM can enable an SNN to maintain both asynchronous transmission and synchronous transmission capabilities, while effectively solving the problem of an excessively high output rate. Also, usage of the "memory mechanism" ensures that an SNM remembers the sum of its transmitted spikes (positive and negative spikes can be offset). Only when the memory value is greater than zero can negative spikes be transmitted to the next layer. By this means, the dynamic of SNM neurons (described by Eqs. (3.6)–(3.10)) are rewritten as:

$$\tilde{v}_j^l(t) = v_j^l(t-1) + \sum_i w_{ij} s_i^{l-1}(t) + b_j, \tag{7.8}$$

$$\tilde{m}_j^l(t) = m_j^l(t-1), \tag{7.9}$$

$$s_j^l(t) = \begin{cases} \theta_j^l, & \tilde{v}_j^l(t) \geq \theta_j^l, \\ -\theta_j^l, & \tilde{v}_j^l(t) \leq -\theta_j^l \quad \text{and} \quad \tilde{m}_j^l(t) > 0, \\ 0, & \text{otherwise}, \end{cases} \tag{7.10}$$

$$v_j^l(t) = \tilde{v}_j^l(t) - s_j^l(t), \tag{7.11}$$

$$m_j^l(t) = \tilde{m}_j^l(t) + s_j^l(t), \tag{7.12}$$

where m_j^l is the memory value of neuron j in layer l.

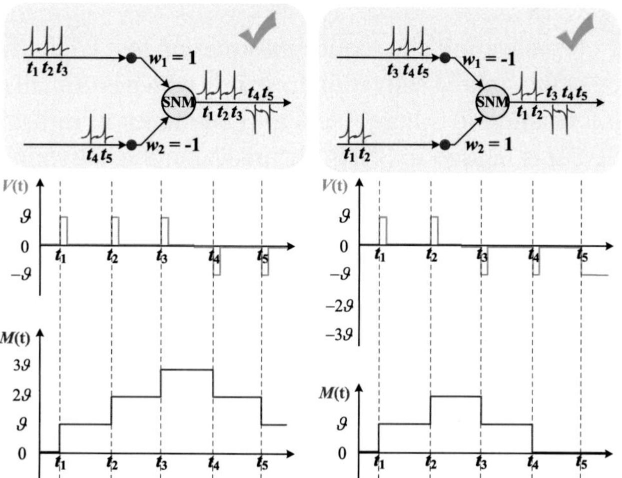

FIGURE 7.2 Exemplification of signed neuron with memory. $V(t)$ represents the membrane potential of the SNM neuron at t, and $M(t)$ represents the memory value of the SNM neuron at t, which equals the sum of currently transmitted spikes.

Let us illustrate the SNM through Fig. 7.2. The examples in green and purple boxes, respectively, correspond to the error conditions of the same color box in Fig. 7.1. For the example in the green box, three spikes are input to an SNM neuron from synapse w_1 at t_1, t_2, and t_3 respectively. At t_3, the neuron membrane potential is 0, and the memory value is 3θ, which is the number of all spikes that have been transmitted. At t_4, the SNM will emit a negative spike since its membrane potential is less than $-\theta$ and the memory value is greater than 0. The same is true at t_5. For the example in the purple box, two spikes input to an SNM neuron from w_2 cause the memory value larger than 0 at t_3, so the SNM can fire a negative spike at t_3. However, the negative spikes fire at t_3 and t_4 cause the memory value to drop to 0, then even if the membrane potential at t_5 is lower than the negative threshold again, it cannot fire a negative spike.

Through the above exemplification, it can be said that the output rate of an SNM is equal to its memory value. An ordinary signed neuron brings new problems, i.e., if more negative spikes are transmitted than positive spikes, then the output rate of a signed neuron is negative, which contradicts the ReLU function. However, SNM can ensure that the firing frequency will not be lower than 0 due to the existence of memory.

7.4 Neuron-wise normalization

In this section, we first show that layer-wise normalization suffers from huge information loss during ANN–SNN conversion, which causes the long inference latency of an SNN. Then, we introduce an optimal solution: neuron-wise normalization.

7.4.1 Problem of long inference latency

A proper parameter normalization can reduce information loss when the ReLU activation function is converted to the spiking activation function, which is critical to shortening SNN inference latency. Information loss here refers to the amount of information that can be transmitted in ANNs but is missed in SNNs. By analyzing the activation value of the first convolutional layer, Rueckauer et al. [RLH+17] made a point that setting a normal scale to the maximum activation value λ^l of an ANN layer l (layer-wise normalization, abbreviated as LayerNorm) results in low firing rates. However, this operation comes with the problem of long inference latency.

A large number of activation values in an ANN are far below the maximum activation value [RLH+17]. Regrettably, the transmission of small values by an SNN requires a longer simulation length. For example, assume the maximum activation value λ of an ANN's input layer is 10, so the firing threshold of neurons in an SNN's input layer will be set to 10. When the input to neuron i of the input layer is 0.01, then T must be greater than or equal to 1000 for neuron i to fire a spike (0.01 accumulated T times). Obviously, a smaller value requires a longer T to transmit, so the limited simulation length will cause a lot of data loss. A simple solution is to add a coefficient α ($\alpha \in [0, 1]$) to the maximum activation value λ before setting a threshold. Lowering the threshold can retain more small data, but fails to distinguish larger data, because the neuron output rate will always equal 1 when the input is greater than $\alpha\lambda$.

In summary, there are two factors that affect the information loss, which are the coefficient α of the maximum activation value λ and the simulation length T. For a given α and T, we formulate the missing information of layer l as:

$$Loss^l = \sum_c^C \sum_w^W \sum_h^H x^l_{c,w,h}, \tag{7.13}$$

$$x^l_{c,w,h} = \begin{cases} a^l_{c,w,h}, & 0 < a^l_{c,w,h} < \frac{\alpha\lambda^l}{T}, \\ a^l_{c,w,h} - \alpha\lambda^l, & a^l_{c,w,h} > \alpha\lambda^l, \\ 0, & \text{otherwise}, \end{cases} \tag{7.14}$$

where, $a^l_{c,w,h}$ is the activation value of the neuron located at (w, h) in channel c of layer l. Obviously, a larger T will result in fewer losses, this is why converted SNNs using layer normalization usually requires T greater than 1024.

7.4.2 The solution: neuron-wise normalization

Many existing works focus on how to select optimal normalization scale [KPNY20,LDD+21, DYTH21,WZCQ22], among which neuron-wise normalization (NeuronNorm) [WZCQ22] is a simple and efficient method. In NeuronNorm, the maximum activation value of each neuron in ANN is recorded separately as the firing threshold of corresponding spiking neurons. Since the maximum activation values of different neurons in the same layer are relatively independent, the amount of information loss is greatly reduced. Therefore Eq. (7.6) should be rewritten as:

$$W^l_{ij} = W^l_{ij}\frac{\lambda^{l-1}_i}{\lambda^l_j}, \quad b^l_j = \frac{b^l_j}{\lambda^l_j}, \tag{7.15}$$

where λ^{l-1}_i represents the maximum activation value of presynaptic neuron i and λ^l_j represents the maximum activation value of postsynaptic neuron j.

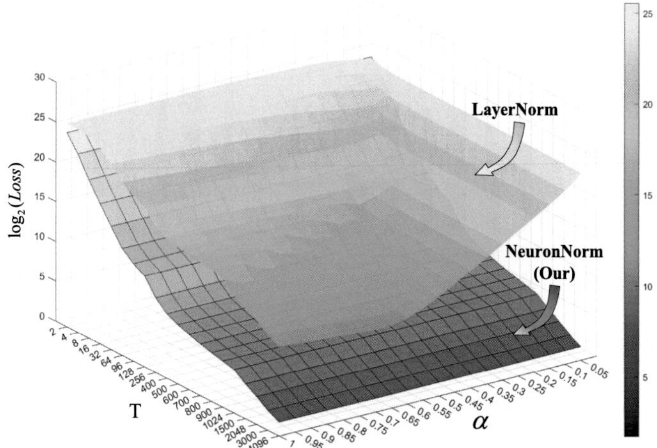

FIGURE 7.3 Comparison of the amount of information loss between LayerNorm and NeuronNorm.

Fig. 7.3 shows the change of loss when applying 20 different T and 20 different α. The vertical axis is the logarithm of the loss calculated by Eq. (7.13) through 9500 samples of CIFAR10 in the first convolutional layer of VGG16. The upper surface is the amount of the converted SNN's information loss using layer-wise normalization, which changes with α and T. The surface below is the amount of the SNN's information loss using neuron-wise normalization. The value of α is fixed to a constant of 1, meaning that NeuronNorm does not perform a parametric search. It can be seen from Fig. 7.3 that the surface obtained by

NeuronNorm is lower than the LayerNorm loss surface of any combination of α and T, which proves that NeuronNorm achieves both simplicity and accuracy.

7.5 Hardware energy consumption analysis

In this section, we will delve into the energy-efficient properties of this method (SNM with NeuronNorm) and the sparsity of network firing. Since the calculation of the SNN depends on the number of spikes, the power consumption of the SNN is proportional to the firing rate of the spiking neurons. We first explore the firing rate of the SNN network with VGG-16 architecture when the inference length is 8 on the CIFAR dataset, as shown in Fig. 7.4. As can be seen from the figure, although the firing rate is higher in the deeper layers of the network, the overall average firing rate is very low. The average firing rate on the CIFAR10 dataset is 0.1857 and on the CIFAR100 dataset is 0.1883.

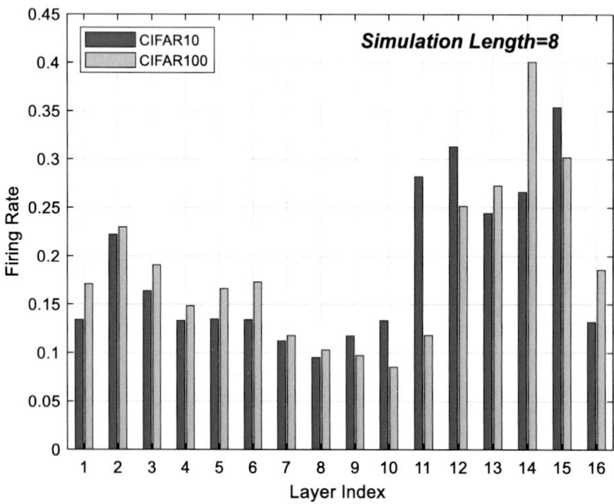

FIGURE 7.4 The average firing rate of VGG-16 when the inference length is 8 on the CIFAR dataset.

In order to more intuitively show the power consumption saving achieved by this framework, we further quantitatively compute the energy reduction using the energy-estimation equation in [RR21]. We first calculate the number of operations of layer l in an ANN and the number of operations of layer l in an SNN by

$$OP_{ANN}^{l} = \begin{cases} k^2 \times c_{in} \times c_{out} \times w_{out} \times h_{out}, & \text{Conv layer,} \\ f_{in} \times f_{out}, & \text{FC layer,} \end{cases} \tag{7.16}$$

$$OP_{SNN}^{l} = \frac{\text{SpikeNum}^{l}}{\text{NeuronNum}^{l}} \times OP_{ANN}^{l}, \tag{7.17}$$

where k is convolution kernel size, c_{in}/c_{out} is the number of input/output channels, w_{out}/h_{out} is the weight/height of the output feature map, and f_{in}/f_{out} is the number of input/output features. The SpikeNum^l and NeuronNum^l represent the total spike numbers over all time steps and neuron number in layer l, respectively.

In an ANN, each operation involves one floating-point multiply accumulate (MAC) operation, whereas, in an SNN, each operation is only one floating-point addition. The energy cost of ANN MAC operation in 45 nm CMOS is 4.6 pJ and SNN addition operation is only 0.9 pJ [Hor14]. Hence, we can calculate the energy reduction of an SNN compared to an ANN through

$$\begin{aligned} Energy\ Drop &= \frac{Energy_{SNN} - Energy_{ANN}}{Energy_{ANN}} \\ &= \frac{(4.6OP^1_{SNN} + 0.9\sum_{l=2}^{L} OP^l_{SNN}) - 4.6\sum_{l=1}^{L} OP^l_{ANN}}{4.6\sum_{l=1}^{L} OP^l_{ANN}}. \end{aligned} \tag{7.18}$$

Since the input of SNN is regarded as the input current of spiking neurons, and there is no additional coding, the first layer in an SNN also uses MAC operation.

The energy consumption reduction results of our framework converted SNN with VGG-16 architecture on the CIFAR dataset are shown in Table 7.1. For 4 time steps, the energy consumption will drop by about 82%. Even for 16 time steps, energy consumption will drop by more than 44%. We also show the drop in accuracy at different time steps in Table 7.1, which is equal to $\frac{Acc_{SNN}-Acc_{ANN}}{Acc_{ANN}}$. It is obvious that accuracy drop and energy drop are positively correlated. As the inference length increases, the accuracy drop decreases less, and the energy drop decreases less, too. It is required to find a balance between accuracy drop and energy consumption drop, and we think it is appropriate to choose a simulation length of 4 for the CIFAR10 dataset and 8 for the CIFAR100. These can give inference power consumption as low as possible while keeping inference accuracy close to that of ANNs.

Table 7.1 Energy efficiency comparison between ANNs and SNNs converted by SNM with NeuronNorm.

		$T=4$	$T=8$	$T=12$	$T=16$
CIFAR10	OP_{ANN}	256.61M	256.61M	256.61M	256.61M
	OP_{SNN}	177.5M±0.07M	351.89M±0.08M	526.09M±0.25M	700.41M±0.26M
	Avg Fire Rate	0.1856	0.1857	0.186	0.1864
	Acc. Drop×100%	−1.60%±0.13%	−0.55%±0.07%	−0.33%±0.08%	−0.23%±0.10%
	Energy Drop×100%	−82.43%±0%	−69.72%±0.01%	−57.06%±0.02%	−44.4%±0.02%
CIFAR100	OP_{ANN}	256.98M	256.98M	256.98M	256.98M
	OP_{SNN}	180.29M±0.03M	352.63M±0.09M	524.96M±0.23M	697.6M±0.12M
	Avg Fire Rate	0.1908	0.1883	0.188	0.1882
	Acc. Drop×100%	−6.09%±0.17%	−1.22%±0.22%	−0.21%±0.08%	−0.09%±0.17%
	Energy Drop×100%	−81.21%±0.01%	−68.76%±0.01%	−56.41%±0.01%	−44.06%±0.01%

7.6 Applications and results

7.6.1 Details

In order to verify the effectiveness of SNM (with NeuronNorm), we use VGG and ResNet network structures to conduct experiments on CIFAR10, CIFAR100,[1] and ImageNet2012[2] datasets. The initialization of ANN network parameters adopts Kaiming normal initialization [HZRS15], and the network training adopts the SGD algorithm with 0.9 momentum followed by milestones learning rate decay. The L2 penalty with a value of $5e^{-4}$ is also added. In addition, to prevent over-fitting, we add Batch Normalization (BN) layers to ANNs. In the SNN inference stage, we use the method introduced by Rueckauer et al. [RLH+17] to fold the parameters of BN layers into convolutional layers. The usage of parameter normalization assumes that train data and test data have the same distribution, so the maximum activation value we choose for neuron-wise normalization is obtained from the training set.

7.6.2 Ablation study

In this section, we will prove that the SNM enables SNNs with higher prediction accuracy and shorter simulation time. The result here is inference top-1 accuracy on the CIFAR10 dataset.

Fig. 7.5(a) and Fig. 7.5(b), respectively, show the SNN inference accuracy of the VGG16 structure and ResNet18 structure when using four different conversion methods. In the benchmark model for comparison, we use the layer-wise normalization with the maximum activation value ($\alpha = 1$) of each layer to normalize weight and bias, which is marked as the green line in Fig. 7.5. After changing the IF neuron of the benchmark model to an SNM neuron, as shown by the orange line in Fig. 7.5, we can see a significant improvement in accuracy at any simulation duration. The black line shows that the role of neuron-wise normalization is significant, it can use 32 time steps to achieve the accuracy of layer-wise normalization with 256 inference time steps.

The blue line shows the effect of combining the two techniques proposed in this work. It can be seen that the inference accuracy of converted SNN now exceeds the accuracy of any method used alone, and there are only 32 time steps to achieve a near-lossless ANN–SNN conversion.

7.6.3 Comparison with related work

To further illustrate the effectiveness of SNM, we use VGG and ResNet structures to conduct experiments on three datasets, and compare top-1 accuracy with some of the best models, as shown in Table 7.2. For CIFAR datasets, regardless of using VGG or ResNet, the accuracy of our model can surpass all previous state-of-the-art models. The VGG16 trained

[1] https://www.cs.toronto.edu/~kriz/cifar.html.

[2] https://image-net.org/challenges/LSVRC/2012/.

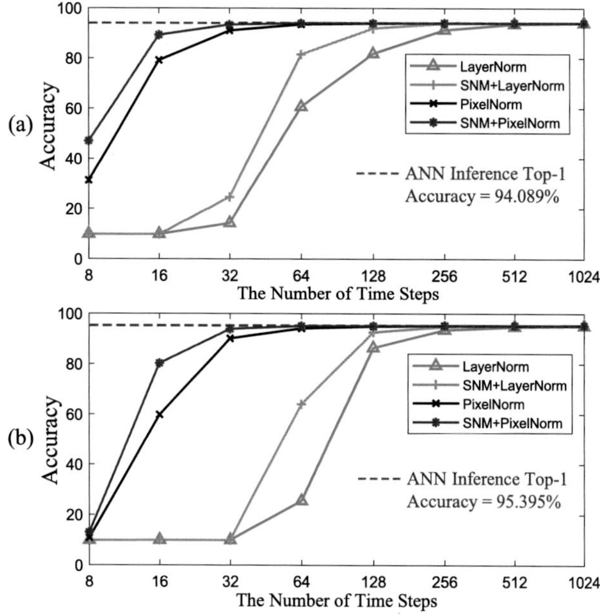

FIGURE 7.5 The inference top-1 accuracy on CIFAR10 dataset w.r.t. different simulation lengths. (a) The accuracy of the network using the VGG16 structure. (b) The accuracy of the network using the ResNet18 structure.

on CIFAR10 can reach a top-1 accuracy of 94.1%, and when trained on CIFAR100 can reach a top-1 accuracy of 74.1%. The ResNet18 trained on CIFAR10 reached a top-1 accuracy of 95.44%, and when trained on CIFAR100 can reach a top-1 accuracy of 78.3%. In order to prove that SNM does not require excessive inference latency ($T > 128$), Table 7.2 also lists the inference accuracy of different time steps, and compares them with other works. The results show that its accuracy is the highest at any number of time steps in CIFAR datasets. Since the ANN we trained on ImageNet is not satisfactory, we further compare the conversion losses that are listed in brackets. The results indicate the accuracy drop of SNM is minimal with any simulation length on the ImageNet dataset.

7.7 Conclusions

In this chapter, we analyzed the conversion error caused by SNN asynchronous transmission, and introduced an ANN–SNN conversion method named Signed Neuron with Memory (SNM), which can achieve accurate and low-latency inference. It ensures the correspondence of the spiking neuron output rate to the ReLU activation value without losing the asynchronous transmission capability of the SNN. On the other hand, the layer-wise normalization will lose much information during ANN–SNN conversion, which severely increases the inference latency of SNNs. On this basis, we introduce the neuron-wise normalization method dealing with this problem, which can significantly reduce the in-

Table 7.2 Comparison with other works. The best accuracy of the same network structure on the same dataset is displayed in bold. The ImageNet dataset additionally lists the conversion loss in brackets under accuracy, which is $Acc_{SNN} - Acc_{ANN}$.

Method	Net. Arch.	ANN Acc.	$T = 32$	$T = 64$	$T = 128$	$T \geq 512$
			CIFAR10			
RMP [HSR20]	VGG16	93.63	60.3	90.35	92.41	93.63(T=2048)
RateNorm [DYTH21]	VGG16	92.9	85.4	91.15	92.51	92.86(Unknown)
Opt. [DG21]	VGG16	92.09	92.29	92.22	92.24	92.03(T=512)
SNM+NeuronNorm	VGG16	94.09	**93.43**	**94.07**	**94.07**	**94.1**(T=512)
RateNorm [DYTH21]	ResNet18	93.06	83.95	91.96	93.27	93.45(Unknown)
Opt. [DG21]	ResNet20	92.32	93.3	93.55	93.56	93.58(T≤600)
SNM+NeuronNorm	ResNet18	95.39	**94.03**	**94.03**	**95.19**	**95.44**(T=1024)
			CIFAR100			
RMP [HSR20]	VGG16	71.22	–	–	63.76	70.93(T=2048)
Opt. [DG21]	VGG16	70.21	56.16	62.93	67.45	70.35(T≥2048)
SNM+NeuronNorm	VGG16	74.13	**71.8**	**73.69**	**73.95**	**74.1**(T=512)
RMP [HSR20]	ResNet20	68.72	27.64	46.91	57.69	67.82(T=2048)
Opt. [DG21]	ResNet20	77.16	51.27	70.12	75.81	77.19(T≥2048)
SNM+NeuronNorm	ResNet18	78.26	**74.48**	**77.59**	**77.97**	**78.3**(T=1024)
			ImageNet			
RMP [HSR20]	VGG16	73.49	–	–	–	73.09(T=4096) (−0.4)
Opt. [DG21]	VGG16	72.4	54.92 (−17.48)	66.51 (−5.89)	69.94 (−2.46)	72.09(T≥2048) (−0.31)
Calibration [LDD+21]	VGG16	75.36	63.64 (−11.72)	70.69 (−4.67)	**73.32** (−2.04)	**75.32**(T≥2048) (−0.04)
SNM+NeuronNorm	VGG16	73.18	**64.78** (**-8.4**)	**71.5** (**-1.68**)	72.86 (**-0.32**)	73.16(T=1024) (**-0.02**)

formation loss, thereby shortening the SNN inference latency. We convert deep neural networks such as VGG16 and ResNet to SNNs with this model, and the converted SNNs can reach new state-of-the-art performances for different simulation lengths on challenging datasets.

References

[DG21] Shikuang Deng, Shi Gu, Optimal conversion of conventional artificial neural networks to spiking neural networks, arXiv preprint, arXiv:2103.00476, 2021.

[DNB+15] Peter U. Diehl, Daniel Neil, Jonathan Binas, Matthew Cook, Shih-Chii Liu, Michael Pfeiffer, Fast-classifying, high-accuracy spiking deep networks through weight and threshold balancing, in: 2015 International Joint Conference on Neural Networks (IJCNN), IEEE, 2015, pp. 1–8.

[DYTH21] Jianhao Ding, Zhaofei Yu, Yonghong Tian, Tiejun Huang, Optimal ann-snn conversion for fast and accurate inference in deep spiking neural networks, arXiv preprint, arXiv:2105.11654, 2021.

[Hor14] Mark Horowitz, 1.1 computing's energy problem (and what we can do about it), in: 2014 IEEE

International Solid-State Circuits Conference Digest of Technical Papers (ISSCC), IEEE, 2014, pp. 10–14.

[HSR20] Bing Han, Gopalakrishnan Srinivasan, Kaushik Roy, Rmp-snn: residual membrane potential neuron for enabling deeper high-accuracy and low-latency spiking neural network, in: Proceedings of the IEEE/CVF Conference on Computer Vision and Pattern Recognition, 2020, pp. 13558–13567.

[HZRS15] Kaiming He, Xiangyu Zhang, Shaoqing Ren, Jian Sun, Delving deep into rectifiers: surpassing human-level performance on imagenet classification, in: Proceedings of the IEEE International Conference on Computer Vision, 2015, pp. 1026–1034.

[KGTM18] Saeed Reza Kheradpisheh, Mohammad Ganjtabesh, Simon J. Thorpe, Timothée Masquelier, Stdp-based spiking deep convolutional neural networks for object recognition, Neural Networks 99 (2018) 56–67.

[KPNY20] Seijoon Kim, Seongsik Park, Byunggook Na, Sungroh Yoon, Spiking-yolo: spiking neural network for energy-efficient object detection, Proceedings of the AAAI Conference on Artificial Intelligence 34 (07) (2020) 11270–11277.

[LDD+21] Yuhang Li, Shikuang Deng, Xin Dong, Ruihao Gong, Shi Gu, A free lunch from ann: towards efficient, accurate spiking neural networks calibration, arXiv preprint, arXiv:2106.06984, 2021.

[NMZ19] Emre O. Neftci, Hesham Mostafa, Friedemann Zenke, Surrogate gradient learning in spiking neural networks: bringing the power of gradient-based optimization to spiking neural networks, IEEE Signal Processing Magazine 36 (6) (2019) 51–63.

[RLH+17] Bodo Rueckauer, Iulia-Alexandra Lungu, Yuhuang Hu, Michael Pfeiffer, Shih-Chii Liu, Conversion of continuous-valued deep networks to efficient event-driven networks for image classification, Frontiers in Neuroscience 11 (2017) 682.

[RR21] Nitin Rathi, Kaushik Roy, Diet-snn: a low-latency spiking neural network with direct input encoding and leakage and threshold optimization, IEEE Transactions on Neural Networks and Learning Systems (2021).

[WDL+18] Yu Jie Wu, Lei Deng, Guo Li Qi, Jun Zhu, Lu Ping Shi, Spatio-temporal backpropagation for training high-performance spiking neural networks, Frontiers in Neuroscience 12 (331) (2018) 1–12.

[WZCQ22] Yuchen Wang, Malu Zhang, Yi Chen, Hong Qu, Signed neuron with memory: towards simple, accurate and high-efficient ann-snn conversion, in: Proceedings of the Thirty-First International Joint Conference on Artificial Intelligence, 2022, pp. 2501–2508.

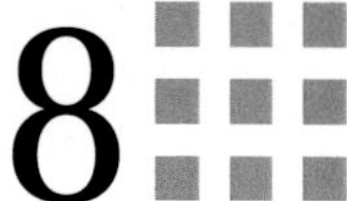

8 Spiking deep belief networks for fault diagnosis

8.1 Preface

Artificial Intelligence (AI) technology has made manipulators more systematic and intellectualized. However, external factors such as noise, temperature, and humidity can lead to accidents [WPY+20], making Fault Diagnosis (FD) a crucial aspect of manipulators [NUS21]. The FD methods for manipulators are classified into three categories: knowledge-driven, model-driven, and data-driven [Fra90,PFC13]. Among these methods, data-driven approaches have become popular for FD with the application of AI techniques [YSXJ21,YLJ20a,YLJ20b,YLXJ20].

Two main approaches are used to address issues in data-driven models: traditional Machine Learning (ML) methods for feature extraction, which have limitations in complex and high-dimensional data, and deep learning algorithms that can approximate complex functions through multiple hidden layers to extract valuable features. While Deep Learning (DL) has a high recognition rate in diagnosing faults, it may not capture time-varying signals and requires significant computational resources for training, making it challenging for real-time interaction with the physical world. To address the limitations of traditional ML and DL algorithms in solving FD problems, researchers have explored using DSNNs for FD in manipulators [TBL+20]. Some of them are developing DSNN-based FD algorithms that improve practical application, minimize resource consumption, and maintain the capabilities of existing DL algorithms [YTTL13].

In this chapter, we introduce an event-driven Spike Deep Belief Network (Spike-DBN), which can be used to improve the FD ability and reduce resource consumption of DSNNs. Leveraging the advantages of DSNNs, we evaluate the classification performance of the event-driven Spike-DBN model on the robot execution failures dataset from the UCI Machine Learning Repository [DG17] and CWRU dataset [Ken18].

8.2 Building blocks of spiking deep belief networks

In this section, we introduce the working mechanism of a Restricted Boltzmann Machine (RBM), and describe how the Siegert neuron model with event-driven strategy operates. Then, a Latency-Rate coding mechanism is given.

Towards Neuromorphic Machine Intelligence. https://doi.org/10.1016/B978-0-44-332820-6.00015-X

8.2.1 Restricted Boltzmann machine

RBM is a key part of Deep Belief Networks (DBNs), consisting of a visible layer and a hidden layer. There are no links between nodes in the same layer, as distinct from the structure of the Boltzmann Model. This makes it better for learning and computing. The RBM stores a joint probability distribution, which is shown by $p(v,h|\theta)$. This distribution depends on an energy model [ONL+13] defined by Eq. (8.1):

$$E(v,h;\theta) = -\sum_{ij} w_{ij} v_i h_j - \sum_i a_i v_i - \sum_j b_j h_j, \tag{8.1}$$

where θ denotes RBM parameters $\{w, a, b\}$. The bias of the visible and hidden units is represented by the scalars a and b (both are set to 0 in the Spike-RBM later). v_i and h_j represent the current states of the ith visible layer neuron and the jth hidden layer neuron, respectively. Neuron states are randomly assigned a value of 0 or 1, based on the inputs. The weights link between v_i and h_j is denoted by w_{ij}. The encoded joint probability $p(v,h|\theta)$ is defined as Eq. (8.2):

$$p(\mathbf{v}, \mathbf{h} \mid \boldsymbol{\theta}) = \frac{\exp(-E(\mathbf{v}, \mathbf{h}; \boldsymbol{\theta}))}{\sum_{\mathbf{v}'} \sum_{\mathbf{h}'} \exp\left(-E\left(\mathbf{v}', \mathbf{h}'; \boldsymbol{\theta}\right)\right)}. \tag{8.2}$$

From Eq. (8.1) and Eq. (8.2), we can calculate the updated state of each neuron according to Hinton's theory [HS86] that each updated state reaches the equilibrium in a lower energy state. Therefore the activation probability of each neuron in the hidden layer is determined by Eq. (8.3) whenever the neurons in the visible layer receive a number of external inputs:

$$p\left(h_j = 1 \mid v, \theta\right) = \sigma\left(b_j + \sum_i w_{ij} v_i\right). \tag{8.3}$$

Similarly, we are able to reconstruct the visible layer as a direct outcome of the one-of-a-kind structure of RBM. As a result, Eq. (8.4) can be used to derive the activation probability of the visible layer:

$$p\left(v_i = 1 \mid h, \theta\right) = \sigma\left(a_i + \sum_j w_{ij} h_j\right), \tag{8.4}$$

where $\sigma(x)$ is the logistic sigmoid function, which can be defined as $\sigma(x) = \frac{1}{1+e^x}$.

The training of one RBM is a crucial step for the determination of parameters. Hinton's work reveals that a Gibbs sampling process can be used to come close to the gradient ascent on the log-likelihood of the weights w_{ij}. Thus we can obtain the rule of updating weights by the Contrastive Divergence (CD) algorithm [HOT06] in Eq. (8.5):

$$\Delta w_{ij} = \eta\left(\langle v_i h_j \rangle_{\text{data}} - \langle v_i h_j \rangle_{\text{recon}}\right), \tag{8.5}$$

where η stands for the rate of learning, $\langle v_i h_j \rangle_{\text{recon}}$ represents the reconstructed model with sampling data, and $\langle v_i h_j \rangle_{\text{data}}$ is the one with real input data.

8.2.2 Siegert neuron model

A Siegert neuron can be introduced into RBMs, which can be regarded as a spiking neuron because its output is approximately equivalent to the output rate of spiking neurons [JLKS12]. In particular, if the state of a unit is 1, we further treat it as a Siegert neuron and calculate its average firing rate λ_{out}. Then, we need to calculate four auxiliary variables u_Q, δ_Q^2, γ, and Γ:

$$\begin{aligned} u_Q &= \tau_m \sum \left(\vec{w}_e \vec{\lambda}_e + \vec{w}_i \vec{\lambda}_i \right), \quad \gamma = V_{rest} + u_Q, \\ \delta_Q^2 &= \tfrac{\tau_m}{2} \sum \left(\vec{w}_e^2 \vec{\lambda}_e + \vec{w}_i^2 \vec{\lambda}_i \right), \quad \Gamma = \delta_Q, \end{aligned} \tag{8.6}$$

where τ_m is the time constant of the membrane potential. $\vec{\lambda}_e$ and $\vec{\lambda}_i$ are used to receive excitatory and inhibitory inputs by a neuron. $\vec{w}_e$ and $\vec{w}_i$ correspond to their respective connection weights. V_{rest} is the resting potential (in our experiment set to zero). Then, λ_{out} is defined as Eq. (8.7):

$$\begin{aligned} \lambda_{\text{out}} &= \Phi(\gamma, \Gamma) \\ &= \left(t_{ref} + \frac{\tau_m}{\Gamma} \sqrt{\frac{\pi}{2}} \cdot \int_{V_{\text{reset}} + ks\Gamma}^{V_{th+ks\Gamma}} \exp\left[\frac{(u-\gamma)^2}{2\Gamma^2} \right] \cdot \left[1 + \operatorname{erfcx}\left(\frac{(u-\gamma)}{\Gamma\sqrt{2}} \right) \right] du \right)^{-1}, \end{aligned} \tag{8.7}$$

where V_{th} is the firing threshold and V_{reset} is the reset potential. $k = \sqrt{\tau_{syn}/\tau_m} < 1$ is set to be less than one, in which τ_{syn} denotes synaptic time constant. $s = |\zeta(1/2)|$, where ζ is the Riemann zeta function. The $\operatorname{erfcx}(x) = \exp(x^2) \cdot \operatorname{erfc}(x)$, where $\operatorname{erfc}(x)$ is the Complementary Error function, and $\operatorname{erfcx}(x)$ approximately equals $\frac{1}{x\sqrt{\pi}}$.

Next, change the output of the Siegert neuron from the average firing rate to spike in Eq. (8.8):

$$s_j(t) = \begin{cases} 1, & \text{if } \lambda_{\text{out}} > v_{mean}, \\ 0, & \text{otherwise}, \end{cases} \tag{8.8}$$

where $s_j(t)$ is the state of the jth neuron's output at the tth time of updating, and v_{mean} is the average value of membrane potential throughout the course of each cycle. Thus the Siegert neurons approximate the activity of spiking neurons, which attempt to mimic biological neurons from a computational perspective. Here, we visualize the simulation process of spiking neurons according to the biological neurons in Fig. 8.1. $s(t)$ denotes a series of spike trains sent by presynaptic neurons. The behavior of biological neurons is shown by the two inner circles: a spike is generated at the current moment when the membrane potential has accumulated to a value greater than the threshold V_{th}. The postsynaptic neuron emits a series of output spike trains $y(t)$ when the process is repeated over and over again.

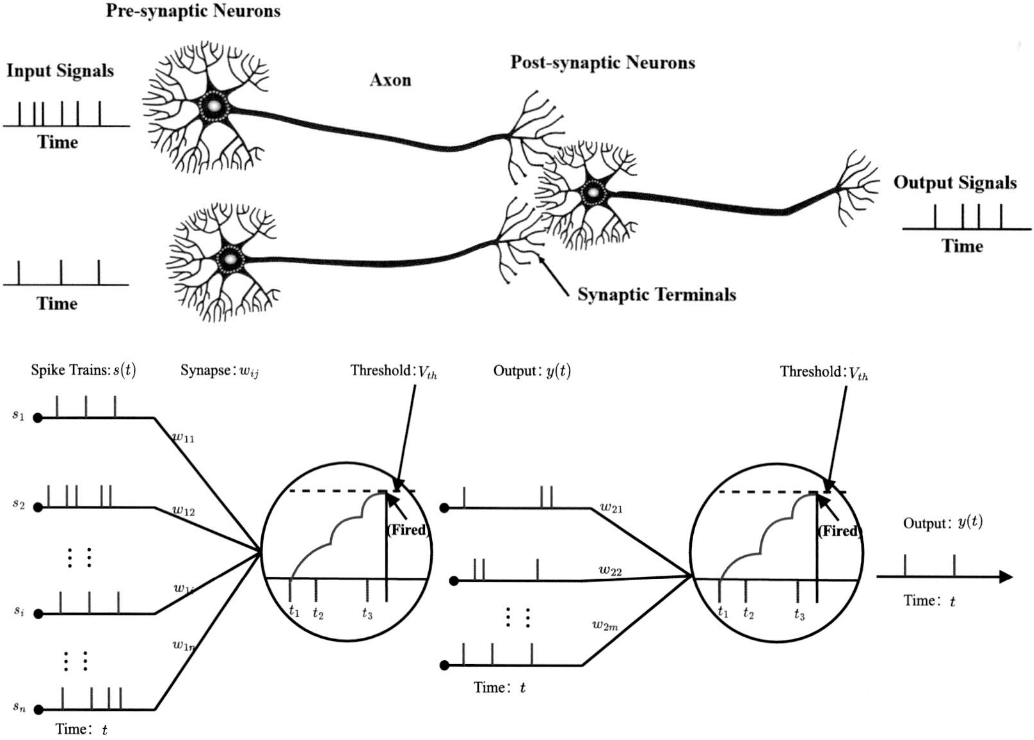

FIGURE 8.1 The simulation process of spiking neurons.

8.2.3 Neuron coding

How to encode the input signals to obtain a series of input spike trains is critical to the model presented next, since neurons in the model communicate via spikes, which differs from traditional ANNs [WWQ+21]. There are two mainstream coding methods in SNNs; rate-based coding and latency-based coding [MLB06]. Rate-based coding mainly determines the spiking frequency based on the intensity of the input stimulus. The advantage of this encoding is the high noise immunity, whereas its disadvantage is not only the high power consumption but also the long learning time, while latency-based coding avoids the disadvantage of rate coding and emphasizes the precise firing time of neurons. However, it is susceptible to noise. Hence, a Latency-Rate coding with dual characteristics based on rate coding and latency coding is proposed to better reflect input features.

Assuming that the input layer receives data x from K sensors, where x_{kj} is the value of the kth sensor at time j. Each x_{kj} $(k = 1, 2, \cdots, K; j = 1, 2, \cdots, J)$ is encoded into a spike train s by a coding neuron, so there are in total $K \cdot J$ encoded spike trains. The start time

T_{start} of a spike train is determined by the input value x_{kj} in Eq. (8.9):

$$T_{\text{start}} = T \times \left(1 - \frac{x_{kj}}{\max(x)}\right), \tag{8.9}$$

where T is the window size of coding. Then, for $t \geq T_{start}$, $s(t) = 1$. For example, assuming $T = 13$ ms and the initial location T_{start} calculated by Eq. (8.9) is 7 ms, spikes are sequentially emitted within the time window following the initial location, i.e., $s = \{0, 0, 0, 0, 0, 0, 0, 1, 1, 1, 1, 1, 1, 1\}$.

8.3 Event-driven spike deep belief network

This section describes the model architecture and its learning methods.

8.3.1 Network design

The overall structure of the event-driven Spike-DBN framework for fault diagnosis of manipulators is presented in Fig. 8.2, which consists of two basic RBMs [HOT06]: bottom RBM and top RBM. The input signal $X = \{x_1, x_2, \ldots, x_t\} \in \mathbb{R}^{t\times m}$ is fed into the model after Difference of Gaussians (DoG). Here, t is the amount of time each sample takes, and m is the total amount of sensors. According to "the dimension of input signals," the best number of spiking neurons is 48, with 32 neurons per hidden layer and 4 each label layer. Moreover,

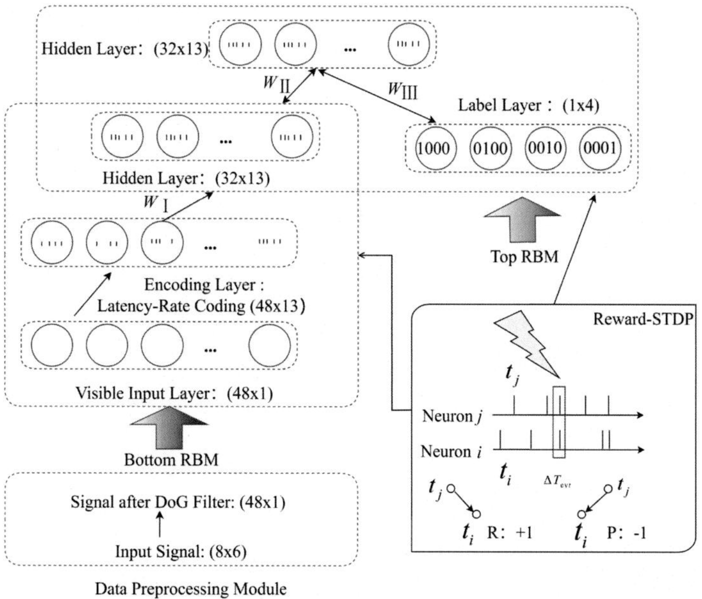

FIGURE 8.2 Event-driven Spike-DBN model structure.

an encoding layer using the Latency-Rate coding is added to convert input data to spike trains. Then, a Reward-STDP learning method is used to extract the features of spike trains. This method combines the effect of reward and punishment throughout the learning window of STDP improving the learning efficiency for spiking neurons. Finally, the Spike-DBN model updates weights in an event-driven fashion using the Reward-STDP learning rule.

8.3.2 Reward-STDP learning rule

In the neuroscience field, theories of memory suggest that neurons convey information through synaptic connections to enable reliable communication between neurons. The spike-timing-dependent plasticity (STDP) rule is considered to be a comprehensive representation of synaptic learning rule [SWW10]. Also, the event-driven strategy and the reward mechanism are introduced to further improve its performance.

8.3.2.1 Event-driven strategy

Taking advantage of spike trains of the modified output in Siegert neurons, the event-driven strategy is put forward to minimize network computation. In this way, the learning process may be triggered only in response to a spike symbiosis event. Eq. (8.10) defines the occurrence of spike symbiosis events:

$$\Delta T_{evt}(t) = \begin{cases} 1, & \text{if } s^h(t) = s^v(t) = 1, \\ 0, & \text{otherwise,} \end{cases} \tag{8.10}$$

where s^v and s^h denote the states of the visible and hidden layers, respectively. $\Delta T_{evt}(t) = 1$ refers to the condition under which learning occurs at time t. It is worth noting that this condition can be satisfied only when the states of a pair of neurons in the visible and hidden layers are both 1 and they fire simultaneously at t.

8.3.2.2 Reward-STDP

The STDP learning method takes into account the relative spike time between pre- and postsynaptic neurons during a learning window [HS21]. Provided that the synaptic weight persistently increases, this process is named Long-term Potentiation (LTP). On the contrary, if the weight decreases persistently, it is called Long-term Depression (LTD) [BPHO06]. The adaptation process of synaptic weight in a common STDP is described by Eq. (8.11) in a learning window:

$$W(s) = \begin{cases} A_+ exp\left(-\frac{s}{\tau_+}\right), & \text{if } s \geq 0, \\ A_- exp\left(\frac{s}{\tau_-}\right), & \text{if } s < 0. \end{cases} \tag{8.11}$$

$W(s)$ is the temporal learning window of STDP. A_+ and A_- determine the enhancement and inhibition procedures of synaptic connections. τ_+ and τ_- are time constants. s represents the time difference of firing spikes between the pre- and postsynaptic neurons:

$s = t_j^g - t_i^f$. t_j^g is the gth firing time of the jth presynaptic neuron, and t_i^f is the fth firing time of the ith postsynaptic neuron.

The STDP learning rule is relatively poor because it does not consider the interaction of multiple spikes over longer simulation durations. To track the entire spike pattern, the STDP learning approach with reward and punishment signals, namely Reward-STDP, was developed. Note that the Reward-STDP is applied only when a spike symbiosis event occurs, and it consists of the following two processes.

A. Local signal capture: Whenever a spike symbiosis event occurs, the Reward-STDP learning rule acquires a local reward (δ^+) in Eq. (8.12) or punishment signal (δ^-) in Eq. (8.13) based on the pre- and post-action potential times within a time window (the length is T_{win}) around the event. Assuming that such an event occurs at t^*, i.e., $\Delta T_{\text{evt}}(t^*) = 1$, then for $t_j^g,\ t_i^f \in [t^* - T_{win}/2,\ t^* + T_{win}/2]$,

$$\delta^+ = \sum_g \sum_f H(t_j^g - t_i^f),\ H(x) = \begin{cases} 1, & \text{if } x \geq 0, \\ 0, & \text{if } x < 0. \end{cases} \tag{8.12}$$

$$\delta^- = \sum_g \sum_f G(t_j^g - t_i^f),\ G(x) = \begin{cases} 0, & \text{if } x \geq 0, \\ -1, & \text{if } x < 0. \end{cases} \tag{8.13}$$

B. Global decision making: This comprehensively decides whether to update the weights by the cumulative results of δ^+ and δ^- in Eq. (8.14):

$$\delta = \delta^+ + \delta^-. \tag{8.14}$$

δ denotes the effective basis for weight update by Eq. (8.15):

$$\Delta\omega_{ij}(t) = \begin{cases} \eta \Delta T_{\text{evt}}(t), & \delta > V_{ct}, \\ 0, & \delta = V_{ct}, \\ -\eta \Delta T_{\text{evt}}(t), & \delta < V_{ct}, \end{cases} \tag{8.15}$$

where η denotes the learning rate. V_{ct} (set to zero in this work) is a control variable that determines the direction of the weight update.

To intuitively understand the Reward-STDP learning rule, four cases are visualized in Fig. 8.3. Fig. 8.3(a) shows the case where the weights should be increased, because the postsynaptic neuron fires a spike later than the presynaptic neuron, resulting in a reward signal, whereas Fig. 8.3(b) shows the opposite situation where the weight should be attenuated. For Fig. 8.3(c) and (d), they show the case of no spikes within the learning window, that is, no need to make any changes. In addition, we also present the pseudo-code of the Reward-STDP learning rule in Algorithm 1.

Algorithm 1: The Reward-STDP.

Input: $S_{siegert}(t) = \left\{ S_j(t)_{j=1}^{M}, S_i(t)_{i=1}^{N} \right\}$

/* $S_{siegert}(t)$ represents the output spike of the j presynaptic neuron and the i postsynaptic neuron at t time, M and N are the number of neurons in the visible and hidden layer. Here, $M = 48$, $N = 32$. */

Init1: period $T = T_{win} \times batchsize$;

/* T_{win} is encoding window. $batchsize$ is number of samples for one training. */

Init2: F_{pos}, $V_{ct} = 0$, $T_{STDP} = 20ms$;

/* F_{pos} is the updated position. */

/* V_{ct} is control variable in learning window. */

/* T_{STDP} is learning window size of the STDP. */

for $j = 1$ *to* M **do**

    /* get the current presynaptic neuron j. */

    for $i = 1$ *to* N **do**

        /* get the current postsynaptic neuron i. */

        Init3: $\delta^+ = 0$ and $\delta^- = 0$;

        for $t = 1$ *to* T **do**

            if $S_j(t) = 1$ *and* $S_i(t) = 1$ **then**

                /* determine whether starting learning progress */

                $t_{min} = \max\{1, t - T_{STDP}/2\}$;

                $t_{max} = t + T_{STDP}/2$;

                Start to call Algorithm 2:

                positive,negative=Learning(t_{min}, t_{max}, F_{pos}, positive, negative, S_j, S_i);

                Learning(getbackwardPos, F_{pos}, positive, negative, S_j, S_i);

                $\delta^+ = \delta^+ +$ positive;

                $\delta^- = \delta^- +$ negative;

        $\delta = \delta^+ + \delta^-$;

        if $\delta > V_{ct}$ **then**

            $\Delta W_{ji} = 1$;

        if $\delta < V_{ct}$ **then**

            $\Delta W_{ji} = -1$;

        if $\delta = V_{ct}$ **then**

            $\Delta W_{ji} = 0$;

Algorithm 2: Learning Function.

```
Function Learning(t1,t2,positive, negative,Sj,Si):
    Init4: positive = 0 and negative = 0;
    for t = t1 to t2 do
        if Sj(t) == 1 then
            for t̄ = t1 to t do
                if Si(t̄) == 1 then
                    negative = negative - 1;
            for Si(t̄) = t to t2 do
                if Si(t̄) == 1 then
                    positive = positive + 1;
    return positive, negative
```

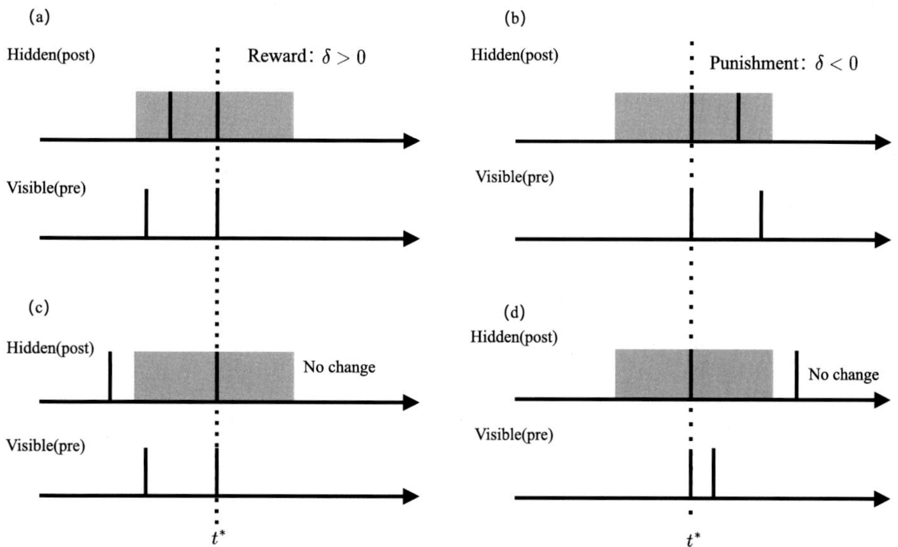

FIGURE 8.3 Reward-STDP Learning Rule. A spike symbiosis event occurs at t^*, the gray box around t^* indicates the Reward-STDP learning window, and its duration is set to 20 ms, i.e., $T_{win} = 20$ ms. (a) Weight enhancement. Exactly before the hidden layer fired a spike, the visible layer had already fired one spike, $\delta > 0$. (b) Weight weakening. The hidden layer fires before the visible layer, $\delta < 0$. (c) and (d) illustrate examples of no changes.

8.4 Applications and results

In this section, we begin by validating the performance of the event-driven Spike-DBN for fault diagnosis of manipulators using the UCI execution failures dataset. Secondly, to explore the feasibility of the proposed method in a practical scene, we use the CWRU dataset provided by Case Western Reserve University. In the end, we evaluate the performance of the suggested technique in comparison to some other methods that are considered to be state-of-the-art and examine the classification results.

8.4.1 Classification of UCI datasets

Table 8.1 Description of each subset problem.

Subset	Instances	Categories	Category distributions	
			Proportion (%)	**Category**
LP1	88	4	24%	Normal
			19%	Collision
			18%	Front collision
			39%	Obstruction
LP2	47	5	43%	Normal
			13%	Front collision
			15%	Back collision
			11%	Collision to the right
			19%	Collision to the left
LP3	47	4	43%	Ok
			19%	Slightly moved
			32%	Moved
			6%	Lost
LP4	117	3	21%	Normal
			62%	Collision
			18%	Obstruction
LP5	164	5	27%	Normal
			16%	Bottom collision
			13%	Bottom obstruction
			29%	Collision in part
			16%	Collision in tool

8.4.1.1 Data description

The UCI execution failures dataset consists of five distinct subsets, namely LP1 (failures during approach to grasp position), LP2 (failures during transfer of a part), LP3 (position of the part after a transfer failure), LP4 (failures during approach to ungrasp position), and LP5 (failures during motion with part). Each subset corresponds to a distinct learning task. As shown in Table 8.1, the number of instances in each subset is inadequate and the distribution of the dataset is unbalanced. To obtain adequate samples, each instance is extended on the premise of ensuring the time-series characteristics.

For example, the subset LP1 stores the force $F(t) = \left((F_x(t),\ F_y(t),\ F_z(t)\right)$ and torque $T(t) = \left(T_x(t),\ T_y(t),\ T_z(t)\right)$, providing 6-DOF (degrees of freedom) measurements that the manipulator receives from the sensors in real time, where the input signal varies with

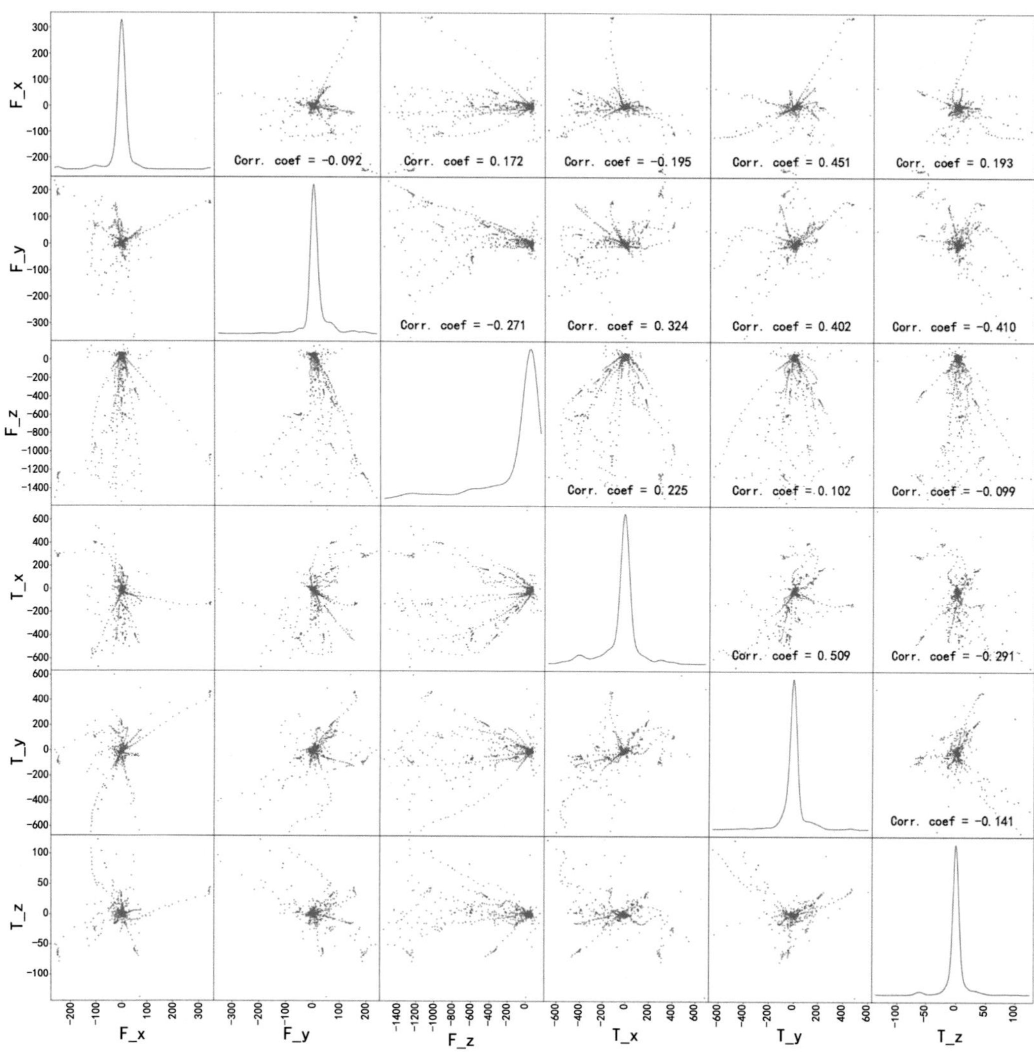

FIGURE 8.4 Density functions (diagonal) after Gaussian kernel density estimation and scatter plot (off-diagonal) showing the correlation between various columns of LP1.

time t. To show the statistical distribution characteristics of the data, the correlation between different sensors is visualized in Fig. 8.4. The subplots on the diagonal are all density function curves after Gaussian kernel density estimation. The scatter subplots on the off-diagonal lines are symmetrical, showing the correlation between various measurements. From the values of the correlation coefficients, the force values of $\{F_x(t), F_y(t), F_z(t)\}$ are strongly correlated in the x, y, and z dimensions, while the correlation with the torque values of $\{T_x(t), T_y(t), T_z(t)\}$ is weak.

8.4.1.2 Data preprocessing

A. Data augmentation: To prevent model over-fitting, a sliding window is applied to every state in the input signals along the time dimension to enlarge the total sample size. For example, in the LP1, the sampling time of sensors T_{signal} is 15 ms (sampling is performed every 1 ms), and the length of sliding window T_{cut} is 8 ms. Then, an instance is cut into $T_{signal} - T_{cut} + 1$ samples by the sliding window. Each sample consists of 8 sampling points, with 6 attributes per point, resulting in a total of 48 attribute values per sample. Such an operation increases the amount of data by eight times without losing time information, and still retains the differences between samples of different class. Table 8.2 displays the quantity of samples in the LP1 subset preceding and following the expansion. For each class, the expanded sample set is split into a training set and a test set in a ratio of 7:3.

Table 8.2 Number of samples before and after expansion of subset LP1.

Categories	Before expansion		After expansion	
	# Samples	# points	# Samples	# points
Collision	17	255	136	1088
Front collision	16	240	128	1024
Normal	21	315	168	1344
Obstruction	34	510	272	2176
Summation	**88**	**1320**	**704**	**5632**

B. Feature extraction by the DoG filter: A mammalian retina-inspired Difference of Gaussians (DoG) filter in the temporal domain is employed to detect disparities in the input signals [ONL+13]. The receptive field kernel (RF) is fashioned to emulate the center-surround properties of retinal ganglion cells, featuring a central mechanism of excitability and a weaker, larger peripheral mechanism that exerts inhibitory effects. Both mechanisms demonstrate characteristics of a Gaussian distribution, as depicted in Fig. 8.5. This method enhances the network's ability to detect features in the input signal, thereby improving the model's fault diagnosis capabilities. It introduces extra parameters into the network that require training [GVT20]. As a result, the convolution kernel design must be thoughtfully considered to ensure it effectively and efficiently extracts the desired input features. The RF using a two-dimensional Gaussian function is defined in Eq. (8.16):

$$g_\sigma(x, y) = \frac{1}{2\pi\sigma^2} \exp\left(-\left(x^2 + y^2\right) / \left(2\sigma^2\right)\right). \tag{8.16}$$

In the experiments, the RF center's and surround's standard deviations are, respectively, set to 0.3 and 0.9. When the RF method is applied in the LP1, the processed data exhibit a symmetric spatial distribution, as depicted in Fig. 8.6(b). Thus the weight is lower when the sensor's value is further away from the input's center, aiding in the encoding window's establishment, which is further described in the subsequent section. In Fig. 8.6(a), the degree of data dispersion in the LP1 under the same condition is presented.

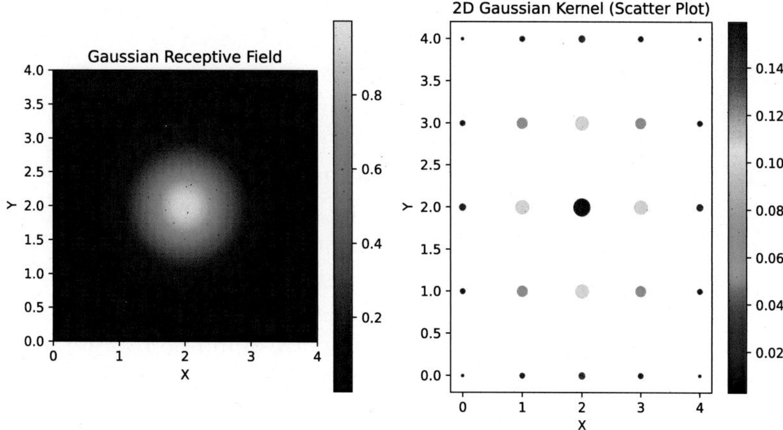

FIGURE 8.5 Gaussian receptive field.

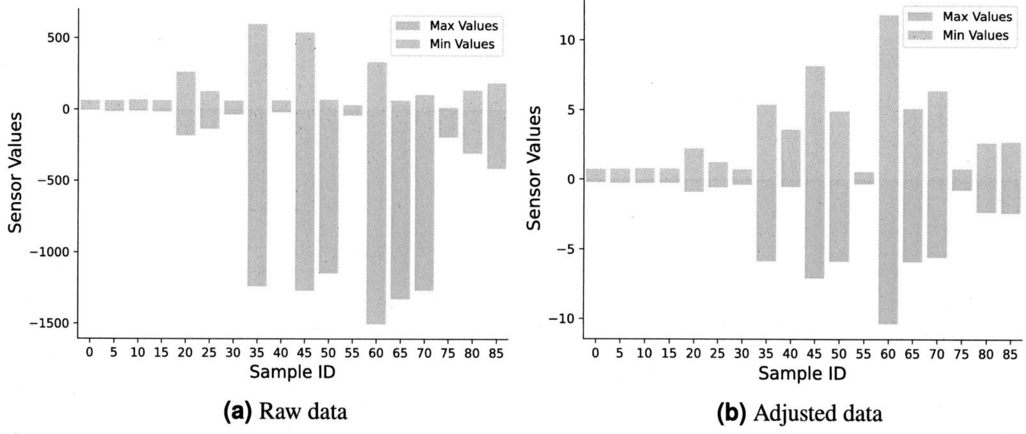

(a) Raw data **(b)** Adjusted data

FIGURE 8.6 The dispersion degree of data.

8.4.1.3 Implementation details

A. Configuration of the encoding window: To train the event-driven Spike-DBN, the input signals need to be encoded by the Latency-Rate approach referred to in subsection 8.2.3. Based on the analysis of data preprocessing, we consider only positive values as input to encode, negative values are discarded. This can be attributed to the usage of binary spike trains to process data in SNNs. In this approach, a sequence at a certain location is assigned a value of 1 only if there is a spike, and 0 otherwise. After applying DoG processing, the obtained features are spatially symmetrically distributed, meaning that the same features appear on both the positive and negative sides of the spatial distribution. As it is redundant to extract the same feature twice, we only consider data with positive characteristics and disregard data with negative values. This approach considers the properties of spiking neurons, which is highly adaptable to input with positive values.

This strategy is highly adaptable to meeting the requirements of spiking neurons, including reducing the duration of the encoding window, denoted by T. Specifically, the value of T is determined based on the peak values of the preprocessing data distribution for each subset. The model first determines the number of subsets to be trained, preprocesses the data for each subset, and then plots the distribution of each subset. Next, the value of T is calculated as the minimum and maximum values of each subset based on these distribution maps. T is set to the higher absolute value. This guarantees that the encoding window is sufficiently long to catch each token's salient characteristics. During training, the model retrieves the maximum value corresponding to the tested subset in Table 8.3 and further adjusts the window length accordingly. Overall, the model's ability to capture the relevant properties of the input data is dependent on the dynamic configuration of the encoding window T, which strikes a balance between accuracy and efficiency.

Table 8.3 Reference the duration of coding window for each subset.

Dataset	Maximum value	Minimum value	Encoding window (T_{win})
LP1	12.91	−11.54	13 ms
LP2	24.57	−28.45	29 ms
LP3	24.57	−28.45	29 ms
LP4	18.74	−19.24	20 ms
LP5	21.50	−22.37	23 ms

B. Configuration of Spike-DBN hyperparameters: The structure of Spike-DBN used in the experiment is based on O'Connor's paper [ONL$^+$13], and the number of neurons in the visible layer V_{neuron} is determined based on the number of input features. The hyperparameters for the model, such as the number of neurons in the hidden layers H_{neuron}, the number of training iterations Pre_{train} and its learning rate Pre_η in the unsupervised pre-training stage, the number of training iterations $Fine_{train}$ and its learning rate $Fine_\eta$ in the fine-tuning stage, momentum SGD_M, and batch size B_{size}, are initialized based on O'Connor's previous Spike-DBN report. However, these hyperparameters are further tuned using a genetic algorithm (GA) in the experiment. As shown in Table 8.4, after 10 iterations of GA optimization, the resulting optimal hyperparameters were $SGD_M = 0.3765$, $Pre_\eta = 0.0679$, $Fine_\eta = 0.0465$, $B_{size} = 41$, $Pre_{train} = 5$, $Fine_{train} = 87$, and $H_{neuron} = 32$. Additionally, the inner parameters of spiking neurons were set to $\tau_m = 5$, $\tau_s = 1.25$, $t_{rest} = 0$, $t_{ref} = 0.02$, $V_{th} = 0.08$, and $t_{decay} = 0.005$.

8.4.1.4 Evaluation metric

The F1-score ($F1$) is computed as the harmonic mean of Precision (P) and Recall (R), with equal weight assigned to each. This allows for evaluating a model using a single score that takes into account both P and R, making it useful for model performance evaluation and

Table 8.4 Output values for each hyperparameter after every iteration.

Iteration	SGD_M	Pre_η	$Fine_\eta$	B_{size}	Pre_{train}	$Fine_{train}$	H_{neuron}
1	0.1557	0.0101	0.0164	27	6	76	26
2	0.1990	0.0495	0.0562	17	15	86	31
3	0.1990	0.0515	0.0562	17	12	85	16
4	0.3364	0.0427	0.1925	29	6	10	20
5	0.3364	0.0427	0.1925	29	6	10	20
6	0.3765	0.0679	0.0465	41	5	87	32
7	0.3765	0.0679	0.0465	41	5	87	32
8	0.3765	0.0679	0.0465	41	5	87	32
9	0.3765	0.0679	0.0465	41	5	87	32
10	0.3765	0.0679	0.0465	41	5	87	32

comparison. In addition to classification accuracy, we also evaluate the effectiveness of the Reward-STDP using P, R, and $F1$. P and R represent the predictive impact on positive cases and are equivalent to examining true positives (TP) from two different perspectives. P is a subjective measure of correctly identifying a positive example, while R is an objective measure of correctly identifying a positive example. As the F1 value increases, the classification accuracy of fault detection improves. The corresponding mathematical formulas are defined in Eq. (8.17):

$$P = \frac{TP}{TP + FP}, \quad R = \frac{TP}{TP + FN}, \quad F1 = \frac{2 \times P \times R}{P + R}, \tag{8.17}$$

where TP stands for true positive, FP presents false positive, and FN is false negative, respectively.

8.4.1.5 Accuracy

We compared the Spike-DBN with other deep neural networks, including Stacked Autoencoders (SAE) [SOC+12], Recurrent Neural Network (RNN) [ZSV14], Convolutional Neural Network (CNN) [LWRL19], and Spike Convolutional Neural Network (Spike-CNN) [LZZ+21], based on precision, recall, and F1-score. We also compared it with other state-of-the-art methods in various signal processing-based DNN, such as EMD-DNN [LLHZ13], wavelet-DNN [CLW+21], Sparse Preservation-DNN (SR-DNN) [SYZC19], and Morphological Filter-DNN (MT-DNN) [ZXY+08]. Finally, the experimental results are presented in Table 8.5.

The results in Table 8.5 demonstrate the superiority of Spike-DBN. Specifically, Spike-DBN achieves higher accuracy, precision, recall, and F1-score than other models on the LP1 dataset, indicating that it has better classification ability on this dataset. On the LP2 dataset, Spike-DBN achieves higher precision, recall, and F1-score than other models, indicating that it can better identify true positive samples on this dataset. On the LP4 dataset, it achieves higher accuracy and F1-score than other models, indicating that it has bet-

Table 8.5 Comparison results of UCI datasets.

Models	LP1				LP2				LP3				LP4				LP5			
	Acc(%)	P(%)	R(%)	F1(%)	Acc(%)	P(%)	R(%)	F1(%)	Acc(%)	P(%)	R(%)	F1(%)	Acc(%)	P(%)	R(%)	F1(%)	Acc(%)	P(%)	R(%)	F1(%)
Decision Tree	88.88	83.33	83.33	83.33	90.00	66.66	75.00	70.00	80.00	62.50	62.50	62.50	80.33	78.54	87.77	81.34	87.87	86.36	83.33	84.00
SVM	57.14	53.84	70.00	60.86	47.61	40.00	44.44	42.10	80.00	71.42	58.33	60.57	62.07	77.78	53.84	63.63	75.57	63.99	72.16	65.61
MFSA [RAF21]	79.00	–	–	–	–	–	–	–	–	–	–	–	81.00	–	–	–	–	–	–	–
DBN [DNNV23]	77.27	–	–	–	80.00	–	–	–	–	–	–	–	82.76	–	–	–	–	–	–	–
SAE	80.00	80.00	80.00	80.00	67.00	67.00	67.00	67.00	71.00	71.00	71.00	71.00	75.00	75.00	75.00	75.00	77.00	77.00	77.00	77.00
RNN	70.21	70.21	70.21	70.21	62.60	62.60	62.60	62.60	60.93	60.93	60.93	60.93	86.70	86.70	86.70	86.70	48.24	48.24	48.24	48.24
CNN [LWRL19]	98.77	–	–	–	82.87	–	–	–	–	–	–	–	61.56	–	–	–	–	–	–	–
Spike-CNN [LZZ+21]	91.07	91.57	91.50	91.52	96.66	100.00	92.85	96.29	–	–	–	–	93.95	93.08	93.86	93.91	–	–	–	–
Wavelet-DNN	83.39	82.20	81.64	80.83	25.07	33.81	26.15	20.19	57.43	47.28	40.66	39.17	77.69	73.98	79.32	75.80	65.07	62.04	60.39	59.64
EMD-DNN	94.53	94.28	94.83	94.48	77.21	65.65	64.50	64.83	92.80	90.14	94.13	91.83	83.25	81.22	74.98	76.90	90.00	89.82	88.33	88.77
SR-DNN	88.96	65.45	75.11	85.37	71.45	61.16	61.08	61.96	87.29	52.80	54.98	55.09	93.24	91.84	87.35	90.58	77.19	65.11	62.74	67.55
MT-DNN	79.49	78.32	77.07	77.44	50.43	33.36	32.11	31.16	65.41	48.38	49.34	48.42	82.42	78.70	76.00	76.54	61.31	59.87	59.58	59.70
Our method	94.09	94.56	89.65	94.54	97.56	97.52	96.55	98.24	96.46	95.73	92.17	93.95	93.81	92.85	96.29	94.54	88.64	89.52	88.12	87.12

ter overall classification performance on this dataset. Additionally, Spike-DBN performed competitively with signal processing-based DNNs.

In addition to comparing classification accuracy, Fig. 8.7 presents the processing time of various models. This information can provide insights into the computational efficiency of each model. As illustrated in Fig. 8.7, Spike-DBN has a clear advantage over other models in terms of processing time, with a processing time of only 13 s. This is substantially faster than other models, indicating that our proposed method is more computationally efficient and capable of processing data quickly. This advantage could make it a better option for practical applications where fast processing times is critical.

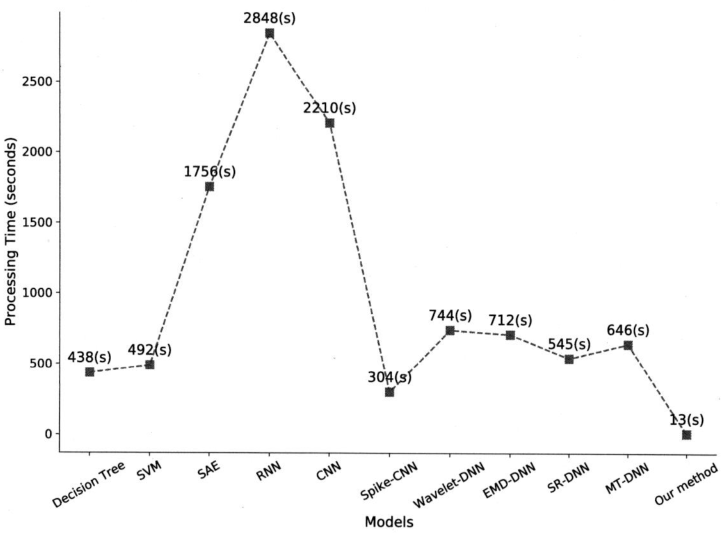

FIGURE 8.7 Processing time of various models on the LP1 dataset.

To visually assess the model's ability to distinguish between different categories, we present a confusion matrix for the test data in LP1 with 10 test runs in Fig. 8.8. The diagonal elements of the matrix denote the count of accurately classified test samples, whereas the off-diagonal elements represent the count of misclassified samples. From the confusion matrix, it is evident that the obstruction category is more distinguishable compared to the other three categories, which exhibit varying degrees of misclassification.

On the other hand, the proposed model's feature extraction capability is demonstrated by visualizing the feature distribution between the bottom RBM and the top RBM using the t-SNE method. The visualization reveals a clustering of samples with the same label, while samples containing various labels are spread out. This is presented in Fig. 8.9.

8.4.1.6 Ablation experiments

To determine which parts of the strategy of Spike-DBN are most crucial, we disable them one by one and monitor the classifier's output. First, we investigate the significance of the

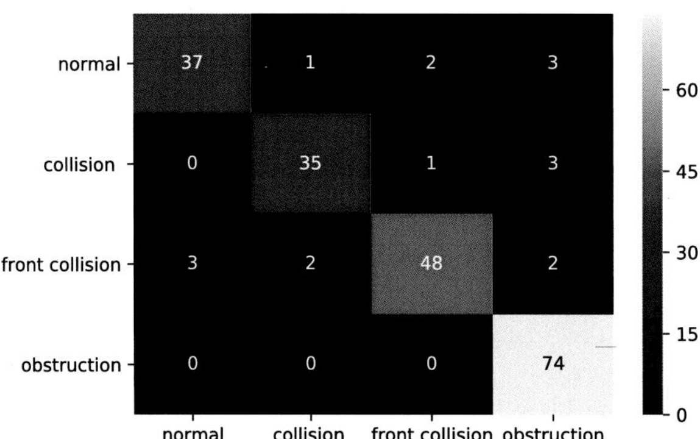

FIGURE 8.8 Confusion matrix for the test set of the LP1 dataset.

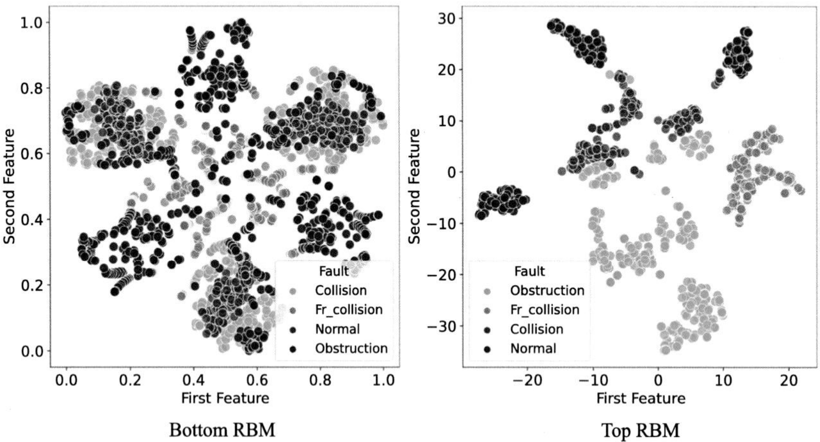

FIGURE 8.9 t-SNE visualization of the LP1 subset.

Reward-STDP by substituting it with a traditional STDP, which updates each step. Then, we disable one of the encoding methods from our proposed encoding strategy. Finally, we use the Spike-DBN model separately without event-driven embeddings to evaluate the time required to train this model.

- **Effectiveness of the Reward-STDP:** When Reward-STDP is replaced with a traditional STDP, there is a considerable drop in model performance. This is likely because the values of the sensors are easily affected by external factors, and focusing on local learning behavior under noise can mislead the model. Therefore the Reward-STDP mechanism is crucial for improving the model's robustness in noisy environments, and the results in Table 8.6 underscore its effectiveness.
- **Effectiveness of the latency-rate encoding:** When the combined coding technique is replaced with the single coding method, there is a degradation in classification perfor-

Table 8.6 Performance of Spike-DBN with different strategies.

Method	LP1(%)				LP2(%)				LP3(%)				LP4(%)				LP5(%)			
	Acc	P	R	F1	Acc	P	R	F1	Acc	P	R	F1	Acc	P	R	F1	Acc	P	R	F1
Our method	94.09	94.56	89.65	94.54	97.56	97.52	96.55	98.24	96.46	95.73	92.17	93.95	93.81	92.85	96.29	94.54	88.64	89.52	88.12	87.12
Traditional STDP	80.41	80.34	79.76	76.83	74.28	74.21	74.15	74.18	82.45	81.38	82.12	80.77	81.21	82.54	80.13	79.23	73.54	73.89	74.52	74.11
Latency coding	83.63	83.59	83.28	84.51	76.39	77.27	77.99	77.67	85.21	84.27	85.36	85.24	84.72	84.89	84.55	84.74	79.21	79.56	78.88	79.37
Rate coding	81.91	81.86	81.76	83.73	79.51	76.06	76.73	76.53	82.69	83.21	84.12	82.57	83.39	83.46	84.05	84.65	74.25	74.56	73.99	74.37

mance, with the effect being more pronounced for the LP2 subset. This suggests that the combined coding technique improves classification performance, particularly for subsets with sufficient sample sizes. The results in Table 8.6 highlight the effectiveness of the combined coding technique in improving the performance of the latency-rate encoding method.

- **Evaluation of event-driven strategy:** After discarding the event-driven embeddings from the Spike-DBN, the computation time on the LP1 subset increases by two to three times, as demonstrated in Fig. 8.10. It is worth emphasizing that the "learning count" here denotes the overall number of training-related occurrences. We are pleased to observe that our model's computation is highly efficient, as evidenced by the low number of learning times required.

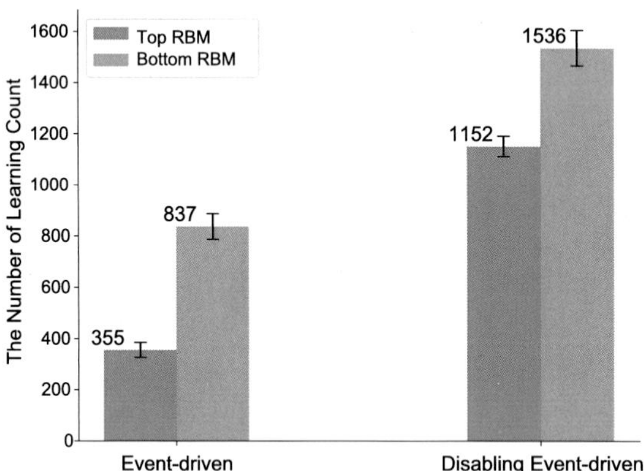

FIGURE 8.10 Learning count of Spike-model under two strategies.

In a nutshell, the Reward-STDP and the Latency-Rate encoding contribute to the superior performance of Spike-DBN compared to baseline methods. Additionally, the event-driven strategy greatly reduces the computation times of Spike-DBN.

8.4.1.7 Evaluation under different noisy environments

To assess the noise resistance of Spike-DBN in real-world applications, we introduced Gaussian white noise into the model during the testing phase. The robustness of the model was evaluated by analyzing its performance under different levels of noise. Also, the degree of signal contamination by noise was quantified using the signal-to-noise ratio (SNR) defined in Eq. (8.18):

$$SNR = 10\log_{10}\frac{P_{signal}}{P_{noise}}. \tag{8.18}$$

The power of the input signal is denoted as $P_{signal} = \frac{1}{n}\sum_{k=1}^{n} s_k^2$, where s_k represents a discrete signal $S = \{s_1, s_2, \ldots, s_n\}$. After determining the SNR, The noise power P_{noise} can be obtained as $P_{noise} = P_{signal}/10^{\frac{SNR}{10}}$. In this test, we use a standard Gaussian distribution to generate a noise sequence of the same length as the original signal. The noise sequence is then scaled to obtain the desired Gaussian noise, which is added to the test set to create test samples with different SNRs.

Table 8.7 Results of the noise resistance.

SNR (dB)	0	−1	−2	−3	−4	−5	−6
Acc(%)	97.40	95.25	93.71	91.34	90.16	89.64	83.9

As shown in Table 8.7, the Spike-DBN is able to achieve relatively high accuracy classification results in both low- and high-noise environments, with a testing accuracy greater than 90% even under an SNR of −4 dB, demonstrating its robustness to background noise.

8.4.2 Classification of CWRU datasets

8.4.2.1 Data description

The Spike-DBN was further evaluated on a larger real dataset, namely the Case Western Reserve University (CWRU) dataset [Ken18]. The dataset provides a realistic and challenging testbed for fault diagnosis algorithms. It contains vibration data from ball bearing experiments under normal and faulty conditions. The dataset includes a normal state dataset captured at a sampling rate of 12 kHz, as well as three fault states: rolling element fault, inner race fault, and outer race fault. The outer race fault is further categorized based on its location, including 3 o'clock, 6 o'clock, and 12 o'clock. The sensor at the drive end captured normal data at 12 kHz and three types of fault data for the experiment.

8.4.2.2 Implementation details

The dataset is divided into four categories based on the type of fault: Normal (labeled as 1), Inner Race (labeled as 2), Outer Race (labeled as 3), and Rolling Element (labeled as 4). Each category contains 480 examples, resulting in a total of 1920 samples in the dataset. Each sample consists of 30 features, which are extracted from vibration signals, making it a high-dimensional dataset. The specific implementation is as follows:

- **Signal processing:** The original signal is decomposed using the Local Mean Decomposition (LMD) [MZL19] method. Part of the feature distribution map is shown in Fig. 8.11.
- **Feature extraction:** The DoG method is used to extract features from the decomposed signal. The feature size of a single sample is (30, 4).
- **Spiking encoding:** The encoding window length $T_{win} = 18$ ms is determined based on the maximum value (16.8594) of the calculated features. Then, the Latency-Rate method encodes the calculated features into a spike sequence with time information.
- **Model initialization:** Visible units = 30, hidden units = 16, Batch size = 16, $\eta = 0.0001$, the weight follows a Gaussian distribution with a mean of 0 and a variance of 0.08.
- **Split the training and test sets:** The 1920 samples of the dataset are split into 1536 training samples and 384 test samples (8:2).
- **Training and testing:** This process is repeated for a total of 1000 epochs.

- **Evaluation:** The performance of the model was evaluated by measuring prediction accuracy, precision, recall, and F1-score.

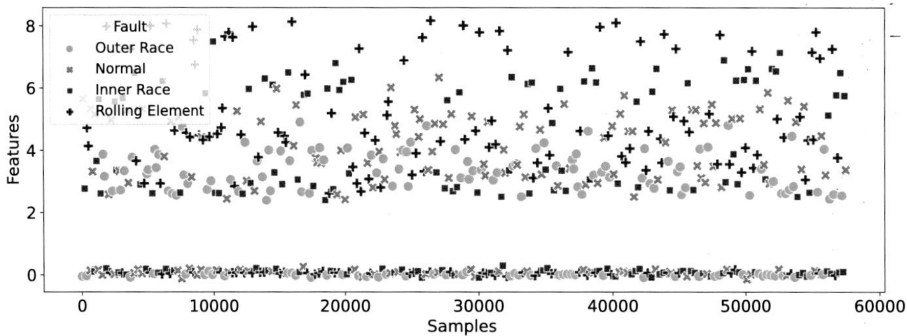

FIGURE 8.11 Distribution map of feature.

8.4.2.3 Visualization of layers

To provide a deeper understanding of the learning process, we visualize the different layers of the Spike-DBN model on the CWRU dataset, as shown in Fig. 8.12. This visualization allows us to observe the flow of the data in each layer during the learning process, shedding light on how the model is able to step-by-step change between different layers.

As depicted in Fig. 8.12, the input layer receives the preprocessed signal and determines the window length for spike encoding based on the signal distribution's peak value. The encoding layer then transmits the spike trains to the RBM for hierarchical feature extraction, with spike timing indicating feature presence. The RBMs optimize neuron connections to increase model accuracy, as seen in the visualization. The bottom RBM decomposes the input signal into lower-level features, while the top RBM combines these features to generate higher-level features.

8.4.2.4 Results on the CWRU dataset

The Spike-DBN model was evaluated using 5-fold cross-validation to adjust any hyperparameters. The model achieved prediction accuracies of 97.63%, 97.02%, 97.88%, 97.56%, and 97.91% across the five folds after 1000 epochs. The mean test accuracy on the CWRU dataset was reported to be 97.40%, with a variance of 0.0787%. Table 8.8 compares with seven models for bearing fault diagnosis on the CWRU dataset. The suggested imbalance-robust DA method combines the know-how of experts with a deep autoencoder that has already been trained. The testing phase involves observing the reconstruction error and cluster assignment of the input data to detect anomalies and identify the fault condition [WTF21]. The deep representation clustering-based approach involves performing K-means clustering on extracted features, which are then used to train a Support Vector Machine (SVM). It is evaluated performance using a 10-fold cross-validation method [LLM20]. The DCDBN-DMLP model uses unsupervised clustering for training. Subse-

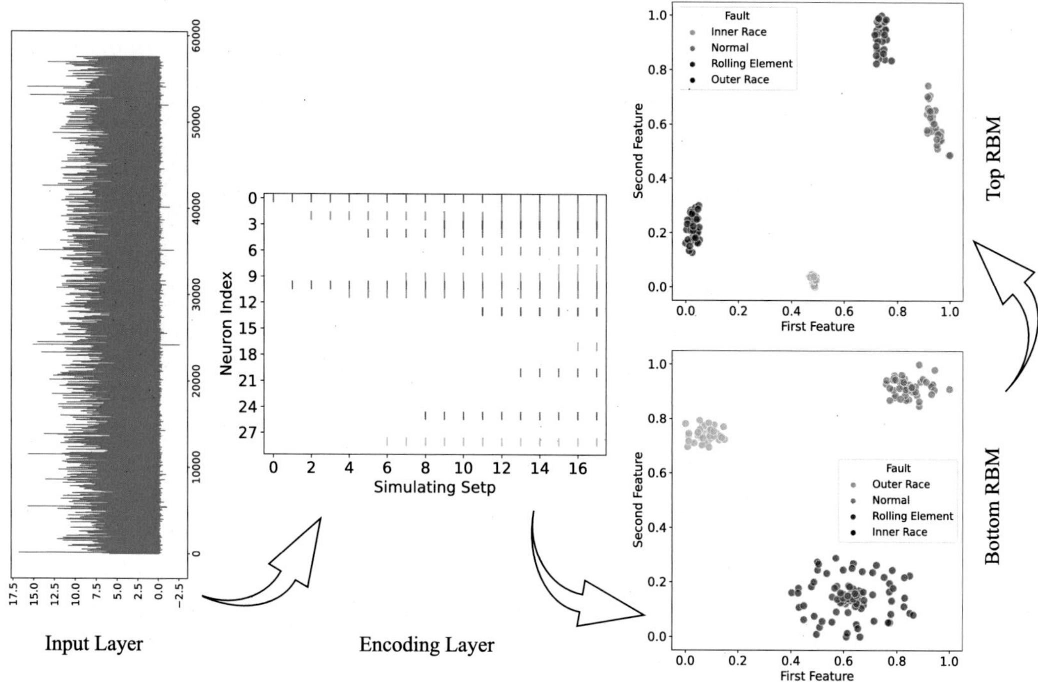

FIGURE 8.12 Visualization of the various layers.

Table 8.8 Accuracy of various methods on the CWRU dataset.

Models	Learning method	Acc. (%)
SNN with tempotron learning [ZZZ+21]	Supervised	99.18
SNN with backpropagation learning [ZXZ+22]	Supervised	99.38
Imbalance-robust DA [WTF21]	Unsupervised	84.18
Deep representation clustering [LLM20]	Unsupervised	95.70
DCDBN-DMLP [SYX+22]	Unsupervised	97.23
Maximum classifier discrepancy [WY22]	Semi-supervised	97.25
Spike-DBN	Unsupervised	97.40

quently, the model diagnoses the fault condition of test data by observing the clustering results [SYX+22]. The maximum classifier discrepancy involves training a domain-invariant feature extractor using adversarial training, which is then used to train a fault diagnosis model. The performance of the model is evaluated by testing it on unlabeled data from the target domain [WY22].

As in Table 8.8, the supervised SNN method achieves a classification accuracy of over 99%, demonstrating the strong capability of SNN processing for time-series signal analysis and fault diagnosis. In this research, the unsupervised Spike-DBN leverages the benefits of

SNN and improves test accuracy to a maximum of 97.30% and an average of 95.47% after 1000 iterations, achieving competitive accuracy in unsupervised learning methods.

8.5 Conclusions

This chapter introduces an event-driven version of the DBN model for detecting manipulator faults. The innovation points of the event-driven Spike-DBN include the infusion of an event-driven method to reduce resource consumption and the proposal of Latency-Rate coding to capture the time-varying feature of input signals by encoding sensor signals into spatiotemporal patterns. Notably, a new Reward-STDP approach is applied to the Spike-DBN for learning. The effectiveness of the Spike-DBN is validated using the UCI dataset and CWRU data. When compared to other methods in the field, Spike-DBN not only uses fewer resources but also achieves better results in terms of precision, recall, F1-score, and accuracy. In a nutshell, this study primarily contributes: (1) Spike-DBN incorporates the dynamics of biological neurons to capture the change in time-varying signals. Due to the binary structure of spike trains, this model is easier to implement in hardware. (2) The Latency-Rate encoding can enable the model to perform tasks such as temporal pattern recognition and event-based processing. (3) The Reward-STDP uses rewards and an efficient spike-timing-dependent plasticity mechanism, which is event driven and focuses on how spiking neurons behave globally, whereas standard STDP focuses on how neurons behave locally.

References

[BPHO06] Daniel Bush, Andrew Philippides, Phil Husbands, Michael O'Shea, Investigating STDP and LTP in a spiking neural network, in: International Conference on Simulation of Adaptive Behavior, Springer, 2006, pp. 323–334.

[CLW+21] Yi Wei Cheng, Man Xi Lin, Jun Wu, Hai Ping Zhu, Xin Yu Shao, Intelligent fault diagnosis of rotating machinery based on continuous wavelet transform-local binary convolutional neural network, Knowledge-Based Systems 216 (106796) (2021) 1–12.

[DG17] Dheeru Dua, Casey Graff, UCI machine learning repository, 2017.

[DNNV23] Pandit Byomakesha Dash, Bighnaraj Naik, Janmenjoy Nayak, S. Vimal, Deep belief network-based probabilistic generative model for detection of robotic manipulator failure execution, Soft Computing 27 (1) (2023) 363–375.

[Fra90] Paul M. Frank, Fault diagnosis in dynamic systems using analytical and knowledge-based redundancy: a survey and some new results, Automatica 26 (3) (1990) 459–474.

[GVT20] Shikhar Gupta, Arpan Vyas, Gaurav Trivedi, FPGA implementation of simplified spiking neural network, in: 2020 27th IEEE International Conference on Electronics, Circuits and Systems (ICECS), IEEE, 2020, pp. 1–4.

[HOT06] Geoffrey E. Hinton, Simon Osindero, Yee Whye Teh, A fast learning algorithm for deep belief nets, Neural Computation 18 (7) (2006) 1527–1554.

[HS86] Geoffrey E. Hinton, Terrence J. Sejnowski, Learning and relearning in Boltzmann machines, in: Parallel Distributed Processing: Explorations in the Microstructure of Cognition, vol. 1(2), 1986, pp. 282–317.

[HS21] Christian Huyck, Carlos Samey, Extended category learning with spiking nets and spike timing dependent plasticity, in: International Conference on Innovative Techniques and Applications of Artificial Intelligence, Springer, 2021, pp. 33–43.

[JLKS12] Florian Jug, Johannes Lengler, Christoph Krautz, Angelika Steger, Spiking networks and their rate-based equivalents: does it make sense to use Siegert neurons, Swiss Society for Neuroscience (2012) 1.

[Ken18] Kenneth B. Loparo, Case Western Reserve University Bearing Data Center, 2018.

[LLHZ13] Ya Guo Lei, Jing Lin, Zheng Jia He, Ming J Zuo, A review on empirical mode decomposition in fault diagnosis of rotating machinery, Mechanical Systems and Signal Processing 35 (2013) 108–126.

[LLM20] Xiang Li, Xu Li, Hui Ma, Deep representation clustering-based fault diagnosis method with unsupervised data applied to rotating machinery, Mechanical Systems and Signal Processing 143 (106825) (2020) 1–18.

[LWRL19] Ying Liu, Xiu Qing Wang, Xue Mei Ren, Feng Lyu, Deep convolution neural networks for the classification of robot execution failures, in: 2019 CAA Symposium on Fault Detection, Supervision and Safety for Technical Processes (SAFEPROCESS), 2019, pp. 535–540.

[LZZ+21] Ying Liu, En Hui Zhou, Wei Zhang, Xiu Qing Wang, Feng Lv, Classification of robot execution failures using a Spike-CNN model underlying stdp learning by reward and punishment mechanisms, Journal of Chinese Computer Systems 43 (6) (2021) 1285–1292.

[MLB06] Sam McKennoch, Ding Ding Liu, Linda Bushnell, Fast modifications of the spikeprop algorithm, in: The 2006 IEEE International Joint Conference on Neural Network Proceedings, IEEE, 2006, pp. 3970–3977.

[MZL19] Yong Hao Miao, Ming Zhao, Jing Lin, Identification of mechanical compound-fault based on the improved parameter-adaptive variational mode decomposition, ISA Transactions 84 (2019) 82–95.

[NUS21] Aneesh G. Nath, Sandeep S. Udmale, Sanjay Kumar Singh, Role of artificial intelligence in rotor fault diagnosis: a comprehensive review, Artificial Intelligence Review 54 (4) (2021) 2609–2668.

[ONL+13] Peter O'Connor, Daniel Neil, Shih Chii Liu, Tobi Delbruck, Michael Pfeiffer, Real-time classification and sensor fusion with a spiking deep belief network, Frontiers in Neuroscience 7 (178) (2013) 1–13.

[PFC13] Ron J. Patton, Paul M. Frank, Robert N. Clark, Issues of Fault Diagnosis for Dynamic Systems, Springer Science & Business Media, 2013.

[RAF21] Mohamed Elhadi Rahmani, Abdelmalek Amine, José Eduardo Fernandes, Multi-stage genetic algorithm and deep neural network for robot execution failure detection, Neural Processing Letters 53 (6) (2021) 4527–4547.

[SOC+12] Hoo Chang Shin, Matthew Orton, David Collins, Simon Doran, Martin Leach, Stacked autoencoders for unsupervised feature learning and multiple organ detection in a pilot study using 4d patient data, IEEE Transactions on Pattern Analysis and Machine Intelligence 35 (8) (2012) 1930–1943.

[SWW10] Harel Z. Shouval, Samuel S-H. Wang, Gayle M. Wittenberg, Spike timing dependent plasticity: a consequence of more fundamental learning rules, Frontiers in Computational Neuroscience 4 (19) (2010) 1–13.

[SYX+22] Hao Su, Xin Yang, Ling Xiang, Ai Jun Hu, Yong Gang Xu, A novel method based on deep transfer unsupervised learning network for bearing fault diagnosis under variable working condition of unequal quantity, Knowledge-Based Systems 242 (108381) (2022) 1–13.

[SYZC19] Ruo Bin Sun, Zhi Bo Yang, Zhi Zhai, Xue Feng Chen, Sparse representation based on parametric impulsive dictionary design for bearing fault diagnosis, Mechanical Systems and Signal Processing 122 (2019) 737–753.

[TBL+20] Aboozar Taherkhani, Ammar Belatreche, Yu Li Hua, Georgina Cosma, Liam P. Maguire, T. Martin McGinnity, A review of learning in biologically plausible spiking neural networks, Neural Networks 122 (2020) 253–272.

[WPY+20] Ya Linv Wang, Zhuo Lin Pan, Xiao Feng Yuan, Chun Hua Yang, Wei Hua Gui, A novel deep learning based fault diagnosis approach for chemical process with extended deep belief network, ISA Transactions 96 (2020) 457–467.

[WTF21] Qin Wang, Cees Taal, Olga Fink, Integrating expert knowledge with domain adaptation for unsupervised fault diagnosis, IEEE Transactions on Instrumentation and Measurement 71 (3500312) (2021) 1–12.

[WWQ+21] Yu Chen Wang, Xiao Bin Wang, Hong Qu, Ya Zhang, Yi Chen, Xiao Ling Luo, Bio-inspired model based on global-local hybrid learning in spiking neural network, in: 2021 International Joint Conference on Neural Networks (IJCNN), IEEE, 2021, pp. 1–8.

[WY22] Hong Shu Wang, Rui Yang, Adversarial based unsupervised domain adaptation for bearing fault diagnosis, in: 2022 27th International Conference on Automation and Computing (ICAC), IEEE, 2022, pp. 1–6.

[YLJ20a] Xiao An Yan, Ying Liu, Min Ping Jia, Health condition identification for rolling bearing using a multi-domain indicator-based optimized stacked denoising autoencoder, Structural Health Monitoring 19 (5) (2020) 1602–1626.

[YLJ20b] Xiao An Yan, Ying Liu, Min Ping Jia, Multiscale cascading deep belief network for fault identification of rotating machinery under various working conditions, Knowledge-Based Systems 193 (105484) (2020) 1–20.

[YLXJ20] Xiao An Yan, Ying Liu, Ya Dong Xu, Min Ping Jia, Multistep forecasting for diurnal wind speed based on hybrid deep learning model with improved singular spectrum decomposition, Energy Conversion and Management 225 (113456) (2020) 1–22.

[YSXJ21] Xiao An Yan, Dao Ming She, Ya Dong Xu, Min Ping Jia, Deep regularized variational autoencoder for intelligent fault diagnosis of rotor–bearing system within entire life-cycle process, Knowledge-Based Systems 226 (107142) (2021) 1–19.

[YTTL13] Qiang Yu, Hua Jin Tang, Kay Chen Tan, Hai Li Zhou, Precise-spike-driven synaptic plasticity: learning hetero-association of spatiotemporal spike patterns, PLoS ONE 8 (11) (2013) 65–87.

[ZSV14] Wojciech Zaremba, Ilya Sutskever, Oriol Vinyals, Recurrent neural network regularization, arXiv preprint, arXiv:1409.2329, 2014, pp. 1–8.

[ZXY+08] Li Jun Zhang, Jin Wu Xu, Jian Hong Yang, De Bin Yang, Da Dong Wang, Multiscale morphology analysis and its application to fault diagnosis, Mechanical Systems and Signal Processing 22 (3) (2008) 597–610.

[ZXZ+22] Lin Zuo, Feng Jie Xu, Chang Hua Zhang, Tang Fan Xiahou, Yu Liu, A multi-layer spiking neural network-based approach to bearing fault diagnosis, Reliability Engineering & System Safety 225 (108561) (2022) 1–14.

[ZZZ+21] Lin Zuo, Lei Zhang, Zhe Han Zhang, Xiao Ling Luo, Yu Liu, A spiking neural network-based approach to bearing fault diagnosis, Journal of Manufacturing Systems 61 (2021) 714–724.

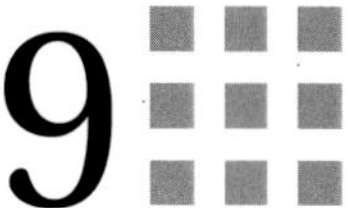

Conclusions

9.1 Summary

Known as the third generation of ANNs, SNNs possess many advantages. First, spiking neurons borrow the information processing and transmission mechanism of biological neurons from the microscopic scale, and have rich spatiotemporal dynamic characteristics, which can handle tasks containing complex temporal information. Secondly, the discrete spike output simplifies the complex floating-point matrix operations in ANNs, evolving into a new computing paradigm characterized by ultra-low-power consumption, suitable for deployment on edge computing platforms with limited resources. Thirdly, the event-driven computation enables the network to achieve a high degree of parallelization, even under current hardware computing modes, greatly reducing computing power consumption. However, the development of SNNs is still subject to various limitations. For instance, most models are simply transplanted from ANNs, but the learning algorithm of ANNs cannot be directly applied. Therefore partial accuracy loss is inevitable when utilizing transplanted methods to train the SNNs. In light of this, this book introduces some new spiking neuron models, learning algorithms, and network models, and their applications in image recognition, speech recognition, fault diagnosis, etc.

SNNs are the theoretical basis of neuromorphic computing and an emerging field in artificial intelligence. As the beginning of the book, we introduce the background and supporting basis of the birth of SNN in Chapter 1, namely the computational theory of the brain and neuromorphic computing. Chapter 2 then introduces three main neuron models in SNNs. Among them, the HH model is not widely used in current SNN models and algorithms due to its computational complexity. In contrast, the LIF model and SRM model are often used in shallow or deep SNNs, including in recurrent and feedforward networks, due to their simplicity in computation.

In Chapter 3, we introduce some new specialized spiking neuron models. They modify the existing neuron models to adapt the algorithm derivation. In the resonate spiking neuron, the neural oscillation and phase-locking mechanism are introduced into the spiking neuron, so that the neuron not only simply transmits the spike of neither 0 nor 1, but also transmits the spike with different sizes, which makes it able to transmit more complex information in the network. Rectified linear PSP neurons modify the PSP function in SRM neurons to be linear, which makes it easy to propagate forward and backward in deep networks. Drawing on the structure of biological pyramidal cells, spiking neurons with multiple dendrites were constructed to process sequence information. Signed neurons with memory are designed for the lossless conversion of ANN–SNN. Negative spikes are introduced so that the converted SNN can maintain the same output frequency as the

Towards Neuromorphic Machine Intelligence. https://doi.org/10.1016/B978-0-44-332820-6.00016-1

ANN. The algorithms and models corresponding to these neuron models are introduced in the following chapter.

In Chapter 4, several SNN learning algorithms designed for shallow networks (no hidden layer or only one or two hidden layers) are introduced. For sequence learning, FE-Learn and RLSBLR learning algorithms are introduced. FE-Learn only updates parameters at the first wrong spike time in each round, which allows it to avoid traversing the entire time window in each calculation, improving efficiency. RLSBLR uses all the historical error information to update parameters whenever an incorrect spike is encountered, and learns multiple times in one traversal of the time window to reduce the learning rounds. For aggregate-label learning, MPD-AL and ETDP learning algorithms are introduced. MPD-AL saves much calculation time by manually selecting the peak point of the membrane voltage to avoid multiple iterations to find the critical threshold. ETDP is driven by the critical threshold, using the error backpropagation to calculate the weight update. It has a stronger ability to deal with the time credit-allocation problem.

In Chapter 5, two SNN learning algorithms for deep networks are introduced, both of which aim to solve the common problems in the direct training of deep SNN, namely, a non-differentiable spike function, gradient explosion, and dead neurons. The deep SNN constructed by resonate neurons outputs the number of ions, and its derivative with respect to synaptic weights can be calculated directly, thus avoiding the problem of non-differentiability. The function $F(V) = V$ also avoids the problem of gradient explosion, and the phase-locking activation function allows the neuron to fire anyway, avoiding the problem of dead neurons. Deep SNNs built from neurons with rectified linear PSP also benefit from their linearly growing PSP, making them immune to non-differentiable spike function and gradient explosion problems, and the neurons are always driven to fire as early as possible, and thus are less prone to the dead neuron problem.

In Chapter 6, two SNN models for episodic memory inspired by cortical neural columns are introduced. BSTM uses the STDP learning algorithm and a new column selection algorithm to encode input elements, and proposes a sequential memory algorithm to store the context, which realizes multi-sentence memory and multi-time step memory. CSTM is proposed for sequences with variable time intervals. It uses a column to represent a specific element, and uses the synapses of the neurons between the columns to connect the sequence elements. Synaptic delays are established to represent the time interval between the elements. The model can memorize a long sequence of thousands of elements after learning the input sequence only once.

Chapter 7 introduces a nearly lossless ANN–SNN conversion method. This method uses signed spiking neurons with memory to solve the inconsistency of information transmission between synchronous ANN and asynchronous SNN in the existing ANN-to-SNN method. This method has almost no accuracy loss during the conversion process and maintains the characteristics of asynchronous transmission in the converted SNN. In addition, a new normalization method, neuron-wise normalization, is proposed, which can significantly shorten the inference delay of the converted SNN. This transformation method is superior to the existing methods in both precision and inference delay.

Chapter 8 introduces a SNN for fault diagnosis called Spike-DBN. This method integrates the event-driven method into the model through the Latency-Rate coding method and the Reward-STDP learning rule. It can effectively capture changes over time in multivariate time-series data, which not only keeps the resource consumption low, but also improves the fault diagnosis ability. Under the same conditions, compared with the spiking convolutional neural network, the accuracy of fault classification of manipulators can be effectively improved, and the learning time can be greatly shortened.

9.2 Future outlook

In addition to the research of the SNN model and algorithm, the spike coding strategy and brain-like hardware of SNN are also worth exploring in the future. A few interesting approaches are listed here, but SNN research is much more than just these:

(1) Simulate biological visual and auditory pathways to build new cognitive SNNs models. The biological nervous system has complex neural pathways, but it performs various perception and cognitive tasks very efficiently and with low power consumption. The entire human brain has a power consumption of only about 20 W. Taking the visual pathway as an example, the input starts from the retina, projects through the lateral geniculate nucleus, and performs basic information processing in the primary visual cortex V1 area. Subsequently, it performs shape and motion recognition through parallel dorsal and ventral pathways, respectively, with very rapid and low power consumption. Simulating the visual pathway to build new SNNs for applications such as action recognition and target detection is expected to achieve more efficient and rapid visual information processing. Similarly, simulating the biological auditory pathway can also build low-power SNNs for tasks such as voice separation and sound source localization.

(2) Build new memory SNNs based on Neural Differential Equations (NDEs). NDEs can be used to describe dynamic systems. Currently, some ANNs based on NDEs have been proposed, replacing the feedforward and feedback calculation processes of the network with numerical solutions of NDEs. Memory can be regarded as attractors in neural circuits, so it is a feasible method to build SNNs that simulate human brain memory functions based on NDEs. Unlike reservoir computing networks that directly describe neural dynamics using differential equations, NDEs describe the dynamics of the entire neural network, and the neural network can have arbitrary structures, making it very flexible.

(3) Explore more efficient spike encoding schemes and brain-inspired hardware. The biological nervous system has very efficient information encoding mechanisms, such as the retina that rapidly encodes the viewed scene into spike streams for various shape or motion recognitions. However, current machine vision still processes pixels, including SNNs that mostly encode pixels in images captured by ordinary cameras. This encoding of visual information causes information redundancy and loss, especially for objects in ultra-high-speed motion scenes. Inspired by biological encoding mechanisms, event cameras detect changes in light intensity with extremely high temporal resolution, converting dynamic information into binary event streams, greatly facilitating the detection of ultra-

high-speed motion. This indicates that by learning biological coding mechanisms while building low-power brain-like hardware devices, some of the existing application limitations can be overcome.

Glossary

Aggregate-label learning: Aggregate-label learning is a class of complex learning problems in SNNs, which aims to excite a specific number of spikes in response to multiple spatiotemporal clues embedded in background noise. During the learning process, neurons spontaneously identify valid clues and emit a designated count of spikes to discern the clue's presence, while remaining silent at other times. Consequently, neurons must acquire the skill of efficiently allocating temporal credits.

ANN–SNN conversion: ANN–SNN conversion is a kind of efficient training approach for SNNs, where the parameters of a pre-trained ANNs are transplanted into an SNN through various design techniques. This approach aims to circumvent the intricate learning process of SNNs and enable the converted SNN to achieve superior performance.

Apical dendrites: Apical dendrites are dendrites that emerge from the apex of pyramidal cells and contribute significantly to memory, learning, and sensory associations by regulating the excitatory and inhibitory signals received by pyramidal cells. In this book, the simulated apical dendrites receive feedback signals from upper-layer neurons.

Artificial Neural Networks (ANNs): An artificial neural network is a nonlinear system composed of a large number of simple computing units. To a certain extent, it can imitate the information processing, storage and retrieval functions of the human brain nervous system, and has intelligent processing functions such as learning, memory, and calculation.

Critical (firing) threshold: The critical threshold refers to the firing threshold that triggers a shift in the number of spikes emitted by neurons. Specifically, if the threshold surpasses this critical value by a marginal amount, the count of spikes emitted will decrease by one (albeit in rare instances, it may decrease by more than one).

Dead neurons: If the neuron receives insufficient input to evoke spiking activity, numerous learning algorithms that depend on precise timing for synaptic plasticity become inactive for those neurons. Consequently, they are unable to participate in the learning process by adjusting the synaptic strengths required to trigger spiking. Therefore, these neurons remain silent, never discharging spikes, and are called "dead neurons."

Distal dendrite: The base of the pyramidal cells gives off some basal dendrites that extend in a horizontal direction. In this book, we refer to the basal dendrites that form synaptic connections with cells in the same layer as distal dendrites, i.e., receiving lateral input from neurons in the same layer.

Firing: The action of a spiking neuron to trigger a spike.

Firing rate/frequency: The firing rate is defined as the quotient of the number of spikes emitted by a neuron within a specific time window and the duration of that time window.

Firing threshold: When the membrane voltage of a spiking neuron surpasses a specific value, i.e., the firing threshold, the neuron becomes activated, generating a spike that is transmitted to other neurons via synaptic connections.

Firing time: Firing time refers to the moment when the membrane voltage of the spiking neuron exceeds the firing threshold, that is, the time to emit the spike.

Gradient explosion: Gradient Explosion refers to the phenomenon that during the training process of neural networks, due to the accumulation of gradients layer by layer during backpropagation, if the gradient itself is large, after multiple layers of accumulation, the gradient value may rapidly increase, resulting in unstable or even nonconvergent training. It usually occurs in deep neural networks, especially when the number of layers in the network is large, the network structure is complex, or inappropriate activation functions or the initial weights are used.

Gradient vanishing: Gradient Vanishing is a problem that arises in deep neural networks, especially when training networks using gradient-based optimization methods such as error backpropagation. During backpropagation, the gradient is multiplied by the derivative of the activation function layer by layer. If the derivative of the activation function is close to zero, then the gradient becomes very small and approaches zero, which results in very slow or even stopped updates of model parameters, making the training process very difficult.

Membrane voltage/potential: This is the electrical potential difference between the interior and exterior of the cell membrane. In spiking neuron models built to simulate biological neurons, the membrane voltage is an internal state variable of the neuron that changes in response to incoming spikes, reflecting the dynamic nature of neuronal activity.

Multimodal task: Multimodal refers to data or information that involves multiple modalities, such as visual, speech, text, etc. A multimodal task refers to a task that requires the simultaneous processing of two or more different types of data. For example, the classification of images is a unimodal task. However, by combining image and speech or text data, more complex tasks can be performed, such as image captioning or visual question answering, which require the simultaneous utilization of information from both the image and language modalities.

Neural column (cortical column): Cortical columns are vertical columnar structures throughout the whole thickness of the cortex, which is the basic functional unit of the cerebral cortex, also known as the functional column. The cerebral cortex contains about 500 million cortical columns, the structure of each column varies in size, between 200 and 500 μm in diameter, and the vertical direction of the cortical column is constructed by 6 layers of cells. It was found that neurons within a vertical column have the same or nearly the same peripheral receptive field and respond to the same type of peripheral stimulus.

Neural oscillation: Research has demonstrated that neurons do not operate in isolation; instead, they collaborate in synchrony to execute particular cognitive functions. Neural oscillation denotes the rhythmic (periodic) alterations in neural activity patterns, arising from the concerted firing of neuron ensembles at specific moments and frequencies.

Neuromorphic computing: Neuromorphic engineering is a discipline that uses an analog, digital or analog/digital hybrid very large scale integrated circuit (VLSI) and its related software to imitate biological neurons, neural circuits and even larger scale neural architecture to create a brain-like chip or circuit. It is used to construct a new device with low energy consumption, closer to biological authenticity, and realize the corresponding function of neural tissue. Neuromorphic computing focuses on the theoretical aspects of neuromorphic engineering, a field that seeks to combine biology, electrical engineering, computer science, and mathematical techniques to create artificial nervous systems with perceptual and processing loads similar to those of the human brain. Neuromorphic computing is also commonly referred to as "brain-inspired computing".

Non-differentiable spike function: When the membrane voltage V exceeds the threshold θ, a spike is fired. If $S(t) = 1$ indicates that a spike is excited at the time t ($V(t) \geqq \theta$), and $S(t) = 0$ indicates that no spike is excited at t ($V(t) < \theta$). Then, the relationship between S and the membrane voltage V can be expressed by a function $S = F(V;\ \theta)$, and F is not differentiable at the time of spike excitation, so it is called the non-differentiable spike function. This function makes it difficult to train SNN based on gradient descent.

Phase locking: Rhythmic stimuli with specific frequencies can synchronize neural oscillations with corresponding frequencies within the brain, causing neural activity to phase lock with external stimuli. This phenomenon is known as neural oscillation–external rhythm synchronization. This synchronization phenomenon is accompanied by periodic fluctuations in the excitability of neuronal clusters within the brain, and is associated with cognitive processes such as rhythm information processing, perception, and attention.

Postsynaptic neuron: If a synapse is formed between two neurons to transmit spikes, then the neuron that receives the spikes is called a postsynaptic neuron, and the spikes it generates are called postsynaptic spikes.

Presynaptic neuron: If a synapse is formed between two neurons to transmit spikes, then the neuron that emits the spikes is called a presynaptic neuron, and the spikes it transmits are called presynaptic spikes.

Proximal dendrite: The base of the pyramidal cells gives off some basal dendrites that extend in a horizontal direction. In this book, we refer to the basal dendrites that form synaptic connections with adjacent layer cells as proximal dendrites, receiving feedforward input from lower-layer neurons.

Postsynaptic Potential (PSP): The postsynaptic potential denotes the alteration in the membrane voltage of the postsynaptic neuron, resulting from the transmission of spikes from the presynaptic neuron to the postsynaptic neuron. The PSP is either positive or negative, depending on the nature and strength of the synaptic connection.

Refractory period: After a neuron emits a spike, it will not generate other spikes for a period of time due to factors such as temporary inactivation of the ion channels. This period of time is called the refractory period. The refractory period includes the absolute refractory period and the relative refractory period.

Sequence learning: Sequence learning in this book refers to training neurons to fire specific spike trains, that is, to fire spikes at specific multiple moments.

Spike coding/encoding: Spike coding is an important part of SNN research. Given that neurons within SNNs primarily receive and transmit spikes (binary signals of 0 or 1), which differ significantly from the natural, analog signals encountered in real-world scenarios. It is necessary to convert these inputs (such as images, speech, text, etc.) into spikes in a suitable way. This process is referred to as spike coding.

Spike train: A series of spikes fired by a neuron at different times is called a spike train.

Spiking Neural Network (SNN): Spiking neural networks are the cornerstone theory of brain-inspired computing and are frequently referred to as third-generation neural networks. SNNs are constructed by the interconnection of spiking neurons. These spiking neurons process information via the "integrate-and-fire" mechanism, facilitating the exchange of information through spikes. Notably, these neuronal units in SNNs become active only when receiving or transmitting a spike signal, embodying an event-driven paradigm that enables energy-efficient computation.

Spike Timing-Dependent Plasticity (STDP): Spike timing-dependent plasticity is a biologically plausible mechanism of synaptic plasticity, where the alteration of synaptic weights is expressed as a function of the relative timing of presynaptic spike arrival and postsynaptic spike excitation. When the presynaptic spike is fired a little earlier than the postsynaptic spike, the synaptic connection of the pair of neurons is strengthened and vice versa. There are many different variants of STDP.

Surrogate gradients: To address the challenge posed by the non-differentiable spike function, which precludes the propagation of gradients in SNNs using standard backpropagation techniques, a surrogate function is introduced as a proxy for the derivative of the non-differentiable spike function. The gradients obtained through this surrogate function are referred to as surrogate gradients.

Synaptic connection: A synapse is the information transmission structure between two neurons, in SNNs, we simply regard it as the connection between neurons, thus called a synaptic connection. Synaptic strength/efficacy/weight is often used to quantify the intensity of a synaptic connection, thereby reflecting the efficiency of information transfer between neurons.

Synaptic delay: A synaptic delay is the time required for neurotransmitters to be released from nerve endings, diffuse across the synaptic cleft, and ultimately interact with the postsynaptic membrane. In SNNs, synaptic delays can be regarded as adjustable parameters of synapses, akin to synaptic weights, that play a crucial role in governing the dynamic behavior of neural networks.

Synaptic plasticity: Synaptic plasticity refers to the (structure and function) adjustable properties of synaptic connections between neurons, which is the most universal law of almost all synapses. It includes classical frequency-dependent synaptic plasticity (long-term potential, long-term inhibition, and advanced plasticity) and firing time-dependent synaptic plasticity. On the basis of the above functional synaptic plasticity, further plasticity changes of synaptic structure may occur.

Temporal credit allocation: The credit allocation discussed in ANNs pertains to the adjustment of weights between layers based on the significance of inputs towards the final output during network training, which is also called spatial credit allocation. In SNNs, the emphasis is on temporal credit allocation due to the varying contributions of presynaptic input spikes at different instants to the firing of postsynaptic neurons. Consequently, the modulation of synaptic connections between pre- and postsynaptic neurons relies on the temporal relationship between spikes. As such, synaptic adjustments encompass not only spatial but also temporal credit allocation, collectively known as spatiotemporal credit allocation.

Index

A

Ablation
  experiments, 179
  study, 158
Accuracy, 177
  classification results, 183
  drop, 24, 149, 150, 157
  learning, 28, 37–39, 41, 42
  loss, 4, 102, 189, 190
  measure, 28
  metric, 40
  ReSuMe, 63
  RLSBLR learning, 58, 60
  test, 135
Action potentials generation, 12
Adaptive learning rate, 97, 109
Adversarial training, 185
Afferent neurons, 22
Aggregate-label learning algorithms, 68
Algorithm
  analysis, 34
  description, 99, 104
Analog neurons, 97
ANN–SNN conversion, 151, 190
Apical dendrites, 117, 118
Artificial Intelligence (AI), 1, 2, 163
Artificial neural network (ANN), 1, 95, 109, 110, 149, 189, 191
  learning algorithm, 189
  network parameters, 158
  neuron, 151, 152
  trained weights, 4
Artificial neurons, 1, 2, 20, 95, 98
Asynchronous spikes, 151
Axon, 11, 21, 22, 117, 118
  neuron, 141
  squid, 13
  terminals, 11

B

Backpropagation (BP), 95
Backpropagation Through Time (BPTT), 4, 27
Basal dendrites, 117
Batch Normalization (BN) layers, 158
Binary spike representation, 19
Biological
  neural networks, 2, 97
  neurons, 1, 2, 11, 13, 25, 29, 165, 189
Biologically plausible Auditory Encoding scheme (BAE), 84
Bionic spiking neurons, 118
Bionic Spiking Temporal Memory (BSTM), 118, 132, 190
  model, 118, 120, 127, 136
  networks, 120
  neuron, 118
Brain
  computational theory, 1, 189
  cortex, 5
  diseases, 1
  nervous system, 1, 11
  projects, 1
  research, 1
Building blocks, 163

C

Caltech face/motorbike dataset, 111
Case Western Reserve University (CWRU) dataset, 163, 171, 183, 184
Cell body, 11, 117, 138
Classification
  accuracy, 48, 88, 113, 177, 179, 185
  accuracy STDBP, 107
  applications, 61
  multimodal data, 44
  UCI datasets, 42, 172
Coding neurons, 42, 43, 166

Columnar-structured model, 137
Computational theory, 1
Contrastive Divergence (CD) algorithm, 164
Contributory synaptic weights, 30, 31
Convolutional
  layer, 101, 102, 154, 155, 158
  SNN, 106, 107, 110, 112
Convolutional Neural Network (CNN), 101, 177

D

Data
  description, 172, 183
  preprocessing, 174
Dead neuron, 95, 97, 98, 103, 190
Decision layer, 3
Deep
  networks, 1, 3, 189
  neural networks, 150, 177
Deep Belief Network (DBN), 163, 164
Deep Learning (DL), 163
Deep spiking neural network (DSNN), 3, 21, 95, 98, 103, 163, 189, 190
Delay
  adjustment, 51–53
  change, 55
  inference, 190
  learning, 3, 27, 49, 51–53, 125
    algorithm, 27, 42, 48
    method, 48, 51
    rule, 51, 55
  property, 137
  rules, 57
  update, 55
  updating learning rate, 32
Delayed feedback, 28, 65, 72, 75, 84
Dendrite, 11, 12, 117, 118, 139
  firing threshold, 143
  matrix, 129
  potentials, 139
  reuse, 145
  spike, 118, 140
  structure, 117
Dendritic spike, 139, 140
Dentate gyrus (DG), 119
  layer, 120, 137
  neurons, 120, 121, 132
Difference of Gaussians (DoG), 167
  filter, 174
  method, 183
  processing, 175
Distal dendrite, 21, 22, 117, 118, 120, 124–128

E

Efficient Threshold-Driven Plasticity (ETDP), 63, 81, 82, 84, 190
  algorithm, 75, 80, 82
  learning algorithm, 75, 77, 79, 190
  rule, 28
Encoded spike, 107
  patterns, 74, 88
  time, 44
Encoding
  layer, 137, 184
  process, 120
Episodic memory, 118–120, 190
Error analysis, 151
Error Backpropagation (BP) algorithm, 3
Evaluation metric, 176
Event-driven spike deep belief network, 167
Exploding gradient prevention strategy (EGPS), 78, 84
Extended first error learning rule, 32

F

Fashion-MNIST dataset, 110
Fault Diagnosis (FD), 163, 167, 171, 174, 183, 189, 191
Feedforward
  input, 21, 22, 118, 127
  input spikes, 22, 118
  networks, 3, 189
  SNNs, 110
Firing
  goal neuron, 138
  instants, 24
  minicolumns, 121
  network, 156
  neuron, 139, 140

patterns, 23
postsynaptic neurons, 142
potential, 139
rate, 37–39, 42, 56–58, 60, 156, 165
spikes, 15, 168
threshold, 23, 29, 35, 37, 48, 51, 77, 96, 97, 103, 139, 150, 151, 165
time, 19, 29, 31, 43, 49, 101, 107, 140, 141
First Error Learning (FE-Learn), 28–30, 32
First error-based supervised learning algorithm, 29
First-Order Reduced and Controlled Error (FORCE) algorithm, 4

G
Genetic algorithm (GA), 176
Goal cluster, 138
Gradient explosion, 35, 37, 97, 98, 103, 190

H
Hardware
architecture, 105
energy consumption analysis, 156
simulation methodology, 104, 106
simulation results, 112
Hidden
layer, 75, 79, 80, 99, 108, 152, 163, 164, 168, 176, 190
layer neuron, 34, 108, 164
neurons, 34, 80, 108
neurons spikes, 79
spiking neurons, 87
Hierarchical Temporal Memory (HTM)
model, 5, 117
neurons, 117, 118
Hodgkin and Huxley (HH) model, 13, 14
Human brain, 1, 2, 29, 79, 87, 137, 142, 191
atlases, 1
memory, 191

I
Inactive
minicolumns, 119, 123
neurons, 120
Incoming spikes, 88, 105
Incorrect
output spike, 49
spike, 49, 51, 54, 190
Inference delay, 190
Inhibitory
input spikes, 66, 77
neurons, 3
PSPs, 12
Input
neurons, 54
spikes, 40
Integrate-Fire (IF)
model, 14
neurons, 24, 150, 151
neurons input, 150
Internet of Things (IoT) systems, 2

L
Layer-wise parameter normalization (LayerNorm), 150, 154–156
Leaky Integrate-and-Fire (LIF)
model, 4, 13–15, 29, 189
neuron, 24
neuron model, 14
Learning
ability, 39
accuracy, 28, 37–39, 41, 42
algorithms, 3, 4, 27, 29, 37, 46, 48, 95, 97, 101, 102, 189
behavior, 180
capabilities, 2, 106
curves, 54, 68, 79
delay, 3, 27, 49, 51–53, 125
difficulty, 53
effect, 37, 59
efficiency, 54, 56, 58, 65, 69–71, 75, 78, 168
epochs, 58, 59, 70, 81, 82
information, 54
mechanisms, 66
methods, 27, 30, 65, 167
multimodal sensory clues, 82
neuron, 29, 35, 37, 40, 67, 81, 83
performance, 3, 37, 40, 48, 58, 60
predictive clues, 71
process, 5, 27, 48, 51, 120, 140, 168, 184

rate, 31, 50, 57, 58, 66, 68, 99, 107, 123, 169, 176
rounds, 190
rule, 2, 32, 54, 57, 77, 99
SNNs, 5
synaptic weight, 32
task, 69, 172
time, 191
window, 168, 169
Local Mean Decomposition (LMD), 183
Long-term depression (LTD), 122, 168
Long-term potentiation (LTP), 122, 168

M
Machine Learning (ML), 65, 71, 75, 82
algorithms, 61
methods, 163
models, 42
Machinery Failure Prevention Technology (MFPT), 64, 65
Mapping, 106
Maximum activation value, 151, 154, 155, 158
ANN, 151, 154
postsynaptic neuron, 155
presynaptic neuron, 155
Membrane potential, 19–21, 23, 29–31, 35, 37, 95–97, 121, 126, 129, 130, 150, 153, 165
contribution, 56
dynamics, 120
minicolumn, 121
neuron, 153
oscillation, 19, 20
traces, 28, 65, 67, 70, 74, 81
Membrane voltage, 4, 12–14, 21, 29, 31, 32, 131, 132, 190
leakage, 14
reset, 16
Membrane-Potential Driven Aggregate-Label (MPD-AL)
learning, 65
learning algorithm, 28, 65
Memory
capacity, 125, 132, 135
mechanism, 23, 24
models, 137
SNNs, 191
time intervals, 137
value, 23, 24, 152, 153
Minicolumn
calculation model, 120
learning algorithm, 122
neuron, 135
organization, 118, 119
postsynaptic, 123
representation, 123
response, 121
selection algorithm, 118
structure, 119
Minicolumn-based model, 118
MNIST, 44
data, 112
dataset, 48, 84, 88, 101, 107, 112
image dataset, 46
Model
accuracy, 184
architecture, 118
MPD-Al learning algorithm, 66
Multi-layer network learning, 33
Multi-layered perceptron (MLP), 101
Multi-Spike Tempotron (MST) algorithms, 27, 28, 68, 71
Multimodal sensory clues, 28, 75, 82, 84

N
Negative
spike, 24, 152, 153, 189
synapses, 51, 152
Network
architectures, 101, 112
design, 137, 167
firing, 156
models, 3, 4, 101, 189
optimization, 103
parameters, 134
settings, 135
SNNs, 156
structures, 3, 101, 102, 107, 118, 127
training, 5, 158
Network-on-Chip (NoC) architecture, 105, 106

Neural
network, 2, 3, 24, 95, 103, 104, 191
network organization, 119
oscillation, 19, 25, 97, 101, 113, 189
synapses, 2
Neural Differential Equation (NDE), 191
Neuromorphic computing, 2, 189
Neuron
ANNs, 151, 152
axon, 141
BSTM, 118
coding, 166
connections, 184
distal dendrite, 125
firing, 139, 140
rate, 151
threshold, 154
time, 166
input spike train, 123
layers, 3
learning, 29, 35, 37, 83
membrane potential, 153
membrane voltage, 14
model, 22, 28, 48, 57, 63, 66, 118, 189, 190
output rate, 152, 154
postsynaptic, 3, 5, 12, 14, 24, 32, 33, 140, 141, 143, 150, 152, 168, 169
potentials, 105
presynaptic, 12, 14, 19, 21, 32, 40, 48, 80, 97, 123, 138, 141, 165, 169
spike, 15
spike time, 21
spiking activity, 95
state, 127, 128, 164
state change process, 127
structure, 118
synaptic delay time, 48
trained, 72, 84
Neuron-wise normalization (NeuronNorm), 154–156, 158
Neuronal
activities, 27, 81, 110
diversity, 13
Non-differentiable spike function, 97, 103
Normalized Perceptron-Based Learning Rule (NPBLR), 3

O

Oscillation Postsynaptic Potential (Os-PSP), 19, 98

P

Perceptron-Based Spiking Neuron Learning Rule (PBSNLR), 3, 41, 42, 52, 53
learning accuracy, 58
Performance evaluation, 57
extended FE-learn, 39
FE-learn, 37
Postsynaptic
minicolumn, 123
neuron, 3, 5, 12, 14, 24, 32, 33, 140, 141, 143, 150, 152, 168, 169
maximum activation value, 155
membrane voltage, 12
spike time, 96
Postsynaptic potential (PSP), 12, 14, 53–55, 95
Power consumption, 1, 2, 112, 149, 150, 156, 157, 189, 191
Precision Spike Driven (PSD), 3
Prediction accuracy, 158, 184
Predictive
neurons, 22, 127–129
sentence, 130, 131
Presynaptic
neuron, 12, 14, 19, 21, 32, 40, 48, 80, 97, 123, 138, 141, 165, 169
firing rate, 80
maximum activation value, 155
PSPs, 48
spike, 15, 79, 138, 139
spike time, 96, 122
Processing element (PE), 105, 106
Projective neurons, 117
Proximal
dendrite, 21, 22, 117–120, 122, 123
input, 139, 141, 142
input stimuli, 140
Pyramidal
neuron, 21, 22, 118
structure spiking neuron, 21

R

Receptive field kernel (RF), 174
Rectified linear function, 21
Rectified Linear Postsynaptic Potential (ReL-PSP), 102, 190
  function, 102
  neurons, 25, 189
  spiking neuron, 20
Rectified Linear Unit (ReLU) activation, 97, 104, 150, 154
Recurrent network structures, 4
Recurrent Neural Network (RNN), 177
Recursive Least Squares-Based Learning Rule (RLSBLR), 28, 48, 51–53
  algorithm, 28, 54, 56, 58, 61
  learning
    accuracy, 58, 60
    algorithms, 190
    curve, 55, 56
    epochs, 58
    rule, 48, 56, 65
  method, 52–54, 56, 58
  performance evaluation, 57
  supervised learning, 49
Remote Supervised Method (ReSuMe), 3, 5, 37–39, 52–54
  accuracy, 63
  learning curve, 56
  weight updates, 52, 56
Reservoir
  computing networks, 191
  structure networks, 4
ResNet network structures, 158
Resonate Spiking Neuron (RSN), 19, 25, 98, 189
  membrane potential, 20
  neurons, 20
Resting potential, 14, 15, 23, 24, 150, 151, 165
Restricted Boltzmann Machine (RBM), 163, 164
Retrieval
  accuracy, 132, 134, 135, 143–145
  process, 127

S

Sequence memory, 137
Sequential
  learning tasks, 28, 40
  memory, 5, 25, 190
  memory algorithm, 118
  memory algorithm LSTM, 136
Shallow
  networks, 3, 190
  SNNs, 3
  SNNs learning algorithms, 3
Siegert neuron model, 163, 165
Signed neuron, 153, 154
Signed Neuron with Memory (SNM), 22, 23, 25, 151, 152, 159, 189
  membrane potential, 24
  neuron, 24, 152, 153, 158
Sparse network connectivity structure, 137
Spatio-Temporal Backpropagation (STBP), 4
Spatiotemporal
  spike patterns, 29
  spike time computations, 73
  subnetwork, 137, 138, 140, 141, 143
Spike
  activation, 3
  activity, 71, 149
  coding strategy, 191
  count, 65, 66, 70, 72, 75, 77
  dendrite, 118, 140
  encoding, 184
  encoding schemes, 191
  events, 100
  excitation, 4
  firing, 15, 168
  generation function, 96, 97
  generation mechanism, 97, 104, 110
  generation process, 11
  metric, 28
  neuron, 4, 15
  numbers, 157
  output, 189
  packets, 105
  patterns, 3, 44, 46, 71, 73, 74, 101, 107, 111, 169
  presynaptic, 15, 79, 138, 139
  response kernels, 15
  sequence, 3, 183

sequence learning, 34
symbiosis event, 168, 169
time, 30, 33–35, 42, 43, 103, 104, 123, 168
derivative, 4
noise, 75
postsynaptic, 96
presynaptic, 96, 122
timing, 29, 102, 106, 108, 113, 184
train, 19, 20, 28, 30, 32, 37–40, 43, 46, 48, 49, 98, 120, 132, 152, 165, 166, 168
firing rate, 60
length, 37
Spike Convolutional Neural Network (Spike-CNN), 177
Spike Deep Belief Network (Spike-DBN), 163
Spike Pattern Association Neuron (SPAN), 3
Spike Response Model (SRM), 15, 120
neuron, 46, 189
neuron membrane potential, 56
Spike-Level-Dependent Backpropagation (SLDBP) learning algorithm, 98, 113
Spike-Threshold-Surface (STS), 75
Spike-Timing Dependent Plasticity (STDP), 3, 27, 122, 123, 168
learning
algorithm, 118, 190
approach, 169
method, 168
rule, 169
method, 120
rules, 3
temporal learning window, 168
weight update, 123
Spike-timing-dependent backpropagation (STDBP), 102, 104, 110
algorithm, 107
classification accuracy, 107
learning algorithm, 104, 107, 108, 112
SpikeProp algorithm, 4
Spiking
convolutional neural network, 191
network models, 3
neuron, 3, 13, 19, 28, 75, 80, 97, 102, 104, 137, 139, 151, 155–157, 165, 167, 176, 189
counterparts, 21, 95
model, 11, 13, 21, 28, 75, 98, 103, 138, 189
output, 150, 159
neuronal, 95
Spiking neural network (SNN), 2, 3, 13, 27–29, 95, 98, 118, 149, 150, 166, 175, 189
deep, 3, 21, 95, 113, 163, 189, 190
feedforward, 110
inference accuracy, 158
learning, 5
learning algorithms, 27, 29, 190
memory, 191
network, 156
trained, 85
training, 95
Squid axon, 13
Stochastic Gradient Descent (SGD), 101
Storing process, 124
Subthreshold membrane
potential, 66, 68
voltage, 43
Supervised learning algorithms, 3
Support Vector Machine (SVM), 184
Synapse, 11, 19, 34, 51, 52, 57, 100, 117, 141
connection strength, 5
contribution, 68
current, 40
delay, 51
Synaptic
current, 29
delay, 2, 5, 27, 32, 33, 99, 101, 137, 190
delay learning, 32, 48
inputs, 37, 38, 41, 58
learning rule, 168
weight, 4, 5, 21, 27, 29–31, 33, 37, 95, 97, 103, 104, 121, 122, 125, 168, 190
adjustment, 3, 123
learning, 32
plasticity, 27
vector, 48

T

Target neuron, 43, 62, 104
Temporal coding, 106
Temporal Credit-Assignment (TCA) problem, 75, 82

Temporal-sequential learning (TSL), 137
Test accuracy, 135
Thalamocortical neurons, 22, 23
Threshold-Driven Plasticity (TDP) algorithms, 27
Tolerance window, 30, 32, 34, 37, 38, 40
Tonic firing, 23
Trained
  model, 107, 110
  model parameters, 102
  neuron, 70, 72, 84
  SNN, 85
  SNN models, 106
Transmitted spikes, 24, 152

U

UCI machine learning repository, 42, 163
Undesired spike time, 49, 52
Unfired minicolumns, 121
Unsupervised learning
  algorithms, 3
  methods, 186
Upstream neurons, 29

V

Visible layer, 164, 176
  neuron, 164
Vision task, 101

W

Weight
  adjustment, 30, 31, 35, 37, 52–54, 99
  learning rule, 49
  update, 34, 48, 50, 54, 55, 123, 169, 190
  update rule, 79
  update STDP, 123
Winning neuron, 62, 65, 139, 140, 144
Wrong
  output spike time, 29
  spike time, 30, 51, 190

X

XOR
  classification task, 85, 86
  input pattern, 101
  problem, 100